Britain, Europe and the Modern World: 1918–1977

Book 5 of the Britain, Europe and the World Series
General Editor: Dennis Witcombe

Britain, Europe and the World series

Britain, Europe and the Modern World 1918—1977

THIRD EDITION

Paul Richardson

 HEINEMANN EDUCATIONAL BOOKS · LONDON

Heinemann Educational Books Ltd
22 Bedford Square, London WC1B 3HH

LONDON   EDINBURGH   MELBOURNE   AUCKLAND
HONG KONG   SINGAPORE   KUALA LUMPUR   NEW DELHI
IBADAN   LUSAKA   NAIROBI   JOHANNESBURG   EXETER(NH)
KINGSTON   PORT OF SPAIN

ISBN: 0 435 31105 0

First published 1970
Reprinted 1972
Second Edition 1975
Reprinted with corrections 1976
Third Edition 1977
Reprinted 1979

Printed in Great Britain by Page Bros (Norwich) Ltd

Contents

Preface

This book appears only two generations after the end of the First World War, but those two generations have witnessed greater and more rapid changes than any other similar period in the history of mankind. For this reason it is not possible to write a 'world history' of the period 1918–77 in the compass of a book of this length. What I have tried to do instead is to look at the main movements of modern history in the Western world and show how they have become increasingly involved in the affairs of the 'third world'. This means, inevitably, that many parts of the world, many great events and many important men are not mentioned, but the book attempts to give an interpretation of those parts of contemporary history which are likely to seem most important to readers in Britain and other parts of the English-speaking world. Of course, the book does involve a good deal of *interpretation* and many of the events it records are too close to us for more than a provisional judgement. Some readers will reach different conclusions from mine, but the book will have achieved its purpose if it provokes serious discussion of this most important period of man's history.

I would like to thank Dr Dennis Witcombe, the general editor of this series; we planned this book together and he has been a constant source of constructive criticism. I must also record my gratitude to my wife for unfailing encouragement and advice in the preparation of the manuscript.

In this third edition the text has been updated to deal with events up to the middle of 1977.

Paul Richardson

11 November 1918

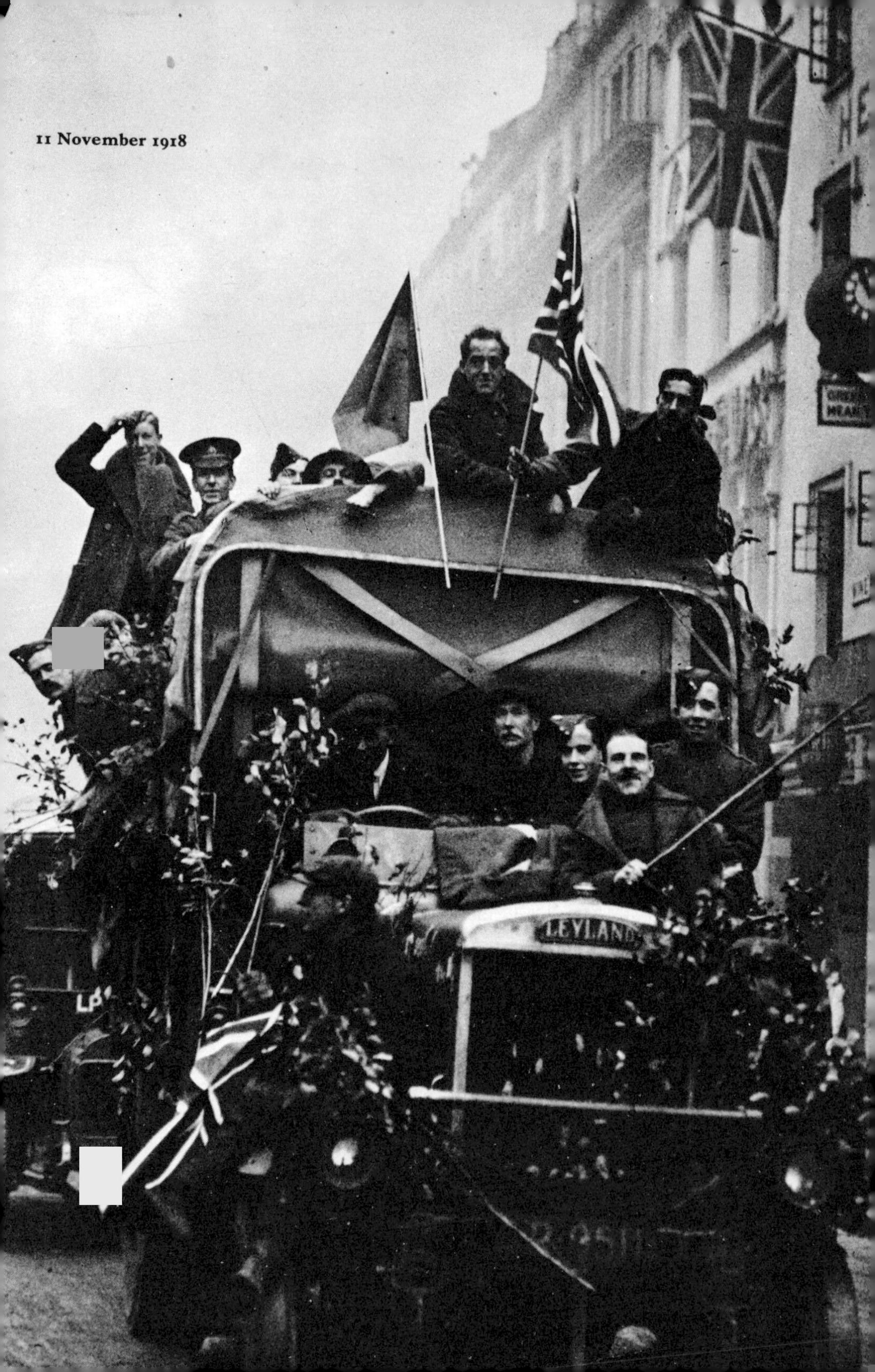

Introduction

Gentlemen, the select classes of mankind are no longer the governors of mankind. The fortresses of mankind are now in the hands of the plain people of the whole world . . .

We are here to see . . . that the very foundations of this war are swept away. Those foundations were the private choice of small coteries of civil rulers and military staffs. Those foundations were the aggression of the great powers upon the small. Those foundations were the folding together of empires of unwilling subjects by duress of arms. Those foundations were the power of small bodies of men to work their will and use mankind as pawns in a game.
President Woodrow Wilson of the United States at the Paris Peace Conference, January 1919

The most terrible war men had ever experienced was over. Ten million men had died in the fighting in four years, more than twice the number that had died in battle in the whole of the previous century. Four great empires, the Ottoman and the Hapsburg, the Hohenzollern and the Romanov had been destroyed. Revolution which had swept through Russia seemed to be spilling over into Germany, Hungary and even western Europe. The United States of America had intervened for the first time in European affairs and its idealistic President had come to settle the future of the Old World at the Peace Conference. This was the context in which Woodrow Wilson made his ringing declaration that the new world was going to be strikingly different from the one which had existed before the war.

A*

'The plain people of the whole world'

When Wilson spoke about the plain people of the whole world he was indulging in a politician's exaggeration. The war did not bring about any immediate alteration in the position of the whole world simply because it had never been a world war. Very few people were directly involved in the fighting outside Europe and the Middle East. There was some non-European intervention in the war, but even this was only on an important scale in the case of the United States and the British Dominions and did not alter the European nature of the war.

The indirect effects of the war were much more far reaching. Uninvolved or nominally involved countries such as Spain, the South American states and Japan all prospered, thanks to the enormous demands of the war and the preoccupation of the other major trading nations in the struggle. Even more important, the war brought a new relationship between Europe as a whole and the United States, as the anti-German powers came to rely more and more upon American goods and credit. In addition both Britain and France were forced by the demands of the war to develop their colonies as sources of raw materials and the war gave an enormous boost to world demand for relatively new materials like rubber and petroleum from previously underdeveloped regions. Thus the world was bound much closer than before by international trading and credit relationships. Yet the fact remains that throughout the post-war years Europe remained politically distinct and the major non-European powers – the United States and Japan – played much smaller parts in European affairs than might have been expected.

'The private choice of small coteries of civil rulers and military staffs'

Before 1914 most of Europe was ruled by the small privileged groups which Wilson described. Only Scandinavia and a handful of western European states were run by governments which were fully responsible to elected assemblies. In Germany, the Hapsburg Empire and Russia and the rest of central and eastern Europe political power lay in the hands of the dynastic rulers, the landowners and the army staffs.

The war seemed to change all this. In Britain all men and some women were given the vote after the war while continental Europe was already sprouting a score of new democratic systems in 1918, which sought to reproduce the best features of the United States Constitution or the hallowed traditions of the British Houses of Parliament. Yet it was soon clear that the superficial political changes the war had brought about were much greater than the changes in the social and economic substructure of European society. One of the most important features of the post-war world was the way in which the 'coteries of civil rulers and military staffs' maintained their political influence under the new systems.

'The aggression of great powers'

In 1914 Europe had been a continent of great powers. Blot out Britain, France, Germany, Austria-Hungary and Russia and what was left? Only the isolated extremities in the north and in the Mediterranean. The new Europe which was the product of the war, the Russian revolution and the Versailles agreements seemed to be quite different. A belt of small states appeared from the Arctic Circle to the Adriatic under the protection of the League of Nations. Yet even in 1918 with Austria-Hungary destroyed and Russia and Germany in eclipse, Europe was dominated by the Big Three (see p.6) and the 1930s were characterised by the 'aggression of great powers upon small'.

'The folding together of empires'

The war of 1914–18 destroyed three European empires and one Middle Eastern one, but amongst the victorious allies Britain, France, Japan, Belgium and Italy were all imperial powers. Despite Wilson's fine phrase they had no intention of dissolving their vast possessions and indeed all of them hoped to increase them at the expense of Germany and Turkey. The representatives of the 'unwilling subjects' of the victorious powers – Irishmen, Indians, Egyptians and Annamese – who came to Paris in search of their freedom were sent away empty-handed.

Of all Wilson's hopes this was probably the most naive. The strongest line of continuity between the world of 1913 and that of 1919 was the continued domination of European–North American civilisation directly or indirectly over the rest of the world. The war had even increased this. It had prompted the colonial powers to extend their administrations into areas which had previously been only nominally under their control and the growth of world trade made the underdeveloped more, not less, subservient to the industrialised nations. In 1919 almost the whole of Africa and most of Asia was either ruled by the European powers or fell within their spheres of political influence and economic exploitation.

The major exception was Japan, and Japan enjoyed her special position because she had matched the European powers in the development of her industrial and commercial potential and in the creation of modern armed forces. In 1904–5 she had defeated the lumbering Russian Empire and laid the foundations of her own empire in the Far East. During the war she had seized German territories in the Pacific and China and forced the feeble Chinese government to accept most of the notorious Twenty-One Demands which gave her wide powers of interference on the Chinese mainland.

In 1919 the empires within Europe had disappeared, but more people in the world as a whole were under alien rule than ever before.

'The power of small bodies of men to . . . use mankind as pawns in a game'

Even in those countries such as Britain and France which had well developed parliamentary systems, it was still true in 1919 that relatively small groups of traditional political leaders wielded considerably more political power than their single vote nominally gave them. But at least this oligarchic power was moderated by the constitutional system. In other countries, such as Germany, the war led to political changes without a social or economic revolution and small oligarchies continued to hold decisive power (see p. 15). Even more striking was the case of Russia where a complete political and social revolution only succeeded in transferring absolute political power from one small group to another (see p. 32). Within fifteen years of the peace, vast areas of Europe were ruled by small groups of men whose power was more despotic than that of any of their royal or feudal predecessors and who were prepared to use their subjects even more ruthlessly as pawns in a game.

So Wilson was over-optimistic in 1919 and the two decades which followed witnessed the destruction of most of what he had hoped for. Moreover in those years it became common to blame this failure less upon the situation the war had produced, than upon the peace which had followed and in which Wilson himself had had so great a part. It is therefore important to start a study of the world after 1919 by looking at the peace treaties and seeing how both the victors and the vanquished faced their post-war problems.

The peace treaties and the defeated powers   I

No settlement which contravenes the principles of eternal justice will be a permanent one. Let us be warned by the example of 1871. We must not allow any sense of revenge, any spirit of greed, any grasping desire to override the principle of righteousness.
Lloyd George, 12 November 1918

The Peace Conference met in Paris on 18 January 1919. The Treaty of Versailles between the allies and Germany was signed on 28 June. The treaties with the other central European powers followed during 1919 and 1920. Considering the complexity of the problems the work was done very quickly, but events in Europe could not wait even that long. While the delegates were debating, the Czechs and Poles were already creating their new nation states; two revolutions swept through Hungary and a host of other issues were being settled *de facto* whatever the statesmen in Paris might say. In any case the representatives of the great powers were not operating in a political vacuum; they had to listen to public opinion in their own countries. In Britain, France and America the people understandably wanted a quick settlement and a speedy demobilisation. All too often they were also motivated by the sense of revenge and the spirit of greed against which Lloyd George had warned. The conference met nine weeks after the last shots were fired, but victory fever was still at its height and the atmosphere in Paris in particular was overcharged with emotion.

The Peace Conference
The membership of the conference was restricted to the allies and the associated powers, such as the states of South America, which had nominally supported them. The defeated powers only attended

when the victors wished to announce their decisions and neither Russia, which had made peace prematurely (see p. 32), nor the neutral nations were invited to join in the discussions.

In fact the authorship of the treaties was even more limited than this suggests. The most important decisions were taken by the Big Three – America, Britain and France – represented by Woodrow Wilson, Lloyd George and Clemenceau. These three men balanced the claims of the lesser powers, heard the pleas of the delegates from the submerged peoples, such as the Czechs, who were aspiring to nationhood, and above all sought to win acceptance from each other for their own particular interests. The result was that the peace was based not on any defined principles, but on a series of political compromises which frequently left everybody dissatisfied.

Paris 1919
Orlando of Italy, Lloyd George, Clemenceau and Wilson.

Personalities and aims

In these circumstances the personalities and aims of the three principal statesmen were of great importance. First there was Clemenceau, the chairman of the conference, an old man with deep and bitter memories of two German invasions of France in his own life-time. Clemenceau was not blindly vindictive as he has sometimes been depicted and as many of his fellow countrymen wished him to be, but he was determined to prevent the rebirth of Germany as a great power. His deep understanding of the workings of European politics and his pessimistic view of human nature led him to believe that France's security could only be assured by punitive measures against her temporarily helpless enemy.

In contrast Woodrow Wilson brought to the conference a high-minded faith in the progress of mankind and the possibility of perpetual peace in Europe. What was needed, he believed, was the separation of the races of Europe into their own nation states; the government of these states by democratic means; the destruction of trade barriers; and a system of open diplomacy through a great international body. Wilson was strong-willed, even dogmatic, and by no means as naive as he is sometimes painted. He was the one leader who was not seeking any acquisitions for his own country and he had behind him the enormous power of the United States which had scarcely been strained by intervention in the last stages of the war. Unfortunately he lacked any real insight into the European political system and he did not have the full backing of his own countrymen.

Finally there was Lloyd George. The British Prime Minister was above all a skilled political tactician. He was moved neither by Wilson's altruism nor Clemenceau's fears and hatreds. His aim was to preserve and enlarge the British Empire and to strengthen his own rather precarious political position in Britain. With his mercurial political abilities and his freedom from either the principles or the prejudices of the other two, he was well equipped to produce expedient compromises and political deals.

The Treaties

The allied powers actually drew up five treaties; the Treaty of Versailles with Germany was signed in June 1919; the Treaties of St Germain and Neuilly with Austria and Bulgaria followed in the same year. In 1920 came the Treaties of Trianon and Sèvres with Hungary and Turkey respectively. Sèvres was radically revised three years later, but the others either recognised changes which had already come about or attempted to bring about permanent alterations in the

European political system. The element of permanence was emphasised by the fact that the creation of the League of Nations was part of the Treaty of Versailles itself. The League was the fulfilment of Wilson's desire for a world peace-keeping organisation, but it was also given the specific duty to preserve the situation created by the peace treaties and its clauses made it mandatory upon all its members to join in this task. This had important implications both for the United States (see p. 20) and for the future of the League itself (see p. 126).

The re-shaping of eastern Europe
It was in eastern Europe that the map was changed most dramatically. The whole area had been thrown into a state of political instability first by the expulsion of the Russians by the Treaty of Brest Litovsk (see p. 32) and then by the collapse of Germany and the disintegration of the Hapsburg Empire a few months later. In this area the peacemakers were able to arbitrate and draw up new frontiers, but the basic course of events was out of their hands. From the old Russian lands emerged Finland, the Baltic republics of Estonia, Latvia and Lithuania and a reborn Poland. The old master races of the Hapsburg Empire, the Austrian Germans and the Hungarian Magyars were left with their homelands. The Czechs and the Slovaks created a new nation and the rest of the empire was parcelled out to the Poles, the Italians, the Romanians and to Yugoslavia, a new composite south Slav state, dominated by the Serbs. These and other minor changes can be seen opposite but no map can convey their true significance.

In the first place an area previously dominated by three great powers had been broken up into a series of small and medium states. These states were plagued, almost without exception, with two problems. The first was political instability. The old states like Austria and Hungary found their former political role had been destroyed and their old markets lost. Their internal politics turned to extremes and they soon reverted to non-democratic forms of government. The new states lacked political experience and inevitably disliked and feared their old masters. There too the new statesmen tried to run western European constitutions without western European social or economic systems.

Economic insecurity, social backwardness and political extremism were all made more dangerous by the second great problem: national minorities. When Wilson had promised national self-determination to Europe he cannot have had a very clear idea of the racial structure

Europe 1914

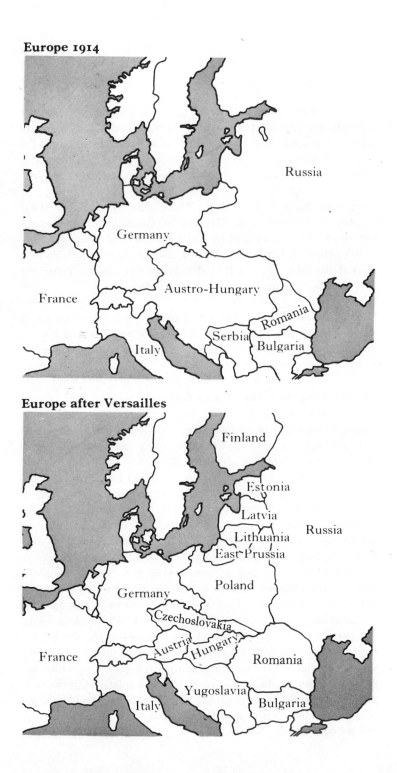

Europe after Versailles

of central Europe. There were no clear-cut lines which separated Czech from German, or Magyar from Slav, and no frontiers could be drawn without leaving minority groups which would be constant sources of friction and a constant excuse for outside intervention. Not surprisingly when the frontiers were finally drawn the largest minority groups were those of the defeated nations and they gave Russia, Germany and Hungary yet another grudge against the Treaty of Versailles. As it was there were 3,500,000 Germans in Czechoslovakia, 1,000,000 in Poland and 500,000 in Yugoslavia. There were 1,500,000 Magyars in Romania and many more in Czechoslovakia and Yugoslavia. There were Germans in Italy, Bulgars in Romania and Magyars in Poland. Poland, now an enormous state with a population of 28,000,000, had millions of non-Polish people within her frontiers. The unsatisfactory division also worked the other way, as tens of thousands of Czechs, Poles and Slavs remained outside their new national states.

Even in 1920 such a situation was dangerous. It became very much worse in the 1930s, when a revived Germany was able to dominate the area and exploit the grievances of these mutually suspicious states to her own advantage.

The resettlement of the Middle East
The break-up of the Ottoman Empire produced a superficially similar proliferation of new states in the Middle East. The public and secret agreements of the allies concerning the Middle East were largely self-contradictory. In 1916 the Sykes–Picot Treaty had secretly arranged to partition large areas between Britain and France. The 1917 Balfour Declaration had publicly promised to found a national home for the Jewish people in Palestine (see p. 229); while in November 1918 the allies had also publicly declared: 'The goal envisaged . . . is the complete and final liberation of the peoples who have for so long been oppressed by the Turks, and the setting up of national governments and administrations that shall derive their authority from the free exercise of the initiative and choice of their indigenous populations.' In the end the settlement was another compromise. Turkey certainly lost her empire. All her Arab lands and parts of Thrace were stripped from her so that she was left no more than Anatolia and a foothold around Constantinople. However, very few of her old colonies became truly self-governing. Only the remote Arabian peninsula was left to its native rulers, while the new states of Syria, Palestine, Iraq and Transjordan became League of Nations mandates (see p. 230), the first under the control of France and the others under Britain.

The Middle East 1914

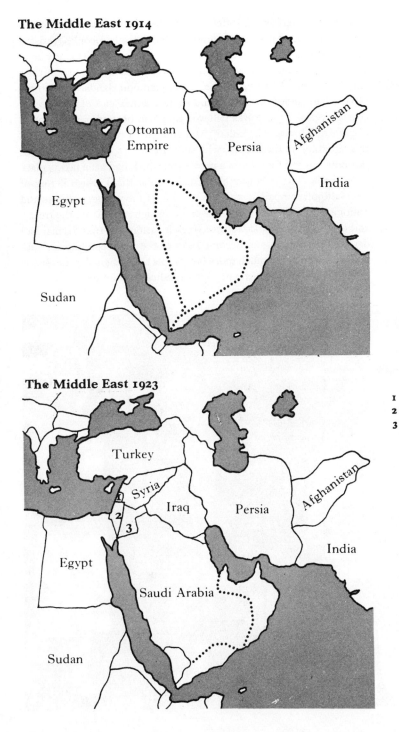

The Middle East 1923

1 Lebanon
2 Palestine
3 Transjordan

The Turkish settlement differed from the others in another important sense. The Turks, alone amongst the defeated peoples, resisted many features of the treaty and managed to reverse them very soon after the war. They were goaded into action not by the loss of their empire, but by the threat to their Anatolian homelands. In 1919 the Greeks had landed at Smyrna and tried to annex part of the western coastal area and the Turks believed they had been wrongly stripped of parts of Thrace. The Sultan, Mohammed VI, was forced to accept this situation by the British, who sent troops to Constantinople, but this only hurried the pace of a revolution which had been taking place in Anatolia. There Mustapha Kemal, one of the Turkish heroes of the Gallipoli campaign, with the backing of the younger officers and politicians, set up a National Assembly which repudiated the treaty, and organised resistance to the Greek invasion. By 1921 Kemal had deposed the Sultan and become head of the new republic. He succeeded in winning a much more favourable treaty signed at Lausanne in 1924 and threw his country into a radical revolution.

The Turkish Revolution
A photograph taken in 1925 to show the revolution in women's fashion in Turkey.

Within a few years Islam had ceased to be the official religion, the Ottoman political system had been destroyed, and a new one-party state created. This was only a beginning: Kemal proceeded to wage war against illiteracy, the subordination of women and the backwardness of the Turkish economy. He encouraged western dress and brought in western technologists and engineers. He could not destroy all remnants of the old Turkey overnight, but he did succeed in building a compact new state with a modern army, a reasonably efficient administration and the foundations for industrial and commercial expansion. His revolution was an early prototype of those which were to shake the rest of the Middle East a generation later (see p. 235).

Germany and peace

The way in which peace came to Germany was later the material for a great deal of Nazi propaganda so it is worth following the true sequence of events. From 1916 onwards power in Germany lay not with the Chancellor, or even with the Kaiser, but with the generals, in particular Hindenburg and Ludendorff, the heroes of the eastern front. It was the military leaders who took the decision to wage unrestricted U-boat warfare which brought the United States into the war, and throughout 1917 and early 1918 they ignored the pleas of the Social Democrats for a negotiated peace. By the autumn of 1918, however, they realised that the war was bound to be lost and there was every indication from strikes and unrest in the navy that it would be followed by a social upheaval. In these circumstances the army chiefs switched policy and ordered the civilian government to make peace at once, while the army was still intact and the enemy still outside German territory. In September they made the liberally inclined Prince Max of Baden Chancellor and he opened negotiations with the allies. On 4 November the sailors at Kiel mutinied, on the 7th Kurt Eisner set up a socialist republic in Munich, on the 9th there were riots in Berlin. Prince Max then resigned in favour of the Social Democrat leader, Ebert, having first forced the Kaiser to abdicate. The Kaiser fled to Holland and on 11 November the armistice terms with the allies were accepted. They were harsh, but the army had insisted that the civilian negotiator Erzberger accept them. In fact the army leaders had achieved their limited aims. Peace had been made, the army had not been defeated in the field, and the armistice had been made by, and could later be blamed upon, civilian politicians. It was a manoeuvre the generals repeated in the following months. They used their forces to preserve the moderate socialist government, but left that government to take all the responsibility for the unpopular peace treaty.

The Versailles Settlement

Germany had to cede territory all round her frontiers. Alsace-Lorraine was returned to France. The rich coal-producing area of the Saar was granted to France for fifteen years to make good the destruction wrought in the industrial areas of north-east France. North Schleswig, a predominantly Danish province, was returned to Denmark and several small areas were given to Belgium. More important, Posen, West Prussia and parts of Silesia were ceded to Poland, and Danzig became a free city. Another port, Memel, was granted to Lithuania. On top of this Germany lost all her colonies and was forced to sign clauses which prevented any future union with Austria and acknowledged the frontiers of the new state of Czechoslovakia.

Apart from the territorial clauses there were a number of other important sections. Germany was to lose her fleet and her air force; the army was to be reduced to 100,000 men and to be forbidden the use of heavy weapons. The Rhineland was demilitarised and certain points occupied by allied forces. The Germans had also to sign clauses acknowledging their guilt in starting the war, agreeing to the trial of war criminals and promising to pay reparations to her enemies which would be fixed at a later date by an allied commission.

These terms came as a terrible shock to the German people. They were terms of absolute defeat yet, because Germany had not been invaded and the German army had not been routed, the Germans did not feel that they had suffered such a defeat. In any case they believed that their political revolution which had overthrown the autocratic monarchy would win them much easier terms. Many politicians favoured the rejection of such a humiliating dictated peace. But the generals knew how vulnerable their position was. To protect Germany from a truly crushing defeat and to safeguard their own organisation and reputation, they forced the government to accept the treaty.

The Weimar Republic

The provisional government over which Ebert presided was predominantly a Social Democrat one since the Social Democrats had been the largest party in the elections of 1912 and clearly represented the people most adequately in the new political situation. However, their position was very far from secure, even after the elections of January 1919 had confirmed Ebert in power.

The government was under fire from two sides and only survived because it suited the army to support it. The first challenge came from the extreme left. In December 1919 the army had to crush mutinous sailors in Berlin and the next month it saved Ebert from a rising of the Spartacists, or extreme left-wing socialists. A communist government in Bavaria was also overthrown with the help of the army and irregular armed units known as the Freikorps. However the suppression of these left-wing movements revealed a second danger – from the extreme right. The Freikorps who crushed the Spartacists had brutally murdered left-wing leaders and the new right-wing Bavarian government was thoroughly disloyal to the central government. In March 1920 right-wing elements staged their *coup* in Berlin, the Kapp *Putsch*, and this time the government received no help from the army. The *putsch* was defeated by a general strike by the Berlin workers instead. Between 1918 and 1922 there were several hundred political murders in Germany carried out by right-wing nationalists. The victims included Erzberger, the Social Democrat Minister of Finance, who had signed the armistice and von Rathenau, the Foreign Minister, who was blamed for the reparations settlement and, as a Jew, was particularly reviled by the nationalists.

The Constitution

Despite this unstable situation the National Assembly, meeting in the calmer atmosphere of Weimar, did manage to produce a new democratic constitution. It was based on universal suffrage and the electorate was to choose a new legislature at least every four years. Proportional representation would allow minority interests a voice and referenda could be held on special issues. The head of government was the Chancellor, who was to be appointed by the President, but responsible to the Reichstag. The President himself was to be elected every seven years by the whole electorate. He was head of state and commander-in-chief of the armed forces; he also held special powers to rule by edict in an emergency.

The system of government created in this way was in most senses admirable and when Ebert became President in August 1919 with a coalition government of Social Democrats, Centre party and Democratic party members (see p. 96), there was the hope that Germany was settling into a genuinely parliamentary system for the first time. Yet the system did have its weaknesses. It allowed the existence of many small parties and this in turn meant that the government always depended upon an alliance of several political groups.

Moreover the political reforms were not accompanied by parallel reforms elsewhere. Although there was a largely socialist government no attempt was made to nationalise basic industries or to break up the power of the great industrial cartels. In the administration the old imperial officials very often remained in power and the new army embodied the ideals and *esprit de corps* of the old.

Reparations

The reparations which Germany was to pay to her former enemies were finally fixed at £6,600,000,000 in 1921. This enormous sum, which was to be paid off in money or goods over a number of years, provoked another outcry in Germany. It also contributed to an uncontrollable inflation. There was a desperate shortage of goods of all sorts and a complete lack of faith in the stability of the economy or the value of the mark. In 1914 the exchange rate had been 15 marks to the £; by 1922 it was 750; in January 1923 it had risen to 72,000 and by the late autumn the mark had become worthless with an official exchange rate of 16,000,000,000 to the £. The crisis, which had been aggravated by the reparations payments, got out of hand when the government suspended further payments, for this provoked an occupation of the Ruhr industrial area by the French and Belgian armies and led to a snowballing political and economic disaster.

Galloping inflation destroyed the savings of the middle class and thousands of workers were thrown out of work. The political effects were immediately apparent in the growth of the extremist parties.

The French in the Ruhr
January 1923. French troops picnic in the Ruhr Coal Syndicate during their abortive debt-collecting mission.

In 1922 there was a communist rising in Saxony and in 1923 a National Socialist one in Munich which first brought Hitler to the notice of most Germans (see p. 100). Once more the régime was saved by the army, but in 1923, five years after the end of the war, the situation in Germany remained unsettled and potentially explosive.

Rethinking the Peace Treaties

The troubles which wracked Germany and other parts of eastern Europe in the early 1920s were by no means all due to the peace treaties but they did focus attention on the treaties and lead more and more people both within the defeated countries and elsewhere to criticise them. In Germany the denunciation of the treaties became one of the most important party slogans for right-wing groups. Even moderate Germans in the centre parties felt that the treaties were unjust and that they fell short of Wilson's own principles. To strip Germany of all her colonies was not, they argued, 'a free, open-minded and absolutely impartial adjustment of colonial claims'. When the allies forbade the Austrian Germans to seek an act of union with Germany itself or put the German population of the Saar or West Prussia under foreign rule, they were not applying the principle of national self-determination. Above all no German could agree to the clause whereby Germany shouldered all blame for the outbreak of war and was consequently expected to pay general reparations. Many echoed the bitter reply of the German delegate at Versailles:

I do not wish to answer reproaches with reproaches, but if it is from us that penance is demanded, then the Armistice should not be forgotten. Six weeks passed before we obtained it, and six months before we learned your conditions of peace. Crimes in war may not be excusable, but they are committed in the struggle for victory, in anxiety to preserve national existence . . . The hundreds of thousands of non-combatants who have perished since the eleventh of November through the [allied naval] blockade were killed with cold deliberation, after victory had been won and assured to our adversaries. Think of that when you speak of guilt and atonement.

These views won some sympathy outside Germany. This was increased by the relentless attitude of Poincaré, the new French Premier, and in particular by his invasion of the Ruhr to collect reparations which Germany could not hope to pay at that moment. Such feelings were strongest in the United States and in Britain, where the greatest critic of the peace was the influential economist J. M. Keynes. Keynes had resigned his post at the Paris Peace Conference because he believed that a harsh treatment of Germany would have a disastrous effect on Europe and he argued his case brilliantly in *The Economic Consequences of the Peace*, published in 1920. In it he painted a vivid and critical picture of the circumstances of the conference:

Paris was a nightmare. A sense of impending catastrophe hung over the frivolous scene; the futility and smallness of man before the great events confronting him; the mingled significance and unreality of the decisions; levity, blindness, insolence, confused cries from without, all the elements of ancient tragedy were there. Seated amid the theatrical trappings of the French Saloons of State, one could wonder if the extraordinary visages of Wilson and Clemenceau, with their fixed hue and unchanging characterisation, were really faces at all and not the tragicomic masks of some strange drama or puppet show.

He also issued a stern warning of the consequences of a harsh peace:

If the European Civil War [the war of 1914–18] is to end with France and Italy abusing their momentary victorious power to destroy Germany and Austria-Hungary, they invite their own destruction also, being so inextricably twined with their victims by hidden psychic and economic bonds.

The victors and the post-war world

Sometimes people call me an idealist. Well, that is the way I know I am an American. America is the only idealistic nation in the world.

When Woodrow Wilson made this claim at Sioux Falls in September 1919 he was not just indulging in a piece of political flattery; he was appealing for American support for the most important creation of his political life – the League of Nations. He was fighting a political crusade, the strain of which brought on a paralytic stroke just one week later and ended his political career. Nor was his boast without some foundation. He had certainly been the most idealistic leader at the Paris Conference and the United States had not sought to win an inch of territory or a dollar of reparations. European cynics might argue that the Americans had won their reward in the enormous profits that American industry had reaped from the war, and that it was easy to be generous when they had never experienced invasion and had suffered relatively few casualties. All the same many Americans felt that their country had fought the war for higher motives than most of the other participants and that their President had brought to the sordid political dealings of Europe a new spirit of righteousness and justice.

However, even in 1918 when Wilson set out for Europe, not everyone in America was behind him. Some people felt that it was wrong for the President to take the unprecedented step of leaving the country during his term of office. Others bitterly resented the fact that he took no members of the Republican party with him in his delegation. Already there was a reaction against 'Mr Wilson's War'. There was a fear of entangling foreign alliances and both conscription and war-time government controls in transport and industry had provoked considerable opposition in a country which had a built-in suspicion of central authority.

Even as Wilson was on his way to Paris, ex-President Theodore Roosevelt issued a warning that, 'Mr Wilson has no authority what-soever to speak for the American people at this time . . . His fourteen points and his four supplementary points and all his utterances every which way have ceased to have any shadow of right to be accepted as expressive of the will of the American people.' The congressional elections which were held while Wilson was in Europe seemed to confirm Roosevelt's words. The Republicans won control of both the Senate and House of Representatives and Wilson returned with a heavy task ahead of him. He had signed the Peace of Versailles and with it the Covenant of the League of Nations, but until he had won approval from Congress by a two-thirds majority his signature had no validity.

For Wilson it was a simple matter of right and wrong: 'The question is whether we can refuse the moral leadership that is offered us, whether we shall accept or reject the confidence of the world.' But his countrymen did not see it in such clear-cut terms. There were many, in both parties, who supported Wilson. There were many more who agreed with his policy in general but feared too close an alignment with the European nations in the League. In particular they wanted a modification of Article 10 of the Covenant which would have bound the United States to 'respect and preserve against external aggression the territorial integrity and existing political independence' of other members. They were not sure that they wished to be bound to defend every aspect of the Treaty of Versailles or to be involved automatically in every European war. There were also those who opposed the whole idea outright. They were led by the millionaire Republican isolationists such as Theodore Roosevelt, Frick and Mellon who believed that America had nothing to gain from intervention in European affairs. Others opposed Wilson on largely personal grounds. His high-handed and self-righteous attitude and his refusal to compromise on the smallest issue earned him the hatred of many leading politicians. Most powerful of these was Henry Cabot Lodge, a Republican senator who had advocated the creation of a world peace-keeping organisation for many years. How-ever in 1919 he was Chairman of the Senate Foreign Relations Committee and his hatred for Wilson led him to swing all the influence of his position against the President's plans.

Wilson might still have won approval for the League had he been prepared to make some concessions to the opposition in Congress. Instead he appealed direct to the people in a nation-wide campaign and it was the strain of this campaign that broke him in September 1919. For the remaining months of his term of office he lay, partially paralysed, in the White House, and his government was left without leadership or initiative. In March 1920 the Senate finally rejected the Treaty and the League. In the autumn the Republican candidates swept to victory in the presidential elections. America had rejected both Mr Wilson's War and Mr Wilson's Peace.

Isolationism

This rejection was expressed in other ways as well. Demobilisation caused considerable unemployment and in 1920–1 there was a brief economic depression. This brought new immigration laws which shut out thousands of Europeans who were seeking a new life away from war-torn Europe. At about the same time there was mounting pressure for more tariffs which would shut out European goods from the rich American market. In fact most Americans neither understood nor were interested in the problems of Europe. America was still a dynamic young society too deeply involved in the problems of her own breakneck expansion to spare much thought for the troubled Old World across the Atlantic.

Great Britain after the war

Britain, like the United States, had not suffered the horrors of invasion and in Britain too there was a traditional suspicion of continental commitments, but Britain had been much more deeply involved in the war both materially and psychologically.

The cost of the war had been terrible in any terms. First the old regular army of the British Expeditionary Force, then the 'first hundred thousand' volunteers from Lord Kitchener's recruiting drive, then the conscript armies had been slaughtered on the battlefields of Flanders. The war had destroyed a generation of young men born in the last quarter of the century with quite noticeable effects on the balance of the population.

The economic effects were incalculable. Direct expenditure on the war raised the National Debt twelvefold in four years. Britain had lost millions of tons of shipping and she had been forced to sell off vast blocks of overseas investments. Even before 1914 Britain was losing ground in the world's markets and during the war countries such as the United States and Japan, which had been less heavily engaged in the war effort, captured many of her trade outlets.

What, apart from military victory, had been gained in return? Britain and her dominions took by far the largest share of Germany's old colonial empire. She gained control of important areas in the Middle East. Finally she had to accept with France the rather unwelcome political leadership of Europe and the League of Nations. It seemed a meagre enough return and most people in Britain wanted above all to be free from further expensive commitments abroad and to begin to tackle the country's grave social and economic problems.

Deaths in Battle 1914-18

Britain and Commonwealth
900,000

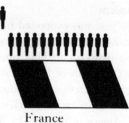

France
1,400,000

Germany
1,800,000

Austria-Hungary
1,200,000

USA
50,000

Russia
1,700,000

The political situation

The elections of 1918 were fought in an overheated political atmosphere when crude slogans like 'Hang the Kaiser' and 'Squeeze Germany till the pips squeak' were more popular than sober statements of policy. The coalition of Conservatives and Lloyd George Liberals which had controlled the country since 1916 romped home very comfortably. In the end they commanded 478 seats against 26 Asquith Liberals and 59 Labour party members. This left Lloyd George more than ever at the mercy of his Conservative allies. On the other hand the Labour party had become strong enough to attract not only the trade union vote, but the support of many middle-class radicals. This might have been even more apparent but for the peculiar circumstances of the election. Although 2,000,000 more men and 8,000,000 women were given the vote, the registers were very out of date and a large number of soldiers never got the chance to vote. In addition the jingoistic atmosphere of the immediate post-war period told against the Labour party which had been deeply divided over the whole issue of the war.

There were other ways in which the political situation had changed. During the war the government greatly extended its authority and although it soon renounced its control over prices, railways, food and coal production, many of its wartime powers remained. Of the ministries created in the war those of Labour, Pensions and Air survived the peace. They were joined by the new ministries of Health and Transport. The University Grants Committee and the British Broadcasting Company (later Corporation) were both products of the immediate post-war years. The government was also responsible for forcing the rationalisation of the railways into four regional companies in 1921–3. All these things were signs of the growing influence of the central government in social and economic affairs.

Social and economic problems

Most politicians and businessmen were anxious to get back to the 'good old days' of pre-1914, while most workers hoped that they really might get the 'homes fit for heroes' which Lloyd George had promised. It was certainly impossible to go back to the old days. It was not just that the economy was disrupted by the wartime interference with international trade or the effects of mass demobilisation. Britain had to face up to a new world situation. She had lost many of her old markets and it was even clearer than before that her basic industries were being outclassed by more efficient foreign competitors. In America and elsewhere British goods were being excluded by tariff barriers, while the British government still hesitated to throw over its old free trade traditions and British industrialists failed to develop new light industries.

In 1919 there was a boom in the old industries such as shipbuilding, steel and textiles as the world sought to make good its wartime losses, but this did not last. Even in the boom, the average working man did not benefit much, as prices outstripped wages, and afterwards thousands were thrown out of work. Parliament was dominated by conservatively minded businessmen and politicians and the government refused to nationalise troubled industries such as coalmining. There were major industrial disputes in the railways, the docks and the mines. In 1919 and 1920 there were 2,000 strikes and an average of 60,000 men striking every day. Even the London police went on strike. By 1920 there were 2,000,000 unemployed, there was a chronic shortage of houses, and discontent was rife not only amongst trade unionists but in many sections of society. Demobilisation brought bitter disillusionment for soldiers who could not find jobs. There was also the disillusion of those who had tasted a better world and then had it snatched from them:

Distress cannot be measured exactly by dividing the amount of
weekly income by the number in the family. During the war and in
the boom the standard of living rose, and many little luxuries came
to be regarded as necessaries – smoking, visits to the cinema, and to
public houses . . .
Report on Unemployment in Manchester

These things were now beyond the means of those who had to live on the meagre unemployment benefit or 'dole' to which they were entitled under the Unemployment Act of 1920.

Ireland
There was not even a real peace; from 1919 till 1921 British soldiers were fighting a ruthless war against the Irish nationalists, a war which brought no honour and which few people could even understand.

The Irish had become increasingly militant after the unsuccessful Easter Rebellion in Dublin in 1916. In the 1919 elections the most extreme party, the Sinn Fein, won almost all the seats, but its members refused to come to Westminster. Instead they set up their own government in Dublin and soon they, rather than the British administration, controlled large areas of rural Ireland, Their leader, de Valera, became self-proclaimed President of an Irish Republic and by 1920 there was a full scale war between the brilliantly organised

guerilla forces of the Irish Republican Army, commanded by
Michael Collins, and the British troops and Black and Tans, an
armed police force who outdid the Irish terrorists in their brutality.
After months of murder and reprisals the nationalists were in considerable financial and military difficulties while the British government was under pressure from public opinion both at home and
abroad to make peace. The treaty which Lloyd George negotiated in
December 1921 made Ireland, with the exception of the six predominantly Protestant counties in the north, a self governing dominion owing a rather shadowy allegiance to the King. The six counties
remained part of the United Kingdom, but had their own parliament
in Belfast to deal with purely local affairs.

Dublin 1916
*The Rising was a failure
but it led directly to the
Sinn Fein victory in the
1918 elections.*

The treaty split the Sinn Fein in two. De Valera and his group
wanted nothing short of a united Irish Republic but Michael Collins
and other leaders, supported by the majority in the Irish Parliament,
were prepared to accept the treaty and the status of the new Irish
Free State. There followed two years of bloody civil war between the
two factions before the Free State was firmly established and in the
meantime the whole Irish business had lost Lloyd George a good deal
of popularity especially amongst the Conservatives.

B

Imperial affairs

It was not only in Ireland that Britain continued to face fighting and disorder. In India the claims of the nationalists had been met by a few concessions (see p. 248), but more impression was made on Indian public opinion by the massacre at Amritsar in which British troops had fired on an unarmed Indian crowd. By 1920 the Indian nationalist movement was becoming a formidable threat to the British administration.

The British also had difficulties in the new Arab mandates and in Egypt where emergent nationalist forces bitterly resented European control. On top of this Lloyd George nearly involved the country in an unnecessary and unjustifiable war with Mustapha Kemal in Turkey in 1921. This incident known as the Chanak crisis, compounded with all the other failures of the Coalition government to bring about the fall of Lloyd George.

The fall of Lloyd George

Like his fellow wartime leaders, Clemenceau and Wilson, Lloyd George suffered a rapid decline in popularity after 1919. By 1922 a large section of the Conservative party had decided that the alliance with Lloyd George had become a political liability. This disaffection in the rank and file reached a climax at a meeting of Conservative Members of Parliament at the Carlton Club in which the majority defied their leader, Austen Chamberlain, and voted to end the alliance with the Lloyd George Liberals. The Coalition government immediately resigned and the leadership of the Conservatives reverted to Bonar Law who formed a wholly Conservative government. Many prominent Conservatives, including Austen Chamberlain and Lord Birkenhead, refused to serve under him and this meant that a number of relatively unknown men were thrust into important positions. Amongst these were Stanley Baldwin, a deeply committed opponent of Lloyd George, who became Chancellor of the Exchequer, and another member of the Chamberlain family, Neville, who was made Minister of Health. It was the beginning of a new age for the Conservative party for these two men were to dominate the political life of the party and the country for the next two decades.

The new society

Even before the war had ended many of the older generation began to realise that Britain would never be quite what it had been before 1914 again. One of the greatest changes which contemporaries noticed was the new status of women. In the war they had taken over men's jobs, they had driven ambulances and they had worked in munitions factories. Their efforts won for them what the suffragette agitation had failed to achieve. In 1918 women over the age of thirty were given the vote and the first woman MPs took their seats in Parliament. For the less seriously minded there were other equally significant changes. In the words of a verse by A. P. Herbert:

In greedy haste, on pleasure bent,
We have no time to think, or feel,
What need is there for sentiment
Now we've invented sex appeal?
We've silken legs and scarlet lips,
We're young and hungry, wild and free,
Our waists are round about our hips,
Our skirts are well above the knee.

The revolution in fashion
Edwardian fashions at the Henley Regatta contrast with post-war bobbed hair and short skirts.

New fashions, short hair, cosmetics and smoking in public were really just as important as the extension of the franchise in emphasising the new position of women. Even more fundamental was the decline in the size of families. For the first time methods of birth control were openly discussed and most young couples chose to have no more than two children. There was also a rise in the divorce rate. In 1910–12 there were, on average, 823 divorces a year; ten years later the figure was 3,619.

There were many signs that the war had produced a less strait-laced society. There was a great expansion in the popular press and in the (still silent) cinema industry. Cars, radios and even aeroplanes were no longer the rare curiosities they had been. (In 1919 Alcock and Brown made the first transatlantic flight.) For the Bright Young Things of 1922 all this was of much greater interest than unemployment in South Wales, or the obscure problems of tariff reform.

Post-war France
Of the major western nations France had suffered by far the most. Between 1914 and 1917 one French soldier had died, on average, every minute. By the end of the war the toll had risen to 1,400,000 dead and 4,250,000 wounded. The material losses were on the same level, for the fighting had swept through her most highly industrialised areas. In the end the French were victorious, a French Marshal was commander-in-chief of all allied forces on the western front and the French Premier was chairman of the peace conference. Yet Clemenceau himself was the first to realise how empty this triumph was. France was only victorious because Britain, and later America had born the brunt of the fighting after 1916. The defeated Germany was still more populous and potentially more powerful than France could ever be.

The French had avenged 1870, they had won back Alsace-Lorraine, they had taken a share of the German colonial empire, but what they really wanted was security and this was much more difficult to achieve. In the pursuit of security Clemenceau and his successors followed two policies. The first was to involve the United States and Britain in European affairs in peace as they had been in the war. In this they failed almost completely. America not only refused to guarantee France's frontiers, but rejected the whole system created by Versailles. Britain was equally unwilling to give the French specific assurances and although she did remain a fellow member of. the League, her attitude towards Germany drifted further and further from that of the French.

In the long run French attempts to cripple Germany were equally unsuccessful. Clemenceau was prevented by his allies from separating the Rhineland from the rest of Germany and the French were not even assured of permanent possession of the Saar. Reparations were fixed at a much lower level than the French wanted and then the inflation and the suspension of payments destroyed their value. In the meantime French politicians came to base their budgets on a notional idea of what reparations should bring in rather than re-form their old-fashioned taxation system. The results were natur-ally disastrous both for government finances and for the long term reconstruction of the country.

Like most other European countries after the war, France was troubled by inflation and industrial unrest. The 1919 elections re-turned an overwhelmingly right-wing government which seemed incapable of dealing with the economic problems or of introducing long needed economic reforms. The new assembly refused to elect Clemenceau as President and his place as Prime Minister was taken first by complete nonentities and then by the inflexible *revanchist*, Poincaré. It was Poincaré who initiated the invasion of the Ruhr to collect reparations, but even this desperate action brought few rewards and, after a few months, the French withdrew again empty-handed.

France, like Britain, was also faced with colonial troubles. In north Africa Abd el Krim led a revolt which took six years to crush; there was unrest in Syria and in 1920 a young Vietnamese, Ho Chi Minh, was getting his first experience of Communist party organisation in Paris and plotting the liberation of his homeland.

French society and politics
The colonial troubles and even the unsuccessful foreign policy would have mattered much less if France had enjoyed political stability at home. In fact the country was plagued by political extremism from which Britain, even in these difficult times, was relatively free. The trade unions and all the left-wing organisations were fatally split between the communists and moderate socialists. On the right there were powerful anti-democratic groups which were quite prepared to resort to political violence like their German counterparts. By the 1930s such groups were a dangerous fifth column which sapped France's determination to resist the menace of Nazism and fascism.

These extremist groups were so troublesome because there was never a strong coalition of centre parties. The two most important, the

Socialists and the Radicals, were uneasy partners. The Radicals represented the small shopkeepers and lower middle classes. They were opposed to government interference in the tax system or the economy and in an economic crisis they tended to become obstinately conservative and unenterprising. The Socialists on the other hand favoured moderate social and economic reform, but were always vulnerable to attacks from the communists and their own left-wingers. Neither group was able to win the support of the basically conservative and Catholic peasantry.

The post-war scene in France was not altogether gloomy. The country remained the cultural centre of Europe. It was the home of the post-Impressionist schools of painting and its literary life was adorned by such brilliant figures as Marcel Proust, Jean Cocteau and André Gide. Paris also continued to attract many distinguished foreign writers and artists such as Ezra Pound and James Joyce who both spent a good deal of time there in the early 1920s. By the mid-twenties it also seemed possible that the country might have a more hopeful political future under the guidance of moderate statesmen such as Herriot and Briand. Unfortunately this was not to be. Even before the Great Depression there were once more signs of frag-mentation of the centre parties and a further drift to political extremism. During the thirties this chronic political instability was to leave France with neither courage nor initiative in European affairs.

The war had put a considerable stress on both the defeated and the victorious powers. It disturbed their economic structure, strained their political systems, and sparked off social unrest. But the changes in western Europe and North America were mild compared with those which convulsed Russia during the same period.

The emergence of Soviet Russia 3

Russia was the first of the great powers to collapse under the strain of the war. By the end of 1916 her forces were in total disarray and the administration was in chaos. The passionate nationalism which had swept the country in 1914 had been dissipated by a corrupt and inefficient government which had led the nation from one disaster to another. In February 1917 a spontaneous revolt by the workers and armed forces overthrew the authorities in Petrograd (now Leningrad; in 1917 it was still the capital of Russia). The Tsar abdicated almost immediately and his power officially passed into the hands of a provisional government of liberals and moderate socialists under the leadership of Alexander Kerensky. Kerensky and his allies intended to introduce constitutional reforms, but their immediate concern was to pursue the war more efficiently. Unfortunately for them the February Revolution had unleashed much more radical forces and their authority was challenged from the first by groups of soldiers, workers and intellectuals who formed their own local committees, or Soviets, and demanded a share in the government.

In April 1917, with the help of the Germans who regarded him as a useful disruptive force, Vladimir Lenin returned from exile in Switzerland to Russia. Lenin was the leader of the most extreme group of socialist revolutionaries and his return transformed the situation. He had no desire to co-operate with the provisional government and demanded instead that all power should be given to the Soviets. With the simple slogan of bread for the workers, land for the peasants and peace for everyone, he sought to build up the backing for the Bolsheviks in the Soviets themselves, especially in Petrograd and Moscow. In the meantime the front was collapsing as Russian troops deserted in their tens of thousands and it was harder and harder to control events in the countryside. In October Lenin and his collaborators staged a brilliantly successful *coup* in Petrograd and Kerensky was driven into exile. The Bolsheviks were still only a tiny group, but their support was concentrated in the two great cities which gave them control of the machinery of government and the centres of communication. Lenin immediately proclaimed himself as head of a new provisional government committed to make peace and to carry through not just a political revolution but the social and economic transformation of Russia.

When a Constituent Assembly was elected in January 1918, the Bolsheviks found themselves heavily outnumbered by the more moderate Mensheviks and the Social Revolutionaries, who still commanded the support of the peasants. But Lenin was not prepared to bow to the wishes of an electorate which, in his view, was still unaware of its true destiny. Once again his control of the centres of power allowed him to dismiss the assembly and perpetuate the one-party domination of the Bolsheviks.

In the meantime the Germans had been advancing into Russia almost unopposed. In this hopelessly disadvantageous position Lenin had to make peace. He knew it was impossible to rally Russian forces and, equally important, he could not fight both the Germans and his political rivals on the home front. But peace could only be bought at a terrible price. On 3 March the Soviet delegates signed a humiliating treaty at Brest Litovsk. Russia lost a quarter of her population, over a quarter of her railway system, a third of her food supplies and three-quarters of her heavy industry. Moreover Brest Litovsk only brought peace with the Germans; for the next three years Russia had to endure the armed intervention of the other powers and a savage civil war.

The civil war
After the first shock of the Bolsheviks' *coup* their opponents soon prepared to stage a counter-revolution. By the summer of 1918 Social Revolutionary and Menshevik leaders had control of parts of the Volga basin; White Army officers were leading a rebellion of the Don Cossacks; and the Ukrainians and Georgians had established separatist governments of their own. Soon afterwards Admiral Kolchak set up a White Russian government in Siberia and claimed, rather ineffectually, to be the supreme leader of all anti-Bolshevik forces.

The civil war which followed was complicated by the intervention of

Moscow 1917
*Lenin the revolutionary
exhorts the people.*

the great powers. The British and French sent forces to Murmansk,
Archangel and the Black Sea; the Americans and Japanese landed in
eastern Siberia and advanced far inland. The powers intervened at
first in the hope of keeping an eastern front open against the Germans,
and later because they feared that the Bolshevik revolution might
spread. Their forces were not supposed to settle the political future
of Russia, but their presence was bound to help the White Russian
armies. A further complication was provided by the presence of the
40,000 strong Czech Legion, a force made up of released prisoners
from the Austrian army. They were on their way back to the western
front via Vladivostok when the revolution broke out and their main
interest was to get out of Russia, but for many months they controlled the Trans-Siberian Railway and they too generally favoured
the Whites. As a result Lenin and his lieutenants were soon in grave
difficulties. For a while their control was limited to little more than
the old state of Muscovy and the White generals were within striking
distance of Petrograd and Moscow. Yet by 1920 the last remnants of
the White armies were being evacuated from the Crimea.

B*

The Russian Civil War

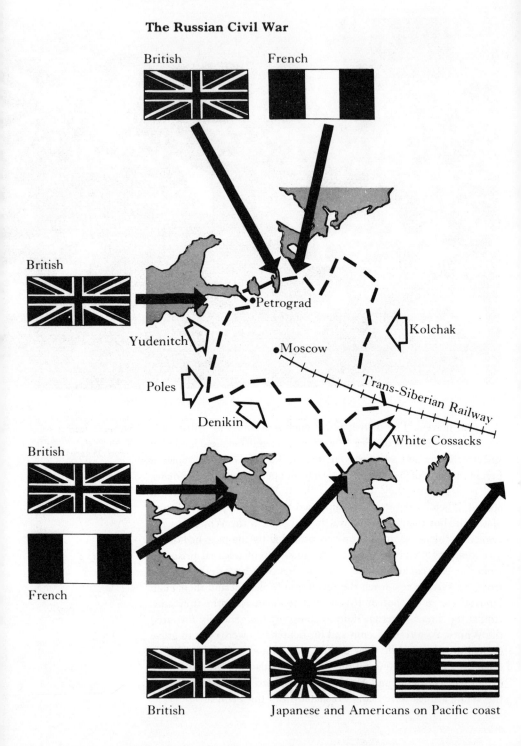

British

French

British

Petrograd

Kolchak

Yudenitch

•Moscow

Poles

Trans-Siberian Railway

Denikin

White Cossacks

British

French

British

Japanese and Americans on Pacific coast

There were several reasons for the Bolshevik victory. Once the Germans had surrendered, the war-weary people of Europe and America were increasingly unwilling to fight in an obscure civil war in which the issues were so unclear and their sympathies deeply divided. The allied governments soon lost all confidence in the irresponsible and deeply divided White leaders. Both sides fought the war with terrible brutality, but the Whites came to be hated by the civilian population even more than the Bolsheviks and they refused to compromise with the peasants over the distribution of the great estates. Finally the Red leaders, especially Lenin and Trotsky, proved to be much more effective as propagandists and military and political strategists.

Early in 1921 the last of the interventionist armies, the Japanese, withdrew; later in the year the remaining White armies collapsed and in the spring of 1922 the Russians made peace with their last effective military opponents, the Poles.

War Communism
Soon after their seizure of power Lenin and his associates began a series of drastic social and economic experiments which became known as 'War Communism'. Factories were taken over by the workers and the produce of the land expropriated by the state. Banks, mines, shipping fleets and finally all concerns employing more than ten people were nationalised. By 1921 private trade and the private ownership of land had been outlawed. Meanwhile the government built up a system of political control through secret police, censorship and propaganda that was both more efficient and more ruthless than that of any of the tsars.

The results of War Communism were disastrous. The peasants refused to grow more food than they needed for themselves; factory production slumped and trade in consumer goods dried up altogether. Even before the end of the civil war the government had to abolish worker control in the factories, but prices still soared until money became utterly worthless. On top of this millions starved to death because of the disruption of food supplies and Russia was ravaged by diseases, such as cholera and even plague, which had been unknown in Europe for generations.

Although the Bolsheviks had defeated their counter-revolutionary enemies most of the population remained passively hostile. Even in the old Bolshevik strongholds there was disaffection. In March 1921 the sailors of the Kronstadt naval base, whose predecessors had played a key part in the October Revolution, mutinied against the Bolshevik government and were only crushed after ten days' bloody fighting.

The New Economic Policy

The end of the civil war and the failure of War Communism led Lenin to change his tactics. At the 1921 Party Conference he admitted that the process of socialisation would have to slow down and for a while Russia would have to allow some private enterprise. The state retained control of heavy industry, transport, banking and foreign trade, but peasant ownership of the land, private internal trade and even small-scale private industry were tolerated. In the factories worker control was replaced with state ownership – often with the old owner and manager in charge once more.

However there was no sign of liberalisation in political matters. Indeed after the Kronstadt Rising things grew progressively stricter. As late as 1920 the Mensheviks and Social Revolutionaries had been allowed to hold their conferences in Moscow but after 1921 the secret police began to make mass political arrests and moderate socialist leaders fled abroad. Lenin's attitude was ruthlessly logical. He, as much as any other socialist idealist, looked forward to a time

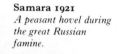

Samara 1921
A peasant hovel during the great Russian famine.

when the machinery of the state would wither away, but he believed that while communism was still beset by so many enemies any form of opposition from within must be crushed at all costs. Ultimately this meant that a few men at the head of the party wielded absolute authority. Lenin himself was head of both the Communist party and the government. After him came Kámenev and Zinoviev the senior party members, Trotsky the brilliant theoretician who became head of the Red Army, Bukharin the most able of the younger thinkers and writers and Stalin, the son of a Georgian peasant, who had been appointed Secretary-General of the party. These six men with Lenin made up the Politburo at the very head of the communist organisation.

The death of Lenin and the struggle for power

Lenin's health began to collapse in 1922 and he died in January 1924. In his last months he was increasingly preoccupied with the problem of his succession. He believed that Trotsky was by far the most able candidate, but also the most dangerous for he was strong-willed and could easily become a military dictator. Kamenev and Zinoviev were his closest friends, but he believed they lacked the courage and drive to lead Russia. Bukharin had not the force of personality and of Stalin he wrote, 'Comrade Stalin holds immense power in his hands and I am not convinced that he will always know how to use that power with moderation.' In fact just before his death Lenin was preparing to remove Stalin from his post as Secretary-General. Since no one man was fitted for the task Lenin could only hope that they would form a collective leadership in which their individual weaknesses would be cancelled out.

No sooner was Lenin dead than a bitter power struggle developed between Trotsky and the triumvirate of Zinoviev, Kamenev and Stalin. Trotsky was manoeuvred out of his post as Minister of Defence and his supporters were purged from the party and government organisations by Stalin who occupied a key position in the struggle.

On one level the struggle was a crude political vendetta, but like most Communist party conflicts it was fought in ideological terms. Trotsky believed that the Russians should place great emphasis on spreading the revolution as rapidly as possible beyond the confines of the Russian state. According to his theory of 'permanent revolution' the Russian revolution itself could only progress if it developed into a general world revolution. Stalin maintained that it was possible to have 'socialism in one country'; that is to say that Russia could advance far along the road to a true communist society alone, though of course other revolutions were to be encouraged. In many ways the ideological differences were much smaller than the personal differences between the two men, but, in any case Stalin was triumphant in both ideological and personal terms.

Then even before he had finally dealt with Trotsky, Stalin turned on his former allies. Within the Politburo he allied with Bukharin and his group to oust Zinoviev and Kamenev. Here again ideological

Trotsky
Theorist and man of action : the Commissar for War in 1923.

weapons were used. Kamenev and Zinoviev were particularly concerned with rapid industrialisation. On the other hand Bukharin's group were more concerned with agriculture and were in favour of slower industrialisation and a continuation of the New Economic Policy. Stalin very ably exploited these differences, and between 1925 and 1927 drove Kamenev and Zinoviev not only from the Politburo and from all positions of power in the government, but from the Communist party itself.

The Five Year Plans
Once his three main rivals had been defeated Stalin flung Russia into one of the most dramatic economic revolutions in the history of mankind. On the tenth anniversary of the October Revolution he announced his proposals for the first Five Year Plan which was to come into effect from the beginning of 1928. He explained the necessity for an enormous programme of strictly controlled economic expansion in these terms:

*She [old Russia] was ceaselessly beaten for her backwardness. She
was beaten by the Mongol Khans, she was beaten by the Turkish
Beys, she was beaten by the Swedish feudal lords, she was beaten by
the Polish-Lithuanian Pans, she was beaten by the Anglo-French
capitalists, she was beaten by the Japanese barons. She was beaten by
all for her backwardness. For military backwardness, for political
backwardness, for industrial backwardness. She was beaten because to
beat her was profitable and went unpunished . . . We are fifty or a
hundred years behind the advanced countries. We must make good
this lag in ten years. Either we do it or they crush us.*

The plan covered many aspects of human activity including the improvement of education and the promotion of equality for women but it rested basically on two economic policies: collectivisation and industrialisation. Both of these policies were diametrically opposed to the ideas of Bukharin and his group and they too were pushed out of office and replaced by loyal Stalinists during the early years of the plan.

Collectivisation. In the first flush of the revolution land was distributed to the peasants and each family cultivated its individual plot. Under Stalin's new plan most land was to be pooled to form large farms of several thousand acres supporting eighty or more families. The farms were run by elected management committees and the produce sold at controlled prices to the state. Such large units were able to use improved methods and the government set up a series of tractor stations staffed by young technical advisers, who could not only improve productivity but also act as propagandists and political supervisors. Some land was not included in these collectives, but formed even larger farms run by the state on which the peasants worked as paid labourers.

Collectivisation had two aims. In the first place it was part of the economic plan to raise more food and support a larger industrial population. In the second place it would destroy the rich peasant or *kulak* class which had become the most conservative social group in the new Russia. The *kulaks* were blamed for poor harvests and the poor peasants were encouraged to seize their lands. Where the *kulaks* resisted they were imprisoned, deported to Siberia or shot wholesale. The policy was carried out with utter ruthlessness, and, despite both active and passive opposition, 60 per cent of the farmland was collectivised and a good deal of the rest incorporated in the vast state farms.

Industrialisation was the other half of the plan. To be strong Russia had to catch up with the western world in industrial production. Huge capital investment was needed and there was no hope of help from abroad. There was a terrible lack of equipment so every man and woman had to be mobilised to fight the battles for steel and electricity, coal and chemicals. This great planned creation of a new society attracted many engineers and craftsmen from all over Europe and America. What they saw both inspired and horrified them, as one western visitor to the great new steel centre at Magnitogorsk described:

A quarter of a million souls, communists, kulaks, foreigners, convicts and a mass of blue-eyed Russian peasants building the largest steel works in Europe in the middle of the Russian steppe. Here men froze, hungered and suffered but the construction went on with a disregard for individuals and a mass heroism unparalleled in history.

This was the Russia of the Five Year Plan: on the one hand fanatical enthusiasm for a great human adventure; on the other savage repression and regimentation of human bodies and souls in the belief that the end justified the use of any means necessary to achieve it.

The first Five Year Plan (1928–32) was in many ways highly successful. Nearly three-quarters of the arable land was collectivised, though at a great cost in human life and not always with any improvement in output. The great industrial centre in the Donetz basin was developed; tractors were produced in their thousands at the newly named southern city of Stalingrad, oil at Baku, steel at Magnitogorsk. The biggest power station in Europe was built at Dneiprostoi and Russia's network of roads and railways was immensely improved.

The second Plan (1932–7) was supposed to concentrate upon providing the people with the consumer goods and food which they had to do without during the First Plan. Some forms of rationing ended and the food shops were a little better stocked. Thousands of new houses were built, though never enough to keep pace with the population. But in fact during these years most resources were still directed into mining, heavy industry, electrification and strategic transport projects such as the White Sea and Volga Canals. Collectivisation also continued so that by 1940 the 25,000,000 land holdings of 1928 had been reduced to 250,000.

The first two plans produced many political strains. The peasants remained bitterly opposed to the changes in agriculture. Sometimes they refused to grow crops on the new collectives and perhaps 10,000,000 people died during the famines of the 1930s. There was discontent even within the party. The secret police had become a permanent and ever more menacing part of the government machine and Stalin's own wife committed suicide under the strain of the killings for which her husband was responsible. Yet the dictator knew when to make concessions. In the mid-thirties the peasants

Industrialisation
The blast furnaces of Magnitogorsk.

were allowed small private vegetable plots and even animals for themselves and the collectives were given better prices for their surpluses. Stores of army grain were distributed in the cities, food was imported, and a great propaganda campaign was waged to win back the enthusiasm of the people.

In a period of rising prices and a desperate shortage of all goods propaganda was very important. Special ginger groups encouraged high production in emulation of the legendary worker, Stakhanov, who was supposed to have mined 102 tons of coal without a break. This campaign emphasised the retreat of the Communist party from some of its ideas of absolute equality. Good workers were offered special bonuses and incentives and the new *élite* of technicians, managers and party officials enjoyed a noticeably better standard of living than the ordinary workers.

The Third Plan began in 1937, but was interrupted by the German invasion of 1941. By the late 1930s it had become obvious that the early plans had led to all sorts of wasteful practices. In the Third Plan emphasis was put on quality of production rather than quantity and speed. A large part of the plan was devoted to armaments and the whole plan became increasingly hard to operate as the forces swallowed up more and more manpower. In 1934 the army had numbered 940,000 men; by 1940 it was 4,000,000 strong.

Taken as a whole the plans had produced an enormous advance in the Russian economy, though *per capita* she still lagged behind the other powers:

1939	Population (millions)	Steel (million tons)	Coal (million tons)
USSR	170	15	165
USA	131	32	395
Germany	73	18	186 (+ lignite)
Great Britain	47	7	227

The lag in Russian light industry was, of course, even more striking.

The party and the Constitution
With the revolution Imperial Russia fell apart and when the various non-Russian areas were once more brought under the control of Moscow they formed part of a federal plan. The main block of territory became the Russia Soviet Federal Socialist Republic, and it was joined by other Soviet republics in Georgia, Armenia, the Ukraine and elsewhere to form the Union of Soviet Socialist

Republics. However the federal structure could not disguise the fact that all important matters were controlled by the central government and the constituent republics had only a theoretical right to secede.

A more complicated constitution was promulgated in 1936. The eleven constituent republics were retained, but power became even more centralised. The new Constitution provided a complicated series of assemblies elected on universal suffrage and it guaranteed the right to work, to freedom of speech, assembly and conscience. In practice there was no democracy and no freedom in the western sense. There was a state controlled press, one political party, one candidate at each election and no opposition in the Supreme Soviet. But for the communist theoreticians this was seen as the fulfilment of democracy. Stalin himself explained, 'In the USSR there are only two classes, workers and peasants, whose interests, far from being mutually hostile, are . . . friendly. Hence there is no ground in the USSR for the existence of several parties and consequently for freedom for these parties.' On the other hand in western society, to quote Lenin, 'Democracy is always bound by the narrow framework of capitalist exploitation and consequently always remains, in reality, a democracy for the minority, only for the possessing classes, only for the rich . . . In the ordinary peaceful course of events, the majority of the population is debarred from participating in social and political life.' In any case Stalin needed absolute control to carry out his plans and power was wielded not so much through the Constitution as through the party structure.

In communist theory the party had always been regarded as the vanguard of revolution. It was the pressure group of politically active workers and intellectuals without which the masses would be help-less. During this period party membership grew very rapidly – from 23,000 in 1917 to 2,500,000. All the same it remained an *élite* enjoying great privileges and all political power. In the party as in the state, all power came from above even though theoretically it had a demo-cratic structure. Congresses were held yearly until 1925 but then only in 1927, 1930 and 1939. Real authority lay with the Central Committee and above all with the Politburo under Stalin's direction.

During the inter-war period the top positions in the party fell more and more into the hands of managers, technical experts and intel-lectuals; very few went to peasants or workers. The party bosses, the army officers and the managers in the state industries were already beginning to form a new middle class. By 1939 14 per cent of the population earned 35 per cent of the national income (though of course this inequality was still much less than in the great capitalist countries).

The great purges
Stalin's own position at the head of the political structure seemed quite unchallengeable in the 1930s and yet in 1935 he began a bloody political purge of unprecedented horror even in Russia.

In 1934 the party chief of Leningrad, Kirov, was assassinated. His death may well have been the work of the secret police (NKVD) with whom he was on bad terms but it was blamed on a Trotskyite plot backed by western European capitalists and fascists. Thousands of people were rounded up and sent to prison and a security commission began to investigate the whole party structure.

In 1936 there was a dramatic development. Stalin staged a series of show trials in which the most prominent old Bolsheviks were forced publicly to denounce themselves as capitalist or fascist spies. Kamenev and Zinoviev were amongst the first to sign their own death warrants in this way and the old Central Committee was virtually wiped out. Of the 140 members in 1934 only fifteen still held their posts in 1937. Nor was it only the leaders who suffered. All those connected with them were suspect. Millions of ordinary people, nomadic tribesmen, minority racial groups, and Russian peasants were imprisoned, sent to Siberia or executed. In 1940 there were still 10,000,000 people under some form of detention in Russia.

In 1937 and 1938 Stalin turned on the army leaders. The civil war hero Marshal Tukhachevsky and a quarter of his officers were executed and thousands more were dismissed. Finally there was a purge of the purgers. Beria took control of the police from Yezhov who died with many of his minions, a victim of his own system.

Stalin's motives are clear enough. He wished to eliminate all those who had played a major part in the October Revolution. These men had not only to be killed, but also discredited. They were forced to denounce themselves and later they were removed from all histories of the revolution. Stalin was left without any rivals, an almost superhuman figure served by men who owed everything to his patronage – Kaganovitch, Zhdanov, Malenkov, Molotov and Kruschev.

The terrible bloodletting was completed in a macabre way. In 1940 Trotsky, in exile in Mexico and still indefatigably denouncing Stalin was battered to death with an ice axe by a Russian agent.

Ideology and society

In the sort of society created by the Russian revolution every aspect of human life was of significance to the state. For the first decade the Soviet government did all it could to destroy the inherited customs and culture of the old Russia. The Bolsheviks encouraged young people to reject the ideas of the older generation and to despise bourgeois values such as respect for parents or the sanctity of marriage. In schools old subjects were replaced by Marxist social studies and discipline often broke down.

Naturally the revolutionaries had no sympathy for the established Orthodox Church. The clergy lost their civil rights and were ejected from their schools and seminaries. Thousands of priests died at the hands of the police and the party encouraged the Association of Militant Atheists to discredit the teachings of Christianity and to humiliate its believers.

All art forms also fell under the supervision of the authorities and many Russian intellectuals went into exile or to prison. New art forms which seemed to reject old values were favoured and Russians showed a great interest in the new medium of the cinema. Directors such as Eisenstein produced films which were not only effective propaganda but very fine examples of cinematography.

However, the self-conscious modernism of the 1920s did not last. With the Five Year Plans there came almost a cultural counter-revolution. Stalin had always been narrowly nationalistic in his attitudes and he saw the need to excite national pride to carry the people through the strains of the economic programme. As a result history ousted Marxist sociology in the schools and patriotism became a virtue. School textbooks acknowledged the greatness of pre-revolutionary Russian national heroes. Eisenstein began his work on the great film trilogy *Ivan the Terrible* for which Prokofiev composed the music and other films honoured Alexander Nevsky the saviour of Muscovy and Suvorov the great eighteenth-century general.

Family virtues were reinstated. Divorce which had been extremely simple after 1917 suddenly became very difficult, while mothers who produced large families were awarded public honours and discipline was tightened in homes and schools.

The revival of patriotism was of course of the greatest importance in the creation of an effective army to defend the Russian motherland. Universal military service was introduced and in contrast to the post-1917 years there was a privileged officer class headed by the *élite* General Staff. Even the Church was partly rehabilitated. Its role in the creation of the Russian state was recognised and the attacks of the atheists abated a little.

The outstanding part of this process was the development of the cult of the leader. As his rivals were displaced Stalin's own position became more and more godlike. In science, art and literature he was the ultimate arbiter of taste and truth. The result was that official cultural activity was often worthless hackwork and servile adulation, while composers, authors and scientists of distinction were likely to see their work proscribed and stood in danger of imprisonment or death. The only safe works were those which concentrated on the cult of the leader:

Tenderly the sun is shining above,
And who cannot but know this sun is you?
The lapping waves of the lake are singing the praises of Stalin
The dazzling snowy peaks are singing the praises of Stalin
The meadows' million flowers are thanking you, thanking you.
The well-laden table is thanking you, thanking you,
All fathers of your young heroes, they thank you, Stalin, too.
Oh heir of Lenin, to us you are Lenin himself;
Beware, you Samurai*, keep out of our Soviet heaven.
Poem by Djambul, an elderly Kazakh poet, published on the front
page of Pravda, *10 March 1939*

* A reference to the Japanese armies which were threatening Russia's Manchurian frontier.

RUSSIA AND THE WORLD

During the inter-war years Russian foreign policy also passed through some dramatic convulsions with far-reaching results. No doubt the long-term aims were always the same, but three distinct phases can be observed between the end of the civil war and the German blitz-krieg in 1941 which flung Russia willy-nilly into the wartime alliance with the western democracies.

Isolation 1920–33
After the civil war relations with the other powers were inevitably very bad. Russia had suffered in quick succession the German invasion of

1916–18, the humiliating peace of Brest Litovsk, the allied interventions and the Polish War. For her own part she was openly seeking to spread revolution to all parts of the world and to stir up colonial peoples against their white masters. In 1919 the Comintern or international socialist organisation was set up in Moscow under Zinoviev to co-ordinate communist tactics in a world campaign under Russian leadership.

However, the new state could not remain completely isolated, especially as there was no sign of a communist millennium sweeping over the rest of Europe. Her first friendly contacts were with Germany. Partly because the Russians had no part in the *Diktat* of Versailles and partly because both countries had grievances against the victorious powers, they aligned themselves by the Treaty of Rapallo. Both parties wrote off all claims for reparations and resumed trade and diplomatic relations. The treaty threw the rest of Europe into confusion for it seemed to be an ominous alliance of the two outcast states. The relationship cooled a little thanks to communist plots against the Weimar Republic and Stresemann's closer links with the West (see p. 94), but they remained reasonably friendly throughout the 1920s.

Relations with the victors of the First World War were much less good. Britain did recognise the Soviet government *de facto* but all through the 1920s there was mutual suspicion. The British resented communist propaganda in Asia and the panicky reaction to the Zinoviev letter (see p. 70) showed how deep-rooted British fears were. American governments showed even less sympathy for the Soviet Union.

The Popular Front 1934–9
The Nazi revolution in Germany (see p. 102) produced a profound change in Russian policy. All military co-operation with Germany ceased and communists were ordered to ally themselves with socialist and liberal parties in the European democracies. In 1934 Russia joined the League of Nations and the next year she signed a mutual defence pact with France which also guaranteed the security of Czechoslovakia. In 1936 and 1937, the years of the Rome-Berlin Axis and the anti-Comintern Pact (see p. 131), the Russians became firm supporters of collective security through the League of Nations, but many European countries remained just as frightened of Russia as they were of Nazi Germany.

The Nazi-Soviet Pact 1939-41

From 1938 onwards co-operation between Russia and the democracies broke down completely. Although Russia had guaranteed Czechoslovakia and offered to act in conjunction with the democracies against Hitler, Britain and France refused to accept the offer and the Poles would not allow transit rights to the Red Army. The Russians were not invited to the Munich meeting (see p. 137) and the betrayal of Czechoslovakia naturally led them to fear that they too might be abandoned in a showdown with Hitler. On top of this the Great Purge had thrown the Red Army into temporary disarray and weakened Stalin's confidence and the confidence of the western democracies in Russia's ability to adopt a tough foreign policy.

Stalin certainly had no faith in the honesty of France and Britain and despite sporadic negotiations throughout the summer of 1939 they could not agree on a guarantee for Poland or upon a common policy against Hitler. In August 1939 the world was suddenly shaken by the announcement of a Nazi–Soviet Pact by which the two arch-enemies came to terms, and secretly agreed to partition eastern Europe between them. The pact threw communists outside Russia into utter confusion and convinced anti-communists of Stalin's complete lack of principle. On the other hand it bought Russia two years' breathing space before the hammer blow of Operation Barbarossa finally fell (see p. 147).

The New Russia

In some senses Russia in 1939 was what it had always been: a vast police state governed by a heavy and ruthless bureaucracy under an absolute head of state. It was a country in which the masses lived in great poverty while a small *élite* enjoyed considerable privileges; a country where political freedoms existed only on paper and the state sought not only to dragoon the bodies of its subjects, but to regiment their minds.

But there were also vital differences. In a matter of just one decade the country had been flung through the early stages of industrialisation, which had taken from five to ten times as long in other advanced countries, and the communists had created a new type of society which had many positive lessons to offer especially to the poorer nations of the world.

The United States: Depression and New Deal 4

The successful establishment of a communist system of government in Russia was one of the most significant events in modern history, but its true importance was hidden for some years by Russia's partial isolation from the main stream of European politics. The same may be said of the emergence of the United States as a dominant world power. America could have taken up this new role at any time after 1918, but many people did not realise that this major shift in the balance of world politics had taken place for more than twenty years.

The Republican Years

The USA presidential elections of 1920 marked the end of an era in American politics. While Wilson lay, half paralysed, in the White House, Cox and Franklin Roosevelt, the Democrat candidates, were trounced at the polls by the Republicans, Harding and Coolidge. The ideals and ambitions of Woodrow Wilson had been decisively rejected by the American people and there followed a dozen years of Republican government which were, perhaps, the least glorious in the history of the Union. Harding, the new president, was an amiable nonentity, the tool of the unscrupulous politicians and financiers who had manoeuvred him into office. Before he died in 1923 his administration had become notorious for its corruption and misuse of public funds. Coolidge, his successor who served till 1929, cleaned up the government, but continued to govern in the interests of big business.

During these years all the initiative that Wilson had taken to build up the powers of the President and create a policy of constructive social and economic reform was lost. Business interests were allowed to control the nation's wealth and dictate government policy. By

1930 half the industry and commerce of the country was in the hands of 200 giant companies. The government poured lavish and unnecessary subsidies into aviation and shipping corporations and allowed the anti-trust laws which were supposed to check monopoly to fall into abeyance.

For a decade this policy seemed to pay off. America had become without doubt the richest country in the world and throughout the 1920s there was an almost unchecked business boom. There was exploitation of labour, there was gross inequality in the distribution of wealth, some groups, such as the small farmers, suffered a steady decline in their standard of living, but the bulk of the population was better off than ever before.

The movies
The great stars of early Hollywood : Rudolph Valentino and Mary Pickford.

American society seemed to enjoy a sudden sense of liberation that

won this age the nickname of 'the Roaring Twenties'. Women were given the vote and were soon expressing their new freedom in other ways – bobbing their hair, smoking in public and wearing daring knee length skirts. This was the 'Jazz Age' which produced so many things that seem typical of American society – big-time baseball and American football, the craze for consumer goods such as refrigerators and vacuum cleaners, hire purchase and mass production. It was the age of Hollywood with the heroes and heroines of the silent screen like Rudolph Valentino, Charlie Chaplin and Mary Pickford. In 1927 came the first 'talkies' with Al Jolson in the *Jazz Singer* and the *Singing Fool*. By 1930 100,000,000 tickets were sold at the movies every week. It was the age of the first mass-produced motor cars: the production of Henry Ford's famous model 'T' increased from 9,000,000 in 1920 to 23,000,000 in 1927.

It was also the age of Al Capone and gang warfare, of bootlegging (the sale of alcohol, which had been turned into a vast criminal racket by the prohibition of its legal sale in 1920), anti-Semitism, of race riots and a revival of the Ku Klux Klan. There were witchhunts directed against socialists and communists who received scant justice in the courts and even died for their political convictions, like Sacco and Vanzetti in a particularly infamous case.

Neither popular prejudices nor the inertia or worse of the government went unchallenged. There were individual politicians such as Senator Norris, the champion of government action in the supply of electricity and in agricultural reform, who kept up lonely struggles throughout these years. There were outspoken newspapers such as the *New Republic* and the *Nation* which were prepared to wage unpopular campaigns against injustice and prejudice. But these criticisms did not do much to divert most Americans from their immediate material preoccupations, nor from their determination to keep their country unentangled with the impoverished and strife-torn world beyond North America.

America and Europe in the 1920s

This new 'isolationism', endorsed at the polls by the electorate and preached by the Republican administration, sprang from several sources. First there was already a powerful reaction against 'Mr Wilson's War'. Secondly there was the problem of war debts. By the early 1920s European states owed the US government alone $10,000,000,000 in war debts and a good deal more to private investors. The European governments argued that the war loans had been spent on a common struggle in which the United States had contributed much less in other ways than Britain or France. The unwillingness of the Europeans to repay convinced most Americans that foreigners were untrustworthy exploiters of American generosity. Yet even given a willingness to pay it is hard to see how America's debtors could have set about it. Their economies had been shattered by the war and the only way they could earn dollars to meet the debt was by selling to America. But this method was closed to them by a series of protective tariffs imposed by the Republicans.

Ironically Europe's instability, to which the tariff policy contributed, forced America to be more active abroad than she had intended. In 1924 under the Dawes Plan, millions of dollars were poured into Germany to prop up the reeling economy and solve the reparations problem and this scheme was extended in the Young Plan of 1928. In 1922, America played a leading role in the limitation of naval armaments at the Washington Conference. Yet the basic isolationism of the country was clearly demonstrated when, for instance, the Senate twice vetoed Coolidge's mild efforts to make the United States a member of the World Court.

President Hoover and the Great Crash
In 1928 Coolidge declined to stand for another term and in his place the Republicans nominated Herbert Hoover. For Hoover it was the climax of a distinguished career in public service. He had filled several important posts in earlier administrations and played an important part in post-war famine relief work in Europe. 'The Great Engineer', as he was popularly known, had an outstanding reputation for efficiency and honesty. The election was held at the most dizzily prosperous point in the 1920s and not surprisingly Hoover routed his Democratic opponent Al Smith. He could say with some justification when he took up office 'We in America are nearer the final triumph over poverty than ever before in the history of mankind.' Yet within six months the whole financial structure of the United States had been shaken to the core and by the end of his four-year term the American dream of the twenties had been shattered and with it the reputation of the President.

In the early months of 1929 there was feverish financial activity. Faith in the irresistible prosperity of the country led to speculation in shares at ridiculous prices: prices which the expected profits could never justify. Then in the autumn confidence began to waver. On 21 October there was a rush to sell. On 24 October 12,000,000 shares were on offer on the New York Stock Exchange and prices

Crime
Al Capone, king of the Chicago mobsters.

Intolerance
Ku Klux Klansmen on the march.

were tumbling. On 29 October the market collapsed as worthless speculative shares dragged down the shares of even the great corporations like Du Pont and General Motors. All this was bad enough, but the effects could not be limited to Wall Street and the ruined financiers. Holding companies collapsed, factories closed their doors, banks stopped business. Millions were thrown out of work. Taxes could not be collected and funds for the welfare services or school-teachers' salaries could not be found. The Great Crash had turned into the Great Depression. By 1932 share prices had fallen by 82 per cent, output by 40 per cent, wages by 60 per cent. Twelve million men were out of work.

At first neither the government nor the people seemed to be able to grasp what had happened. Hoover and the experts kept assuring people that this was merely a financial upset and that things would soon return to normal; instead they got steadily worse. It became more and more clear that the government had to do something, but government interference in the economy went against all Hoover's most deep felt principles. The President was prepared to tinker with the credit rates or juggle with the details of the economic system but to interfere with the fundamental structure of the economy was not only against the conservative policies of his party; it seemed to be a threat to the system of unbridled competition on which he believed American democracy was founded. When, for instance, Senator Norris once more sought to get a government development plan for the Tennessee Valley, one of the most depressed areas in the Union, Hoover replied, 'For the Federal Government to go out and build up . . . power and manufacturing business is to break down the initiative and enterprise of the American people; it is destructive of equality of opportunity amongst our people; it is the negation of the ideals upon which our civilisation is based.' His answer to the Great Depression was economy and stoical acceptance of nation-wide hardship until the course of business took a turn for the better. For the unemployed, the mortgaged farmers and the ruined small businessmen this was cold comfort. In default of government action they looked elsewhere for some hope of improvement. Like the people of Europe under similar circumstances they sought a saviour, someone to rescue them from the collapse of the American dream.

Why had the dream of the twenties ended with such a grim awakening? Why was the Great Crash followed by the Great Depression? The traditional explanation was simply that production outran purchasing power and produced a glut, but the problem was more

VOL. LXXIX....No. 26,206.   ✳ ✳ ✳ ✳

PRICES OF STOCKS CRASH IN HEAVY LIQUIDATION; TOTAL DROP OF BILLIONS

PAPER LOSS $4,000,000,000

2,600,000 Shares Sold in the Final Hour in Record Decline.

Thyroid Determines if a Man Should Be Flier, Says Dr. Asher

Special to The New York Times.

BALTIMORE, Md., Oct. 23.— Upon perfect thyroid condition depends an airplane pilot's efficiency, declared Dr. Leon Asher, Professor of Physiology at the University of Berne, in an address last evening before the Biological Society School of Medicine of Maryland University.

complicated than that.

First, it was not just that production was growing faster than buying power, but that wealth was very unequally shared so that too large a part of it was in too few hands. Professor Galbraith has explained what this meant in *The Great Crash:*

In 1929 the rich were indubitably rich. The figures are not entirely satisfactory but it seems certain that the five per cent of the population with the highest incomes in that year received approximately one third of all personal income . . . This highly unequal income distribution meant that the economy was dependent on a high level of investment or a high level of luxury spending or both. The rich cannot buy great quantities of bread. If they are to dispose of what they receive it must be on luxuries or by way of investment in new plant and new projects . . . This high bracket spending was especially susceptible one may assume to the crushing news from the stock market in October 1929.

Secondly the business structure of the United States was especially vulnerable in this sort of collapse. The banks were generally small units which loaned money too easily and went bankrupt equally easily in a financial panic. Large sections of industry were controlled by monopolies and holding companies which were highly speculative ventures. These were the companies which collapsed first in 1929 and dragged down otherwise sound firms with them. On top of this the administration's tariff policy had provoked retaliatory action and the administration could not or would not produce an economic policy to meet the crisis. Central government had renounced its initiative and local government was overwhelmed by the size of the problem. It was in these circumstances that the Americans sought a national saviour.

Roosevelt comes to power
There were many strange claimants for this role. Some Americans looked to the ideologies of Europe – to communism or fascism – but America also produced its own batch of miracle workers. There was Father Coughlin, the popular 'Radio Priest' from Chicago who advocated all sorts of dramatic social reforms. There was Huey Long, the political boss of Louisiana and hero of the poor whites in this impoverished state, who had much in common with the European Fascists. There was Father Divine who claimed to be God himself. However, the most serious contender was a much more orthodox, though no less colourful figure, Franklin Delano Roosevelt.

Roosevelt's background was extremely conventional. He came from a wealthy east coast family and had been educated at exclusive private schools and Harvard. He was a distant cousin of Teddy Roosevelt, the progressive Republican president of the early years of the century. He started his political life in New York State where he championed the farmers against the political bosses in the city. In 1912 he was made Assistant Secretary to the Navy and proved to be an able and energetic administrator. He supported Wilson's entry into the war and later American membership of the League of Nations. Indeed on this issue he fought alongside Cox in the 1920 elections. Within a year of their defeat Roosevelt was struck down by poliomyelitis. His political career appeared to be in ruins.

However, with the help of his able wife, Eleanor, he fought his way back to political prominence, though he remained partly paralysed for the rest of his life. In 1928 he was elected Governor of New York State. Here in the face of the disasters of the Depression he was prepared to try out all sorts of new policies. His comparative success

F.D.R.
Roosevelt campaigning before his illness.

was in sharp contrast to the inaction of Hoover's government and it won Roosevelt the Democrat nomination in the 1932 elections. In his speech after nomination he said: 'I pledge you, I pledge myself to a new deal for the American people.' It was an open challenge to Hoover, who had become identified with the years of disaster.

In his election speeches Roosevelt managed to convey the impression that he was a moderate reformer who offered a slightly better chance of recovery than the discredited Republicans without being a dangerous revolutionary. In the end he won forty-two of the forty-eight states, the most crushing victory in American electoral history at that time. Then followed the most frustrating time in Roosevelt's life. He had been elected in November, but according to American law he had to wait five months, till March 1933, before he could take up office. In the meantime the Hoover administration lingered on with no policy of their own except to obstruct any plans their successors had for the future of the nation.

The New Deal
Roosevelt's administration opened at last with a dramatic 'hundred days' in which a great mass of legislation was rushed through to deal with the nation's ills. The new laws dealt with agriculture, industry, banking and social welfare and with them came a revival of hope. At last something was being done.

Roosevelt had always been deeply concerned with agriculture and one of the most famous of his early bills was the Three 'A's (Agricultural Adjustment Act) which was designed to control surpluses and prevent gluts and ruinously low prices for the farmers. He also sought to provide the farmers with better credit and to give security of tenure to tenants and mortgagees. He set up the civilian Conservation Corps, a body of young men who were provided with useful work fighting soil erosion and preserving the natural resources of the nation.

There was also legislation dealing with industry and commerce – bills to take America off the Gold Standard, to stabilise the banks, to control stock exchange practices, and to mobilise federal funds to prevent a new financial collapse. Equally important, the new president fought unemployment, low wages and the exploitation of labour. The Federal Emergency Relief Act supplied funds for work on public schemes and helped the local authorities to do the same. Unlike Hoover and many conservative European statesmen, Roosevelt saw that to fight the Depression the government had to be generous not economical, optimistic not cautious, energetic not passive.

One of the most famous pieces of labour legislation was the National Industrial Recovery Act – the Blue Eagle Act – so called because of the blue eagle seal which became a symbol of the charter of labour embodied in the act. This act along with the 1935 Wagner Act tried to give a new deal to labour with proper conditions of work, reasonable wages and the right to union bargaining. It sought this moreover not by coercion but by negotiation with the employers.

In all this New Deal legislation Roosevelt was not just legislating for the immediate future. He had a vision of America as a great and wealthy country in which people could achieve a proper standard of life under a democratic system. Nor was this just idealistic theorising. Roosevelt was trying to make it true by his massive backing for public works, by his labour codes, by his schemes for old age and sickness insurance, by his help to students through the National Youth Administration and above all by restoring people's faith and giving them something to strive for. Nowhere was this fusion of high ideals and practical policies better illustrated than in the work of the Tennessee Valley Authority.

The Tennessee Valley Authority (TVA)

The TVA was not typical of Roosevelt's work; indeed it was a unique project in American history, but it was all the same the embodiment of the best of the New Deal – radical reform by consent. The valley of the Tennessee River was one of the most backward and impoverished areas in America. Its agriculture was primitive and its once fertile soil was badly eroded. The great complex of rivers frequently brought disastrous floods. There was little industry and a low level of education. Even in the twenties the area had been depressed and Senator Norris had struggled in vain to get the government to put the great dam at Muscle Shoals to some use.

In 1933 Norris's dream began to come true; the Tennessee Valley Authority was created. It was a government corporation whose job was to build great dams to control the floods, to produce hydro-electricity, to set up fertiliser factories, to help farmers to save their land and improve their methods, and less directly to encourage private industry.

The achievements of the authority affected the people of the valley in many ways. A series of thirty great dams were built and the power of the rivers harnessed. In 1933, 3 per cent of the farms in the area had electric power; twenty years later the proportion was 93 per cent. Eleven million dollars of flood damage per year was prevented and 300,000 acres of arid land reafforested. Tens of thousands of farmers were introduced to new methods and given credit to buy new machinery. All this was achieved without coercion. The Authority did not seek to extend its power, but to co-operate with other local authorities. The farmers were not forced to use new methods, but volunteers tried out the ideas and then taught their neighbours. Roosevelt saw the whole project which had started from the dam and factories at Muscle Shoals as a demonstration to the world that democracy could plan and that free enterprise could achieve the common good – a theory that the crash had seemed to discredit. As he said:

Muscle Shoals is more today than an opportunity for the federal government to do a kind turn for the people in one small section of a couple of states. Muscle Shoals gives us the opportunity to accomplish a great purpose for the people of many states and indeed the whole union. Because there we have an opportunity of setting an example of planning not just for ourselves but for the generations to come, tying industry and agriculture, forestry and flood prevention, tying them all into a unified whole over a thousand miles so that we can afford better opportunities and better places of living for the millions of yet unborn.

This achievement was all the more remarkable because in America far more than in Europe there was a deep-rooted suspicion of government interference in the economy. But Roosevelt's reaction to any charges on that score were characteristically pragmatic. When asked if the TVA was a form of socialism he replied, 'It is neither fish nor fowl, but whatever it is it will taste awfully good to the people of the Tennessee Valley.'

The opposition and the later reforms
Roosevelt's work did not, however, pass unopposed, or in the long run unchecked. On paper he controlled a decisive majority in Congress but there were powerful forces aligned against him. The Republican minority naturally fought his legislation at every stage but there were also conservatives within his own party who conspired against him. The petty demagogues like Coughlin and Long denounced him when he rejected them as allies and his old rival for the leadership of the Democrat party, Al Smith, tried to undermine his position. And although none of these groups were powerful

The Tennessee Valley Authority

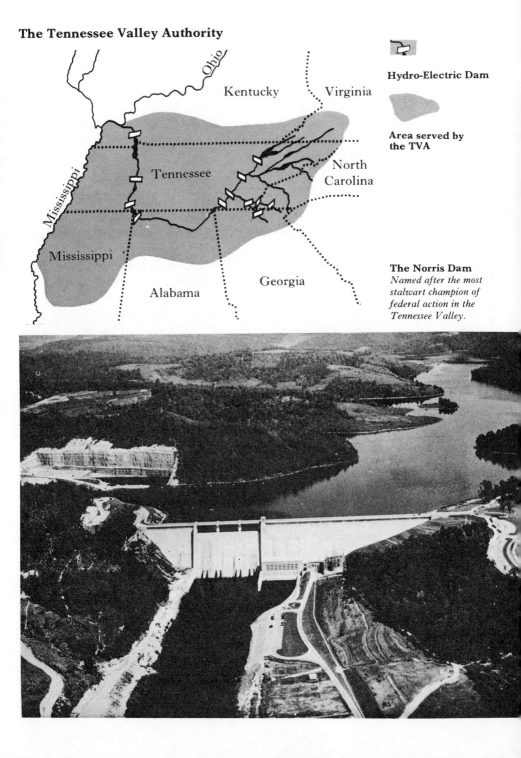

Hydro-Electric Dam

**Area served by
the TVA**

The Norris Dam
*Named after the most
stalwart champion of
federal action in the
Tennessee Valley.*

enough to baulk the President there was one body which could – the Supreme Court.

The nine judges of the Supreme Court had the power to annul any government action or Congress legislation which they believed contravened any of the basic principles laid down in the American Constitution. This was a perfect weapon to use against Roosevelt, for the majority of the judges were Republicans and even if they did not wish to enter into party political battles their judgements tended to favour the conservative side.

At first the Court upheld a number of government actions but between 1933 and 1936 twelve decisions went against federal laws and many more against New Deal legislation passed by individual state legislatures. The Blue Eagle Act and the Three 'A's were amongst the laws destroyed. The main claim against the New Deal legislation was that it interfered in areas specifically reserved in the Constitution for the state legislatures or that it contravened the Fifth Amendment which said that no man could be deprived of 'life, liberty or property' without due process of law. Thus attempts to fix agricultural prices or labour relations were taken to be incursions on the rights of liberty and property.

The President's position was extremely difficult. In 1936 he won the greatest electoral victory of all time – his opponent Landon captured only two states out of forty-eight. But the Supreme Court was able to dismantle his programme often by only a majority of five to four. Roosevelt prepared to counter-attack with characteristic vigour. He proposed that extra judges should be appointed and he toyed with the idea of seeking a constitutional amendment to limit the Court's power. But this time he was on uncertain ground. Even devoted supporters of the New Deal wavered when he threatened to tamper with the Constitution and his enemies were able to depict him as a would-be dictator trying to erode the sacred liberties of the individual.

In the end the President gave way and there was a tacit compromise. The NIRA and the Three 'A's were replaced by less controversial and in many ways more effective legislation and the Court did not block any other major pieces of his programme.

Roosevelt continued his work in the late thirties. There were useful acts dealing with housing and social security, farming and the consolidation of the TVA, but the original impetus was lost. In 1937 and 1938 there was a new wave of depression and Roosevelt was unwilling to spoil his attempts to balance the budget by handing out more relief. When the economy surged forward again in 1939 it was due as much to the demands of the war in Europe as to Roosevelt's efforts.

Judgement on Roosevelt

One of the most enthusiastic observers of Roosevelt's work was the English economist, J. M. Keynes, who devoted much of his career to the study of the economic weaknesses of the capitalist world and their cure. In 1933 Keynes wrote to Roosevelt, 'You have made yourself the trustee for those in every country who seek to mend the evils of our condition by reasoned experiment within the framework of the existing social system. If you fail rational change will be gravely prejudiced throughout the world leaving orthodoxy and revolution to fight it out.' Later, when the strength and weakness of Roosevelt's methods were clearer Keynes wrote: 'Mr. Roosevelt may have given the wrong answers to many of his problems but he is at least the first President of modern America to ask the right questions.'

Keynes's judgements give several clues to the real nature of Roosevelt's work. Roosevelt was concerned with the possibility of practical reform which would get the country out of the depression without destroying the existing social and economic structure. In one of his famous 'fireside chat' broadcasts in 1934 he rejected the charge that he was anything more than a commonsense reformer:

A few timid people who fear progress will try to give you new and strange names for what we are doing. Sometimes they will call it 'Fascism', sometimes 'Communism', sometimes 'Regimentation', sometimes 'Socialism', but in so doing they are making very complex and theoretical something that is really very simple and very practical.

On the other hand just because he rejected any idea of doctrinaire revolution it did not mean that he would ignore the evils in society as it stood. Unlike his immediate predecessors he was ready to take vigorous action even at the risk of making mistakes. In his own defence he said: 'Better the occasional faults of a government that lives in the spirit of charity than the constant omission of a government frozen in the ice of its own indifference.' In the political context of twentieth-century America this was the only possible approach even though it made reform piecemeal and inconsistent. Each action was an answer to a specific problem. The TVA was not the first step in a plan to nationalise electricity production but a special cure for a special difficulty.

The results of this moderation were paradoxical. Roosevelt was the saviour of big business because he made revolution unnecessary. In fact his enemies, the monopolistic corporations, emerged stronger than ever. In 1937 three firms controlled 80 per cent of car production and another three 60 per cent of steel. On the other hand some of those he meant to help were little better off. The impoverished tenant farmers of the deep south still eked out miserable existences and there was still terrible urban poverty especially for the Negroes. It was not even clear that the New Deal had conquered the Depression: when America entered the war in 1941 there were still 6,000,000 unemployed.

Within these limitations Roosevelt was responsible for a sort of revolution. At the beginning of the century two vigorous presidents, Theodore Roosevelt and Woodrow Wilson, had increased the power of the federal government and the office of the President at the expense of the states' governments and Congress. During the twenties the Republicans had allowed this power to go by default. Roosevelt's four terms as President made the office more powerful and important than it had ever been and this time the change was permanent. Local government had failed to control the disaster and this had provided one good reason for increasing federal control over social and economic affairs. It had also failed to control crime and violence and here again federal powers were increased. The FBI (Federal Bureau of Investigation) was founded under J. Edgar Hoover and the law altered so that federal law officers could operate more effectively. The new 'G-men' rounded up the notorious gangsters of the twenties and early thirties such as Dillinger, Baby Face Nelson and Machine Gun Kelly. In addition the collapse of Wall Street had given the federal government the excuse to extend its control over business and the credit system.

All over the world governments were extending their powers at this time, but the New Deal, unlike Hitler's 'Economic Miracle' and Stalin's 'Five Year Plans', was basically democratic. Whatever his failures, Roosevelt had sought to show that a democratic state could survive the Depression, could take effective steps to care for its underprivileged, could preserve the best of its old institutions without revolution or dictatorship. What Roosevelt proudly boasted of the TVA could be applied to the New Deal as a whole:

*These fine changes we have seen have not come by compulsion, for
thousands of people have met together in a common effort. They have
debated it and discussed it. Participating in the processes of their
government – state government, local government, Federal
government – they have altered the looks of their towns and their
counties. They have added fertilisers to the soil. They have improved
their industries. No farmer was forced to join this conservation
movement. No workman was compelled to labour here under
onerous conditions or for less than a rightful wage. No citizen lost
one single one of those human liberties that we prize so highly in this
democracy. This is a demonstration of what a democracy can do,
of what a people uniting in a war against waste and insecurity
can do.*

International affairs in the thirties

The one way in which 1933 did not mark a sharp break with the
past was in the conduct of foreign policy. Indeed, in the early years
Roosevelt seemed even less constructive in this field than Harding,
Coolidge and Hoover had been. Almost immediately after taking
office he wrecked the slim hopes of success that the London World
Economic Conference had had. He firmly believed that America
needed to solve her own problems in her own way and rejected any
idea of a world economic plan. During the years that followed,
when the fascist and Nazi dictatorships were advancing on every
front in Europe and the Far East, America was more isolationist
than at any time since 1914. Roosevelt certainly showed no desire to
take up his 1920 election programme of American membership of
the League of Nations. This is not to say that he was unaware of the
dangers of the growth of totalitarianism, but both the President and
the people were absorbed in their own economic problems and
Roosevelt knew that his massive electoral support was not a mandate
to embark on foreign adventures.

Of course individual Americans were deeply involved in European
affairs. Many fought in the Spanish Civil War, especially on the
Republican side. The majority however felt even more remote from
the affairs of Austria and Czechoslovakia than the French and
British did. In this sense Roosevelt was merely reflecting the mood
of the people. What was more surprising was the supine attitude of
both the people and the administration to the Japanese invasion of
China which had always been regarded as a sphere of particular
interest for America. Roosevelt's own sympathies were known to be
with the democracies, but he refused to go far ahead of public
opinion. By 1940 this had hardened and the President openly con-

demned Italy's attack on France. At the same time he promised Britain all aid short of war.

In the autumn of 1940 Roosevelt stood for election for a third term. No previous President had stood more than twice but the international situation made continuity in government seem vital. Roosevelt was still promising 'Your boys are not going to be sent to any foreign wars', but by now American sympathies were increasingly behind the allies. In June, when Hitler attacked Russia, aid was even extended to Stalin. In August Roosevelt met Churchill at Placentia Bay in Newfoundland. There they signed the Atlantic Charter (see p. 357) which affirmed their determination to seek democratic rights for all peoples of the world. Yet America was still not at war.

In the meantime relations between America and Japan had deteriorated. Public opinion was outraged by reports of Japanese atrocities in China. Talks dragged on for months between the two countries, but by December 1941 they reached a complete deadlock, a deadlock that was resolved by the Japanese attack on Pearl Harbor. Ironically it was this unparalleled disaster which allowed Roosevelt to unleash the whole energy of the United States upon the side of the European democracies.

Britain between the wars   5

In the recurrent crises of the inter-war years, and in particular in the grim years of the Depression, nations on both sides of the Atlantic found themselves in the grip of events which threatened their whole social and economic security. In the face of this challenge each nation threw up its own style of national saviour. In the United States there was the ebullient Roosevelt, a doctrine-free economic planner buying his way out of the Depression; in Russia the austere and relentless leadership of Stalin; in Italy the tragi-comic dictatorship of Mussolini; in Germany the terrifying tyranny of Hitler. Britain's 'saviours' in these years were men of a very different calibre – Stanley Baldwin, James Ramsay MacDonald and Neville Chamberlain. They were all good parliamentary politicians and they were all hailed in their time as the champions of the nation's security. Later, like most of the other national saviours, they were to be reviled as vigorously as they were once acclaimed.

The politics of the post-war years
'Tranquility and freedom from adventures and commitments both at home and abroad', this was the promise of Bonar Law when he formed the first purely Conservative government for sixteen years in 1922 (see p. 26) and this was to remain the ideal of all governments in the inter-war years. It was a cautious slogan well suited to a period dominated by unadventurous politicians. The brilliant but unreliable figures of the previous era – Lloyd George, Churchill, Birkenhead – had been consigned to the back benches. The government front bench was filled with loyal but unimaginative Tories and facing them were the Labour party leaders, looking remarkably unrevolutionary. Though few people realised it yet, this was to be the pattern for most of the period up to 1940.

Bonar Law's own triumph was short lived. In 1923 he resigned and died very soon afterwards. His successor was not his able senior minister, Lord Curzon, but the much less well-known Stanley Baldwin who had, however, played a major part in destroying the Lloyd George Coalition. Curzon was personally unpopular, but the decision was really a recognition of the new political situation in the country. It was impossible to have a Prime Minister in the House of Lords where the main opposition party was virtually unrepresented.

British General Elections 1918-35

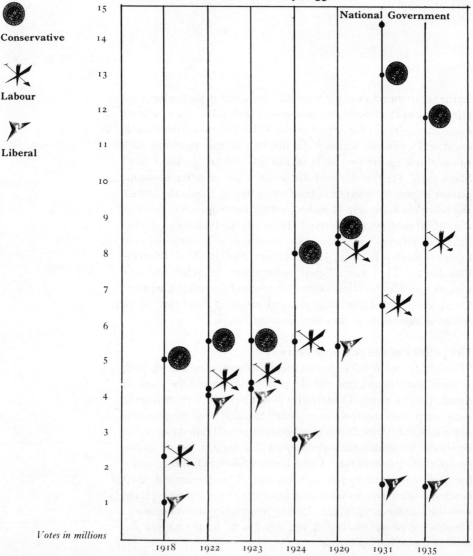

The new Prime Minister might have remained in office for several years, but he chose to call an election almost at once and to fight it on the controversial issue of the introduction of protective tariffs which had helped to lose the election of 1906 for the Conservatives. Baldwin believed that protection would help to solve Britain's post-war economic problems and he knew that a programme of protection would prevent a new alliance between the Conservatives and the Lloyd George Liberals. In the short run however it led to a setback. The Conservatives emerged as the largest single party but without an overall majority (see fig. p. 68). They were defeated on a vote of confidence and the King had no choice but to call upon Ramsay MacDonald, leader of the next largest party, to form a government.

The first Labour government

It was a totally unexpected turn of events. Clynes, a member of the new Cabinet, marvelled at the chance which had brought 'Mac-Donald the starveling clerk, Thomas the engine driver, Henderson the foundry worker and Clynes the mill hand to this pinnacle'. But it did not herald the political and social revolution which the more extreme members of the Labour party expected. In fact the government could scarcely have been more moderate. The new Prime Minister was handsome, charming and eloquent; he was also a little beguiled by the glamour of his new position. To the horror of many of his followers, the first working man's Prime Minister wore a top hat like any Tory when he went to visit the King. He held most of his colleagues in contempt, insisted on taking over the Foreign Office as well as the premiership, and appointed many Liberals to senior posts. The only left-wing member of the Cabinet was Wheatley, the Minister of Health. Ironically it was Wheatley who carried out the most important legislation of this brief ministry – an act which laid the basis for municipal housing schemes and produced 500,000 houses over the next ten years.

In the meantime MacDonald, the wartime pacifist, agreed to the building of five new cruisers and Snowden, the Chancellor of the Exchequer, was acting with as much caution as any City banker. Yet despite all this the government could not escape the stigma of red revolution. MacDonald's decision to open diplomatic relations with Russia was bitterly attacked. Then the government was defeated in a vote of confidence over its failure to press charges against a communist paper which had been inciting indiscipline in the army. MacDonald, weary of the frustrations of minority government, called new elections even though it was clear that his party had little chance of winning. The result was clinched by the publication of the

'Zinoviev Letter' in the *Daily Mail* just before the election. The letter, which was certainly a forgery, was supposed to reveal a communist plot to stage a revolution in Britain. Baldwin was returned with an overwhelming majority (see p . 68), but Labour polled more votes than ever before and it was the Liberals who really suffered – losing to both left and right.

The Baldwin years

Baldwin had returned in triumph, this time for a full five years, and the Conservatives who had spurned office in 1923 were ready to serve under him. He was even able to bring the erratic Churchill, who had been elected as an Independent, into the Cabinet in the unlikely position of Chancellor of the Exchequer.

Baldwin's main concern was to preserve Britain from the class conflict and social unrest which was plaguing post-war Europe. He was not a vigorous leader except when defending his own position as party chief and he had little interest in foreign affairs. He liked to pose as an ordinary, bluff, pipe-smoking countryman and although he was much more astute than he pretended, he was not a man to apply imaginative new policies. Such impetus as there was for reform came from the Minister of Health, Neville Chamberlain. With the co-operation of Churchill he carried out a series of important welfare reforms including the extension of widows', orphans' and old-age pensions. The climax of his work was the 1929 Local Government Act which virtually destroyed the old Poor Law system and placed the administration of social services under the County Councils. Unfortunately the situation in the mid-twenties called for more than the benevolent inaction of Baldwin and the progressive conservatism of Chamberlain.

The economy and the coal crisis

The difficulties of the British economy in the post-war world have already been described in Chapter 3. There were never less than a million unemployed in the twenties and the worst hit sectors of the economy were the basic heavy industries which had been the backbone of British prosperity in the nineteenth century. Their position was actually made worse by government policy. In 1925 after a brief boom, Churchill, backed by the rest of the Cabinet, decided that Britain should return to the Gold Standard which had been abandoned during the war. This meant that the pound sterling was freely convertible into gold or any foreign currency. The intention was to demonstrate the stability of the pound and reassert Britain's position as the centre of world finance. Unfortunately it left the pound in a very vulnerable position in a crisis and the rate of exchange was fixed at an unnaturally high level. As a result British goods seemed to be very expensive on foreign markets and foreign goods cheap in Britain.

The coal industry was particularly hard hit by foreign competition. During the war the mines had been placed under government control and miners had been paid high wages. A post-war commission had recommended permanent nationalisation, but this was not carried out and relations between the owners and miners deteriorated as the demand for coal fell off. There was heavy unemployment and miners' wages were soon lower in real terms than they had been in 1914. There was constant unrest in the industry and neither employers nor miners seemed capable of grasping the need for reform and rationalisation.

In 1925 the owners announced that there would have to be a cut in wages and longer working hours. The mineworkers' union at once prepared for a strike. An immediate confrontation was only averted when Baldwin stepped in and offered to subsidise the miners' wages until a commission, headed by Sir Herbert Samuel, had had time to investigate the needs of the industry.

The Samuel Commission reported in March 1926. It was strongly critical of the structure of the industry and recommended major reforms which the owners ought to carry through. At the same time it advised that the subsidy should not be renewed and that the miners should accept lower wages on an agreed national scale. None of the parties involved would agree to the report and despite the efforts of both the government and the TUC (Trades Union Congress) the coal mines were paralysed by strikes and lock-outs by the end of April. Then, through bungling and misunderstanding on both sides, the TUC talks with the government collapsed on 3 May. At once the TUC called out its front line unions – in transport, railways and heavy industry.

The workers struck with almost 100 per cent solidarity. Docks, railways and factories were immobilised. Food had to be carried through the streets of London in armoured convoys. Many members of the goverment declared that the strike was not an industrial action at all but an unconstitutional threat to democracy and national security. In the words of the government news sheet (there were no newspapers during the strike), the *British Gazette*, edited by Churchill:

*There can be no question of compromise of any kind. Either the
country will break the General Strike or the General Strike will
break the country. His Majesty's Government will not flinch from the
issue, and will use all the resources at their disposal . . . to secure in
a decisive manner the authority of Parliamentary government.*

This was a very partisan interpretation of the strike, but it was widely
believed, especially as the government monopolised the radio and
used it for its own propaganda purposes.

The middle classes rallied behind Baldwin with gusto. Under-
graduates and businessmen drove buses and even trains. A hundred
and thirty thousand men enrolled as special constables. The government had made adequate plans and had all the powers of the state at
its disposal. The TUC was surprisingly unprepared for the strike
and had only limited funds for strike pay. In fact the government
were only prevented from seizing the unions' bank balances by the
intervention of the King and the unions did not even have the open
support of Ramsay MacDonald who found the whole affair a
political embarrassment.

In the end it was left to Samuel to mediate between the TUC and
the government. The strike ended on 13 May, but the settlement
was a compromise only in name. The government gave the vaguest
promises in return for a resumption of work and even these were not
honoured. The miners fought on, embittered by the collapse of their
fellow workers, until their funds ran out in November. Then they
too were forced to accept all the owners' terms, including longer
hours and lower wages without even a national agreement. The King
noted in his private papers: 'This old country of ours can well be
proud of itself, as during the last nine days there has been a strike in
which four million men have been involved; not a shot has been
fired and no one killed; it shows what a wonderful people we are.'
But in the aftermath of the strike there was little cause for pride.

The strike was a disaster for the unions. Their membership slumped
and they had spent £4,000,000 on strike pay. The strike also affected
Baldwin's own leadership. He saw in it signs of the class conflicts he
dreaded so much and he did nothing to restrain his more extreme
colleagues in dealing with it. He allowed the passage of the 1927 Trade
Disputes Act which outlawed sympathetic strikes and forbade the
payments from union funds to the Labour party without specific
written agreement by the union members. This legislation, coupled
with the vindictive actions of the employers after the strike, caused

bitter class resentment and hardened the attitudes of the unions for years to come.

The General Strike
An armoured car in Oxford Street during the General Strike.

The second Labour government

Britain's economic position did improve during the twenties and the condition of the people did benefit from Chamberlain's reforms. Yet most improvements were due to the general boom conditions in the western world rather than the initiative of the government. Within the Conservative party the younger members were dissatisfied with Baldwin's nerveless leadership. He had been hailed as the nation's saviour in 1926 but his popularity with the middle class waned and the working classes were united against him. In the 1929 elections Labour won a greater part of the popular vote than ever before and even the Liberals made a partial recovery (see fig. p. 68). This time MacDonald found himself at the head of the largest party at Westminster though still without an overall majority.

If anything his new Cabinet was even more moderate than that of 1924. In place of Wheatley at the Ministry of Health there was Margaret Bondfield, the first woman Cabinet minister; otherwise there were the same men – Thomas, Clynes, Henderson and Snowden – and as before, a sprinkling of former Liberals. There were a few reforms – an increase in unemployment benefit and a new housing programme – but within months the situation was swinging out of control as the first effects of the Depression hit Britain. In June 1929 unemployment stood at 1,164,000; by January 1930 it had risen to 1,760,000 and by the end of 1930 to 2,500,000. Exports which had stood at £729,000,000 in 1929 had fallen to no more than £389,000,000 in 1931.

The economic crisis

It was some time before people began to realise that this was a crisis on an unprecedented scale. The traditional reaction of handing out unemployment money and riding out the storm would not work over a long period. The government began cautiously to make wider plans. Thomas, the Minister for Unemployment, proposed a modest public works scheme to absorb some of the workless. His ambitious and impatient young lieutenant, Sir Oswald Mosley, had drawn up a much more fundamental scheme for government controls and massive public spending to boost the economy. It was rejected and Mosley stormed out of the government and the Labour party.

In fact the government was soon under fire for even the modest extension of the housing programme and unemployment benefit. As the number of workless soared, so the bill for the benefit rose beyond the expectations of the government. The opposition attacked public extravagance and MacDonald answered by appointing the May Committee to investigate the whole field of government spending. The committee reported that the government was running into a deficit of £120,000,000 and recommended increased taxation, a reduction in public spending, and cuts in both the unemployment benefit and the wages of many public servants. For Snowden, MacDonald and the traditional economists of the Treasury and the City, there seemed to be no alternative but to accept the proposals. Loans had been raised in France and America, but they were soon swallowed up. There was an alarming drain of gold from the country which threatened to force Britain off the Gold Standard. The country was in financial difficulties and the logical answer seemed to be economy and retrenchment.

But most of the Labour party, including several Cabinet members could not agree to a cut in unemployment benefit and criticised the other May proposals which suggested much greater reductions for teachers, the police and the ranks in the services than for higher public servants like judges and admirals. There were also some economists led by Keynes who held that public spending rather than retrenchment was the answer to Britain's problems.

Faced with a major economic crisis, a minority position in Parliament and a divided Cabinet, MacDonald abandoned party government. In August 1931 he forced the Labour Cabinet to resign and then formed a National government with four of his Labour colleagues, Thomas, Snowden and Sankey; four Conservatives led by Baldwin, and two Liberals. He was denounced by the rest of his Labour colleagues and later expelled from the party, but in the country as a whole he was acclaimed for a great act of statesmanship which would save the economy and the pound sterling. The electorate granted him and his new Conservative and Liberal colleagues an overwhelming mandate (see fig. p. 68) to carry through the May proposals. The Labour

British Unemployed in the 1930s

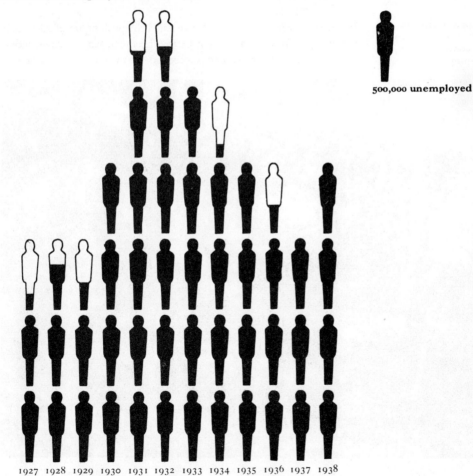

 500,000 unemployed

1927 1928 1929 1930 1931 1932 1933 1934 1935 1936 1937 1938

party was reduced to fifty-odd seats and lost nearly all its old leaders.

The National government

Faced with a desperate national crisis the country had rallied around the 'safe' men – MacDonald, and the real power behind him, Baldwin. But the safe men of the National government (from which both Churchill and Lloyd George were excluded) had little in common beyond their opposition to adventurous policies and the situation continued to deteriorate. The government economies provoked some opposition within the Civil Service and there was unrest amongst the sailors at the naval base at Invergordon. This so-called mutiny was sufficient to send confidence in the pound reeling and lead to a further drain on the gold reserves. As a result the government had to abandon the Gold Standard in 1931 – the very thing it had been formed to prevent.

Unemployment
The Jarrow marchers at a soup kitchen on their way to London.

In the same year unemployment reached the peak figure of 2,800,000 but the government had very little to offer in the way of constructive policy. Neville Chamberlain succeeded Snowden as Chancellor of

the Exchequer and introduced a 10 per cent protective tariff to cut down imports and protect British industry from foreign dumping. He also convened the Ottawa Conference to arrange special preferential trading agreements within the Empire. In 1933 unemployment began to fall slightly and world trade as a whole very slowly picked up in the mid-thirties, but even this partial improvement was only felt in some parts of the country. In the old industrial areas of South Wales, the North and Scotland, which relied heavily on coal, iron and shipbuilding, there was very little improvement before 1939. The most famous example of long term depression was the shipbuilding town of Jarrow, where almost the whole male working population depended on a shipyard which was forced to close by the economic crisis, but there were many other cases which were as bad and tens of thousands of working men were unemployed, through no fault of their own, for a decade or more.

The government was slow to accept the idea of subsidies, spent little on public works schemes in the depressed areas and made only feeble efforts to help the decaying industries to reorganise and rationalise. After 1935 there was a more marked improvement in British industry as a whole. There were new industries: carmaking, chemicals, electrical goods and service industries; there was also a boom in private house building, but all these developments came first and most noticeably in the south and the Midlands which had never suffered so badly from the effects of the Depression. As a result there was a double standard in the country, with permanent unemployment and industrial decay in some areas and a rising standard of living and thriving new industries in others.

It was because of this that the Conservatives retained their hold on Parliament in the elections of 1935. Their share of the vote fell and that of Labour increased, but the Labour vote was concentrated and won a disproportionately small number of seats. For most people MacDonald and Baldwin still retained their high reputation and in the face of threatening developments in Europe (see p. 130) people were unwilling to vote for the Labour party which had still not recovered from the effects of the 1931 split. MacDonald gave way to Baldwin at 10 Downing Street and the National government was more obviously an almost entirely Conservative affair, but there was no major change in policy and no new sense of purpose in the Cabinet. Such drive for reform as there was in the government came from Neville Chamberlain, an able and hard working administrator who was to succeed Baldwin as Prime Minister in 1937, in time to earn his own reputation as the saviour of the nation.

The abdication crisis

Before Baldwin retired he was involved in one more internal crisis from which he emerged yet again with an enhanced reputation. During the reign of George V the monarchy achieved a new peak in popularity and respectability. The King was not a man of great imagination or charm, but he was guided by a powerful sense of duty

The monarchy
Edward VIII with his mother Queen Mary.

and on several occasions exercised a beneficial moderating influence on the activities of the politicians. His Silver Jubilee in 1935 was celebrated with great pomp and the King's death the next year was deeply mourned throughout the country.

His heir, Edward VIII, was a totally different character. He was gay, charming, relaxed. In fact his lack of formality had long caused concern in traditional Court and government circles. Almost as soon as he had acceded to the throne he was involved in a crisis by his decision to marry Mrs Simpson, an American *divorcée*. Baldwin and many other leading public figures were determined to prevent the marriage which they believed was utterly unsuitable and unacceptable. The King resolved the intolerable situation by offering to abdicate. Churchill, the newspaper magnates Beaverbrook and Rothermere, and a few other Conservatives tried to rally support for the King, but despite wide popular sympathy for Edward most people seemed to believe that Baldwin was right. It was a final triumph for the Prime Minister before he retired amidst the general praises of the press and the politicians.

Britain and the Empire

One area of moderate and constructive policy in which Baldwin was involved during the inter-war years was the Empire. In a formal sense the British Empire reached its greatest territorial extent in 1919, but this was a period of growing national self-awareness amongst the peoples of many British dependencies and one in which most British politicians came to accept that political power would have to devolve upon the indigenous peoples of her Imperial territories sooner or later.

The process went furthest in the 'white dominions' which already enjoyed internal self-government in 1914. After the war they were recognised as fully independent sovereign states. They had their own representatives at the League of Nations, South Africa and Australia both held League of Nations mandates in their own right and Canada made her first separate treaties with the United States. The whole concept of dominion status was also extended by the creation of the Irish Free State. Ireland was in effect a completely independent nation after 1923 and in the thirties she was in all but name a republic with a foreign policy which differed considerably from that of Britain.

The position in the non-white colonies was still rather different. In the Middle East Britain was already under fire from Arab nationalists and eventually her occupying forces in Egypt and Iraq were reduced to a minimum and the countries given internal self-government. Even more important clashes with local nationalist organisations occurred through these years in India which was by far the largest and most important Imperial possession (see p. 248). Both Conservative and Labour governments struggled with the intractable problems of India but the concessions they offered always lagged behind the demands of Gandhi and Nehru, the Indian leaders. Yet most parts of India enjoyed considerable local self-government and the British had offered the first stage of dominion status to the country as a whole by 1935 (see p. 250). The theory that Indians should enjoy some form of Home Rule was accepted by almost everyone except for Churchill and a small group of reactionaries.

The idea of the Empire, like the idea of the Monarchy, enjoyed a good deal of popular support at this time but in practice the economic crisis encouraged a concentration on domestic issues and a general attitude of isolationism.

Britain and the outside world

After 1920 there was a reaction in Britain against Lloyd George's adventurous interventionist policies just as there was against Woodrow Wilson's international ambitions in the United States. Yet Britain was inevitably involved as one of the great European powers and Britain and France alone of the great powers remained on the League of Nations Council throughout the period. Britain did, indeed, make some serious contributions to the settlement of European problems from the very first. The two Labour Foreign Secretaries of these years, MacDonald himself and Arthur Henderson, were both dedicated supporters of the League ideal and made several efforts to strengthen it. The Conservatives showed rather less faith in the League, but Austen Chamberlain was one of the authors of the Locarno Pact (see p. 126) and with Briand of France and Stresemann of Germany played a major part in rehabilitating Germany in international affairs. There was a difference of emphasis between the policies of the Labour and Conservative governments of the 1920s, but they were agreed upon keeping the country fairly uninvolved in close alliances and both were ready to modify the terms of the Treaty of Versailles in order to improve European relations.

This attitude of benevolent detachment was much harder to maintain with the growing tension and aggression in world affairs that came with the economic crisis. But although the new situation called for a more positive policy, it also made British politicians less willing to act firmly in the face of international aggression. The Japanese invasion of Manchuria, which was the first great challenge to the authority of the League, came in 1931 at a moment when British politics were in turmoil and the government wholly preoccupied with economic problems. Thereafter the direction of affairs fell more and more under the control of Baldwin who showed little understanding of the European situation. He was unwilling to put the resources of the country behind the League of Nations or to provide Britain with an effective defence system of her own. Yet though this implied an appalling misjudgement of the threat to Britain's security which Hitler and Mussolini posed, it showed a shrewd appreciation of public opinion at home. In fact one of the most powerful slogans of the 1935 elections was Baldwin's promise that there would be no great expenditure on armaments.

That year was the year of the Italian invasion of Abyssinia (see p. 129), an issue on which British public opinion was certainly aroused. The press reflected the general popular sympathy for the plucky underdog, Abyssinia, and the Peace Ballot organised by the League of Nations Association showed that an overwhelming majority of the people were in favour of collective security for all nations through the League. When it seemed that the British government were making a shabby deal with the Italians in the Hoare-Laval Pact (see p. 130), the Foreign Secretary was forced to resign in the face of a public outcry.

But apart from such sporadic outbursts the British people were not deeply committed to the idea of Britain taking on the heavy burden of peacekeeping. There was a strong vein of pacifism at this time, not least in the Labour party itself. The general abhorrence of war was strengthened both by the spate of anti-war novels and plays that appeared after 1918 and by the widely held belief that a war involving modern bombers would lead to a holocaust which would destroy the whole continent of Europe. As a result there were concessions to both Germany and Italy and some half-hearted attempts to re-equip the forces, but all was done without any sense of purpose and without any effective co-operation with France, the natural partner in checking the aggression of the dictators.

This certainly changed in 1937 when Baldwin retired. Neville Chamberlain threw himself energetically into the task of developing a coherent defence and foreign programme but, tragically, it was based on a disastrous misconception of what was happening in Europe. Chamberlain expressed his policy in these words, 'I believe the double policy of rearmament and better relations with Germany and Italy will carry us through the dangerous period.'

The results of both parts of his policy were soon apparent. The air-force was built up from less than 3000 war machines to more than 8000. The navy was overhauled and re-equipped. At last something was done to develop a civil defence organisation and the invaluable radar screen around the south and east coast was completed. On the other hand Hitler was spending 25 per cent of his budget on the army in 1938 while Chamberlain spent only 7 per cent.

The Prime Minister showed even more vigour in the application of the other part of his policy. Unlike Baldwin he was only too anxious to throw himself into the business of international negotiation. He believed that the problems of Europe could be settled by limited and reasonable concessions to Germany. The series of concessions he negotiated, seemed to him to be strokes of enlightened statesmanship. He obstinately held to this idea that a terrible European war could be avoided by these means at least until March 1939 and even in September of that year only declared war on Germany very reluctantly (see p. 140).

Chamberlain's policy of appeasement has now become notorious, but it is important to remember how little effective opposition there was to it at that time and with what rapturous acclaim his negotation of the Munich agreement, which led to the destruction of Czecho-slovakia, was received (see p. 137). The Labour party did attack his failure to defend European democracy and to co-operate with Russia against Germany, but the party was itself deeply divided over the attitude it should adopt to rearmament. Churchill and a handful of Conservative backbenchers did keep up an attack on Government policy throughout the thirties, but Churchill was a discredited figure at this time, a man whose post-1918 record as a minister was far from glorious and who had throughout the inter-war years adopted reactionary and apparently misguided attitudes to many great issues.

The politics of protest

The overwhelming majorities commanded by National and Con-servative governments throughout the 1930s rendered orthodox opposition relatively ineffectual. There were instead some unusual forms of political protest. Some, dazzled by the success of the totali-tarian régimes in Europe, joined their rather feeble imitations in Britain. By far the most important of these was the British Union of Fascists, led by Sir Oswald Mosley. Mosley had walked out of the

Labour party to form his own New party with several socialist colleagues, but he soon turned to ape the activities of the Fascists and Nazis. He dressed his followers in black uniforms and adopted anti-Semitic slogans. However after a number of violent fascist clashes with workers in the East End of London, the organisation of uni-formed political parties was banned by the government and Mosley's movement dwindled into insignificance.

Of more permanent importance were the various movements of the Left. Many intellectuals, disillusioned with the main political parties joined the Communist party or fellow-travelling organisations. After 1933 they agitated for Popular Front alliances of all left-wing organisations against the fascist menace and although faith in com-munism was shattered both by the Great Purges and by the Nazi-Soviet Pact, the left-wing groups provided the most cogent and literate criticism of government policy both at home and abroad in these years. Many outstanding socialists and liberals went to fight for the Republicans in the Spanish Civil War and a good deal of the best literature of this period showed a great awareness of social and political problems. The most important organ of the literate left wing was the Left Book Club. This organisation was founded by the publisher, Victor Gollancz, to distribute cheap editions of selected books, especially those with relevance to contemporary social and political problems. The club's membership rose to 60,000 at one time and its limp-bound orange books were an important educational force.

Yet, after all, communism and fascism, anarchism and pacifism and all the other political protest groups of the inter-war years only in-volved a vocal minority of the people. Most were either too contented or too hungry for these activities.

Social change
For the middle class and many of the working class a new pattern of life was developing in the inter-war years. Families were smaller and though there were fewer servants, life was probably a good deal easier for the women who lived in the new suburban estates which sprawled out around the big towns. Three million homes had electricity in 1920 and 9,000,000 in 1937. Many middle-class housewives were able to afford the new electric carpet sweepers and often their husbands were able to buy their first car. Cars were being produced at a rate of 500,000 a year in 1937 and Austin, Morris and Hillman built their business on cheap family models. These things and many other small luxuries were bought on hire purchase which increased

Politics of violence
*British fascists salute
their leader, May 1938.*

twentyfold between the wars.

There was also a great increase in the variety of popular entertainments and a consequent decline in drunkenness. By the 1930s 20,000,000 cinema tickets were bought every week. By 1939 all workers were entitled to one week's holiday with pay a year. As a result a new cheap holiday industry grew up; both Butlin's holiday camps and the Youth Hostels Association were products of the thirties. Sport of all kinds was immensely popular. Wembley Stadium and the first greyhound race tracks were built in the twenties and the first football pools established a few years later. Wimbledon, the Boat Race, the Cup Final and the Grand National were all firmly established as national events and attracted a wider audience with the development of the radio and the expansion of the popular press. It was also a golden age of cricket. In the fateful winter of 1932–3 there was probably more interest in Britain in the controversial bodyline bowling of Larwood in the test matches in Australia than in events in Germany.

The extension of public communications was also very important during this period. Thriving on the growing income from advertisements for new luxuries and on the general improvement in literacy, the popular daily newspapers reached new peaks in circulation and their owners wielded considerable political power. Dawson, the editor of *The Times*, exerted influence within the political establishment and was an important supporter of Chamberlain's foreign policy. Lord Beaverbrook of the *Daily Express* and Lord Rothermere of the *Daily Mail* played active roles in Conservative party politics and waged their own eccentric political campaigns. Both tried to oust Baldwin on several occasions and both supported Edward VIII in the abdication crisis. In their political campaigns they were generally unsuccessful but their readerships kept on growing and they waged cut-throat battles to boost their circulation.

The BBC was an equally powerful and more high-minded cultural force in these years. Under the iron control of its first Director-General, Sir John Reith, the Corporation sought not only to broadcast light entertainment but to run talks, concerts and educational programmes to instruct public taste as well as to pander to its immediate demands. It became a serious political medium with the first broadcasting of campaign speeches in 1924 and the government monopoly of the radio during the General Strike.

The educational value of the press and radio were all the more important because in formal education there was very little progress between the wars. Educational reform was set back by government economies after the war and the teachers were amongst those whose wages were heavily reduced in 1931. The state provided free education only up to the age of fourteen in elementary schools and for those who could not afford the fees there was only a slim chance of a scholarship to a grammar school. Even more remote was the chance of further education. The universities were the preserve of the middle classes and Oxford and Cambridge in particular were dominated by entrants from the public schools.

Despite this there can be no doubt that the condition of life improved considerably between the wars. Even in 1932 it was possible to pass through large areas of England without noticing many signs of economic crisis. After 1935 life for millions of people in Britain was generally satisfactory and in the austere years after 1945 people would look back nostalgically to the good old 'pre-war' days. But there was one all important qualification to this – life was only good for the employed.

New entertainments
Brooklands race track
Easter Monday 1923.

Butlins Skegness camp
in 1939.

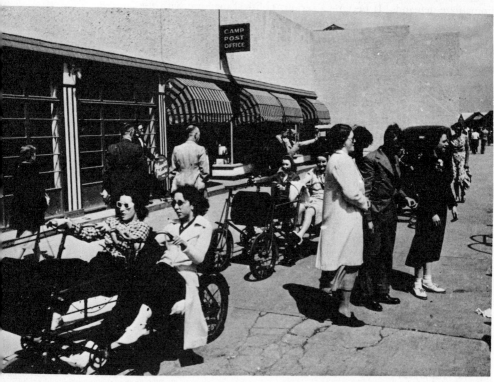

Life on the dole

When the hollow-cheeked shipbuilders from the dying town of Jarrow passed through the Home Counties at the end of their famous Hunger March in 1936, they seemed like strangers from another land. One of the most poignant features of the Depression was that there might be no more than fifty miles between areas of comparative prosperity and those of abject poverty. For much of the time the difference between standards of living tended to increase rather than diminish. It was in those areas which were already in difficulties in the twenties that the effects of the Depression were most keenly felt, and those which were most prosperous that recovered first. A glance at the map of unemployment (see p. 88) demonstrates this quite clearly. The same sort of picture emerges from a study of unemployment in individual trades. In the north there were many men who worked for no more than a few months in eighteen years. Families had to eke out a living for year after year on the unemployment benefit and upon Public Assistance. To qualify for this the family had to submit to the humiliating 'means test' – a test which debarred those who had accumulated a few savings and deducted from families even if they had only one son or daughter in work.

Average weekly wages, 1931

Coal miners	45s. 11d.
Textile workers	45s. 3d.
Farm workers	31s. 4d.

Unemployment benefit

Unemployment benefit	1931	After cuts
Single man	17s.	15s. 3d.
Married man	26s.	23s. 3d.
Married man with two children	30s.	27s. 3d.

With poverty went a collapse of morale. Men were left, without work or money, to loiter in the streets. The unemployed were at the mercy of the bullying bureaucrat and rent collector: they were forced to give up all forms of expenditure which were not absolutely essential and in those days before the National Health Service illness was a nightmare. Unemployment brought a host of other disadvantages – bad housing, inadequate diet, insufficient clothing. The towns in which the unemployed were concentrated were already unattractive places. With the mass unemployment came a fall in rates and a decline in the public services. Those who could left for more prosperous areas or emigrated. Those who remained often lost all hope.

George Orwell in *The Road to Wigan Pier*, J. B. Priestley in *English*

Areas of Unemployment 1936

1 **Scotland** 18%
  Textiles
  Shipbuilding
  Heavy Industry

2 **Northern Ireland** 23%
  Shipbuilding

3 **North West** 16·2%
  Textiles   Shipbuilding

4 **North East** 16·6%
  Iron and Coal

5 **Wales** 28·5%
  Coal and Iron

6 **Midlands** 9·4%
  Light Industry

7 **South West** 7·8%
  Light Industry

8 **London** 6·5%
  Light Industry
  Finance

9 **South East** 5·6%
  Light Industry

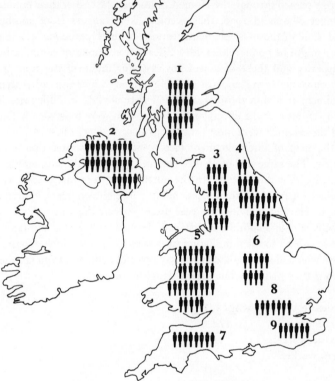

Journey and Walter Greenwood in *Love on the Dole* and many others wrote about the horrors of long term unemployment. Politicians of all affiliations who represented the depressed areas, from the fiery left winger, Ellen Wilkinson, MP for Jarrow, to the radical young Conservative MP for Stockton-on-Tees, Harold Macmillan, demanded special treatment to revive the decaying towns. Journalists from the south reported on conditions:

I saw a man, prematurely old, crouching over a stove in a dark room, the light of the fire touching his features as he coughed and coughed . . . One woman sank in a chair, her form wasted, and death written more plainly on her face than I have ever seen it. Her unemployed husband stood by, trying with a tattered shawl to warm a baby three months old. He smiled proudly down at it. His teeth were rotten with decay.

A few blocks away I found a widow and four sons in a house that
was literally crumbling apart . . . Outside ran a ditch that had once
been the feed for a factory. The factory rots now and the feed is
choked. Only rats breed there.
Dudley Baker in the Evening Standard, *1936, on a visit to the*
North-East

Yet people outside the depressed areas could never really understand what life was like there and though the government provided
what the experts regarded as a basic subsistence for everyone, it
acted without imagination or vigour and all too often treated the
human problems of the unemployed with stony indifference. As
George Orwell wrote of this period: 'However one may hate to
admit it, it is almost certain that between 1931 and 1940 the National
government represented the will of the mass of the people. It tolerated slums, unemployment, and a cowardly foreign policy. Yes, but
so did public opinion.'

What is, in retrospect, surprising is that there was so little political
instability during the Depression itself in Britain. In this respect
many countries in continental Europe were less fortunate; there
economic crisis and political violence all too frequently went hand in
hand.

The defeat of European democracy $\quad$ 6

The establishment of national democracies had been one of Wilson's most treasured ideals but the first decade of peace showed how hard it was to put his dream into practice. The new European states found that their hurriedly created democratic constitutions were unable to cope with their enormous social, economic and political problems especially in the face of powerful forces of both the extreme right and the extreme left who were opposed to the whole idea of a parliamentary system. Within ten years of Versailles, Poland, Hungary, Spain, Portugal and several Balkan states had fallen under some sort of dictatorship. In most cases the authoritarian régimes were merely the creation of powerful conservative groups – the army, the Church and the landowners – which, despite the upheavals of the war, had never been destroyed. But there were also examples of a new style of despotism of a far more complete and overbearing kind which was not merely the tool of entrenched reactionaries. Of these the prototype was the fascist dictatorship in Italy.

Mussolini and the growth of Italian fascism

Italy had picked the winning side in the war but she was amongst the aggrieved parties after Versailles. She had made a few gains, but the war performance of the country had been poor and the country was thoroughly demoralised. There was a raging inflation and the corrupt and discredited party politicians seemed quite incapable of providing a vigorous reconstruction programme. There was brigandage and social unrest in both town and country which led the propertied classes to fear they would soon be engulfed by either anarchy or Bolshevism. This unhappy state of affairs was cleverly exploited by an ambitious demagogue, Benito Mussolini.

Mussolini
Il Duce exhorts his people during the harvest on reclaimed land in the Pontine Marshes.

In 1919 Mussolini, who had been a well-known socialist journalist, founded a new political group in Milan, called the *Fascisti*. The new movement was supposed to be revolutionary, but it was also highly nationalistic and bitterly opposed to the communists and the old socialist parties. Despite its grandiloquent propaganda the party made a miserable showing in the 1919 elections and Mussolini turned at once to violence. Fascist squads, dressed in black shirts, fought running battles with socialists and strikers in the streets of Milan. They broke up communal farms in socialist villages and sought to create a state of political tension. In return for their efforts against the communists they won the financial backing of various big business interests and the support of the frightened middle classes. They even enjoyed the tacit co-operation of many of the police and magistrates. Yet by 1921, when the economic situation was improving, the fascists won only 35 seats out of over 500 in the elections.

At this stage Mussolini's political future might have been very dim, but for the irresponsibility of the established politicians. They ignored the menace of fascism and squabbled continually amongst themselves making stable government impossible. In 1922 Mussolini organised a mass march on Rome by fascists from all over Italy. It was a desperate gamble which he himself believed might end with his arrest, but the government caved in before him. Instead of being imprisoned he was invited to head a right-wing coalition ministry. The King and the army leaders, who despised the upstart rabble leader and could have stopped him, allowed this to happen because they disliked the traditional parties still more. They believed they could use Mussolini for their own ends; his conservative allies believed the same.

Mussolini in power

Within two years of taking office Mussolini had twisted the electoral laws to assure himself an absolute majority in the assembly. In 1924 he had his most persistent critic, a socialist deputy called Matteotti, murdered and he survived the subsequent political storm. It proved to be the last flicker of organised opposition. Thereafter the fascist leader, or *Il Duce* as he was called, was in office as long as his luck held. And it was a matter of luck: when he came to power he had neither a political programme nor any great ability as a statesman (though a great deal as a propagandist and conspirator). Only when he was in power did he try to give his brand of totalitarianism a coherent political philosophy and even then it was no more than a façade. Mussolini lived and died a political bandit.

Between 1924 and 1929 he silenced all criticism of his régime. Political parties were broken up or absorbed into the fascist movement. He introduced a strict censorship, abolished the jury system, set up a secret police force and placed all key administrative posts in fascist hands. Nominally the country was still a monarchy, but Mussolini and his henchmen wielded all effective power. His greatest triumph came in 1929 when he signed an agreement, or concordat, with the Pope which seemed to set the seal of the Church's approval on his regime. Yet despite his despotic methods he was widely regarded as the saviour of Italy and a bulwark against communism. Indeed it is often said that if he had died before 1935 he would have been regarded as one of Europe's greatest modern statesmen. On what was this reputation based?

He imposed order on Italy – just as he had bred disorder before he came to power. The strikes and the street fighting ended, the Mafia was curbed, the brigands were rounded up. But this order was bought at the price of political paralysis. In the place of parliamentary government he erected the 'corporative state' in which the interests of the individual were regarded as of much less importance than the greatness of the nation. The government was supposed to balance the aspirations of all classes; thus fascist officials were supposed to harmonise the interests of employers and workers, but the corporate state was a fraud in which the will of the upper classes generally prevailed and in which the rights of the individual were treated with scant respect.

Mussolini did clean up some of the corruption in the administration, but he replaced it with a top heavy and inefficient bureaucracy. He tried to deal with unemployment by encouraging agriculture and engaging in grandiose public works such as the draining of the Pontine Marshes. But the living standards of the Italian peasant were hardly affected. Much of his apparent success was a triumph of propaganda and his flamboyant self-glorification was played out against a backcloth of intimidation, censorship and defiance of the rule of law. Above all his régime was characterised by its aggressive nationalism which won Il Duce some popularity at home and made Italy the bully of the Mediterranean in the thirties (see Chapter 8).

And yet for a while at least, Mussolini seemed to offer something positive to Italy. He promised social reform without the destruction of capitalism; an end to class warfare without a Bolshevik revolution; a planned economy and a revival of national pride. Although much of this may now seem to be an illusion, at the time it was of the greatest importance and stimulated the growth of totalitarian movements all over Europe.

GERMANY 1924-39

The Stresemann years 1924-9
After the troubled years of its birth the Weimar Republic enjoyed a brief period of political and economic stability. It was governed by a series of coalition governments, but there was considerable continuity both in their policies and membership, and all of them included one statesman of great ability, Gustav Stresemann. Stresemann was a tough industrialist, a former monarchist and an ardent German nationalist, but he was no fanatic. He was prepared to work democratically in Germany and by negotiation in Europe. In the years 1924-9, when he controlled German foreign affairs and exercised a powerful influence in internal affairs, united Germany enjoyed its one brief period of effective democracy.

German election results 1919–33, showing percentage of votes

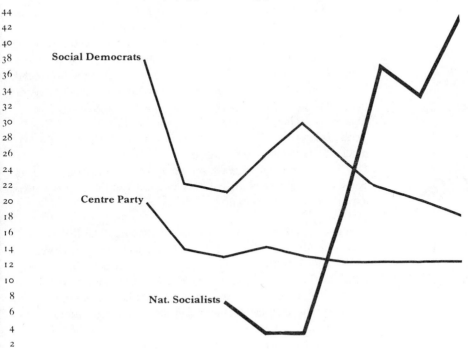

	1919	1920	1924	1924	1928	1930	1932	1932	1933
Nationalists	10	15	20	21	14	7	6	8	8
People's Party	4	14	9	10	9	5	1	2	1
Democrats	19	8	6	6	5	4	1	1	1
Centre Party	20	14	13	14	13	12	12	12	12
Bavarian Catholics		4	3	4	3	3	3	3	3
Social Democrats	38	22	21	26	30	25	22	20	18
USPD	8	18							
Communists		2	12	9	11	13	14	17	12
National Socialists			7	3	3	18	37	33	44

Notes on the Parties

Nationalists   Right-wing conservatives, the party of the landowners, former monarchists and the nationalistic middle class.

People's Party   Also a conservative party but more the party of business interests especially in western Germany.

Centre Party   The Catholic Party especially strong in the Rhineland. The *Bavarian Catholics* were a parallel group in that highly separatist province.

Democrats   The party of the liberal middle class.

Social Democrats   The party of organised labour; it stood for very moderate parliamentary socialism.

USPD   A temporary breakaway group of more radical socialists. Some of its supporters drifted back to the Social Democrats, others moved on to the Communists.

Things began to improve quite suddenly in 1924. The French withdrew from the Ruhr. The worthless German currency was reformed and foreign investment began to flow in attracted by high interest rates. At the same time the United States government backed the Dawes Plan under which America made vast loans to Germany with which to redevelop her economy and pay off the reparations. In the second election of 1924 the anti-democratic forces of both left and right suffered sharp setbacks. Industrialists like Thyssen, Stinnes and Krupp soon re-established Germany's heavy industries and firms such as Farben and A.E.G. recaptured her predominance in the manufacture of chemicals and electrical goods. The middle classes who had lost their savings in the inflation began to recoup some of their fortunes and the working men enjoyed high wages and social benefits such as unemployment insurance, which was introduced in 1927. At the same time, thanks to Stresemann's astute statesmanship, Germany regained an honourable position in European affairs. Stresemann was one of the architects of the Locarno Pact (see p. 126) and he took Germany into the League of Nations in 1926. The allies withdrew all their troops and the control commission from German soil and quite good relations were maintained with Russia.

However even during the Stresemann years there were some disturbing signs. The army continued to enjoy its pre-war prestige and throughout these years it was steadily growing in defiance of the Versailles agreements. Von Seeckt, the first Weimar War Minister, built up the crack nucleus of a major army and there were many para-military organisations and a large armed police force as well. Pilots were trained in secret in Russia and a special armaments office

developed heavy weapons which were forbidden by Versailles. A
second weakness was that the booming economy existed on foreign
loans and investment and was therefore particularly vulnerable to
any recession or loss of confidence on the world markets. Thirdly,
thanks to the lack of co-operation between the socialists and communists, Marshal Hindenburg was elected President in 1925.
Hindenburg was an ageing conservative militarist, dominated by his
military cronies and totally inexperienced in either politics or economics. In the mid-twenties he behaved correctly as a constitutional
head of state, but he was not a man well fitted to steer the country
through a crisis. Finally the anti-democratic forces in Germany were
never completely submerged. Throughout the twenties there were
powerful groups who rejected the terms of the Treaty of Versailles
and constantly worked to subvert the Weimar Constitution.

Germany and the Great Depression

In 1928 Chancellor Müller declared that the Weimar Republic was
'firm and unshakable'. On 3 October 1929 Stresemann died; on 29
October came the Wall Street Crash; within a few months all the
achievements of the Stresemann years were in jeopardy.

The effects of the Crash were immediate and disastrous in central
Europe. American loans dried up, investment ceased and confidence
was shattered. The middle classes lost their investments and bank
savings and the workers lost their jobs. By 1932 wages had dropped
by as much as two thirds and a year later one man in three in
Germany was unemployed.

The Depression had been disastrous enough in the relatively stable
context of American politics; in Germany it was much more dangerous. Captain Bruning, the Chancellor and Centre party leader, tried
to cut back the welfare services and at once lost the support of his
socialist allies. He continued to govern but without a majority and
utterly dependent on the emergency powers wielded by President
Hindenburg. At the time this seemed a necessary evil to meet the
crisis but it set a dangerous precedent, by-passing the elected
assembly. The longer Hindenburg used his powers to rule by edict,
the more democratic procedures were eroded.

At the same time the government was discredited by its failures in
foreign affairs. The French blocked Bruning's plan for a customs
union with Austria and adopted an unbending attitude towards
Germany's desire for equality of status with the other powers in
armaments. In these conditions the propaganda of the extremist

D*

parties took on a new validity. They all benefited and none more dramatically than the National Socialists.

The growth of National Socialism

The National Socialist or Nazi party began as an obscure group of ex-soldiers and working-class intellectuals in post-war Munich; in fact it was almost entirely without significance until Adolf Hitler became a member. Hitler was born in 1889, the son of a minor Austrian official. He had been an impoverished and unsuccessful artist in pre-war Vienna; he had fought in the Bavarian army, had been wounded, and had been discharged with the rank of corporal. In 1919 he showed few signs of becoming a world figure – he was poor, ill-educated, and devoid of any intellectual originality. However even in those days he had a terrifying fanaticism and he soon

Hitler

developed remarkable powers as a demagogue and political organiser.

The policies of the new party were a hotch-potch of ideas borrowed from the less reputable parts of nineteenth-century German philosophy – nationalism, anti-Semitism, militarism and reverence for strong leadership. The full theory of Nazism was only gradually developed by fanatical anti-Semites such as Streicher and Rosenberg, but from the first there were many points in their programme which appealed to the Germans. For instance the Nazis never accepted the *diktat* of Versailles and diligently propagated the myth that Germany had been betrayed but never defeated. In the great inflation of the early twenties they appealed to the workers and the lower middle class by their attacks on 'Jewish' big business and won the approval of the extreme conservatives by their implacable hostility to 'Jewish' Bolshevism.

Hitler and his circle showed a flair for propaganda. They copied the uniforms of the Italian *Fascisti* and adopted the ancient Nordic symbol of the swastika as their badge. In post-war Germany there were many para-military organisations and the Nazis organised the most efficient and violent of these, the brown-shirted SA, under a former army officer, Roehm. They broke up the political meetings of their rivals and organised impressive rallies of their own throughout Bavaria. In Hitler's own words: 'Mass demonstrations must bring it home to the little man's mind that although he is only a petty worm, he is nevertheless part of a great dragon.' In other words he gave the unemployed working man and ruined shopkeeper an identity and a sense of importance by dressing him in a uniform and feeding him the propaganda he wanted to hear. That this was generally the grossest distortion of the truth was not important:

In the big lie there is always a certain force of credibility . . . the broad masses . . . more readily fall victims to the big lie than the small lie, since they themselves often lie in small matters but would be ashamed to resort to large scale falsehoods . . . The grossly impudent lie always leaves traces behind it even after it has been nailed down.
Adolf Hitler, Mein Kampf

So Hitler spread the big lie about 'the stab in the back' that had defeated Germany, about the international 'Jewish' plot against the German people, about the threat of the Bolsheviks, about the treachery of the 'November Criminals' (the politicians who had accepted the Armistice in 1918). All this won the Nazis a good deal of notoriety and some support in Bavaria in the twenties. In 1923 they tried to seize power in Munich. The *putsch* was a miserable failure and the Nazis were the first to run when they came under fire. Hitler was arrested but did manage to use his trial to publicise his ideas and got off with a light sentence.

While in gaol he wrote *Mein Kampf* in which he outlined his plan to win control of Germany and dominate Europe, but few people took any notice of the book at this time. He was released after nine months and resumed control of his party. However in the mid-twenties things went badly. Nazi membership fell as economic conditions improved and they won only a dozen seats in the 1928 elections.

The Nazi road to power
After October 1929, however, events swung increasingly in the Nazis' favour. While Bruning struggled with insuperable economic problems the Nazis offered simple solutions. They promised full employment, they promised to revenge the humiliation of Versailles, they set up the Jews and communists as convenient scapegoats. They fought street battles with left-wing groups and won financial support from big businessmen. Hugenberg, the Nationalist leader, and even Hindenburg came to regard them as distasteful but useful tools in their own political machinations.

As the economic situation deteriorated they began to win striking electoral successes. In 1930 the moderate parties lost heavily to the extremists of both the left and right (see   p. 95). In 1931 the Nazis won control of the provincial assembly in Brunswick which incidentally meant that they could grant Hitler (an Austrian) German citizenship in that state. In 1932 Hitler stood against Hindenburg in the presidential elections. He lost but only after a second vote and he polled over 13,000,000 votes. Then in July came the greatest electoral victory. Bruning had been sacked by Hindenburg and replaced by von Papen who commanded very little support in the Reichstag. The new Chancellor held elections in the hope of improving his position. In this he failed abjectly but the Nazis polled 37 per cent of the vote and became the largest party.

However, Hitler could not form a government on his own and he would not ally with other parties. He knew that it would be hard to retain his electoral support and almost impossible to increase it under normal circumstances. Moreover his funds were running short. The radical wing of the Nazi movement, especially Roehm and the SA, were pressing him to seize power, but he was well aware that a 'March on Berlin' in imitation of Mussolini would be crushed by

Hindenburg and the army.

Hitler comes to power
Hitler the politician. The Chancellor shakes hands with President Hindenburg.

In November 1932 von Papen held a second election and Hitler's fears were confirmed. The Nazis lost seats and their popular vote fell by 2,000,000. Then at this most difficult moment the road to power was cleared for him. In December von Papen was ousted by the ambitious General Schleicher who commanded even less support in the Reichstag than his predecessor. But Hindenburg needed a government with at least a respectably large block of seats in the assembly to cloak his own arbitrary use of the emergency powers and von Papen was anxious to get his revenge on Schleicher. So von Papen made a deal with Hitler. Hitler was to form a coalition government with von Papen as his Vice-Chancellor and other prominent conservatives in key posts. Von Papen was to use his influence with Hindenburg to persuade him to accept the upstart corporal as Chancellor of Germany. The deal worked and in January 1933 Hitler was sworn in as head of a new government.

The failure of the Weimar Republic
Hitler always claimed that he had come to power by constitutional means and this was formally true. Yet the Nazis had won their way

to prominence by their ruthless use of violence and intimidation and their leader was appointed Chancellor through a back-stairs political deal.

But why had this been allowed to happen? Perhaps in the first place because parliamentary democracy had such shallow roots in Germany. The military autocracy of the Hohenzollerns had been swept away in 1918 but many political attitudes remained the same. Most Germans were prepared to accept the way in which Hindenburg wielded his powers and in any case the traditional parties were ill-equipped to defend their rights in the Reichstag. They were deeply divided by regional and religious differences and consistently under-rated Hitler until it was too late. The other powerful revolutionary party, the Communist party, was prepared to stand aside and watch him destroy democracy because they believed that he would clear the way for their Marxist revolution.

Beyond these weaknesses within Germany there were important external factors. Few Germans accepted the international arrangements created at Versailles and Locarno and it seemed that the traditional parties were quite incapable of wringing concessions out of Germany's intransigent neighbours. On top of this came the disastrous effects of the Depression which were very largely beyond the control of German politicians. Yet when all this has been taken into account was it inevitable that Hitler would come to power? It could be argued that by late 1932 the Nazi tide was receding and their leader became Chancellor not through the irresistible forces of history but through the failures of individuals – of von Papen, of Hugenberg, of Hindenburg – who in the pursuit of their own petty ends released a force far beyond their control upon Germany and upon Europe.

The consolidation of power
In January 1933 only three Nazis, Hitler, Goering and Frick, held Cabinet posts and they were outnumbered by von Papen and his conservative allies. But this balance meant nothing in practice. The Nazis easily outmanoeuvred their colleagues. Elections were fixed for February but shortly before polling day the Reichstag building was burned to the ground. Nazi propaganda at once blamed the communists, although the fire was almost certainly the work of the Nazis themselves. Hindenburg was persuaded to exercise his emergency powers again and the elections were fought in an atmosphere of violence and intimidation. Not surprisingly the Nazis won a majority, but despite the fact that the communist deputies were expelled from

the Reichstag, Hitler still did not have the two-thirds majority he
needed to change the constitution. There followed a further wave of
arrests and political intimidation until finally the Centre party and
some of the smaller groups were bribed and bullied not to stand in
the Nazis' way. Finally, in March, the deputies passed the Enabling
Act which gave Hitler power to rule without the Reichstag. Four
hundred and forty-one votes were cast in its favour and only ninety-
nine against. The politicians had signed their death warrant and the
Nazi revolution had begun in earnest.

The Enabling Act was followed by the destruction of all organised
opposition. The Nationalists were absorbed into the Nazi party, the
Social Democrats dissolved and the other parties forced into
'voluntary' liquidation. The unions were submerged into the Nazi
'Labour Front' and the provincial assemblies replaced by Nazi
governors. Hess, the party boss and Roehm, the chief of the SA,
joined the Cabinet. The police and law courts were supervised by
Nazi officials and the press and radio put under a rigid censorship.

The destruction of Roehm
Yet two all-important forces were still beyond Hitler's grasp; the
army and the presidency (which carried with it the supreme command of the forces). By the summer of 1933 it was clear that the aged
Hindenburg would not live more than a few months and Hitler was
determined to succeed him. But he knew that the army officers would
never accept him as their commander while he was associated with
Roehm and the SA, for the generals looked on Roehm as a cheap
upstart and rightly feared that he wished to build up the SA as a
military force which would rival the army itself. Quite apart from
this Hitler had his own reasons to be rid of Roehm. Before 1933 the
SA had been a useful force to fight street battles and intimidate non-
Nazis but after 1933 they were no longer necessary. Roehm had
become a liability and a potential rival.

Once again Hitler made a deal, this time with the generals. It was
more or less openly agreed that if he overthrew Roehm he would be
accepted as Hindenburg's successor. On the night of 29–30 June
1934 Hitler struck. With the help of his closest followers including
Heinrich Himmler who commanded the *élite* corps of blackshirted
SS guards, he had Roehm and the SA leaders liquidated and paid off
a number of other political scores at the same time. This 'Night of
the Long Knives', a series of murders unashamedly organised by the
Chancellor, left Hitler with absolute power. When, soon afterwards,
Hindenburg died, the army not only accepted Hitler as President and

Chancellor combined but even agreed to a new oath of loyalty for their soldiers:

I swear by God this holy oath: I will render unconditional obedience to the Führer [Hitler's new title] of the German Reich and people, Adolf Hitler, supreme commander of the armed forces and will be ready as a brave soldier to stake my life at any time for this oath.

The last independent force in Germany had surrendered to Hitler.

The 'Thousand-Year Reich'

Yet for Hitler the seizure of absolute power was only a beginning. He, more than Mussolini or any of the other fascist dictators, aimed at total control of men's minds as well as their bodies. Goebbels, the pervertedly talented Minister of Propaganda, subjected Germany to a flood of Nazi publicity. The ever more stifling censorship and the persecution of the Jews drove some of Germany's greatest men – Albert Einstein, Thomas Mann, Bertold Brecht, Otto Klemperer, Walter Gropius – into exile. To the rest of the world the flight of such men was an overwhelming condemnation of the Nazi régime, but the Nazis themselves placed little value on these supposedly 'decadent' intellectuals. Their own education policy deliberately halved the university population in five years. Boys were encouraged to follow

Der Führer
Hitler salutes a massed parade in Nuremburg.

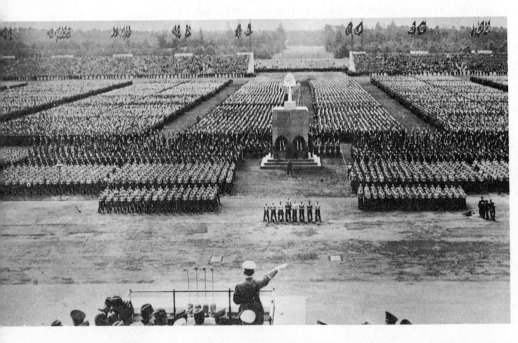

physical pursuits and to join Nazi organisations run on military lines. After 1936 Baldur von Schirach's Hitler Youth became compulsory and replaced the traditional youth organisations such as the Boy Scouts. Women and girls were not expected to take higher education; their role was to raise good young 'Aryans' in a good Nazi home.

Not only the schools and universities but even the churches fell under state supervision. The Catholics of the Centre party had traded their votes for the Enabling Act in order to protect their religious liberty; now they realised, too late, that there was no protection against the ruthless and pagan régime whose leaders were later to scoff at the slave religion of Christ. The Protestant churches were even more vulnerable because they had no international organisation to support them. They were placed under a Nazi administrator and ordered to preach in favour of the regime. A few brave individuals like Pastor Niemöller defied the government and were imprisoned or forced into exile, but most churchmen and their flocks had to pay lip-service to the semi-deification of the Führer.

Racialism

Behind the censorship and the propaganda, behind the destruction of the rule of law and the murderous activities of the secret police,

Aryanism
A defaced Jewish shop in Vienna.

one thought was paramount – the belief of the Führer and his followers in the superiority of the Aryan race. It was this racialism that marked off the Nazis from most of the merely nationalistic fascist movements. The belief that the Germans were somehow racially superior was the justification for their aggression against their 'debased' Slav neighbours and for unbelievably terrible persecution of the Jews. Phoney science and phoney history were produced to support this violent racialism which blamed all Germany's ills on an international Jewish-Slav conspiracy.

As early as 1922 Hitler had proclaimed:

The Jew has never founded any civilisation, though he has destroyed hundreds. He possesses nothing of his own creation to which he can point. Everything he has stolen . . . He has no art of his own; bit by bit he has stolen it from other peoples . . . Already he has destroyed Russia; . . . now it is the turn of Germany, and with his envious instinct for destruction he seeks to disintegrate the national spirit of the Germans and pollute their blood.

In the years that followed his obsession grew more fanatical. Jews were beaten up in the streets and humiliated; their goods were seized and in 1935 the Nuremberg Laws legalised persecution, while a venomous stream of propaganda sought to sow the seeds of anti-Semitism in every 'good Aryan' heart. From the end of 1938 the pogroms had become systematic and all those Jews who could fled the country. But many could not escape and they were soon to suffer the ultimate atrocities of the Nazi death camps where 6,000,000 Jews were shot or gassed during the war – often after being subjected to the most appalling tortures and experiments in the interest of 'Aryan' science.

The economic miracle
The worst of these features of the Nazi régime were partly disguised until the war began and it was possible for the ordinary German to turn a blind eye on those excesses which made no immediate impact on his private life. It was all the easier because of the improvement in the economic situation which followed the Nazi seizure of power. Some of this improvement would presumably have come in any case since all over Europe the worst years were 1932 and 1933; however Hitler naturally claimed all the credit for the 'economic miracle'.

The Nazis, like the other totalitarian regimes of both left and right, exercised a much closer control over the economy than their democratic predecessors. They instituted a series of Four Year Plans (one year faster than the communists!). These involved programmes of public works, including the construction of the autobahns, encouragement to agriculture and state aid for industry. Hjalmer Schacht, director of the state bank and Economics Minister, made trade and currency agreements which gave Germany a dominant position in the Balkans and central Europe. The Nazis had started as a party of the lower classes, but they actively encouraged the centralisation of industry in the hands of the great corporations such as Krupps, though the top industrialists themselves were all subject to Nazi directions. After 1935 all youths were liable for compulsory labour service and the state expropriated vast amounts of Jewish property.

However, none of this would have achieved the dramatic improvement in the employment figures if there had not also been a massive rearmament programme after 1935. It was this that led to the boom in heavy industry and though it made a balanced budget quite impossible Hitler was well pleased. He placed the country on a war economy because he intended by conquest or negotiation to extend his empire in a way that would bring to Germany an ever increasing flow of agricultural goods and raw materials. During the late thirties this plan seemed to show every sign of succeeding. (See pp. 134-40).

Opposition and success
It is impossible to believe that Germany was populated by an entire nation bent upon destruction, war and mass murder. Yet there was very little opposition to Hitler once he was in power. Only a fraction of 1 per cent of the population went to the concentration camps or into exile for opposition to the Nazi régime. On the other hand two-thirds of the male population joined a Nazi organisation for one reason or another. Moreover throughout the thirties Hitler frequently placed his actions before the judgement of the people in referenda. No doubt the overwhelmingly favourable results were achieved by dubious means but many millions of Germans, perhaps the majority, voted 'yes' because they believed Hitler was right.

One reason for the lack of effective opposition was the speed and efficiency with which Hitler destroyed all the normal channels of protest and the unprecedented ruthlessness with which he crushed all signs of opposition. Resistance of a sort lasted longest and was most effective in the army, the one body which kept its traditional organisation and some of its authority after 1933. But even the army surrendered step by step from the acceptance of Hitler as commander-in-chief to the overthrow of the Minister of Defence, von Blomberg, and the army commander, von Fritsch, on trumped up vice charges in 1938. Certain generals continued to plot against Hitler, though not from particularly liberal motives. They were especially active after 1938, when the Führer's international adventures seemed to be heading for disaster. However, Hitler's gambles always paid off and the expected confrontation with the western democracies came too late to spark off a *coup*.

Yet the ruthless use of absolute power was only half the explanation for Hitler's success. He also gave the Germans something they wanted and in return they were prepared to sacrifice their democratic rights and ignore the persecution of their Jewish fellow countrymen. When he came to power the country was faced with an appalling political and economic situation which the Weimar politicians seemed incapable of resolving. Hitler gave the bewildered Germans simple and acceptable explanations for their plight. He loaded the blame for all their disasters on other people: the Jews, the French, the Bolsheviks, and Woodrow Wilson. Once he came to power he seemed to have all the right answers as well. He turned political chaos into order; he performed the economic miracle. Finally, he not only revenged the humiliations of Versailles, but he made Germany more powerful in Europe than she had ever been (see Chapter 8). When his grand design began to go wrong the country was involved in a total war and it was much too late to resist.

Beyond all this, most potent at the time and most intangible for later generations, was the force of Hitler's own personality. Somehow this vulgar and half-educated little man overawed generals, diplomats and economists of great ability and experience, so that they served him even when the Reich was crashing in ruins around him. One of Hitler's most bitter opponents, Gregor Strasser, described his hypnotic power over the German people in these terms:

Hitler responds to the vibrations of the human heart with the delicacy of a seismograph, enabling him, with a certainty which no conscious gift could endow him, to act as a loudspeaker proclaiming the most secret desires, the least admissible instincts, the sufferings and personal revolts of the whole nation . . . Adolf Hitler enters a hall. He sniffs the air. For a moment he gropes, feels his way, senses the atmosphere. Suddenly he bursts forth. His words go like an arrow to their target, he touches each private wound on the raw, liberating the mass unconscious, expressing its innermost aspirations, telling it what it most wants to hear.

Revolution and crisis in Asia 7

For the peoples of Africa, Asia and South America the conflict of 1914–18 was a European civil war and even those countries which eventually declared for the allies did not feel deeply involved. Despite this, the war and its aftermath did have considerable effects in the non-European world. The solid front with which the imperial powers had faced their subject peoples was irreparably breached, and when the powers once more had time to give their attention to their colonies, it was with much less confidence in their right to rule. Their declared war aims had promised 'national self-determination' and the new left-wing parties of western Europe were ready to champion the rights of the native populations. At the same time one major power, Soviet Russia, was avowedly anti-imperialistic and the revolutionary example of the Bolsheviks was soon being studied by nationalist intellectuals, at least in Asia.

The empires of France and Britain, the Netherlands and Italy reached their greatest territorial extent between the wars but in some ways European influence was already in retreat. The old order was changing and although this change was still almost imperceptible in Africa it was both dramatic and violent in the Far East.

Peacemaking in the Far East 1918–22
Although both China and Japan were nominally victorious powers at the end of the war, they occupied very different positions at the peace conference. Japan, represented by her ablest elder statesman, Saionji, was one of the big powers who controlled the inner workings of the conference. Her participation in the war and her intervention, with the other powers, in the Russian civil war gave her a powerful voice in the settlement of world affairs, especially in the Pacific area.

The Chinese delegates represented a weak country, divided between two rival republican governments and a host of warlords. The 'Big Five' whom the Chinese were petitioning were all her former exploiters, and all still enjoyed important economic controls and territorial concessions in China.

The Japanese based their claims on a secret treaty of 1917 with Britain and France by which they were entitled not only to Germany's former colonies in the Pacific but to the German concessions in Shantung which they had seized during the war. Despite President Wilson's opposition the Japanese successfully insisted that the treaty should be honoured. This part of the settlement as much as anything else discredited Versailles in the eyes of the Americans and provoked the first genuine outburst of nationalist feeling in China, the 4 May student riots in 1919. But although Japan was successful in this she also suffered a humiliating rebuff from the other powers which was not easily forgotten: her demands for a clause in the Versailles Treaties on racial equality was successfully blocked by the white powers, led by Prime Minister Hughes of Australia.

The final settlement in the Far East was reached at the Washington Naval Conference in 1922. There the British, American and Japanese governments agreed to a balance of warships in the ratio 5:5:3. America and Britain also agreed not to build any more naval bases in the Far East except at Hawaii and Singapore, which made Japan the greatest naval power in the China Seas. On the other hand Japan had to accept two more setbacks. As part of a Nine Power Treaty to guarantee China's independence, she had to return Shantung to China and drop the Twenty-One Demands (see Chapter 1). At the same time Britain refused to renew the Anglo-Japanese Treaty which had been the basis of Japanese foreign policy since 1902. Thus, although Japan was a great power in 1922, she was isolated and conscious that she was not treated as an equal by the other powers. In 1924 her nationals were excluded by the US Immigration Law as they already were by the 'White Australia' policy. Not only was Japanese national feeling wounded by these measures, her economy was adversely affected and it was not surprising that with her growing population and limited land and resources, she took increasing interest in her weaker neighbours on the mainland of Asia.

JAPAN

Economic development and party government in the 1920s

In 1914 Japan had been on the verge of bankruptcy but the war years had given an enormous boost to her economy. She had been able to capture markets in India and China while her competitors diverted their resources elsewhere. In the four war years her merchant navy more than doubled. There was a short recession immediately after the war but the twenties were a period of rapid industrial expansion. In 1925 the population was 59,750,000, by 1930 it was 64,250,000. Agriculture was still the most important occupation but over the same period the number of workers in urban industry grew from 1,000,000 to 5,000,000. Electricity consumption increased fourfold in the twenties and most of the increase was taken up by new mines and factories. Industrial output trebled between 1914 and 1929 and finished textiles provided a third of the country's exports. The units of production were growing too, especially the great industrial corporations, or *zaibatsu*, such as Mitsui and Mitsubishi.

With the new factories and expanding cities there came many social changes. For the first time there was a sizeable business and professional class who consciously copied western culture as well as western industrial techniques. Prices doubled between 1920 and 1929, but wages increased threefold and urban workers were both more militant and more prosperous than ever before. 'Mobos' and 'Mogas' (modern boys and girls) danced to American pop music and aped western fashions while the more serious-minded students became 'Marx-boys' under the influence of the Russian revolution. This urban population was generally anti-militarist and strongly influenced by western liberal and socialist ideas. Yet these changes were less revolutionary than they seemed. Even in the towns the traditional tea shop still flourished alongside the dance hall just as the family workshop still competed with the Mitsubishi textile mill. In the countryside the old military values of the *samurai* and the traditional veneration for the family and the Emperor were scarcely touched by European and American culture.

Yet in 1920 it did seem that Japan, like many European nations, might develop a form of parliamentary government as she became wealthier and more industrialised. The franchise was doubled in 1919 to 3,000,000 and in 1925 there was full manhood suffrage with an electorate of 13,000,000. The two main parties were led by members of the westernised middle classes and in the early 1920s for the first time a commoner became Prime Minister and there was a majority of commoners in the Cabinet. Hirohito, Regent from 1922 and Emperor after 1926, was still regarded as a semi-divine leader but with the help of the pre-war elder statesman, Saionji, he tried to act as a constituional monarch. It seemed a good omen when the gentle and intelligent Emperor, more interested in marine biology than politics, took the name 'Showa' or 'enlightened peace' as his reign title.

There were many other encouraging signs. Not only did Japan join the world-wide system of naval disarmament but in 1922 and 1925 she considerably reduced her army. Diplomatic relations were established with Soviet Russia and Japanese troops were withdrawn from Siberia (1922) and North Sakhalin (1925). The Japanese government adopted a much more friendly attitude towards China and during the 1920s Japan was an active member of the Council of the League of Nations.

The conservative reaction and the Great Depression
However, even in the 1920s the parliamentary system was under fire from the strongly entrenched forces of conservatism in the House of Peers, the civil service and the armed forces. Many of the older generation were horrified at the breakdown of traditional values in the cities and few people had much respect for the political system which was so obviously corruptly manipulated by the rival business interests of Mitsui and Mitsubishi and which allowed unseemly brawls in the parliament building itself.

As early as 1919 a fanatical reactionary, Kita Ikki, had produced his plan for the 'Reconstruction of Japan', a strange mixture of traditional religious beliefs and modern fascism. Kita's ideas were enthusiastically adopted in the army, especially amongst the junior officers drawn from the families of the small landowners. They developed the idea of the 'Showa Restoration' in which the Emperor and the army would overthrow the power of the hated bourgeois political parties and big business interests just as the Meiji restoration in the nineteenth century had curbed the great feudal landowners. Western influences would be driven out and Japan would return to the traditional military values of the *samurai*. From 1927 the young officers were forming secret societies to put these ideas into practice. In 1928 a group in the Kwantung army which guarded Japanese-owned railways in Manchuria blew up the Manchurian warlord, Chang Tso-lin, because of his hostile attitude to Japanese economic and political influence in his country. There was an international outcry but the General Staff protected the offenders and an evil precedent for political violence had been set.

However, as in Europe, it was the economic crisis which finally undermined parliamentary government. A minor crash in 1927 which forced thirty-six banks to close their doors and ruined hundreds of small businessmen drove many to join either the communists or the more vocal and violent parties of the extreme right. When the Depression hit Japan this process became even more marked. As world demand slumped, not only the urban workers and business-men suffered. Raw silk was the second crop on almost every farm in Japan. In 1929 it made up 36 per cent of her exports, mostly to America. By 1930 silk had fallen to a third of the 1925 price. Thou-sands of farming families, from which most of the army officers came, were ruined as a result.

The Prime Minister was Hamaguchi, the last strong civilian premier of the thirties, but in Japan as elsewhere parliamentary democracy seemed unable to cope with the problems of the Depression. Hamaguchi took two disastrous steps. First he put Japan back on the Gold Standard at just the wrong moment and then tried to economise by cutting civil service pay. Secondly he enraged the conservatives by pledging the country to naval reductions at the 1930 London Conference despite the advice of the Naval Staff. Soon afterwards he was shot and fatally wounded by a fanatic and the government drifted helplessly, unable to deal with either the econ-omic crisis or the open disaffection in the armed forces.

At this critical point Japan did not turn, as many European countries did, to a 'saviour', a Duce, or a Führer; instead the right-wing fanatics and army officers collectively usurped control from the discredited parliamentarians by a policy of assassination and political disobedience. In March 1931 the young officers staged an un-successful coup d'etat in Tokyo. In September a similar group in the Kwantung army were more successful. After 1930 the 'Young Marshal', Chang Tso-lin's son and successor in Manchuria, had begun to reunite his province with the rest of China under the new nationalist government of Chiang Kai-shek. Since the Japanese government seemed unwilling to save Manchuria for Japanese con-trol and exploitation, the army took the initiative. On the flimsiest of excuses and without any orders from Tokyo, the Kwantung army seized the great industrial city of Mukden and began to overrun the whole of southern Manchuria.

The conquest of Manchuria and the triumph of militarism

The Mukden incident produced a fantastic situation in Japan. The civilian government was quite unable to control the army; the senior officers were afraid of their own subordinates and refused to countermand their orders; only the Emperor could have called back the conquest, but his advisers feared civil war and persuaded him not to intervene. The government, deeply embarrassed by what had happened, tried to convince the rest of the world that the whole affair was a limited police action while the army drove the 'Young Marshal' south of the Great Wall into China and conquered the northern part of Manchuria which had previously been regarded as a Russian sphere of influence. In 1932 Japanese troops also attacked Shanghai and Pu Yi, the last of the Manchu Emperors of China, was made head of a state which covered Manchuria and parts of Inner Mongolia. In 1934 he was formally declared Emperor of the state of Manchukuo, but he remained a puppet of the Japanese army.

World opinion was outraged by these acts of aggression. The Lytton Commission, sent to investigate by the League of Nations, condemned Japan, and the United States and many other powers refused to recognise the legality of Manchukuo. However, the Japanese people were only angered by this hostile world reaction and the conservatives strengthened. The country withdrew from the League of Nations and renounced all her naval and disarmament agreements, and however much they disapproved the other powers seemed too preoccupied with their own political and economic problems to take any concrete action in the Far East.

Meanwhile civilian government in Japan was paralysed by the activities of groups such as the League of Blood who assassinated politicians opposed to the army. Militaristic and racialist doctrines were taught in the schools and preached in the press. 'Asia for the Asiatics' became the most popular slogan as Japan sought to win the leadership of the whole continent against western influences. Liberals were hounded from political life and western ideas, recently so popular, were rejected in a wave of aggressive nationalism. The reactionaries were immensely strengthened, in Japan as in Europe, by the dramatic economic recovery in the mid-1930s due in this case to the massive programme of rearmament and the exploitation of Manchuria's rich natural resources.

In February 1936 there was a bloody military rising in Tokyo itself, led by officers who were still not satisfied with the government's policies. At last the Emperor ordered that firm action should be taken and many rebel leaders, including Kita Ikki, were executed. But it was too late to prevent the drift to military government. In 1936 it was the army not the Foreign Office that negotiated the Anti-Comintern Pact with Hitler.

In April 1937 the last pre-war elections were held. The middle-class parties still won a majority of the seats and the moderate left-wing parties alone polled over 1,000,000 votes but the new Prime Minister, Admiral Konoye, was no more able to control the armed forces than his civilian predecessors had been. The army was merely spurred on by the election results to seize the initiative once more. In 1937 Japanese patrols clashed with Chinese guards at the Marco Polo Bridge just north of Peking and provided the army leaders with the excuse to commit Japan to another great act of aggression. This time it was to be no less than the conquest of China.

CHINA

China after the revolution
The political history of China between the overthrow of the last Manchu emperor in 1912 and the Japanese invasion in 1937 was even more turbulent than that of Japan. The last of the Manchus had been followed by a military strongman, Yuan Shi-kai, but after his death in 1916 China disintegrated. The Republican government in Peking was controlled by Chang Tso-lin and a shifting alliance of northern warlords while in the south each province had become a separate warring state. In such conditions the lot of the peasantry was worse than in the worst days of the Empire. The urban middle classes and the workers were almost as badly off and the more educated of them looked for salvation to the one democratic leader with a national reputation, Sun Yat-sen.

Sun was a doctor who had travelled widely in Japan, America and Europe. He was a veteran revolutionary who had once been dramatically saved from the Chinese Imperial embassy in London where he had been kidnapped by Manchu agents. He was greatly impressed by western technological achievements and by western democracy, but almost equally influenced by the achievements of the Russian people in their own revolution. Under these influences he produced a revolutionary programme for China based on the Three Principles of Nationalism, Democracy, and People's Livelihood. These meant in effect an end to foreign intervention in China, an elected government and a more equitable social system, especially for the peasants. However, at first Sun and his supporters had very little influence and they were scarcely able to hold their tiny democratic republican base in Canton against their warlord neighbours.

In 1923 Sun met a Russian agent who offered to help to build up a revolutionary nationalist party in China. Soon after, Sun, advised by Comintern delegate, Borodin, and helped by the tiny Chinese Communist party (founded in 1920), reorganised his supporters into a new party, the Kuomintang. As part of the plan Blucher, a Russian general, established a military training school in Canton with a young nationalist officer, Chiang Kai-shek, as its first commandant. Some communists, such as Chou En-lai, gave political instruction in the academy, while others such as Mao Tse-tung were sent north to stir up the peasants in preparation for a nationalist campaign against the warlords.

This campaign did not begin until after the death of Sun Yat sen in 1925 by which time the Kuomintang was already deeply divided between the right-wing military leaders under Chiang Kai-shek and the left-wing politicians. The quarrel was not resolved when the Northern Campaign began in 1926, but the Kuomintang armies were enormously successful. Everywhere they were joined by the downtrodden peasants and deserters from the armies of the hated warlords.

By the spring of 1927 the nationalists had reached the River Yangtse. In April Chiang advanced on China's greatest industrial city, Shanghai, and there he allied himself with the rich bankers and industrialists who offered to finance his movement if he would get rid of the left-wing leaders. Everywhere the communists and the trade unionists were rounded up and shot, the Russian advisers expelled, the Communist party machine broken and those leaders who survived driven into hiding. Freed from his unwelcome left-wing allies, who received no help from Stalin, their former patron, Chiang succeeded in winning the unwilling obedience of the northern warlords and driving Chang Tso-lin north of the Great Wall. When, in 1930 the 'Young Marshal' recognised Chiang as his overlord, the nationalist leader could claim to have the great majority of the Chinese people directly or indirectly under his control.

However, the Kuomintang government in Nanking, the new capital, did not fulfil the Three Principles of its founder. No effort was made to give the Chinese an elected government nor were any measures taken to improve the dreadful condition of the peasants. Chiang had allied himself with the landowners and big businessmen and their interests remained paramount as before. He did achieve something

in freeing his country from the last vestiges of European political privileges. The western powers recognised China's right to control her own tariffs and postal services and agreed in principle to the ending of their other special rights in China. Britain gave up all her bases except Hong Kong and apart from the gunboat patrols on the Yangtse and the international zones at Shanghai and Tientsin, China had achieved national sovereignty at last. Perhaps, given time, Chiang might have fulfilled more of the Kuomintang programme, but time was denied him for his régime was soon being challenged by two formidable enemies, the Japanese army and the Chinese communists.

Sun Yat-sen
The nationalist leader with his officer corps at Whampoa Military Academy, Canton.

The rise of the communists
In 1927 the Chinese Communist party seemed to be completely shattered. Mao Tse-tung, one of the few surviving leaders, tried to stage a popular rising, the Autumn Harvest Rebellion, which was crushed very easily. The remnants of the Central Committee under instructions from Moscow then ordered a series of urban rebellions which were even more disastrous. However, there was a gradual recovery. Mao with a few hundred followers went into hiding in the wild mountains of Kiangsi and drew to him little groups of survivors. As their numbers grew they extended their control over the surrounding countryside until, at its peak, the Kiangsi Soviet was a small state controlling several million people.

Mao Tse-tung, the leader of the soviet, was the son of an illiterate peasant from the traditionally rebellious province of Honan and even before his experience in Kiangsi, he had developed a theory that, contrary to Marxist doctrine and the experience of the Russian revolution, the peasantry were the most revolutionary class in China. Now in Kiangsi he sought to win the support of the peasantry, for whom the Kuomintang had done nothing, by distributing the land of the local gentry and freeing them from the grasp of corrupt officials. His ideas were a great success but he had acted contrary to the party line dictated by Stalin and the Moscow-trained Chinese of the Central Committee who said that the revolution must start in the towns. For this he was nearly expelled from the party; moreover by 1930 Chiang had completed his work in the north and was ready to deal with Mao's soviet and other smaller groups in central and southern China.

The communist leaders
Mao Tse-tung (left) and his military chief, Chu Teh, at their northern base in 1938.

Between 1930 and 1934 Chiang launched four great 'annihilation campaigns' against the communist bases but each time Mao's forces defeated numerically superior armies by skilful guerilla tactics. So intent was Chiang on defeating the communists that he ignored the threat of the Japanese in Manchuria. Finally in 1934 he attacked for a fifth time with nearly 1,000,000 men and 200 planes. This time his well-equipped forces guided by German generals forced the communist army to abandon their base. In October 1934 the 90,000 strong Red Army from the Kiangsi Soviet set out on its famous Long March from south-east China for 6,000 miles to a new base in the north west. The journey took the main body almost exactly a year and was achieved against overwhelming odds and in the most gruelling physical conditions. In the early stages after a series of major disasters Mao and the generals deposed the old Russian-dominated leaders on the Central Committee and Mao became the

The Long March

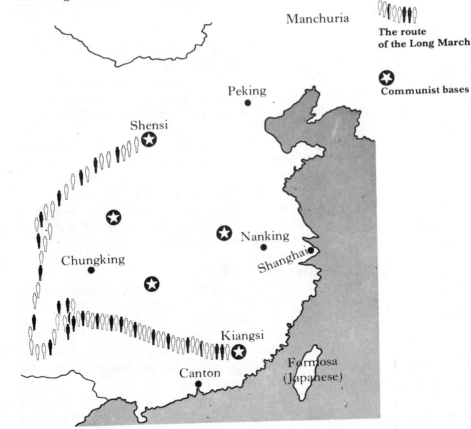

Manchuria

The route
of the Long March

Communist bases

Peking

Shensi

Nanking

Shanghai

Chungking

Kiangsi

Canton

Formosa
(Japanese)

acknowledged leader of the Chinese communist movement.

Under his leadership the retreat was completed and in view of the amazing difficulties it is not surprising that he wrote soon afterwards with justifiable pride:

For twelve months we were daily under reconnaissance and bombing from the air by scores of planes. We were encircled, pursued, obstructed, and intercepted on the ground by several hundred thousand men; we encountered untold difficulties on the way but by keeping our two feet going we swept across a distance of more than 20,000 li [3 li=c. 1 mile] through the length and breadth of eleven provinces. Well, has there ever been in history a long march like ours? No, never!

Only 20,000 men survived the ordeal and reached Shensi just south of the Great Wall, but the retreat had been turned to victory by the enormous prestige the March won for the communists. As Mao wrote later:

Without the Long March how could the broad masses have known so quickly that there are such great ideas in the world as are upheld by the Red Army? The Long March is a seeding machine. It has sown in eleven provinces many seeds which will sprout, grow leaves, blossom into flowers and yield a great harvest in the future.

In addition to this the communists were now strategically well placed to take a direct part in the struggle against the Japanese which Chiang had neglected and through which they hoped to win still greater popularity with the Chinese people. In the end, in 1936, Chiang Kai-shek was forced by his own supporters to drop his attack on the communists and join them in presenting at least a semblance of unity against the Japanese.

The Sino-Japanese War 1937-41

The war which broke out after the incident at the Marco Polo Bridge (see p. 115) was almost a dress rehearsal for the world war that followed it. The massive attacks by mobile armoured columns, the bombing of open cities, the brutal treatment of civilians all heralded the horrors of total war in a technological age. The Chinese fought back with more vigour than they had shown for a century in their clashes with foreigners, but they could not save Peking, the northern plains or Shanghai. Chiang appealed to the League of Nations, but although Japan was condemned she ignored all threats and pleas and the European powers were too preoccupied by the crisis in Europe to take action. In December 1937 Nanking was taken with appalling atrocities.

Chiang would not make peace and retreated behind the Yangtse gorges to set up a new capital far inland at Chungking. He, and the communists in Shensi, could do no more than cling desperately to their positions in the hope that the war would spread and bring them help from outside. When the war broke out in Europe Japan strengthened her links with Hitler and in 1940 was able to move into Indo-China and bully the British into stopping supplies passing through Burma into nationalist-held parts of China. By this time only one power seemed to threaten Japan's hold on the whole of the Far East,

Japanese aggression
*Japanese troops
advance through
Manchuria, 1931.*

the United States. Negotiations between the two countries dragged on throughout 1941 until, in December, the new Japanese Prime Minister, General Tojo, sought to break the deadlock by the fateful attack on Pearl Harbor and the seizing of Hong Kong, Malaya, Singapore, the Philippines and the Dutch East Indies in the early months of 1942.

The non-European world between the wars

This chapter has concentrated upon the Far East because in many ways this area was setting the pattern for the post-war world. The political development of the rest of Asia and of Africa during these years is dealt with in later chapters, but it is worth noticing that even at this time these other areas were powerfully influenced by events in the Far East. Most attention was focused on the phenomenal success of Japan. Although many Asian nationalists such as Gandhi and Nehru disapproved of Japanese militarism, non-European peoples could scarcely fail to be impressed by the way in which this Asian state had come to rival the white powers both militarily and economically. They also observed that Japan had been able to copy many western technological skills without destroying her own ancient culture.

The example of China was less impressive, but even here an exploited and backward country was making the first steps towards genuine independence. Even more significant, though few people can have realised it at the time, Mao Tse-tung was developing the theory and practice of communism to make it relevant not only for urban and industrialised states but also for the predominantly agrarian communities of the non-European world.

The League of Nations and international relations 1923-39

8

For Woodrow Wilson, and for millions of ordinary people in western Europe, the conflict of 1914–18 was 'the war to end wars' and the Versailles settlement was a permanent and just rearrangement of European affairs. It is therefore not surprising that Wilson devoted so much energy to the creation of an international peace-keeping body and that the first duty of that body should have been the preservation of the Versailles treaties.

The constitution of this new organisation was laid down in the Covenant of the League of Nations.

The constitution of the League
The task of preserving world peace lay with two bodies, the Assembly and the Council. The Assembly was really a forum for debate in which all members were represented and had one vote. However the Assembly could not be a very effective watchdog. Not only was it too large to work quickly, but it was not always in session and on most important matters it could only act on a unanimous vote. This left the real initiative with the Council. The Council comprised four permanent members (later five) and four non-permanent (later six and later still nine). This body was in more or less permanent session in Geneva and could take action on a majority vote. Its duty was to investigate cases of conflict or aggression brought before it and to recommend action to the other members. In this respect the most important clause of the Covenant was Article Ten which laid down that:

The members of the League undertake to respect and preserve as against external aggression the territorial integrity and existing political independence of all members of the League. In case of threat or danger of any such aggression the Council shall advise upon the means by which this obligation shall be fulfilled.

The Council might suggest either economic sanctions or military action; however it did not possess any permanent forces itself or the machinery to raise an international peace-keeping army, so ultimately all decisions still lay with the member governments.

The League of Nations

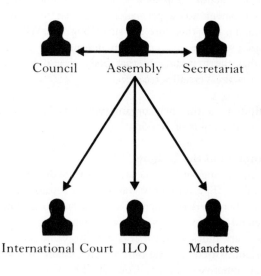

Council   Assembly   Secretariat

International Court   ILO   Mandates

Special commissions on drugs, slavery etc.

Membership of the League

Initially the Covenant was signed by the allied and associated powers at Versailles, and it was soon signed by a number of wartime neutrals so that membership rose to forty-two in 1924 and sixty by 1934. However, the United States never joined and Germany was only a member between 1926 and 1933. Russia did not join until 1934 and one of the last actions of the League was to expel her for aggression against Finland in 1939. Of the four original permanent members of the Council both Italy and Japan walked out of the League in the 1930s, so that only Britain and France, amongst the leading powers, were members of the League throughout its history. In fact the League was neither an all-inclusive body nor a limited alliance of similarly minded nations. The absence of the United States was a particularly crippling handicap for it left the burden of defending peace and democracy on the shoulders of France and Britain, who were not equal to the task either in material resources or in political resolution.

The successes of the League

Despite its disabilities the League and its agencies did achieve some good work. Its special commissions fought the illegal trade in narcotics, cared for refugees, and drew up many international conventions on non-political matters. In 1922 a World Court was set up at The Hague to handle international disputes and the League's International Labour Office which sought to improve working conditions throughout the world was so successful that it survived the collapse of the parent body and later became an agency of the United Nations.

However, the League must ultimately be judged by its success as a peace-keeper. From the first it intervened in international disputes – for instance between the Yugoslavs and Albania in 1921 and Greece and Bulgaria in 1925. But from a very early date there were doubts about its effectiveness. In 1923, during a dispute between Italy (a permanent member of the Council) and Greece, Mussolini seized Corfu without any recourse to the League and although the League eventually arbitrated in the case, Mussolini came off best. Even in those early days it seemed that the confident aggressor had little to fear.

International relations in the 1920s

European politics in the inter-war years were dominated by the manoeuvrings of Britain, France and Germany in search of three fairly constant goals. Britain wanted peace and stability, France security, and Germany a revision of the Versailles settlement. The main difference between the 1920s and the 1930s was the means which Germany used and the sort of reaction with which Britain and France met her claims.

It was always clear that the League could not guarantee peace and the preservation of the *status quo* in the face of German unwillingness to comply, and the unsuccessful French invasion of the Ruhr showed that unilateral military action was no alternative. The French therefore sought some additional guarantee and their first attempt was the Draft Treaty of Mutual Defence drawn up in 1923. The treaty was to give the League the right to name an aggressor in a dispute and to make military action against the named party automatic and obligatory for its members. Such an agreement might have made the League a formidable body but it foundered almost at once on the unwillingness of Britain and several other states to commit themselves to compulsory military action. They felt that France was trying to force them into a rigid defence of the Treaty of Versailles which they were no longer convinced was altogether just.

The next year a new French Prime Minister, Herriot, and his new British counterpart, Ramsay MacDonald, produced a slightly milder version, the Geneva Protocol. This would have made it compulsory to submit any dispute to the League for arbitration. If one or both of the parties involved refused to accept, military sanctions would be applied. Yet once again the scheme was shelved. Many nations feared its implications – for instance the Australians feared that their dispute with Japan over their refusal to accept non-European immigrants might be brought before the League.

However, in 1925 there was a more concrete development as a result of the work of three outstanding foreign ministers – Briand of France, Stresemann of Germany and Austen Chamberlain of Britain. Between them they drew up the Locarno Pact which was, in effect, a partial rewriting of the Versailles settlement. The three powers and Italy agreed to the permanence of Germany's western frontier as it stood – that is to say they reaffirmed the Versailles settlement. They also undertook that any revision of Germany's eastern frontier could only take place by arbitration with France and the eastern European states. Finally France gave specific guarantees to Poland and Czechoslovakia that she would help preserve their independence and integrity. The settlement appeared to be an advance because it reflected the improved relationship between Germany and France but it had dangerous implications. It suggested that Versailles *might* be revised in eastern Europe and that in any case Britain would not give specific promises to the states in this area. It also left France with responsibilities that she could never honour on her own.

These implicit weaknesses in the Locarno Pact were disguised by the friendly relationship which was built up at the conference between the foreign ministers and which was to be an important factor in international politics during the next four years. In 1926 Germany joined the League and took a seat as an additional permanent member of the Council. In 1928 Briand and the American statesman, Kellogg, drew up an agreement which was signed by sixty-five nations including Russia and the United States. All those who signed agreed to renounce war as an instrument of policy. In that year the American Young Plan seemed to offer a final solution to the problem of reparations and in 1930 the last allied troops withdrew from Germany.

Yet already the international scene was growing gloomy once more. In 1929 Briand and Chamberlain were thrown out of office and Stresemann died. Within days of his death the Wall Street Crash heralded the beginning of the Great Depression which was to have such a devastating effect on European affairs in the coming months. In 1930 the French began building their great defensive system, the Maginot Line, and the Nazis won 100 seats in the Reichstag elections. All these events marked the end of the hopeful phase of European politics which was nicknamed the 'Locarno Honeymoon'.

The mounting violence in international affairs in the 1930s gave the impression that an entirely new phase had begun, but this was misleading. Locarno was a pre-Hitler revision of the Treaty of Versailles and the events of the 1920s showed that Britain was unwilling, and France unable, to defend the *status quo* in Europe long before the age of 'appeasement'. There had been an improvement in international relations, but this rested on no firmer basis than the goodwill of the governments concerned. The rise of Hitler made the Kellogg–Briand Pact and even Locarno almost totally meaningless and it became painfully clear that no international system had been developed to preserve peace.

The Depression and armaments
The Depression helped to destroy parliamentary government in Germany and to complete the discrediting of the Versailles system and the reparation agreements in the eyes of the German people.

On the other hand the effects of the Depression helped to sap the democratic states of their initiative in foreign affairs. The United States became even more isolationist, the French were paralysed by internal conflict and government scandals, while the British cut back their defence expenditure and concentrated on their internal problems.

All nations, whether democratic or totalitarian, became increasingly nationalistic in their economic policies. They raised tariff barriers, controlled currency exchange, and imposed import quotas. This naturally helped to break down good international relations still further and strengthened the position of aggressive ultra-nationalist parties everywhere. Such efforts as were made to improve relationships came too late. Political and economic conditions also blighted the hopes of the Geneva disarmament conference. Initially the French refused to reach any compromise with the Germans, and, by the time they were ready for concessions, it was too late. The Weimar Republic had been destroyed and Hitler walked out of the conference altogether.

The Manchurian affair

The first real test for the League and the idea of collective security in these difficult new conditions came in 1931. In September the Japanese began their invasion of Manchuria (see p. 113) and Chiang Kai-shek appealed to the League and to the United States for support. Both the Americans and the League reacted sharply in words but did nothing. By the time the League's Lytton Commission produced its damning report on Japanese activities all the other powers were absorbed by problems nearer home. In 1933 the Japanese walked out of the League and extended their control further into northern China. Yet there was no attempt to check the Japanese by military action. Russia and the United States, the two largest powers in the Pacific area, were not members of the League and neither Britain nor France had either the will or the physical resources in the Far East to act alone.

The rise of the Nazis

Japanese militarism went unchecked partly because Germany presented a much more immediate threat to most League members. Hitler's accession to power marked a watershed in European politics less because his immediate aims differed from those of his predecessors, than because of the ruthless energy with which he was prepared to fight for them. Almost at once he withdrew his country from the League and from the Disarmament Conference. Early in

1934 he signed a ten-year peace pact with Poland which had been an important member of France's system of alliances in eastern Europe. The Pact was significant because it showed that some states in eastern Europe were still more frightened of the Russians than the Germans, and certainly placed little faith in the League to defend them from either.

In July the authoritarian Catholic Chancellor of Austria, Dollfuss, was assassinated by Austrian Nazis and a Nazi *coup* was only prevented by the prompt action of Dollfuss' successor, Schuschnigg, supported by Mussolini. In September the Soviet Union joined the League as a direct result of these events and Communist parties all over Europe were ordered to co-operate with their socialist and liberal counterparts.

Abyssinia and the League
Mussolini and Hitler were far from being natural allies. Both were new-style dictators and both had aggressive expansionist ambitions which involved a revision of the Treaty of Versailles. But Italian fascism and German Nazism were very different ideologies and Italy and Germany were rivals in several parts of Europe. In 1935 Mussolini joined the British and French at the Stresa Conference in reaffirming his support for the Locarno Pact. Yet even while the three powers were meeting at Stresa the whole idea of a united front against Hitler was being destroyed by Italian activities in East Africa and by the unco-ordinated reactions of Britain and France.

In 1925 Abyssinia had become a member of the League with the support of Italy. Three years later the Italians signed a peace treaty with the Emperor, Haile Selassie. Yet in a matter of years Abyssinia was chosen as Mussolini's first victim in his grandiose attempt to create a new 'Roman' empire. Its geographical position and its status as almost the last scrap of independent territory in Africa made it an obvious target and the Italians had the defeat at the battle of Adowa in 1896 at the hands of the Abyssinians to revenge.

Late in 1934 there were a series of border incidents between the Italian colony of Eritrea and Abyssinia. Despite attempts to settle the dispute peacefully there were more clashes the next year and on 3 October Mussolini's troops began an invasion. Four days later the League condemned Italian activities and all the members except Mussolini's allies, Austria, Hungary and Albania, agreed to impose economic sanctions. Although the sanctions did not include the all-important embargo on oil, there was confidence that they would cripple Italy and force Mussolini to make peace. But the result was quite different. Mussolini's modern guns and planes routed the Abyssinian tribesmen much more quickly than anyone had expected. By May 1936 the country had been overrun and in July the League members gave up their useless embargo on Italian trade. But this was not the only reason for the defeat of the idea of collective security. The leadership of the League depended upon France and Britain and their attitudes to the Abyssinian crisis had been fatally different. Laval, the French Foreign Minister, believed that Mussolini was much less of a threat than Hitler and was quite prepared to appease him by concessions in Africa in return for support in Europe. Laval even persuaded the British Foreign Minister, Sir Samuel Hoare, to agree to an arrangement which would have given most of Abyssinia to the Italians.

This agreement never came into effect. When it became known in Britain it provoked a massive public protest which led to Hoare's resignation. Not only were the British horrified at a betrayal of the Abyssinians; they had enormous interests in the Middle East to protect against Italian encroachments and were prepared to reach some sort of an agreement with Hitler in Europe so that they could deal with Mussolini in the Mediterranean. In the end neither the French nor the British policy paid off; Mussolini conquered Abyssinia, but the economic sanctions had driven him into a closer alignment with Hitler, while the British embarked on a series of concessions to the German dictator which only ended in September 1939. In the meantime the League was completely discredited. Haile Selassie had appeared in person to appeal on behalf of his country; right was clearly on his side; the whole principle of collective security was at stake; yet nothing effective was done. Individually and collectively the members of the League had been unequal to their task and the body was of no importance in European affairs thereafter.

The German problem

At no time since 1919 was the international position of Germany absolutely stable. Her statesmen had consistently sought a revision of the Versailles settlement and Stresemann had been partly successful in this. For most of the time they had also evaded the armaments regulations to which Germany was supposed to be subject. However, it was only with the rise of Hitler that Germany launched a frontal attack on the whole European system. This was the attack which many Frenchmen had been fearfully expecting for years but initially it provoked a quite different reaction in Britain. The British did not understand the enormity of Nazism and they had never suffered a German invasion. Ever since Keynes had resigned from the Paris peace delegation in 1919 there had been a strong tradition of opposition to the terms of the settlement and this opposition was strengthened by the economic crisis. In any case Britain was too preoccupied with her own internal problems, with the threat of the Italians in the Mediterranean, with the Indian nationalists and with the Japanese to want to get involved with a dispute with Germany.

Thus, just when the French were vainly trying to build up a series of alliances to contain Germany – first with Russia and then with Italy – Britain gave up all attempts to defend Versailles or even Locarno at all. In 1935 the National government signed a naval agreement with Hitler which recognised his right to a fleet of 35 per cent of the strength of the British navy. The pact was signed without any attempt to consult Britain's Stresa partners, France and Italy, and was an open admission that all previous European agreements were open to renegotiation.

1936: The democracies in retreat
The year 1936 witnessed a series of retreats on all fronts in the face of Italian and German aggression. The Italians completed their conquest of Abyssinia. Their conquest was then officially recognised by Hitler who scored a major triumph of his own soon afterwards. At Versailles it had been laid down that the German Rhineland should be a demilitarised zone, but in 1936 Hitler marched his troops in. Many of his military and diplomatic advisers had warned him that this would provoke a violent reaction from France and Britain and he was prepared to withdraw at the first sign of real opposition. But nothing happened and his position in Germany and Europe was immensely strengthened while the alliances that were supposed to contain him continued to crumble. The Belgians feared that their alliance with France could bring them nothing but the enmity of Germany and so declared their complete neutrality. This action left the flank of the French system of defences, the Maginot Line, completely exposed.

On the other hand Germany was constructing her own system of alliances. Mussolini and Hitler declared their friendship and in November Germany and Japan signed the Anti-Comintern Pact. In the meantime yet another part of Europe was being thrown into a war which the anti-democratic powers were only too willing to exploit.

The Spanish Civil War

After the collapse of the Spanish monarchy in 1930, Spain had been ruled by a series of unstable left- and right-wing governments in rapid succession. In February 1936 the elections gave a substantial majority to a Popular Front alliance of socialists and communists. The new government was soon being harassed by anarchists and separatists on the one hand and the fascist Falangists on the other. The situation was exploited by the traditional conservatives – the army, the Church and the landowners – and in July 1936 the army in Spanish Morocco mutinied. The leadership of the revolt passed into the hands of General Franco and the rebellion of conservative and Falangist forces spread to Spain itself. The country split in two between the Republican government in Madrid which controlled most of the economic resources and had massive popular support' and the rebels who controlled most of the army and air force.

The war which followed was marked by appalling atrocities on both sides which were made very much more grave by outside interference. The Republicans received encouragement and some aid from the USSR and a stream of supporters from all over the world who fought in the International Brigade. This body of communists, socialists, anarchists and liberals numbered 40,000 at its peak and included many writers and intellectuals from Britain and America. On the other hand Franco enjoyed almost unlimited support from Hitler and Mussolini. They sent arms and equipment and by 1938 Franco had 100,000 Italian 'volunteers' and the support of the German Condors, a contingent of planes and pilots, who wreaked havoc in

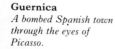

Guernica
A bombed Spanish town through the eyes of Picasso.

Republican towns.

It was obviously undesirable that the war should be extended in this way and Britain and France tried to get a general agreement on non-intervention. In the end their efforts damaged the Republican cause for it meant that its sources of supply were restricted while Germany and Italy were quite prepared to flout their promises to give aid to Franco. A further result was that the Republicans came to rely more and more on communist support internally and internationally. This in its turn led to clashes between the communists and the anarchists and liberals in Spain, and it was hardly surprising that they steadily lost ground until the whole country was under Franco's control by 1939. The war was one more victory for the anti-democratic alliance. For Hitler it served another purpose. It kept Mussolini deeply involved in the western Mediterranean while Germany expanded into areas which had been Italian spheres of influence.

The expansion of Germany

Although both Hitler and Mussolini were heavily committed in Spain, neither of them was ready for a general war. Except in the

The people in arms
A Spanish republican farmer defies a rebel attack.

Far East, 1937 was a breathing space during which both sides prepared for the next and even more serious crisis in international affairs. In Britain Neville Chamberlain replaced Stanley Baldwin as Prime Minister and speeded up the rearmament programme which had been sadly neglected for several years. The French were also rearming, though by this time her leaders were obsessed by the defensive 'Maginot' mentality which was tactically misguided and weakened the confidence of their allies in eastern Europe in their willingness or ability to defend them.

1937 was also a year of preparation for Hitler. In November he held a secret meeting of his military chiefs. He explained that the country must be brought to a full war footing by 1943 at the latest and that in the meantime they must be ready to exploit the weaknesses of the enemy wherever possible. Germany, he claimed, needed more living space and must extend her control over the inferior Slav races of eastern and central Europe: 'There have never been spaces without masters and there are none today; the attacker always comes up against a possessor. The question for Germany is: where can she attain the greatest gain for the lowest cost.' There were several possibilities. Danzig and West Prussia were formerly parts of the German Empire. Czechoslovakia had a large German minority group and Austria was an entirely Germanic state. Hitler had no exact plans of conquest, but he was ready to move into any of these areas if the opportunity arose.

The generals were alarmed by his plans for they believed that expansion in any of these directions would lead to a head-on clash with the other powers for which Germany was not yet ready. But Hitler was determined; those who opposed him were replaced by loyal Nazis. By the end of the year Hitler's team was ready for the creation of a new empire in Europe at the first opportunity.

Anschluss

In fact Austria was the first victim and the date 1938. In January 1938 Schuschnigg, crushed an abortive Nazi *coup* in Vienna, but he was forced by Hitler's threats to appoint the Austrian Nazi leader, Seyss Inquart, as Chief of Police. The Austrian Chancellor then tried to strengthen his position by holding a plebiscite on the question of union with Germany, which he hoped would give him a mandate to defy Hitler. In fact the German dictator moved troops to the Austrian frontier and Schuschnigg, was browbeaten into resigning in favour of Seyss Inquart. The latter ruled as Chancellor for one day and then called in the Germans on 12 March. *Anschluss* (union with Germany) was completed without a war and a subsequent plebiscite taken amongst all the German people gave overwhelming support for it. In 1932 the French had prevented the customs union with Austria, but now they stood by helplessly while Hitler flouted Versailles and Locarno.

Anschluss not only began the creation of a 'Greater Germany'; it opened the way for German expansion into Danubia and the Balkans and outflanked Czechoslovakia. In Austria itself 80,000 people disappeared into concentration camps and prisons in a matter of weeks; the Austrian Jews were subjected to the full rigour of Nazi anti-Semitism and even the powerful Catholic Church found it expedient to obey the Führer.

Czechoslovakia

Czechoslovakia was obviously the next victim, but she was apparently a lot less vulnerable. The country was a successfully functioning democracy with a powerful army and armaments industry. Czechoslovakia was the most industrialised state in central Europe and her independence was guaranteed by both the Russians and the French. On the other hand the country did have several important weaknesses. There was some friction between the Czechs and the Slovaks and there were important national minority groups who were always a potential source of trouble. There were Poles, Magyars and even Russians, but the largest group was the 3,000,000 Germans led by a Nazi, Henlein. Yet these weaknesses only became fatal because of the attitudes of Czechoslovakia's so-called allies.

During 1938 Henlein provoked a series of disturbances amongst the Sudeten Germans, as they were known, demanding the creation of an independent state. The Czech government naturally refused, but President Benes offered considerable privileges to the minority. Hitler at once threatened military action, but was forestalled by a firm warning from Neville Chamberlain. Chamberlain insisted that the case must be put to arbitration and despatched Lord Runciman, an industrial negotiator with no diplomatic experience, to investigate the situation. By implication he was already admitting that Czechoslovakia could not be defended as it stood, but that a compromise could be reached without recourse to war.

Czechoslovakia and appeasement

Chamberlain was convinced that war was imminent. He also believed that the Germans had at least some justification and that some of their demands should be met. He acted at this stage not through

fear of Germany but because he really believed that he was negoti-
ating a reasonable and just compromise which would assure peace in
that part of Europe. In fact he completely failed to see that Hitler's
demands knew no limit and that any compromise would merely be
accepted as a temporary expedient.

The Expansion of Germany

1935 *Germany
regains
the Saar*

1936 *Rhineland
remilitarised*

1938 *Austria seized,
Sudetenland
seized*

1939 *Bohemia
seized
Memel seized*

The British Prime Minister's first move was a dramatic journey to Berchtesgaden on 15 September for a face-to-face meeting with Hitler. His absolute incomprehension of the real situation was reflected in the statement he made afterwards: 'In spite of the hardness and ruthlessness I thought I saw in his face, I got the impression that here was a man who could be relied upon when he gave his word.' He flew home, and on the 19th he and the French Premier, Daladier, told the Czechs that they must be prepared to cede territory to Hitler. For Benes this was quite unacceptable especially on the terms Hitler demanded; in the face of the deepening crisis Chamberlain met Hitler again on the 22nd. By this time he was growing increasingly disillusioned by the way Hitler's demands kept increasing and by additional claims from Poland and Hungary, but he did persuade Hitler to delay any military action while Chamberlain drew up yet another compromise agreement.

On 24 September a new Czech government mobilised their army and during the next four days the French called up their reservists, the British fleet prepared for action and the Germans moved up to the Czech border. Chamberlain reacted with horror at the thought of a general European war. As he said in the House of Commons: 'How horrible, fantastic, incredible it is that we should be digging trenches and trying on gasmasks here because of a quarrel in a faraway country between people of whom we know nothing.' Although he was an old man in poor health he made one more desperate journey in the cause of peace. He called a conference which met in Munich with Hitler, Mussolini and Daladier. The Czechs were not invited, nor were their other allies, the Russians. Stalin was still willing to join France and Britain in the defence of Czechoslovakia, but the Poles would not allow his troops transit rights and in any case Chamberlain did not want such an alliance. The last thing he was seeking was a military confrontation with Hitler. At Munich Chamberlain and Daladier signed away northern Bohemia together with Czechoslovakia's defence system. Benes, completely betrayed by his allies, resigned and the Germans marched in. Hitler declared 'I have no more territorial claims to make in Europe' and Chamberlain flew home tired but triumphant:

This means peace in our time. We regard the Munich aggrement as a symbol of our two peoples' determination never to go to war with one another again.

And most people in Britain and France shared his relief. Only a few were prepared to listen to Churchill when he declared:

Peace in our time
*Neville Chamberlain
returns from Munich.*

*The German dictator instead of snatching the victuals from the
table has been content to have them served to him course by course . . .
a disaster of the first magnitude has befallen Britain and France.*

After Munich

If Chamberlain's analysis of the European situation had been correct,
the Munich agreement should indeed have brought peace. But after
Munich even Chamberlain began to have his doubts and changed
his ground slightly. He claimed that justice had been done, but he
added that in any case Britain was not sufficiently rearmed to stage
a showdown with Germany yet. He also began to search for allies.
But the situation had become considerably less favourable as a result
of Munich. France was hopelessly unstable and had fallen back on a
completely defensive foreign policy. Roosevelt and most Americans
had drawn the conclusion that it was best to keep clear of European
politics altogether. The Russians had lost what little faith they still
had in joint action with the democracies after Munich and Chamberlain was still most unwilling to align with the communists. In any
case he was still seeking to reach a peaceful settlement with Hitler,
not to crush him.

However, Hitler's next move completely undermined Chamberlain's positions. At Munich he had specifically guaranteed the truncated state of Czechoslovakia but in a matter of months Hitler was once more threatening its existence. The new President, Hacha, had tried to pull the country together, but he was faced with a Slovak separatist movement and further demands from the Hungarians. On 13 March Hacha was summoned to Berlin and forced by Hitler to sign away his country's independence. The Germans absorbed the rest of the Czech lands into Germany; Hungary took another slice of Ruthenia and the rest became a puppet Slovak state.

Thereafter there could be no pretence that appeasement could bring anything more than a breathing space. Within days Hitler forced Lithuania to cede Memel to Germany and the Nazis stirred up trouble amongst the Germans in the international port of Danzig. Chamberlain at once offered a guarantee to Poland, but Hitler and even his cautious generals had ceased to pay much attention to Chamberlain's threats. At Easter Mussolini invaded Albania and the British government extended its promises to Romania, Turkey and Greece.

Even Chamberlain had come to realise that such treaties could mean little without the co-operation of the USSR. But the Red Army was still being reorganised after the great purges and the Russians were obsessed by the fear that they would be deserted by the western powers just as Czechoslovakia had been. For their part the British underrated Russia's military might and were influenced by the Poles whose fears of Russia were even at this time blinding them to the threat from Germany.

By May 1939 Hitler had signed a new alliance with Mussolini, the Pact of Steel. Mussolini told the Führer that Italy was far from ready for war, but Hitler was quite sure that neither France nor Britain would go to war over Poland since they had not done so over Czechoslovakia. He had only to make sure that he did not provoke a military reaction from Russia. In August he was assured of this by the Nazi-Soviet Pact (see p. 48) by which Russia gave Germany a free hand in western Poland and Lithuania. Despite the doubts which his generals still expressed, he seemed to be on the brink of yet another easy victory.

After manufacturing a border incident, Hitler declared war on Poland. He was so confident that he had not bothered to wait for the reluctant Mussolini who was only too aware of Italy's military inadequacies. However, to Hitler's surprise and anger, Britain and France finally took a stand. Despite Mussolini's attempt to stage another 'Munich', they delivered an ultimatum to Hitler. When it ran out unanswered on 3 September, they declared war.

The unwanted war

When Chamberlain broadcast the news of the war to the nation he had no doubts where the blame for the tragedy lay: 'We have a clear conscience, we have done all that any country could do to establish peace, but a situation in which no word given by Germany's ruler could be trusted, and no people or country could feel themselves safe, had become intolerable.' On the other hand it has been suggested that the Second World War was an inevitable product of the Treaty of Versailles and the Great Depression. Yet Hitler certainly did not want war in 1939 and Mussolini wanted it still less. Germany was not due to reach her military peak for three more years, and although Hitler expected to fight a major war with Russia sooner or later, the Nazi–Soviet Pact showed that this was not his immediate aim. The war actually occurred when it did because Britain and France finally, and still reluctantly, abandoned their policy of appeasement. The tragedy was that if only they had made a similar stand in 1934 or 1936 or even 1938, Hitler's aggression might have been scotched without war and, even if war had followed, Germany would have been in a much less advantageous position. It was their failure to support the League or to provide genuine collective security for the small nations of Europe which earned Chamberlain and his supporters a share in the responsibility for the war. It was a responsibility which must also be borne in part by the Americans. In 1939 Roosevelt declared, 'I could scarcely believe that such things could occur in the twentieth-century civilisation', but these things had been allowed to happen partly because Americans had turned their back on their responsibilities for world peace. Within a short time they were to learn that they could not remain safely in aloof isolation. In the same way Russia helped to bring the horrors of Operation Barbarossa (see p. 147) on herself by agreeing to the Nazi–Soviet Pact, though there were good reasons why the Soviet Union should have been unwilling to defend a Europe created by the Treaties of Brest Litovsk and Versailles or trust alliances with the authors of the Munich débacle.

Churchill, who had kept up a lonely campaign for firm action against Hitler throughout the 1930s, was later to label the struggle which followed 'the unnecessary war' and a full year before it broke out he analysed the fateful development of international affairs since the rise of Hitler, in characteristically trenchant style:

When I think of the fair hopes of a long peace which still lay before Europe at the beginning of 1933 when Herr Hitler first obtained power and of all the opportunities of arresting Nazi power which have been thrown away . . . I cannot believe that a parallel exists in the whole course of history. So far as this country is concerned the responsibility must rest with those who have undisputed control over our political affairs . . . They exploited and discredited the vast institution of the League of Nations and they neglected to make alliances and combinations which might have repaired previous errors, and thus they left us in the hour of trial without adequate national defence or international security.
Churchill to the House of Commons after Munich

May 1940
*Churchill at his
moment of destiny.*

The world at war 9

In some senses the war of 1939–45 was no more a world war than that of 1914–18 had been. It was, in fact, two wars fought at roughly the same time and with roughly the same contestants, but for much of the time without a world-wide strategy on either side. One war was fought in Europe and the Mediterranean coastlands. Initially it was between Germany on the one hand and France, Britain and various smaller countries on the other. Later it also involved the United States, the Soviet Union and Italy (which fought on different sides at different stages of the war). It is commonly regarded as a war between the democracies and fascism–Nazism, though fascist Spain remained neutral and the largest part of the anti-German struggle on land was borne by Russia, which was the most completely totalitarian regime in the world. The second war was fought in the Far East. It really began in 1937 with unrestricted Japanese attacks on China, but it only involved Britain, America and the Commonwealth after 1941, and the Russians did not declare war on the Japanese until a few days before the general peace in 1945.

The first thing that made this war so very different was its scale; it involved some 55,000,000 casualties and cost more than all previous wars in mankind's history combined. The second distinguishing point was its totality; for those countries which did take part there was a complete involvement for every individual. Governments extended their powers of direction and coercion into almost every aspect of the individual's life – and this was true even in the democracies. The civilians of Coventry, Dresden and Nagasaki had to face the horrors of death and destruction just as surely as the soldiers in the front line. Finally, although the fighting was not world-wide, its effects were. Even the drastic reshaping of Europe in 1918 cannot compare with the profound alteration in the balance of power which the war of 1939–45 wrought in every continent.

The following pages give a very brief account of some of the major military movements of the war and of their immediate significance. The long-term effects will be dealt with later.

THE WAR IN THE WEST

Part 1: The Phoney War. September 1939–April 1940

No one, perhaps least of all Hitler, wanted a war in September 1939, and apart from the conquest of western Poland, Hitler took no offensive action for some months. France and Britain were ill-prepared and unaggressive. There were some engagements at sea, minor clashes along the Maginot Line, but little to indicate that the most terrible war in history had begun. In Britain there was food rationing, the new anti-air raid precautions and some children were evacuated from the towns to the countryside or even to America. There was little elation on either side.

War broke out quietly and as if under a cloud. There were no
frenzied people in the streets such as we had read about in 1914. No
flags, no processions. No cheering and marching troops and flowers
. . . There was only a dull sense of waiting.
Werner Herz, a Berlin journalist

My soul revolted at what was happening. France and Britain stood
still while Germany swallowed Poland . . . We waited patiently to be
attacked and during all this time occasionally bombed Germany with
leaflets. If this was war, I did not understand it.
General Montgomery with the troops in France

Part 2: The blitzkrieg in the West. April 1940–Winter 1940

From April 1940 Hitler scored a series of sensational victories. In a matter of months he succeeded in conquering all his enemies in western Europe with the exception of Britain. Britain withstood his attacks but this did not worry the Führer. He believed that the English could be bombed or starved into defeat while he was engaged in a plan which interested him far more – the extension of his empire to the Urals.

In early April Neville Chamberlain had assured the British that 'Hitler has missed the bus'. On 9 April, however, German troops swept into Denmark and began to invade Norway. British and

French troops also moved into Norway, but the campaign was a failure and they were all withdrawn by May.

The troops lacked aircraft, anti-aircraft guns, anti-tank guns, tanks, transport and training . . . There were neither snow-shoes nor skis – still less skiers . . . Thus began this ramshackle campaign.
Winston Churchill on the Norway campaign

As a result of this many Conservatives finally turned against the Prime Minister and he resigned on 10 May after a dramatic debate in the Commons. Churchill formed an all-party coalition government

The Blitz
St Paul's through the ravages of the second fire of London.

and at once sought to reinvigorate the country:

I would say to this House as I said to those who joined this govern-
ment:
'I have nothing to offer but blood, toil, tears and sweat . . . You
ask what is our policy? . . . It is to wage war . . . with all our might
and with all the strength God can give us . . . You ask what is our
aim? I can answer in one word: Victory.'
Churchill's first speech to the House as Prime Minister

The same day the Germans invaded Belgium, the Netherlands and
Luxembourg. Ten days later they reached the French channel ports.
The French front crumbled and between 26 May and 4 June
300,000 troops, the remnants of the routed allied armies in northern
France, were evacuated from the beaches of Dunkirk. On 10 June
the Italians declared war on France and Britain. Four days later
Paris fell and on 22 June a new French government under the aged
Marshal Pétain signed a peace treaty with Hitler. Pétain's right-wing
puppet government was allowed to rule southern France from a new
capital at Vichy while the rest of the country was taken over by
the Germans. But one French general, Charles de Gaulle, fled to
England and became the self-appointed leader of a Free French
government determined to fight on and redeem France's honour:

Has the last word been said? Must we abandon all hope? Is our
defeat final and irremediable? To all these questions I answer – No
. . . Whatever happens, the flames of French resistance must not and
shall not die.
de Gaulle's first broadcast to France from London

With his empire stretching over most of Europe from Warsaw to the
Pyrenees Hitler prepared to launch Operation Sea Lion, the invasion
of Britain. Between mid-August and mid-September the Luftwaffe
staged a series of raids against British airfields in order to clear the
path for the army. But the RAF never lost control of the air and
destroyed hundreds of enemy planes. On 17 September Hitler
postponed Sea Lion indefinitely. Britain had staved off the threat of
invasion but London and the other big cities continued to suffer from
heavy bombing raids at night. Moreover she was still the only great
power at war with Hitler and her lines of supply were always in
danger. Her only comfort in the winter of 1940–1 was the defeat of
the Italians in Ethiopia and Tripoli and the destruction of a large
part of Mussolini's fleet at the battles of Taranto (November 1940),
and Matapan (March 1941).

The Axis Empire

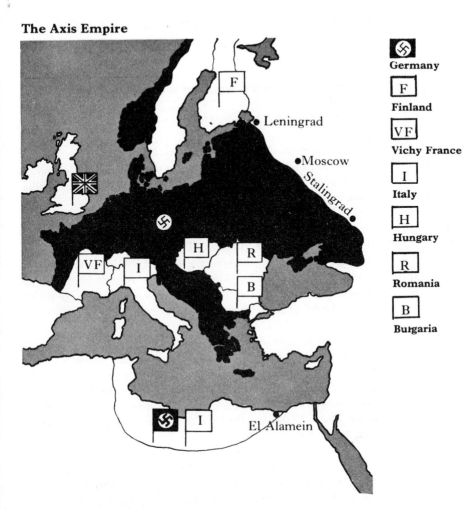

Germany

F
Finland

VF
Vichy France

I
Italy

H
Hungary

R
Romania

B
Bulgaria

Part 3: The flood tide for the Axis. January 1941–January 1942

The year 1941 will bring the completion of the greatest victory in our history.

Adolf Hitler's New Year message to his troops

1941 was indeed a year of amazing victories for Hitler, but the decision he took to attack Russia was in the long run a disastrous one. The subjugation of the 'inferior' Slav people was an essential part of his vision of a new Europe and from the beginning of the year he was absorbed with 'Operation Barbarossa' as the blitzkrieg in the east was to be known. Yet even before the campaign began there were divisions in the high command.

*When Barbarossa commences the world will hold its breath and make
no comment.*
Hitler, 3 February 1941

*This war with Russia is a nonsensical idea to which I can see no
happy ending.*
Field Marshal von Rundstedt, May 1941

In the meantime Mussolini's inability to deal with his military
commitments forced Hitler to intervene on his behalf in the Balkans
and, though the Germans scored some remarkable victories, Barbarossa itself was fatally delayed.

In March General Rommel with his crack Afrika Korps regained all
the ground the Italians had lost in Tripoli and drove the British over
the Egyptian border. In April the Germans were forced to send
troops to Greece and Yugoslavia where the Italians were also un-
successfully involved. Yugoslavia was soon overrun and the British
were driven first from Greece and then Crete.

At last, on 22 June, Barbarossa began. An immense and very well
equipped German army drove the Russians back through eastern
Poland. For Britain at least this was a welcome development for it
gave her an ally and relieved the pressure in the west. Churchill, the
arch anti-communist of pre-war days at once offered what aid he
could give to Stalin and the Russian dictator desperately sought to
rally his people.

All the same the Germans drove deeper and deeper into Russia along
a vast front and were also threatening to strangle Britain in a relentless submarine campaign which destroyed 9,000,000 tons of allied
shipping before the end of the war. The war in the east was even
more bitter than the blitzkrieg in the west had been, as a German
soldier home from the front reported:

*Rudolf stared at me, and said, ' You can take my word for it, Else,
if the Russians should ever knock at this door and only pay back one
half of what we have done to them you wouldn't smile or sing again'.*
Else Wendel, a Berlin housewife

However despite the ferocity of the attack the victory in the east was
not complete:

Now when Moscow itself was almost in sight, the mood of the

commanders and troops changed. With amazement and disappoint-
ment we discovered in late October and early November that the
Russians seemed quite unaware that as a military force they had
ceased to exist . . . Then the weather broke and the full force of the
Russian winter was upon us.
General Blumentritt, Winter 1941

Moreover, not content with taking on the Soviet Union, Hitler
completed the year by declaring war on the United States. The
occasion was the Japanese attack on Pearl Harbor, but the reason was
not just loyalty to his Asian ally. He might well have preserved peace
with America for many more months, but both the British and
Russians were receiving more and more aid from the United States
and it seemed only a matter of time before Roosevelt formally
declared war.

By the end of 1941 the scope of the war had been enormously extended. The immediate advantage was still with Hitler and his allies,
but it was very necessary for them to win the war quickly before the
vast resources of America and Russia could be mobilised. Once that
was done the strategic balance would turn inexorably against the
Axis.

Part 4: The great turning point. January 1942–January 1943
The next twelve months saw another series of Axis advances in
Russia, the Mediterranean and the Pacific. But by the beginning of
1943 the allies had scored three great victories: El Alamein, Stalingrad and Midway which marked the end of Axis expansion.

The year opened with the lightning conquest of the Far East by
the Japanese and further German advances into Russia. With
the Germans at the very gates of Moscow and Leningrad, Stalin
appealed desperately to Roosevelt and Churchill to open up a second
front in Europe. However, Rommel, in a brilliant campaign, had
once more rolled back the British troops through North Africa and
was threatening to break through to the Suez Canal. In these circumstances the British had to concentrate on their vital lifeline to the
Middle East and Asia.

Between 31 August and 3 September Rommel's invasion of Egypt
was checked at Alam-el-Halfa. Then, having built up an armoured
force which heavily outnumbered Rommel, the new British commander, General Montgomery, launched a counter attack at El
Alamein.

A real hard bloody fight has gone on now for eight days . . . I think he (Rommel) is now ripe for a real hard blow that will topple him off his perch . . . If we succeed it will be the end of Rommel's army.
General Montgomery to General Alanbrooke, 1 November

Dearest Lu,
Very heavy fighting again, not going well for us. The enemy with his superior strength is slowly levering us out of our position. That will mean the end. You can imagine how I feel. Air raid after air raid after air raid.
General Rommel to his wife, 2 November

Within another fortnight the 60,000 men and 500 tanks of the Afrika Korps had been thrown back 700 miles through the desert and Rommel was never to take the offensive again. On 8 November the Anglo-American First Army landed in Morocco and by the spring of the next year, allied troops closing from the east and west had retaken the whole of North Africa.

North Africa was not the most important field of conflict. It was to Hitler what the Peninsular War had been to Napoleon, a dangerous side campaign, and for Hitler as for Napoleon the decisive war was in Russia. Throughout 1942 the Russians suffered horribly:

The spectacle of someone dying of hunger in the snow-covered street was by no means rare. Pedestrians . . . sometimes did not even stop since there was no help they could offer.
Leningrad, 1942

But the Russian will to resist was unbroken. The Germans advanced farthest in the south and it was here that Hitler hoped to make the decisive breakthrough. On 15 September the German Sixth Army under General von Paulus reached the outskirts of Stalingrad, the key to Southern Russia.

The Russians are finished. In four weeks they will collapse.
Hitler, September 1942

But somehow the Russians hung on and the siege of Stalingrad turned into the greatest battle in the history of mankind. The Germans poured in all their resources for this titanic struggle and fought, street by street, into the desolated city. As the winter advanced they suffered more and more.

Every seven seconds a German soldier dies in Russia. Stalingrad –
mass grave.
Phrase repeated over and over again on Moscow Radio

Troops without ammunition or food . . . eighteen thousand wounded
without any supplies of dressings or drugs . . . further defence
senseless . . . collapse inevitable . . . Army requests permission to
surrender in order to save the lives of the remaining troops.
Von Paulus to Hitler, 24 January 1943

Surrender is forbidden. 6th Army will hold their positions to the last
man and the last round . . .
Hitler to von Paulus, 24 January 1943

War in the Western
Desert
The scene of Britain's
first decisive victories.

The Russians stand at the door of our bunker. We are destroying our

equipment. This station will no longer transmit.
Last broadcast from 6th Army HQ, 31 January 1943

The reconquest of Europe
American troops landing in Normandy.

Carrying out your orders the troops on the Don front at 4 p.m. on 2nd February 1943 completed the rout and destruction of the encircled group of enemy forces at Stalingrad. Twenty-two divisions

have been destroyed or taken prisoner.
Lieutenant-General Rokossovsky to Stalin

Part 5: The Axis in retreat 1943

During 1943 America turned a large part of her effort to Asia once more, but it was also in this year that the allies began the liberation of Europe. On the Eastern front the defeat at Stalingrad forced the Germans to shorten their front and take up a more defensible position. Yet the pressure of the Red Army was now irresistible and Hitler's determination never to concede an inch of ground forced his generals to fight on unfavourable terms. Slowly but surely the Russians retook their lost cities – Kharkov in August, Smolensk in September, Kiev in November. At the same time German civilians began to feel the direct effects of the war in a new and terrible way as the British began heavy bombing of industrial centres like Cologne, Hamburg and the Ruhr.

In the west the allies made less progress than they had hoped but some important ground was won. In May, a quarter of a million Axis troops surrendered in North Africa and on 10 July Anglo-American forces moved back into Europe by securing a beachhead on Sicily. By 25 July they had advanced through Sicily and Mussolini was dismissed by the King of Italy. Marshal Badoglio took over the government with a view to making peace with the allies. On 3 September the allies landed on the mainland and Badoglio surrendered. The Germans at once seized control with their troops in Italy and continued to block the allied advance up through the peninsula. In October, the Badoglio government officially declared war on Germany. Shortly afterwards the Germans managed to free Mussolini from captivity and make him the puppet head of a North Italian Republic, but the old dictator was a broken man. All the same German resistance in Italy was very effective and it was clear that Germany could not be conquered from this direction.

Part 6: The liberation of western Europe. 1944

In 1944 the western allies were at last ready to open a second front in Europe which would crush Hitler between its forces and those of the Russians.

On 6 June an immense force in 4,000 ships under the supreme command of General Eisenhower landed in Normandy. Within a week 325,000 troops had disembarked and the beachhead was secured. Both sides were hindered by the difficult Normandy countryside but soon the immense material superiority of the allies began to hammer

F

The Eastern Front
*Russians advance
through the snow.*

the Germans into submission.

In Germany a group of distinguished civilians and army officers
decided that the war must be stopped and Hitler killed before
Germany was destroyed. Led by the respected General Beck, they
succeeded in placing a time-bomb in Hitler's conference room. However, by a quirk of fate the bomb failed to kill him and the Führer
carried out a terrible purge through the higher ranks of the forces.

Meanwhile the allies advanced on all fronts. In May they entered
Rome and in August Florence. In the same month the French
Resistance staged a rising in Paris and allied troops led by the Free
French entered the city. Within a week they crossed the Seine and
swept into Belgium.

The Germans answered with two final thrusts. In early September
they began to launch their devastating V2s, the first guided missiles,
against south-east England, but the rocket sites were bombed or
overrun before the terrifying new weapon could really have a great
effect. Then in mid-December they flung a last whirlwind offensive
through the Ardennes. The allies were hurled back many miles, but

when the fury of the attack died out in mid-January the Germans had spent all their reserves and the way to Germany itself lay open.

During this same period the Red Armies were engulfing eastern Europe. During July and August the Russians crossed the Niemen and the Vistula. The Polish Resistance staged a desperate rising in Warsaw but the Russians did not advance on the city until the Germans had virtually destroyed it. However, during August they invaded Romania and in September, Hungary. The eastern front too was crumbling.

Part 7: The fall of the Thousand-Year Reich. 1945
In March the Anglo-American troops crossed the Rhine. As they advanced the world learned the full horror of the Nazi New Order in Europe. In April the Americans liberated Buchenwald concentration camp and soon afterwards the British reached Belsen.

No one had been able to compile a register of the patients. Many, of course, had forgotten their identity. I visited the human remains lying on straw palliasses, covered with filthy blankets. At first glance we were unable to define their sex. Several were lying on top of their blankets, their heads shorn, the agony of their sufferings showing clearly in their expressions with eyes sunken and listless, cheekbones prominent, too weak to close their mouths, with arms extended in an appalling manner . . . There was not an open window, the floor was filthy, straw littered with human excreta. Thousands of flies were recreating the typhus circle by settling on potato peelings picked up from the garbage bins. Broken cups and plates held pieces of black bread, turnip tops and very sour milk.
A British medical officer at Belsen

In the east the Russians were discovering the even more terrible mass extermination camps such as Auschwitz in which Hitler and Himmler had planned to wipe out all the Jews in Europe and in which, in fact, over 6,000,000 people had been destroyed.

On 21 April the Anglo-American forces halted to allow the Russians to reach their agreed lines along the Elbe. A week later Hitler committed suicide. He had already heard of the death of his fellow dictator, Mussolini, at the hands of the Italian Resistance fighters and the Russians were advancing through Berlin itself. His guards burned his body in the garden of the Chancellery as the last fragments of the Reich toppled before advancing armies from the east and west. By 2 May the Russians completed the capture of Berlin:

Belsen

Russian and American troops linked up across the Elbe and the German army in Italy surrendered. On 7 May General Jodl signed the armistice before the allied representatives.

With this signature the German people and the German armed forces are for better or worse delivered into the hands of the victors . . . In this hour I can only express the hope that the victor will treat them with generosity.
General Jodl, 7 May 1945

THE WAR IN THE EAST

Part 1: Japan in the ascendant. 1937–42
The Japanese invasion of China in 1937 provoked little response from the European democracies or Russia or America. Chiang Kai-shek and the communists were left to defend themselves as best they could in the interior. After the fall of France, the Vichy government were forced to allow the Japanese into Indo-China and the British sought to buy time by closing the only land route to Nationalist China, the Burma Road. The European empires which covered a great part of South-east Asia were in no position to defend themselves,

let alone restrain the Japanese imperialists. Only the United States could mobilise a force in the Pacific which could challenge Japan's New Order in Asia.

Roosevelt's government was well aware of the threat the New Order constituted to their own interests, and the American people were increasingly disturbed by Japanese atrocities in China. The government began to exert economic sanctions against the Japanese and alerted their forces in the Pacific. Throughout 1941 there were constant rumours of war before the blow fell.

A member of the embassy was told by my Peruvian colleague that from many quarters including a Japanese one, he had heard that a surprise attack on Pearl Harbor was planned by the Japanese . . . My colleague said he was prompted to pass this on because it had come to him from many sources, although the plan seemed fantastic.
US Ambassador in Tokyo to US government, 27 January, 1941

Yesterday, 7th December, 1941 – a date that will live in infamy – the United States was suddenly and deliberately attacked by naval and air forces of the Empire of Japan.
Roosevelt to Congress

The Japanese succeeded in crippling the great fleet at Pearl Harbor and destroyed many aeroplanes. The same day Germany declared war on the United States and Japan attacked the British and Dutch Empires in South-east Asia. By the end of January they had taken Hong Kong, driven all British troops out of Malaya and sunk two of Britain's finest ships in the Far East, *Repulse* and *Prince of Wales*. A fortnight later the reputedly impregnable base at Singapore surrendered and the Japanese completely overran the Philippines and the Dutch East Indies. By the spring the new empire was at its zenith. It extended far out into the Pacific Islands, westward into Burma and south to cover most of New Guinea. The US commander, General MacArthur, was forced to retreat to Australia and the Australians themselves prepared to face invasion. On 4 May the American and Japanese fleets met in the battle of the Coral Sea. Technically it was a Japanese victory, but they were badly mauled and their advance through New Guinea was halted.

Part 2: The slow fight back. June 1942–July 1945
On 9 June 1942 the Americans and Japanese fought another great naval battle, mostly between carrier-borne planes. The result was a crushing defeat for Japan. This battle, Midway, was the real turning

The Defeat of Japan

Area still under Japanese control in August 1945

point in the East. In August the US Marines secured a foothold at Guadalcanal; desperate fighting followed until the Americans won another smashing naval victory off the coast of the island. The Japanese were having to make their first withdrawals and their plans to conquer New Guinea were finally scrapped.

During 1943 MacArthur began a great thrust up through the islands to recapture the Philippines.

The Japanese are now speaking of the successful evacuation of Salamua. These successful evacuations are getting the upper hand with the Axis . . . The Axis powers in the course of one year have done so much successful evacuating that a large part of their former war potential has been lost.
Dr Goebbels in a private note

In the meantime the British had fought off an attack on India and the Americans began to pour in aid by air to the beleaguered forces of Chiang Kai-shek.

During 1944 the inner ring of the Japanese Empire began to crumble. Australians and Americans landed at Saipan and Guam. In a desperate gamble to save the situation the Japanese introduced the *kamikaze* or suicide planes. However this was not enough; on 24

October at the battle of Leyte Gulf the Americans won an overwhelming victory which really marked the end of the Japanese navy.
All the same the army still held vast areas of Asia.

In January 1945 the Americans re-entered Manila and were able to
keep mainland Japan under constant long-range bombing. This
became even more intense after February, when in some of the most
bitter fighting of the war the Americans took Iwo Jima – a vital
stepping stone to Japan itself. In April they attacked Okinawa. In a
last fling the Japanese poured in the remnants of their navy and air
force and 100,000 picked troops. All were lost. During the same
period the British were reconquering Burma and reopening the land
route to Chungking.

By the summer of 1945 Japan had clearly lost all hope of holding
back her enemies, especially after the collapse of Germany. Yet many
of the militarists would still not countenance surrender. The Emperor
himself was convinced that the country must make peace, but the
decision was not his alone and, as long as the allies insisted on
unconditional surrender, he found it hard to persuade his ministers.

Part 3: The sudden end

Even in the early summer of 1945 it still seemed possible that the
Japanese forces in China and in their homeland could hold on for at
least another six months or a year and that their defeat would be
extremely costly in allied lives. However on 16 July American
scientists exploded the first atomic bomb at Los Alamos, New
Mexico. Ten days later the allied leaders, meeting at Potsdam,
threatened Japan with prompt and complete destruction unless she
surrendered immediately and unconditionally. They agreed amongst
themselves that, unless their demand was met, another bomb should
be dropped, this time on Japan itself, and that the Soviet Union
should declare war on Japan within a matter of weeks.

Even at this stage scientists suspected that the atomic bomb might
have side effects which were not present in the heaviest conventional
bombing. A number of them who had made the development of the
bomb possible pleaded with President Truman not to drop it. However, the President believed that on balance less lives would be lost
if the war was brought to a rapid conclusion and he believed the
Japanese could only be persuaded to accept unconditional surrender
if one of their cities was bombed. On 6 August the bomb fell on the
city of Hiroshima. Eighty thousand people died.

Hiroshima

Sixteen hours ago, an American airplane dropped one bomb on Hiroshima. That single bomb had more power than twenty thousand tons of explosive. It is an atomic bomb. It is harnessing the basic power of the universe. We are now prepared to obliterate more rapidly and more completely every productive enterprise the Japanese have above ground in any city.
Broadcast by President Truman, 7 August 1945

On 6th August there wasn't a cloud in the sky above Hiroshima, and a mild hardly perceptible wind blew from the south. Visibility was almost perfect for ten or twelve miles.

At nine minutes past seven in the morning an air raid warning sounded and four American B-29 planes appeared. To the north of the town two of them turned and made off to the south and disappeared in the direction of the Shoko Sea. The other two, after having circled in the neighbourhood of Shukai, flew off at high speed southwards . . .

At 7.31 the all clear was given. Feeling themselves in safety, people came out of their shelters and went about their affairs and the work of the day began.

Suddenly a glaring pinkish light appeared in the sky accompanied by an unnatural tremor which was followed almost immediately by a wave of suffocating heat and a wind which swept away everything in its path.

Within a few seconds the thousands of people in the streets and gardens in the centre of the town were scorched by a wave of searing heat. Many were killed instantly, others lay writhing on the ground screaming in agony from the intolerable pain of their burns. Everything standing upright in the way of the blast – walls, houses, factories, and other buildings – was annihilated and the debris spun round in a whirlwind and was carried up into the air. Trams were picked up and tossed aside as though they had neither weight nor solidity. Trains were flung off the rails as though they were toys. Horses, dogs, and cattle suffered the same fate as human beings. Every living thing was petrified in an attitude of indescribable suffering. Even the vegetation did not escape. Trees went up in flames, the rice plants lost their greenness, the grass burned on the ground like dry straw.

Beyond the zone of utter death in which nothing remained alive, houses collapsed in a whirl of beams, bricks and girders. Up to about three miles from the centre of the explosion lightly built houses were flattened as though they had been built of cardboard. Those who were inside were either killed or wounded. Those who managed to extricate themselves by some miracle found themselves surrounded by a ring of fire. And the few who succeeded in making their way to safety generally died some twenty or thirty days later from the delayed effects of the deadly gamma rays . . .

About half an hour after the explosion whilst the sky all around Hiroshima was still cloudless, a fine rain began to fall on the town and went on for about five minutes. It was caused by the sudden rise of over-heated air to a great height where it condensed and fell back as rain. Then a violent wind rose and the fire extended with terrible rapidity because most Japanese houses are built only of timber and straw.

By evening the fire began to die down and then it went out. There was nothing left to burn. Hiroshima had ceased to exist.
From Marcel Junod, Warrior without Weapons

F*

On 8 August Russia declared war on Japan and began to invade Manchuria. On 9 August another bomb was dropped, this time on the city of Nagasaki. On 14 August the Japanese surrendered unconditionally and on the orders of the Emperor their forces all over China and South-east Asia laid down their arms. Finally on 2 September the armistice was signed. The war was over.

Postscript
Thirty million people had died and many millions more had suffered unspeakable horrors. Eventually the war had been won, as usual, by the biggest battalions. The Axis powers had been successful while their enemies were divided and unprepared. After 1941 when both the United States and the Soviet Union were involved it was almost inevitable that sooner or later Hitler and his allies would be defeated.

The world had been changed almost beyond recognition in the course of just six years:

The overwhelming material superiority of the United States and the Soviet Union, which had been disguised in the twenties and thirties was at last revealed.

Europe had ceased to be the centre of world affairs. The European Empires in Asia, Africa and the Middle East had all been shaken and Europe itself was in the process of being divided into spheres of interest by the two super powers.

The war had led to the creation of the United Nations.

In Europe and the Far East communism had made enormous strategic advances.

The world had been given a taste of the absolute powers of destruction which men could now wield.

These developments will provide the main themes for the chapters which follow.

From World War to   10
Cold War

Long before victory was certain the allied leaders were discussing the way in which they would resettle Europe and the Far East at the end of the fighting. In Moscow, Tehran, Cairo and Casablanca they not only settled the strategy for victory, but drew up plans for the creation of the United Nations and discussed the treatment of Germany and her allies. However, they did not get down to details until the Big Three – Stalin, Roosevelt and Churchill – met at Yalta in February 1945.

The Yalta Conference
The decisions taken at Yalta were a clear reflection of the strategic situation at that time. The Russians were ploughing far into eastern Europe, while the British and Americans were only just recovering from the onslaught in the Ardennes. In addition it still seemed possible that the war with Japan would drag on for months or even years, so Russian help was badly needed in the Far East. Finally the war had changed the balance of power in Europe. The German Reich was on the point of collapse, France was ruined and demoralised, Britain was exhausted by the enormous efforts of the past five years. On the other hand Russia and the United States were stronger than they had ever been. The fate of Europe lay in their hands and it was still not clear, at least to the Americans, that the two new giants would become the most bitter enemies. Indeed at times during the negotiations Roosevelt seemed more inclined to trust the revolutionary leader, Stalin, than the old imperialist, Churchill.

Against this background the conference dealt with three main problems. Firstly the leaders settled the various details for the creation of the United Nations (see p. 358). Secondly Stalin agreed that the French should be given a zone of control in Germany after the war. Finally there was the thorny problem of the resettlement of eastern Europe and in particular of Poland. Officially Poland was an ally against Hitler with a government-in-exile in London, but as the Russians advanced into the country they set up a rival provisional government. Eventually Stalin agreed that some of the London leaders, such as Mikolajczyk, the head of the Peasant party, should be allowed into a new coalition government. On the other hand the Russians were able to force the allies to agree to a drastic re-allocation of territory. Russia took over a great swathe of eastern Poland while the Poles were compensated with most of East Prussia and the German lands east of the Oder and Neisse rivers (see p. 168). As the US Secretary of State explained: 'By February 1945 Poland and all East Europe except for most of Czechoslovakia was in the hands of the Red Army. As a result of this situation it was not a question of what Great Britain and the United States would permit, but of what these two countries could persuade the Soviet Union to accept.'

Even at this stage there was a good deal of thinly disguised mutual suspicion. The western powers had been extremely secretive about the development of the atomic bomb while Russia had consistently broken the spirit of earlier agreements in eastern Europe. For Stalin the alliance had been for the duration of the war not for all time and he placed little faith in the friendship of the other leaders:

Perhaps you think that because we are Allies of the English, we have forgotten who they are and who Churchill is. They find nothing sweeter than to trick their allies. And Churchill? Churchill is the kind who if you don't watch him, will slip a kopek out of your pocket . . . And Roosevelt? Roosevelt is not like that. He dips his hand only for bigger coins.
Stalin to Djilas, the Yugoslav communist

However, Roosevelt and later Truman did their best to retain reasonable relations with the Russians. In fact during the spring they allowed the Red Army to 'liberate' Berlin, Prague and Vienna and withdrew their own troops to the west bank of the Elbe to fulfill the Yalta agreement even though the military situation no longer made such concessions necessary.

The Potsdam Conference
In July 1945 the powers held their first meeting after victory in Europe in Potsdam just outside Berlin. By this time Truman had succeeded Roosevelt and in the middle of the conference Attlee re-

placed Churchill (see p. 207). Not only the characters had changed; complete victory was followed by a steady deterioration in allied relations. However, some important decisions were taken over the future of Germany. The country was to be demilitarised and leading Nazis brought to trial. Until a new form of government could be devised, the state was to be run jointly by the allies with only local government at the lowest level in the hands of 'democratic' Germans. However, it was clearly stated that the country's unity should be preserved and that reparations were to be levied at a reasonable rate agreed by all the allies.

The other settlements
Not only Germany, but the whole of eastern and central Europe had to be resettled. Austria was regarded as a 'liberated' state but it too was divided into four zones. The Russians stripped their zone of valuable industrial goods but they did agree to the establishment of a single democratically elected coalition government. Czechoslovakia was also a 'liberated' state and she was reconstituted with most of her former territory and a democratically based coalition govern-

ment. On the other hand the Baltic states of Estonia, Lithuania and Latvia, which Russia had seized at the beginning of the war, were re-absorbed into the USSR as Soviet Republics.

The Red Army also occupied countries which were classed as Axis allies – Romania, Bulgaria, and Hungary – and here they were free to impose their own terms. Strict Russian political control was imposed and frontier corrections were made in Russia's favour. Finland was treated more leniently. She lost some territory and had to agree to onerous economic conditions which made her heavily dependent upon Russia, but she was not occupied by the Red Army and did preserve a precarious political independence. Finally there was the problem of Italy which was beyond Russia's grasp. The western powers were inclined to be generous since Italy had eventually become a co-belligerent, but the Russians insisted on reparations which were quite out of proportion to the damage Italian troops had done on the eastern front.

Peace with Japan

The Americans were in an even more dominant position in the Far East than the Russians in eastern Europe. They had won the Asian war and they granted to General MacArthur, their commander in occupied Japan, all the powers of a victorious Roman proconsul.

MacArthur faced a difficult problem. Japan had been devastated by heavy bombing and stripped of the empire on which a good deal of her economic expansion had been based. However, the Americans did not wish to destroy their former arch-enemy. Even at the end of 1945 it was obvious that Russia might be an even greater menace to American interests in the Pacific than Japan had been. So MacArthur had to try to turn the ruined and bewildered country into a stable, pro-American, democracy. The new Constitution that he imposed granted full adult suffrage and the parties were supposed to be free from the military and commercial pressures of the thirties. Hirohito, alone amongst the defeated heads of state, was not overthrown, although he lost his semi-divine status and became merely a highly-respected constitutional monarch.

The American attitude to Japan became increasingly friendly with the communist successes in China. The US government helped to rebuild the shattered economy and even allowed the re-creation of the great *zaibatsu* (see p. 111). When the Korean War broke out, Japan became a key strategic base and has remained a vital link in the American string of defences around the coast of East Asia. In 1951

America and Japan signed a mutual defence pact and the country was encouraged to develop its own conventional armed forces.

During the same period and afterwards the Japanese economy enjoyed an unbroken boom. Within two decades Japan was once more a major steel and textiles producer. It developed far and away the most successful shipbuilding industry in the world and Tokyo became the world's largest city. Japan is once more one of the world's most important industrial states and is playing an ever more important part in the economic development of Indonesia and other parts of East Asia.

The Cold War

Relationships between Russia and the western allies grew steadily worse as the British and Americans reacted against Russian activities in Poland and Germany. The Russians, who had suffered so terribly during the war, were seeking to rebuild their shattered economy and to establish a cordon of buffer states between their homeland and their potential enemies to the west. The elections which Russia had promised to hold in Poland were deferred until 1947 by which time the presence of the Red Army had assured a communist victory. Soon afterwards non-communist leaders, such as Mikolajczyk, were forced to flee abroad or face imprisonment. In eastern Germany Russian behaviour was even more dismaying. They steadily stripped their zone of food and industrial equipment and then demanded reparations from the more industrialised areas of western Germany as well. In their own zone they established a rigid censorship and political control which effectively split the country in two in defiance of the Yalta and Potsdam agreements.

Nor was this all. In the United Nations the Russians used their veto to block the entry of new members who they feared would help to out-vote the communist bloc. Although the Americans offered to control atomic weapons, which they alone possessed, the Russians would not agree to a disarmament treaty. So, at a time when all the western powers were hurriedly demobilising, the Russians maintained their huge armies all over eastern Europe and these armies exercised a decisive political influence in the countries they occupied.

The communists were also engaged in political subversion beyond the areas the Red Armies had conquered. Greece had been allocated as a British sphere of influence and in 1945 the British had helped the Greek monarchists to crush a rising by native communists. However, in 1946 fighting broke out again and this time the rebels drew support from Greece's communist neighbours. Britain was no longer able to bear the burden of supporting the anti-communist régime and appealed to the Americans for help. President Truman reacted with his famous doctrine which pledged the United States to 'support the free peoples of the world' against subversion (see p. 289).

In April 1947 the Foreign Ministers' Conference in Moscow was wrecked by the intransigence of Molotov. Soon afterwards the Russians rejected Marshall Aid both for themselves and those states under their control, though some, especially Czechoslovakia, would have welcomed it (see p. 177). By the end of 1947, in Churchill's words, an 'iron curtain' had descended across Europe.

The Iron Curtain

British

French

US

The Iron Curtain

Russian Satellites

R

Russian Gains

The Czechoslovak coup

The decisive blow to East–West relations came in Czechoslovakia. Since 1945 the Russians had been strengthening their hold on the states of eastern Europe, but most of these had never been effective democracies and the process provoked comparatively little reaction in the West. In contrast Czechoslovakia had been a genuine democracy before 1938 and after 1945 it once more had a parliamentary government with a socialist-communist coalition. Despite the presence of the Red Army the communists won only 38 per cent of the votes in the first general election and the presidency was restored to the pre-war leader, Benes. But in February 1948 the communists staged a *coup d'état*, forcing Benes to resign. A month later the only remaining socialist minister, Masaryk, Foreign Minister and son of the Czech national hero, was found dead in highly suspicious circumstances. To the democracies of Europe the events of February and March seemed to be a warning that none of them were safe from communist subversion and forced them to draw together for protection.

The background to the Atlantic alliance

Despite the threat which the Russians obviously posed, the states of Europe were still dominated by fear of Germany in 1945 and this was reflected in the post-war treaties. For instance in 1947 France and Britain signed the Treaty of Dunkirk which was clearly aimed against a revived Germany. However, this attitude gradually changed. In March 1948 the Dunkirk powers were joined by the Benelux countries in the Treaty of Brussels, which was directed against both German and Russian aggression. However, the weakness of western Europe was still woefully apparent. Against the communist bloc's 250 divisions the Brussels Pact could only put a dozen into the field. Moreover the situation became increasingly tense in 1948 as the Russians blockaded the western sectors of Berlin and tried to force their secession to East Germany. In these circumstances the West obviously needed a more powerful and closer-knit military organisation, which would include the United States. In April 1949 the five Brussels powers allied with the United States, Canada, Norway, Iceland, Denmark, Italy and Portugal in the North Atlantic Treaty Organisation. They were joined in 1952 by Greece and Turkey and in 1955 by West Germany.

The North Atlantic Treaty Organisation

The new organisation was by far the closest peace-time alliance that had ever existed between European states. What is more it committed the United States to a quite unprecedented peacetime involvement outside her own continent.

The alliance also had an unusually close political structure and its members bound a large part of their national forces under international commands. However, this could not hide the fact that it was an American-dominated system. The United States had been the moving force in its creation and always supplied the Supreme Commander. America provided more than three-quarters of the costs and the military effectiveness of the alliance always depended not upon its own forces but upon the vast nuclear arsenal behind it, which was under purely American control.

Nor did the treaty include all the free states of Europe. Finland, Sweden, Switzerland, Austria, and Eire all chose to remain uncommitted. Spain, on the other hand, might once have liked to join, but was excluded because of the fascist nature of its government.

The aims of NATO
The members of NATO declared their faith in the United Nations, but they also proclaimed that they would co-operate within this special alliance to protect democracy in the North Atlantic area. In fact they were admitting that the United Nations alone was quite incapable of providing general protection. Moreover the NATO alliance was soon to become a key part of the global strategy of the western powers led by the United States. NATO was linked to SEATO and CENTO (see pp. 135, 257) by the common memberships of a number of states, by the common purpose of the containment of communism and by a common dependence on American backing. NATO's purpose in Europe was to prevent the advance of communism into the western democratic states by infiltration or invasion. In purely military terms it never reached its targets. Its founders had planned a NATO army of 100 divisions, but the organisation never had more than thirty at its disposal. Plans for a NATO parliament and common NATO economic and social links never came to anything. It is true that in the years after 1948 tensions eased a good deal. The Berlin blockade was broken early in 1949, the communist bloc was badly shaken by the defection of Yugoslavia, and after 1950 the main battle ground between communists and anti-communists shifted to Korea and the China seas. Yet none of these things were the direct result of NATO action and during the early fifties the organisation failed to find a satisfactory answer to the German rearmament problem (see p. 192) which was one of the reasons for its military weaknesses.

However, NATO was not simply a failure from start to finish. In the first place this real attempt to create collective security had a considerable psychological effect in both halves of Europe and led western statesmen to behave with much greater firmness of purpose than they did in the thirties when their position was relatively stronger. In the second place this firmness of purpose was not just an empty bluff, because it was backed by the enormous military might of the United States. Conversely the American government was ready to commit itself to a forward policy, because it seemed that the European nations were prepared to play a responsible part in their own defence.

However, once the communist threat to western Europe began to recede, it became clear that there were many tensions between the partners. The failure of the European Army Plan (see p. 193) left a residue of ill-will between Germany and France. The crisis in Cyprus after 1955 led to strained relations between Britain, Greece and Turkey, and Britain and France cut themselves off from their allies by their Suez adventure in 1956 (see p. 235). Finally there were still many powerful interests in America who believed that their government was pouring unnecessary sums of money into Europe at the expense of American interests in the Pacific. In fact it was probably only the renewed tensions in eastern Europe in the mid-fifties which postponed an even greater crisis in the Atlantic alliance.

The Russians and the Cold War
It has been common in the West to regard the Cold War as the direct result of Stalin's lust for power and the desire of the Russian communists to subvert democratic-capitalist states throughout the world. Both these factors were important, of course, but they alone do not explain Russian attitudes.

Russia had suffered from German aggression to a degree which even the French could hardly understand, let alone the British or Americans. They were therefore determined to exact whatever they could from their former enemies to rebuild their own frontiers to prevent for ever a repetition of Operation Barbarossa. However, Russian actions were dictated by suspicion of the western allies just as much as by fear of a resurgent Germany. There was an inheritance of mis-understanding and mistrust from the late thirties which had left East and West in disarray against Hitler. There was also a strong feeling that the western powers had delayed launching a second front in 1942 and allowed millions of Russians to die so that the West could preserve its strength and dominate post-war Europe. From 1938 to the very end of the war Russians were never quite free from the fear that the western powers and Hitler might unite against them.

After 1945, when the German menace had temporarily receded, there was a new fear – the fear of the atomic bomb about which the western powers had been so secretive. Many of these suspicions may seem unreasonable to westerners, but they were real enough for the Russians. Indeed it can be argued that Stalin's foreign policy after 1945 was almost entirely defensive.

The creation of the Russian satellite empire
When the Red Armies swept through eastern Europe they occupied some states which were Hitler's allies and some which were his victims but their policies in both were more or less the same.

In the early stages of reconquest they displaced all Nazi influences and installed provisional governments. In most cases these were Popular Front coalitions of socialists, peasant leaders and communists, many of whom returned to their native countries in the wake of the Red Army. (The only states in which this was not true were Yugoslavia and Albania where communist partisan leaders managed to establish themselves with little or no help from the Red Army.) In these early days the native communists and even the Russians were quite popular but it was not long before the old class and regional differences reasserted themselves and the fear of the Russian domination was reawakened. Before these feelings could be channelled into organised opposition the Russians ditched their Popular Front allies and imposed rigid political controls. In some states, such as Bulgaria, the establishment of a full communist government was very rapid, in others, particularly Czechoslovakia, it did not take place until some time after the war. However, sooner, or later popular non-communist leaders such as Maniu in Romania, Mikolajczyk in Poland, Benes and Masaryk in Czechoslovakia, were pushed out of office, driven into exile or even killed.

The purge of the party leaders
However, Stalin's nominees were not always anxious to obey orders from Moscow once they were in power. Some were tempted by the offer of Marshall Aid; others found a close dependence on Russia was making them unpopular at home. Foremost amongst those who were unwilling to subordinate their own national interests to those of Russia was Tito of Yugoslavia. Tito had once been a notably loyal Stalinist, but he created the communist government in Yugoslavia without Stalin's help and by 1948 he was refusing to obey Stalin's orders unquestioningly. He was denounced by Moscow as a fascist traitor, but his hold over his own party and people proved stronger than Stalin had thought. Moreover Yugoslavia was well placed to

receive outside aid and the western powers were only too pleased to encourage a break away from the communist monolith. Yugoslavia remained a communist state, but Tito was soon receiving much needed western aid and developing a highly individual brand of Marxism.

The successful defiance of Tito presented Stalin with a formidable threat which he met by drastic action. To prevent the spread of Titoism he overthrew the most prominent communists who might serve as a focus for national independence in the satellite states. Dimitrov (Bulgaria) died in suspicious circumstances in 1949, Gomulka (Poland) and Dej (Romania) both lost their posts as first secretaries of their national parties, Anna Pauker (Romania), Rajk (Hungary) and Slansky and Clementis (Czechoslovakia) were all executed between 1949 and 1952. They were replaced by lesser-known Russian nominees and trusted Stalinists.

During the same period Stalin sought to reunite his empire by a continued offensive against the non-communist world. In 1948 he began his blockade of Berlin which kept Europe in a state of tension for nearly a year. In 1950 he encouraged the North Koreans to cross the 39th Parallel and he proceeded to build up a series of defence agreements with the satellites which were eventually formalised by his successors into the Warsaw Pact (1955).

Control and resistance
Within the states of eastern Europe there was a steady tightening of control over every aspect of life. Non-communist parties were suppressed, communist leaders themselves were cowed and all political opposition was driven underground. Yet the states of eastern Europe were particularly resistant to at least some aspects of communist society. The peasants, who were by far the largest social group in all these states, had welcomed the communists because they had broken up the great nobles' estates and distributed the land. However, when their communist rulers, often acting unwillingly on Stalin's orders, tried to introduce collective farming they met with stubborn resistance. This opposition, which owed nothing to non-communist political parties, was so tenacious that it completely prevented the implementation of the policy in many areas. It was indicative of the political and social development of these areas that the middle classes had failed to protect their political liberties, but the peasants successfully defended their land.

The second special factor in several states of eastern Europe was the strength of the Catholic Church. In Hungary and Czechoslovakia two-thirds of the people were avowed Catholics. In Poland the percentage was much higher. The dogma of communism was faced by an equally uncompromising doctrine which it could neither tolerate nor crush. Even in Hungary, where the Catholic leader Mindszenty lost popularity through his opposition to the break-up of the Church estates, the Catholic Church survived. In Poland the popular Cardinal Wyszynski demonstrated again and again that the Church retained the loyalty of most of the population despite all attempts to discredit or persecute it. In 1966, after nearly a generation of communist control millions of Polish churchgoers celebrated the thousandth anniversary of the foundation of Christianity in Poland. For them the Church was not only a religious institution but a symbol of Polish nationhood.

Thus, at the time of Stalin's death in 1953, eastern Europe was still in most senses part of a monolithic empire which stretched from the Elbe to the Pacific. On the other hand Tito had shown that under certain circumstances a communist leader could break away from the control of Moscow and survive. Within the member states of the Russian empire Moscow-controlled leaders were generally successful in imposing their will both inside and outside the Communist party. Yet on specific issues there was still an effective grass-roots opposition. The Catholic Church, despite many restrictions, was still a powerful force and even in Bulgaria, where the process had advanced furthest, only 40 per cent of the land was collectivised. The western alliance was threatened by all sorts of internal tensions but the communist bloc also had its inner stresses, though these were less obvious to the outsider. With the removal of the iron grip of Stalin and the consequent power struggle in Russia itself, the satellite states were ripe for change.

The European movement II

If Europe is to be saved from infinite misery, and indeed from final doom, there must be an act of faith in the European family and an act of oblivion against all crimes and follies of the past . . .

What is the sovereign remedy? It is to recreate the European family or as much of it as we can, and to provide it with a structure under which it can dwell in peace, safety and freedom. We must build a kind of United States of Europe . . .
Winston Churchill, speaking at the University of Zurich in 1946

By the end of 1945 there were something like 25,000,000 people in Europe without homes or possessions, wandering like nomads, living in cellars or ruins, or sheltering in hastily constructed refugee camps. Everywhere industry and commerce had been disrupted, governments overthrown and the whole fabric of society broken down. Already the threat of a new war, this time between Russia and the western powers, was looming over the continent. In 1939 Europe had still been the hub of world affairs; six years later it was a devastated no-man's-land between the two super powers, Russia and the United States. In these circumstances Churchill's words were by no means an overdramatic statement of the dilemma facing the European nations. Yet, as he suggested, there was a way out. Europe occupied only 2 per cent of the world's land surface but it contained 10 per cent of its people and this population was the most literate and the most experienced in trade and industry of any in the world. Moreover, despite all the bitterness of the past half-century they shared a common cultural background. If they could create a federation of Europe, there was no doubt that the European nations could form the richest and most powerful bloc in the world. This idea of a united

Europe became the common vision of many post-war statesmen and, while they were primarily concerned with the reconstruction of the political and economic life of their own countries, many of them were also working towards this wider goal.

Marshall Aid and the OEEC

The impetus came from several directions. On the one hand the states of western Europe drew together for mutual protection against the advance of Russian influence in Europe which reached its climax with the Czechoslovak *coup* in 1948 (see p. 169). On the other hand they were offered positive encouragement to co-operate by the United States. In both these cases the driving force was political and military, and the European states reacted by forming the military alliances from the Treaty of Dunkirk to the North Atlantic Treaty which were described in the last chapter. However, they also began to co-operate in economic affairs and this; in the long run, was to be the more significant development.

Initially economic aid to war-shattered Europe was distributed by the United Nations Relief and Rehabilitation Administration, but in 1947 this form of aid came to an end. To make matters worse Europe suffered a particularly bitter winter and it was obvious that economic reconstruction could never be completed without more outside help. The Americans, who had provided most of the UNRRA aid, were quite prepared to sink much more in Europe, but only if the Europeans would work together for their own recovery. In 1947 the American Secretary of State, George Marshall said:

It would be neither fitting nor efficacious for this government to undertake to draw up unilaterally a program designed to place Europe on its feet economically . . . The role of this country should consist of friendly aid in the drafting of a European program and of later support of such a program . . . The program should be a joint one, agreed by a number, if not all, of European nations.

Marshall's speech laid the foundations of the new Europe. On the one hand Stalin refused American aid for all areas under his control and early in 1948 set up the Council for Mutual Economic Assistance (Comecon) to produce a separate development plan for the communist states of eastern Europe. On the other hand a number of western European nations led by statesmen such as Ernest Bevin, the British Foreign Secretary, and de Gasperi, the Italian premier, took up Marshall's challenge. In April 1948 Congress voted $5,300,000,000 aid for Europe and a new organisation, OEEC

(Organisation for European Economic Co-operation) was set up to distribute it. Initially it covered sixteen countries of western Europe with the western part of Germany as an associate member. In 1961 the organisation was changed into the OECD (Organisation for Economic Co-operation and Development) covering the whole of western Europe with USA and Canada as full members and Finland, Yugoslavia and Japan as associates.

The organisation had a permanent administrative staff and a number of specialist advisory committees to deal with co-operation in trade, agriculture, power supplies, fisheries and transport. It successfully distributed millions of dollars of aid and brought about an economic rebirth in the states of western Europe which could never have been accomplished so quickly or so effectively by individual countries working alone. Yet for many people this was only a beginning for all decisions had still to be approved by the individual governments concerned. It was co-operation but not unity. Those who still hoped for a truly united Europe placed more faith in another body conceived at the same time, the Council of Europe.

In May 1948 political leaders from ten democratic European states met at The Hague and produced a plan for a European parliament. Many of them wanted this to be a true parliament with its members elected directly by the people. However, in the end, largely because of British objections, the assembly thus created was a congress of delegates from each of their own national parliaments. The body was called the Council of Europe and met three or four times a year at Strasbourg. The original members were Britain, France, the Benelux countries, Norway, Denmark, Sweden, Italy and Eire. Later Greece, Turkey, Iceland, Austria, Cyprus, and West Germany joined. Countries without democratically elected parliaments were not eligible for membership. But the Council too was soon a disappointment to many of its supporters. Once again all decisive power remained in the hands of the member governments and the Council, which they had hoped would become the parliament of Europe, was little more than a debating chamber for the exchange of ideas.

The functional approach to unity

In the early 1950s, a number of European statesmen who still believed in the idea of European unity began to approach the problem from a different direction. If Europe could not be united at one stroke, then they believed that unity could be achieved by joining the nations in an ever-increasing number of specialised organisations. This idea, known as functional unity, was meant to show the way in which a wider unification could work and to foster a sense of community amongst the countries that took part. Leaders from several countries were associated with this idea – Monnet in France, Spaak in Belgium, Adenauer in Germany and de Gasperi in Italy – but the first successful project took its name from the French minister who first proposed it, Robert Schuman.

The European Coal and Steel Community (ECSC)

In 1950 Schuman, a French cabinet minister, startled the rest of Europe by proposing that France and Germany should pool their resources in coal and steel under a joint authority. Other nations would then be invited to join the pool. French motives were undoubtedly very mixed. They were anxious that the great industrial areas of the Ruhr and Saar basin should never again supply armaments to be used against France and, since they could not prevent the economic recovery of Germany, they wished to control it. Yet there was also a genuine desire to improve the efficiency of European heavy industry by putting it under a single authority. Both American advisers and European economists had pointed out that the great industrial core of western Europe would be enormously stimulated if it was serving a European market of 200,000,000 people rather than a series of much smaller national markets. With such a market firms could be on a larger scale, they could afford to use the most up-to-date methods and inefficient units would be forced to modernise or go out of business. In fact the heavy industries of the area would be operating under conditions more like those of the United States.

At first it was hoped that Britain, the largest coal producer and the second largest steel producer in Europe, would join France, Germany, Italy and the Benelux countries in this scheme. But once the British government realised that the controlling commission would be able to wield real powers they pulled back, and regretfully the other six powers went ahead on their own. In July 1952 they created the ECSC (European Coal and Steel Community).

This new body was in many ways the prototype for all other attempts to build a united Europe. At its head was a High Authority of nine experts appointed by the six governments for a period of six years, but not directly responsible to them as ministers would be. There was a permanent secretariat to administer the High Authority's orders and a Court of Justice of seven international jurists to whom appeal could be made against the Authority's decisions. A Consultative Assembly made up of the representatives of the six countries at the Council of Europe had the power to pass recommendations to the Authority and to dismiss it by a two-thirds majority. Finally there was a consultative committee of fifty-one delegates of the employers and workers in heavy industry who represented their interests to the Authority.

The High Authority was a most unusual body because it had real international control. It had its own income derived from dues paid by the industries involved and it had the right to interfere in the economic organisation of the countries involved. For instance, if subsidised rail charges gave the steel industry of one country an advantage over the others, the Authority could intervene. The council of foreign and economic ministers which works with the Authority could help and recommend but it could not block the Authority's decisions.

Under the chairmanship of Jean Monnet, the Authority proved very successful. It stimulated output in steel, brought together supplies of ore and coal and helped old-fashioned firms to modernise. It has widened its scope to deal with such matters as housing and social security for migrant labour in the heavy industries. Steel production has reached record levels since the Community came into existence and steel trade within the group increased fourfold during its first ten years. Some of this increase would have taken place in any case, but there seems to be no doubt that the Authority has proved its value. In the coal industry the situation was rather different. In 1952 the Authority had to do all it could to stimulate production to meet growing demand. Output rose fast until about 1956, but thereafter the industry was hit by competition from oil and natural gas. Since 1956 production has fallen again and it has been the job of the Authority to minimise the hardship this was bound to cause and it has given special aid to depressed sectors of the industry such as the uneconomic deep-level Belgian mines. This solid achievement of the ECSC helped to create the next steps towards European unity, Euratom and the European Economic Community (EEC or the Common Market).

Euratom
The development of Euratom was very similar to that of the ECSC. In the field of nuclear research the advantages of European co-operation were particularly obvious for only through joint action could the European states ever hope to keep pace with the Americans and Russians. It was also particularly important to win the support of Britain, by far the most advanced European state in this field.

However, for this very reason, Britain was unwilling to share her knowledge with less advanced partners or to hand over control to an international commission. So once again the six states had to go ahead with their own scheme, signed in 1957. This set up a High Authority very like that of the ECSC. In this case it had the power to hold stocks of fissile material, to set up reactors, and to promote research into the peaceful application of atomic power. The Authority was advised by a Council of Ministers, a scientific and technical committee and a social and economic committee. As with the ECSC there was provision for co-operation with Britain and other members of the OECD, but the closest links were naturally within the group itself.

The European Common Market

In the same year as the Euratom agreement came the boldest experiment of all, the European Economic Community or Common Market. This body, created by the Treaty of Rome, was an attempt by the six states to apply the ideas of the ECSC on an even wider scale. Initially the Common Market was to be a customs union: over a number of years all tariff barriers were to be removed between the member states and there was to be a free movement of goods, capital and labour between them. The whole area was to be surrounded by a uniform and reasonably low tariff wall. However, the idea was meant to develop beyond this. In order to control hidden tariffs or subsidies the central authority would eventually have to interfere in the social and economic policies of the individual countries. Governments would have to sign away more and more sovereignty to the common authority and a genuine political union might emerge.

The common authority was the European Commission set up in Brussels under the chairmanship of Professor Hallstein. Apart from its secretariat and other special committees, the Community also had an Assembly, a Council of Ministers and a Court of Justice all of which coincided with those of Euratom and the ECSC, forming a series of interlocking organisations which eventually merged into a single European Community. The European Commission was not a sovereign body like the High Authority of the ECSC because its decisions had to be approved by the Council of Ministers, and thus by the individual governments. On the other hand because its field of activities was so much broader it became by far the most influential body in Europe and in 1967 it was agreed to merge the ECSC and Euratom with it.

The advantages of the system were obviously those which applied to

the other co-operative schemes. A vast new market was created and
a pool of men, money and resources, unrestricted by customs and
frontiers, could be deployed in the most efficient way. An Investment
Bank was set up with a fund of $1,000,000,000 in order to develop
the backward parts of the Community, such as southern Italy, and
to redevelop old declining industrial areas such as the Ruhr and
southern Belgium. There was also a common fund to help the
movement of labour and provide migrant workers with social
security benefits. Finally there was an Overseas Development
Fund to invest in the overseas dependencies of the six powers and
other associated non-European states. Beyond all these economic
advantages there was also the hope that it might help to make men
think of themselves as 'Europeans', to destroy the centuries-old
enmities and to build a third force in the world which was not
dependent on either the Soviet Union or the United States.

Obviously there would also be difficulties. Certain industries in
certain areas would suffer badly when they were left unprotected
against more efficient competitors in other parts of the Market.
During the period of transition there might be sudden changes in
price levels, for instance areas with low food prices might find these
rising to come into line with average prices throughout the Market.
Agriculture posed a special problem because all the members of the
Community had their own system of subsidising and protecting their
farmers. However, it was agreed that full agricultural integration
would be achieved slowly over a period of ten or more years.

The European Free Trade Association (EFTA)
Most of the leaders of the six member states of the EEC hoped that
other countries, especially Britain, would join them in their great
project. However Britain, once a leader in European co-operation,
was faced with special difficulties (see pp. 216-17). As the centre of
the sterling area, linked to a world-wide system of trade, especially
with the Commonwealth, the country could not fit easily into the
tight-knit pattern of the EEC and there was still a powerful strain of
isolationism in British policy. Some countries like Denmark and
Eire were so closely tied to the British economy that they were bound
to follow Britain's lead. Others such as Switzerland and Sweden
were afraid that membership of the EEC would compromise their
traditional neutrality.

In 1956, while the negotiations for the Common Market were still
going on, the British government proposed a much more limited
alternative scheme. They suggested that the European states should

form a free trade area in which they would progressively lower their tariffs. The most obvious differences from the EEC plan were first, that agricultural goods would not be involved at all; second, that the countries concerned would not have to have a common policy towards outsiders so that Britain could retain her preferential terms within the Commonwealth; and finally, that there would be no signing away of sovereignty to a supranational authority. The governments of the Six expressed no interest in this idea and their own scheme began to operate in 1958. Britain and the other non-members, however, pursued the idea and seven of them – Britain, Denmark, Sweden, Norway, Austria, Switzerland and Portugal – set up the European Free Trade Association.

The development of the European groups
But the Seven could never really rival the Six. They formed a much less natural economic or geographical group. Their combined populations and resources were much smaller and the group was dominated by Britain who was still really interested in finding some way into the EEC without giving up too many of her other interests.

In 1961 the possibility of British entry was reopened and a number of her trading partners in EFTA also applied for membership or association. After months of negotiation and considerable controversy within Britain (see pp. 216-17) the talks broke down. Part of the blame lay, no doubt, with the British. They had abdicated the leadership of the European movement years before and they had clearly not believed that the Treaty of Rome would produce the dramatic economic advantages which the Six had in fact come to enjoy. Then when they came to apply for membership at this late date they still sought to protect all their outside interests. Even so their application would probably have been accepted but for the immovable opposition of President de Gaulle. De Gaulle claimed that British membership would destroy the whole close-knit organisation of the EEC and that the British were still not sufficiently 'European' in their attitudes to be accepted. Beyond this de Gaulle was also obviously worried that Britain would take over from France the leadership of the group and that British membership would involve the EEC too closely with the United States.

After de Gaulle's final rejection in 1962 there were almost five years' stalemate. The members of the EEC progressively lowered their barriers and though their agricultural policy ran into difficulties, the organisation was clearly a success in economic terms. EFTA also had its successes; in fact in the mid-sixties the group was expanding its internal trade faster than EEC. Yet there was no obvious direction for further development within the Free Trade Association as there was for the EEC.

In 1967 Harold Wilson, the British Prime Minister, and George Brown, the Foreign Secretary, staged a full-scale campaign within Europe to win support for their application to join. Once again most of the member governments were in favour of British entry, but there was still unbending opposition from de Gaulle and some other leaders. Britain's application seemed in many ways more convincing than in 1961. The government was ready to enter into negotiations without any previous conditions concerning Britain's other inter-national commitments and, in contrast to 1961, both the major political parties supported Britain's application. On the other hand the Six had five more years of integration and the admission of another large power would pose many problems. Even more serious were the implications of Britain's economic crises in the mid-1960s. In de Gaulle's eyes these made Britain more dependent than ever upon the United States and therefore unsuitable as a partner in the EEC.

The expansion of the EEC
Despite two rebuffs many British politicians remained committed to the idea of joining the ECC and a White Paper, published in early 1970, still seemed to indicate that on balance Britain would gain economically from membership. However it was the British general election of June 1970 that revolutionised the situation. Edward Heath had taken a leading part in Britain's first attempt to negotiate entry and had remained an utterly committed 'European' ever since. Now, as Prime Minister, he was determined to carry negotia-tions to a successful conclusion and in this he was aided by a change of attitude in France. He was soon to achieve a close understanding with President Pompidou, who no doubt saw in a Conservative government in Britain an effective counterweight to the Social Democrat government of Brandt in Germany, France's main rival for the leadership of the Community.

At all events Heath immediately put new negotiations in hand and he was joined in this by the governments of Denmark, Norway and the Irish Republic, all close trading partners of Britain. These negotiations eventually concluded in January 1972 with the signature of the treaty of accession to the Community. Subsequently, after a negative vote in a referendum on entry, Norway withdrew but the others joined the Six as full members of the EEC in January 1973.

During this period there was intense debate about the advantages of membership for the newcomers and about the effects of expanding the community on the original members. In Britain, public opinion polls indicated that the majority of the people were at no time in favour of membership. On the other hand, most Conservative MPs, all the Liberals and a substantial number of Labour members were in favour. The evidence was complex and inconclusive. The economic arguments were certainly far from clear cut. It was obviously true that the British economy had been growing much more sluggishly than that of the Six and that the Six had in particular shown a tremendous growth in trade amongst themselves. On the other hand it could be argued that this was due to quite separate factors. In both France and Germany the beginnings of economic renaissance could clearly be traced back to a period before the effects of EEC membership could have been felt. It is also worth noting that in the most recent period the fastest economic growth in Europe was recorded in the relatively underdeveloped non-members, such as Spain and Portugal.

Some businessmen argued that British exports would find a huge new market within the European tariff-free area; others feared (as indeed proved to be the case in 1973–4) that, on the contary, European goods would flood into the British home market. Other interest groups were also divided—some farmers welcomed the idea of guaranteed prices, others feared competition. There were fears of a massive rise in food prices for the consumer and of a flight of British investment into European financial and industrial enterprises. Many trade unionists feared that multinational companies would find it easier to switch production within the community from country to country regardless of national interests, and many people in the economically depressed regions such as Northern Ireland and Scotland feared that they would suffer still more as a result of their distance from the core of the market.

There were also political arguments. On the one hand it was maintained that only in such a community could the old rivalries which had twice in the twentieth century ripped Europe apart be forgotten and a true European cultural and political unity emerge. Some held that the new Community would be a force capable of standing aside from the power blocks of America and Russia (and interestingly the Chinese government have expressed their approval of the Community apparently on these very grounds). Others have countered that it would be a rich man's club and that Britain, in particular, would be turning her back on her traditional world-wide links in the third world through the Commonwealth. Again it was pointed out that far from uniting Europe there might develop a more rigid distinction between the members and the non-members, particularly those in Eastern Europe.

There was also the highly emotive issue of national sovereignty. The British were perhaps particularly sensitive about the fact that law-making powers would be passed from Parliament to the European Commission. But even amongst the original members there was a division between those who saw the Community as a union of convenience between separate nations, in de Gaulle's words 'L'Europe des Patries', and those, notably the Dutch, who seemed to have developed a genuine sense of being 'Europeans' first and foremost.

	The Nine	U.K. alone*	U.S.A.	U.S.S.R.	Japan
Population 1971 (millions)	253	55·5 (2)	207	242	104
Gross National Product 1971 in million $	692	134 (3)	1068	288	219
Growth rate					
1969–70	4·7%	2·8% (9)	4·0%	—	11·0%
1970–71	3·0%	1·6% (7)	2·8%	—	6·3%
Imports as % of World total	39·2%	7·2% (2)	13·9%	3·8%	6·0%
Exports as % of World total	40·6%	7·1% (2)	14·1%	4·4%	7·7%
Steel production million tons	128	24 (2)	111	120	88
Private Cars per 1000 population	232	222 (5)	447	6	102
TV per 1000 population	227	284 (1)	399	127	214
Telephones per 1000 population	198	253 (3)	567	50	194

* Rating within the Nine in brackets

The crisis of the Community

The extension of membership was followed by a most unhappy period for the Community. Now that it had been enlarged, and particularly with British membership, many of the inherent problems of the Community became even more obvious. First amongst these was the Common Agricultural Policy. This policy had been devised to maintain price levels for the benefit of farmers, who made up a much higher proportion of the population in the Six than in Britain. The relatively less efficient French farmers had most to gain from this system and in any case the Six had long been countries geared to fairly high food prices. Britain, on the other hand, had a tradition of low food prices brought about both by government subsidies to farmers and by cheap tariff-free imports from Commonwealth food-producing countries such as New Zealand for lamb and dairy products and the West Indies for sugar. Britain was now agreeing to

G

phase out these cheap imports (and thus also to abandon her old trading partners). During the period immediately before and after membership food prices rose sharply in Britain and this was widely, though unfairly, blamed on the Community. In fact world prices were at that time rising faster than Community prices; on the other hand as world commodity prices began to flatten out in 1974, Community prices showed every sign of remaining very high, to Britain's cost. In addition the inefficiency of the Community policy was dramatically demonstrated by the fact that huge surpluses of beef and butter were produced in 1973 and 1974 and these had to be stockpiled or sold off cheap outside the Community in order to maintain high prices inside the Community. This problem stemmed from the divergence of interest between the more industrialised and the more agricultural states within the Community. Another divergence of interest became apparent over regional policy. One of the original attractions of membership for Britain had been the promise of large-scale investment from the Community to help the depressed regions. However, in practice, Germany, who stood to gain little from the regional fund, but was expected to contribute heavily, insisted that the regional programme should cut back thus frustrating hopes in Britain, Italy and Ireland. In other fields too it was clear that national self-interest frequently triumphed over Community concerns. The much heralded target of a unified currency system by 1980 seemed utterly remote when in 1973-4 Britain, Italy and France flew in the face of community policies in order to defend their own currencies. An even more blatant example came with the oil crisis of 1973-4 when all the major European states sought to establish advantageous deals with the Arabs and showed no interest in giving effective Community support to the Dutch who were for some time victims of an Arab oil embargo because of their supposedly pro-Israeli attitudes.

Another common criticism of the Community was that it was overbureaucratic and overcentralised. Political power was being removed to remote Brussels while the European Parliament had no real powers over the Commission. The parliament was weakened by the slow progress in changing it from a talking-shop for representatives of the various national parliaments into a directly-elected assembly with a mandate from the people of the Community.

By the middle of 1974 the Community had also suffered a setback by the removal from the political scene of some of its most powerful exponents. In Britain Heath had been replaced by a Wilson government, committed to renegotiation of Britain's entry terms. In

Germany Brandt, one of the most dedicated of the European leaders, had been replaced by the tougher and more pragmatic Schmidt and in France Pompidou had given way to Giscard d'Estaing. These two were, of course, still committed to the idea of the EEC but were even more likely to insist on the maintenance first and foremost of national self-interest. Meanwhile in Italy the devasting effects of inflation, particularly in oil prices, had brought the country to the verge of economic collapse and political paralysis.

On the other hand when Britain held a referendum on membership in 1975 the electorate followed the advice of the Wilson government and voted by a majority of two to one to stay in the EEC. Many people in Britain remained unenthusiastic about the Community, though in 1977 there was some renewed interest when the former Labour Cabinet minister, Roy Jenkins, became Chairman of the EEC Commission. A further extension of the Community became likely when, in the mid 1970s, Greece, Spain and Portugal all regained some form of parliamentary government after years of authoritarian rule.

The Council for Mutual Economic Assistance
The countries of eastern Europe were even more disrupted by the war than those of the West and they were always less highly industrialised. In 1948, these states were also offered a chance to receive Marshall Aid, but Stalin prevented this and created Comecon instead. The organisation was supposed to integrate the economies of the whole area but very little was done while Stalin lived and most states were left to press on as best they could with their own industrialisation and agricultural development plans.

After 1953, Comecon became more active. It was obviously inefficient for the satellites to push through a series of unco-ordinated Five Year Plans, especially as these were meeting a good deal of internal opposition. In the mid-1950s Kruschev and the other Russian leaders therefore tried to persuade the countries of eastern Europe to abandon the attempt to develop all sides of their economies and to concentrate instead on those economic activities to which they were best suited, or which fitted most conveniently into the overall Russian plan. Czechoslovakia and East Germany, for instance, were to specialise in the development of heavy industry, while Romania, Bulgaria and Hungary were to be suppliers of food and raw materials. Russia herself was not an integral part of the scheme but was to be associated with it, drawing up plans and providing technical assistance.

Kruschev soon encountered problems. In his speech to the Communist Party Congress in 1956 he said: 'It is impossible to have developed everything everywhere simultaneously. Unfortunately we have often spoken in vain. Hungarians, Poles, Romanians have tried to build everything by themselves ... The sooner and better we develop the division of labour between countries the greater our economies will be.' But the less industrialised states were not content merely to supply raw materials. They saw that the division of labour would only increase the difference between them and their more industrialised neighbours and make them permanently dependent on them. As it happened the Russians were trying to increase their powers of economic direction at the very time that their political control was breaking down (see p. 319) and they soon found it was impossible to compel unwilling states to play their designated part in Comecon plans.

Romania led the opposition. The country had been given the role of a supplier of oil, salt, chemicals, timber and corn and was not supposed to divert her capital into her own heavy industries. However, Gheorghiu Dej, who had regained control of the Romanian Communist party after Stalin's death, was not prepared to accept this. In the early 1960s he was able to exploit the quarrel between the Russians and the Chinese to free Romania from Comecon control. The Romanians did build their own modern steel works and in 1963 began to buy machinery from western Europe. In the same year they set up a joint hydro-electricity project on the Danube with the Yugoslavians, who, of course, were not members of Comecon at all.

The other members of the group were also to varying degrees unhappy about Comecon, at any rate so long as it was obviously under Russian direction. Both Poland and Czechoslovakia have been increasingly attracted by the advantages of trade with the West, and Hungary and Bulgaria may well be tempted to follow the example of the Romanians. It was certainly the aim of those behind the liberalisation movement in Czechoslovakia in 1968 to increase trade with the West (see p. 329), and even after Russian intervention they were not completely deflected from this course.

The command economies of Eastern Europe were not proof against the economic problems of 1970s or the conflict between national economic needs and popular expectations. For instance, twice in the 1970s the Polish government had to drop unpopular food price increases in the face of violent riots.

Divided Germany and the new France   12

The rapid rise and fall of the Nazi empire threw the political life of Europe into confusion. In a handful of north European states democratic régimes were restored without much delay in 1945; Italy began upon her first period of effective parliamentary government with universal suffrage. Elsewhere the changes were more revolutionary. The whole of eastern Europe fell under communist régimes, while Greece, the birthplace of European democracy, passed from a bitter civil war in 1945–7 through twenty years of unstable parliamentary government to a military *coup d'état* in 1967. Yet, as always in modern European history, the most significant changes came in the two dominant states, Germany and France.

GERMANY

The problems of post-war Germany
At the Yalta conference the Big Three agreed to divide Germany into four zones of occupation, but to preserve the essential unity of the country under a joint administration. In fact this agreement never came into effect. The four zones were set up and Berlin was split into four sectors, but the victors could not agree on a common policy. France and Russia adopted much harsher methods in their zones than Britain and America and there was almost no co-operation between the allies except in bringing the surviving Nazi leaders to trial at Nuremberg.

While the conquerors argued, the Germans suffered. During the winter of 1945–6 thousands were homeless; there was a desperate shortage of food and fuel and the currency system collapsed. All these problems were made much worse by the streams of refugees from eastern Europe, especially from the former German territories east of the Oder-Neisse Line. The Russians stripped their zone of food and capital equipment to make good their own losses and demanded further compensation from western Germany. In the spring of 1946 the Americans drew up a plan for the reconstruction of the prostrate country, but neither the Russians nor the French would co-operate. The winter of 1946–7 was even worse and the British and Americans agreed to a unification of their zones as a first step to getting life back to normal. The Americans were also willing to provide capital for economic redevelopment, but nothing could be done until the worthless currency had been reformed. As the Russians would not agree to any reforms the country was soon split between the east and the west for both economic and political purposes. This split became permanent after May 1948 when Stalin refused land access to the western sectors of Berlin. The western allies kept their beleaguered sectors alive by an enormous airlift of food and fuel until the following March when the blockade was lifted once more. By that time it was clear that both Berlin and Germany itself would be divided for a long time to come.

Germany in ruins, 1945

The reconstruction of the western zones

The currency reform and the influx of American aid had an immediate effect. They created the conditions in which the Germans could once more apply their great industrial skills and capacity for hard work. Professor Erhard, a brilliant economist, was appointed to direct the economic affairs of the three western zones in 1948. The area included one of the richest industrial concentrations in Europe and the western zones were soon enjoying a hectic boom. By 1950 production was back to the level of 1938 and the country once more led Europe in the output of steel, electrical goods and chemicals. With American help, the Germans were able to build their new industrial plants with the most modern machinery and methods.

Divided Germany

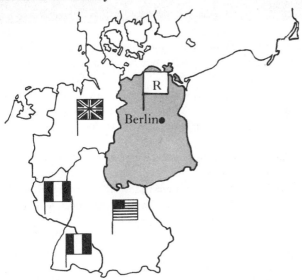

British Zone

French Zone

American Zone

R
Russian Zone

Berlin

French Sector

British Sector

American Sector

R
Russian Sector

Germany restored, 1961
The five millionth Volkswagen alongside the original model.

Before long they were not only absorbing the steady stream of refugees from eastern Germany, but were welcoming migrant labourers from Italy, Spain and Turkey. Modern production methods, good design, hard selling: these were once more their recipe for success, a recipe which has, for instance, made Volkswagen the greatest motor manufacturer outside the United States.

During the same period the first steps were taken to reconstitute the country's political life. At a very early stage the Germans were allowed to take over local government in the villages and towns. The next step was the creation of the Landtags, or provincial assemblies, which were given wide powers in education, welfare work and the provision of public services. Finally, in May 1949, the German Federal Republic was set up to run the affairs of the three western zones and the western sectors of Berlin (though here especially the allied commanders retained wide powers). The new Constitution was deliberately constructed to avoid some of the weaknesses of Weimar Germany. The Landtags retained many important powers, the Chancellor was made fully responsible to the Bundestag, or parliament, in the capital at Bonn, and the President was elected indirectly and given strictly limited powers as head of state.

Rearmament
The rapid rehabilitation of West Germany and the continued threat of Russian expansion soon raised the thorny problem of German rearmament. Without German men and resources NATO could never be an effective defence system. On the other hand many European states, especially France and Belgium, were fearful of a

revival of German militarism. In 1951 it seemed that a compromise solution could be reached through the Pleven Plan, which would have brought German troops under international control as part of a European army. But when the British refused to pool their forces in such an army the French vetoed the plan for they feared that in the absence of Britain, Germany would be the preponderant power in the force. In 1954 yet another formula was found in the Western European Union. This alliance of Britain, France, West Germany and the Benelux states allowed Germany to become a member of NATO and to control her own conventional weapons. In 1956 the Federal Republic became a fully sovereign state and although allied troops remained in the country, it was as part of the western defence system rather than an army of occupation.

The Saar

The responsible behaviour of the Federal Republic and the conciliatory work of the Council of Europe allowed the settlement of another outstanding issue between France and Germany. In 1945 the coal-rich Saar was detached once more from Germany and placed under French control. The French did all they could to integrate the area with their economy, but the sympathies of the native population remained German. In 1957 the area was politically reunited with Germany after a plebiscite and by 1959 its economy had been reintegrated with that of the Federal Republic too. This peaceful change did much to reduce tension between France and Germany and was a concrete example of the way in which European co-operation had softened the old rivalries.

Reunification

Few Germans were prepared to accept that their country should be permanently divided even when the creation of the East German Democratic Republic in 1949 made the existence of two Germanies an irrefutable fact. The western allies and the Bonn government refused to recognise East Germany as a state and vainly sought some formula under which the country could be reunited. The withdrawal of the Russians from Austria in 1955 only emphasised the anomalous position of Germany still further.

The Russians insisted that before the two parts could be joined once more the whole area would have to be demilitarised. Clearly the communists believed that western Germany with its population of over 50,000,000 would completely swamp the 13,000,000 East Germans (who were, in any case, of doubtful loyalty to communism) and the NATO alliance would be allowed to advance its frontiers to

G*

the banks of the Oder. On the other hand the western powers believed that demilitarisation would be much more damaging to their strategic position than to the Russians. In any case the Bonn government for long refused to countenance such a plan and would not renounce categorically their claims to the lands east of the Oder-Neisse Line.

In all the tensions between East and West the position of Berlin has been particularly important. This island of 2,000,000 'West Germans' is completely surrounded by East German territory and so has been used by the communist bloc as a vulnerable pressure point in any crisis with the West. After Stalin's unsuccessful attempt to squeeze the Western powers out in 1948–9 there was an uneasy peace until 1958 when it seemed that there might be an open clash between Russia and the NATO powers over its status. In 1961 the East Germans and Russians built a wall through the city to prevent the outflow of refugees to the West and there was another crisis in 1962. For their part the West Germans have done all they could to establish the fact that West Berlin is part of the Federal Republic. In fact the city has remained by far the most dangerous trouble spot in Europe and Germany itself is still an unresolved problem – its present status satisfies almost nobody.

The political development of western Germany
The first Chancellor of West Germany was the Christian Democrat (conservative) leader, Konrad Adenauer, a former mayor of Cologne who was imprisoned by the Nazis. He was already seventy-three when he took office, but he remained in command of the new state until 1963 and his skilful and tenacious leadership during the period of reconstruction led Churchill to call him 'the greatest German since Bismarck'. With his Economic Minister, Erhard, he was able to preside over the economic renaissance of western Germany, but his role in international affairs was much more difficult. The ultimate aim of West German foreign policy under Adenauer and Erhard, who succeeded him from 1963–6, was obviously to reunite Germany. The difficulty was to choose a policy which might achieve this. For most of the time the Bonn government opted for a close alliance with the United States, but some statesmen in Germany have felt that there was more hope for a united Germany in the less firmly committed Europe which de Gaulle was trying to create. This policy division also involved attitudes towards the Common Market. Some Germans supported the Gaullist attitude towards Britain while others have sought to bring Britain into the Community as a counterweight to de Gaulle's influence.

The Wall
*A divided street in a
divided city. Children
on the western side of the
Wall.*

Konrad Adenauer
*The architect of West
Germany.*

The disagreements about foreign and defence policy and serious set-backs which the German economy had suffered in the mid-1960s seriously weakened the Christian Democrat party and led to the overthrow of Chancellor Erhard in 1966. He was replaced by another Christian Democrat, Kiesinger, but this time the government was a coalition of Christian Democrats and Social Democrats with the popular Social Democrat and former mayor of West Berlin, Willy Brandt, as foreign minister. The intention of this Grand Coalition of the major parties was to give the country a greater stability with which to face her difficulties in foreign relations and economics.

The Grand Coalition certainly succeeded in restoring the health of the economy: by 1968 the German mark was the most stable currency in Europe and the country was enjoying a massively favourable balance of trade once more. As a result of this economic strength at a time when the other major industrial powers were in great difficulties West Germany also began to exercise the political authority in Europe which was due to her as the largest and richest state in the area. The West Germans were now increasingly ready to take initiatives in foreign affairs after many years of dependence on the United States, Britain and France for military protection and diplomatic support. However, the Grand Coalition was only a temporary expedient. In 1969 Willy Brandt succeeded in forming the first Social Democratic government of the Republic. However, electoral setbacks were later to make him dependent on the liberal Free Democrats for a majority.

The new Germany

Under the Social Democrats the economic boom was to continue at least until the world economic crisis of 1973-4, but what was even more remarkable was the vigour with which Brandt began to tackle the intractable problems of West Germany's *Ostpolitik*, the relationship with eastern Europe and in particular the German Democratic Republic. With both parts of Germany prospering, tensions along the border had diminished and there was growing commercial and cultural contact between East and West. In a major diplomatic offensive Brandt succeeded in reaching an agreement with the USSR which wiped out Germany's old territotial claims in eastern Europe and gave full recognition to the Democratic Republic which previous Christian Democrat governments had resolutely refused. The 1973 Treaty on the Bases of Relations opened the way for both parts of Germany to take seats in the United Nations later that year. Brandt was recognising, in effect, that there might be two Germanies for a long time to come and that 'nothing indicates that the frag-mented German nation could be restored in its old form'.

The renunciation of the old claims in the east and the increasing stature of Brandt as an international statesman did much to allay recurrent fears of a resurgence of Nazism. In 1967 there was inter-national consternation at the success of the National Democrat Party in provincial elections, for it was believed to have close connections with old Nazi groups. However the movement did not gather momentum and showed no signs of ever doing so as long as the economy remained in a reasonably healthy state. In the 1970s this was certainly the case as Germany became the leading state, economically, within the European Community.

In 1974, to the dismay of Germany's partners in Europe, Chancellor Brandt resigned over a security scandal. He was succeeded by Helmut Schmidt, a former Social Democrat finance minister. Despite Germany being in an enviable economic situation com-pared with the rest of Europe, the Social Democrats lost ground in the 1976 elections and remained in power, as before, thanks to a precarious coalition alliance with the liberal Free Democrats.

FRANCE
Post-war France
The humiliating defeat of 1940 and the shameful collaboration of the Vichy government damaged France both materially and morally. In the months after liberation 40,000 people were killed without trial as resistance fighters and others paid off old scores, and for some time it was as much as de Gaulle, head of the provisional government could do to bring some law and order to the country and to organise French forces to take part in the last stages of the war against Hitler.

In October 1945 the government was at last put on a firmer footing. The French people voted overwhelmingly against the revival of the Third Republic and at the same time elected a constituent assembly to provide the country with a new system of government. In these elections the communists, socialists and MRP (Mouvement Répub-licain Populaire – liberal Catholics) all won about a quarter of the vote with the rest going to the Radicals and various right-wing groups. The communists had played a great part in the resistance and were the largest party in the assembly but clearly could not form a govern-ment. De Gaulle, the one generally accepted leader, was therefore made the head of a coalition government made up of the three main parties.

The leader out of power
De Gaulle after his resignation in 1946.

Charles de Gaulle

The new head of government was a soldier, not a politician. Charles de Gaulle was a highly conservative Catholic who had fought with distinction in the First World War. In the inter-war years he had won the patronage of Marshal Pétain, the most respected soldier in France, but it was a period of frustration for him. He believed that France would have to fight another great war within his life-time and that it would be quite different from the static trench warfare of 1914–18. But his pleas for the creation of mobile armoured divisions were ignored, with disastrous results in 1940. When France capitulated to Hitler, de Gaulle refused to support Pétain but fled instead to London where he became the self-appointed head of the Free French movement. At first he had hardly any troops, no bases and no international recognition. He was snubbed and ignored by Churchill and Roosevelt and the latter won de Gaulle's undying hatred by seeking to deal behind his back with other French leaders. Yet, in the end, de Gaulle came to control a Free French army and the French Empire in Africa; he was recognised by the French resistance movement and when Paris was liberated in 1944 there was no one else who could possibly have been chosen to head the provisional government.

Through all his difficulties in the war he was borne along by his unbending belief that France was necessarily the centre of European

The leader restored
*De Gaulle at a press
conference in 1966.*

civilisation and that she should never be submerged either by
German conquest or by the influence of the English-speaking powers.
As he wrote at the beginning of his memoirs: 'All my life I have kept
alive in myself a certain idea of France . . . I early came to believe
that France . . . had an eminent and exceptional destiny . . . I am
convinced that France is really only herself when she is in the front
rank. France cannot be France without greatness.' His remarkable
faith in the France of St Louis, Joan of Arc, Louis XIV and Napoleon
was to have considerable effects on European politics in the 1960s.

The Fourth Republic

Despite his faith, de Gaulle was ill at ease as head of government. He
rushed through a mass of legislation: nationalising the Bank of
France, public utilities and the great Renault works; extending the
vote to women; laying the basis for the welfare state. But he was
incapable of the compromises necessary to hold together his ill-
assorted coalition. He also found that the independent role he had
hoped to play in mediating between America and Russia was impossible because France was so dependent on American aid. He
therefore resigned in January 1946 and although he did try to stage
a political comeback in the late forties, he had virtually retired from
politics by the mid-fifties.

In the meantime France was enjoying a great economic boom. With the help of Marshall Aid and under the wise guidance of economists such as Monnet and Schuman, production rose half as high again as the 1938 level by 1953. The population, which had been static or declining in the twenties and thirties, was growing faster than any other in northern Europe. France played a leading part in all co-operative economic ventures in Europe and undertook major schemes in railway reconstruction, electrification, and the development of industry.

Unfortunately her economic health was not matched by political stability. The new Constitution provided no firmer basis for government than that of the Third Republic and all parties showed the old tendency to split and quarrel amongst themselves. There were no less than twenty-four coalition ministries between 1946 and 1958. This prevented the government from dealing effectively with the problems of social reform and the inflation which had come with the rapid economic expansion. Worse still, it left France with a weak and indecisive leadership at a time when she was engaged in a series of disastrous colonial wars.

The French colonial wars
The war had undermined French authority in practically every part of her vast empire. Syria was never recovered and in Indo-China the veteran Communist leader Ho Chi Minh declared independence in 1945. For the next nine years France was involved in a terrible blood-letting in South-east Asia which only ended after a series of humiliating military defeats. Eventually in 1954 the reforming socialist premier, Pierre Mendès-France, liquidated all France's interests in Indo-China. He also began to tackle the problem of withdrawing from Tunisia and Morocco (completed in 1955), but before he could complete his work he fell victim of the irresponsible party manoeuvres of his enemies. His downfall in 1954 was followed by a period of even more unstable government during which France became completely bogged down in the worst of her colonial campaigns.

The Algerian war
From 1954 onwards the overriding problem of all French governments was Algeria. This vast area of North Africa was officially part of metropolitan France with over a million white settlers. However, in 1954 the Arab leaders in Algeria followed the example of their neighbours in Tunisia and Morocco and launched a military revolt. Within a few years 15,000 guerilla fighters had an army of 350,000

The Algerian tragedy
*French troops in the
violence torn streets of
Algiers.*

Frenchmen tied down in a war in which both sides resorted to the
most appalling terrorism and torture. Many Frenchmen were horrified at the brutality of their own soldiers and the breakdown of the
rule of law, but no French government felt strong enough to defy
the demands of the white Algerian settlers who were determined that
the province should remain French, or to curb the activities of the
right-wing army officers who were prepared to use any means to
crush the Algerian FLN (Front Libération National). When at last
the French Cabinet seemed to be considering negotiations with the
rebels which would put an end to this struggle, which was so damaging to the economy, morale and international standing of France,
the colonists and the army in Algeria openly defied the authorities in
Paris. The mutiny spread to Corsica and it seemed that France itself
might be flung into a civil war in 1958. This was de Gaulle's moment
of destiny. Both sides trusted him and both believed they could use
him for their own ends. The colonists and army believed he would
provide a strong government while they continued the war. The party
politicians believed that he alone might be able to control the defiant
rebels. To de Gaulle it all seemed perfectly natural. When the
colonists took up the cry 'de Gaulle au pouvoir' he commented:

*Now the Algerians shout 'vive de Gaulle' just as the French also do
in moments of acute anguish and yet are carried on the wings of hope.*

Nearly all the political parties united to vote him extraordinary temporary powers with which to re-establish order. In the meantime his advisers drew up a new constitution for the Fifth Republic in which de Gaulle became President, wielding great authority and often virtually free from the control of elected assemblies.

De Gaulle and the French Empire

Once in power de Gaulle showed scant gratitude to those who had put him there. He brought the army to heel and began to open negotiations with the Algerian nationalists. Peace did not come until 1962 and in the meantime the President had to face another colonists' revolt, an unsuccessful *coup* by dissatisfied army officers and the terrorist activities of the OAS (Organisation de l'Armée Secrète), an extreme right-wing group. But he was utterly unmoved even by numerous attempts on his life. He granted self-government to almost the whole of the French African Empire between 1958 and 1960. Thanks to this bold policy France was transformed from the most reviled colonial overlord to the most acceptable of the western powers amongst the new nations of Africa and Asia. He granted French aid to many underdeveloped nations and sought to extend French cultural leadership in both Africa and Latin America. In all matters affecting the non-European world he sought to preserve a strict neutrality. In his attempts to win the friendship of the non-aligned powers de Gaulle was at particular pains to dissociate his policy from that of the United States:

We are helping these countries and they like France as a result. In their view the contrast between us and the United States has become immense. While we are helping them the Americans are using all their brilliant new technological inventions to exterminate in the most terrible way thousands of these poor long-suffering Vietnamese who merely want to be left alone.
de Gaulle, April 1965

De Gaulle and the 'Anglo-Saxons'

The hostile reference to the Americans is of great significance. Once de Gaulle was back in power he was determined to revert to his old policy of cutting away from the Anglo-American alliance which dominated Western politics. He wished to lead other European nations in an independent force which was politically and culturally separate. It was because of this that he vetoed British entry to the EEC (see p. 217) and for the same reason he decided to break the American-dominated NATO alliance, which he believed had no part to play in the Europe of the 1960s and which prevented friendly relations with Russia and eastern Europe.

The French developed their own nuclear weapons and refused to be bound by the Russian-American-British nuclear test ban treaty of 1963. He poured scorn on the British for their dependence upon American weapons and rejected the American proposals for a multilateral nuclear force which would have given NATO nuclear weapons but under ultimate American control. In 1967 France withdrew almost completely from NATO.

The converse of this policy was his attempt to establish his leadership in Europe and in particular in the EEC. It was de Gaulle who blocked British entry to EEC in 1962 and it was de Gaulle who decided on the pace and direction of the development of the Common Market though this frequently led to bitter clashes.

The crisis of 1968 and the fall of de Gaulle
At least until 1968 de Gaulle was able to follow a relatively independent foreign policy despite the disapproval of the United States, Britain and even his EEC partners of many of his actions. At the risk of offending the West Germans he attempted to develop his own *détente* with the Russians and paid a much publicised visit to Moscow in 1966. In 1965 he recognised the communist régime in Peking and used the moment to launch an open attack on US policy in Vietnam. It appeared that France, in contrast to Britain, had managed to establish herself in an enviable position of military, economic and diplomatic autonomy.

At the same time de Gaulle's hold on France itself seemed unshakable. In 1958 his wide powers had been approved by 80 per cent of the electorate. Further referenda produced majorities of anything from 75–90 per cent. In elections to the assembly Gaullists did less well and in the 1965 presidential election de Gaulle only defeated his socialist opponent on the second ballot, but even these slight setbacks never really threatened his almost monarchical position in French public life.

In 1968 however three separate events struck heavy blows at his authority and the logic of his policies. One of these was in the international field; the Russian action in Czechoslovakia (see p. 329) threw doubt upon de Gaulle's contention that nothing stood in the way of a general European *détente* apart from American intransigence. The crushing of liberal communism in Czechoslovakia convinced many western Europeans that there was still a threat from the East and that de Gaulle's dismissal of NATO had been premature.

The second crisis came near to toppling the whole Gaullist system. In May 1968 student demonstrations, ineptly handled by the authorities, snowballed into a general expression of opposition to the government in which workers took over factories and rioters took over the streets of Paris. It seemed possible that de Gaulle would resign in the face of such violent hostility. In fact, however, he showed his old courage and self-confidence. By an appeal to national unity and law and order and by well-timed promises of social reforms, he split the opposition of revolutionary students, cautious trade unionists and the traditional opposition politicians, In a snap election he won the support of the great mass of French people and almost annihilated the opposition in the assembly.

It was another great Gaullist victory in the teeth of disaster, but the effects of the riots could not be so easily dispelled. They had shaken confidence in the franc and many people felt that the country could not afford to pay for the concessions that de Gaulle had offered to the unions. The result was the steady erosion of the vaunted gold

The May Days, 1968
The aftermath of student riots in the Latin Quarter of Paris.

reserves of France as currency speculators, and indeed ordinary French businessmen, unloaded their holdings of francs in exchange for safer currencies – in particular the German mark.

In November 1968 Europe was in the midst of a major currency crisis in which it seemed that the shaky franc was endangering the pound and even the American dollar. At a meeting in Bonn the Germans were pressed to revalue the mark to take pressure off the franc but they refused to do this. De Gaulle was equally adamant that he would not devalue the franc. In the end the Germans made some trading concessions while de Gaulle had to accept huge international loans. He avoided the humiliation of devaluation, but only at the price of massive economies at home which included a drastic cutback in the French nuclear arms programme. Even so it was not certain that France would not have to devalue in the long run and in many ways de Gaulle's reputation suffered more through this crisis than the riots of June.

The crises of 1968 made the question of de Gaulle's successor more urgent than ever. The long years of his government, the official control of radio and television and the comparative helplessness of the opposition in the assembly had made it very difficult for an alternative leader to emerge from outside de Gaulle's own circle.

Yet even amongst his ministers he had delegated very little authority. The only one to exercise anything approaching independent political power was M. Pompidou and he was dropped as Prime Minister after the June riots.

The May Days, 1968
The forces of law and order reassert control.

The President's faith in the destiny of his country remained as complete as ever and he believed he embodied that destiny. As he said in his television speech during the Algerian colonists' revolt in 1960:

Finally I want to say a few words to France. Well, my dear old country, here we are again facing a heavy ordeal. In virtue of the mandate given me by the people and in the name of that legitimacy I have incarnated for twenty years, I ask all my countrymen and countrywomen to support me whatever happens.

But the events of 1968 had destroyed much of the old magic. Early in 1969 the President decided to put a thoroughgoing reform of the Senate and of regional government before the people. Probably unnecessarily, he turned the referendum into yet another vote of confidence – and lost. At once de Gaulle resigned. After more than a decade one of the giants of European politics had been unseated and yet this sensational event had come about in a quite unsensational and orderly way. It seemed that France had grown tired of the General and as always, he was not a man to make compromises in order to retain power.

Yet if France had grown bored with de Gaulle the subsequent elections were a vindication of Gaullism and a proof of the fundamental conservatism of the majority of the French people. Pompidou emerged from retirement to defeat the divided parties of the centre and the left. Moreover, though his less grandiose and more sophisticated style constrasted with that of the General, France's policies were to show remarkable continuity. At home Pompidou followed the technocratic, semi-authoritarian, right-wing policies which had apparently been so successful in rebuilding the nation's prosperity. In foreign policy France remained aloof from NATO.

Pompidou reached a close accord with Heath in Britain and consequently agreed to what de Gaulle had for so long opposed, British membership of the EEC. On the other hand France's attempts to establish special relationships with Russia and China were outflanked by Brandt's *Ostpolitik* and Nixon's even more dramatic diplomatic manouvres. Moreover, after a period of unprecedented economic growth and personal prosperity France found herself gripped as remorselessly as her neighbours in the massive inflation of the 1970s. The sudden death of Pompidou early in 1974 was followed by the election of the non-Gaullist right-winger Giscard d'Estaing to the presidency after a very narrow victory over the Socialist-Communist candidate, Mitterand. It was the true end of the Gaullist period.

Britain in the post-war world 13

Alone amongst the great powers Britain was involved in the full six years of the Second World War, and although her military losses were only about one-third of those in 1914–18, this was even more a struggle for survival. So, although there was some planning for the future while the fighting was still going on (notably the Beveridge Report and the 1944 Education Act), it was not until the middle of 1945 that the politicians and the people were really able to take stock of their new situation.

It was certainly not a happy one. After the years of hardship the people expected better food, better homes, and improved social welfare services. But an incalculable sum had been swallowed up in the unproductive effort of the war, equipment had been worn out, markets lost and resources squandered. It was the same in international affairs. The British Prime Minister might sit with Truman and Stalin at Potsdam and the British Empire might still straddle the world, but these were only the trappings of power. Britain's influence in the world had been eclipsed by that of Russia and America, and the empire had survived the menace of the Axis only to face the internal challenge of resurgent African and Asian nationalism. Britain, which had weathered the inter-war years with so few fundamental reforms, could resist change no longer.

AUSTERITY AND REFORM

Even before the end of the war there was something of a political upheaval. In July 1945 the Conservatives suffered their worst political defeat for forty years and, for the first time, there was a Labour government with a clear majority in the Commons.

There were many reasons for the landslide. The young especially hoped that a new kind of Britain would emerge from the war and there was little evidence that Churchill, despite his personal popularity, was likely to carry through the necessary reforms. On the other hand the Labour party had recovered from the disasters of 1931 and its new leaders – Attlee, Bevin, Morrison, Greenwood and many others – had proved their ability to govern as members of the wartime coalition. They were the party of reform, committed, unlike the Conservatives, to the Beveridge Report (see p. 210), and the electors refused to be stampeded by Churchill's exaggerated and emotional warnings that socialist government 'would have to fall back on some sort of gestapo'.

As a result the Labour government enjoyed five years of complete domination in the Commons. The Conservatives still controlled the Lords, but when the upper house became too obstructive the government reduced its delaying powers from two years to one. In fact the main checks upon the government's plans were not imposed by parliamentary opposition but by the weakness of the economy and the pressure of international affairs.

The problems of reconstruction

In April 1945 the American wartime aid programme came abruptly to an end leaving Britain with a terrible balance of payments problem. The government managed to negotiate a loan of £1,000,000,000 from the United States, but only on condition that Britain would remove all restrictions on her currency and stand on her own feet by 1947. They had bought two years' grace, but the difficulties were enormous. Most of Britain's overseas investments had been sold off and the country could not rely upon a high level of income from invisible exports such as shipping, banking and insurance services, which had kept her balance of trade favourable before the war.

In order to achieve the necessary economic growth through planned development, the government greatly extended state control over the economy. On the one hand they attempted to take over the 'commanding heights' of the economy by nationalising public utilities and key industries. The Bank of England, civil aviation and the coal mines were taken over in 1946, electricity and public transport and road haulage in 1947, gas production in 1948, and, after a long struggle, iron and steel in 1949. On the other hand, the 80 per cent of British industry which remained in the hands of private enterprise was directed by a complex series of import quotas, currency restrictions and building licences, and the people had to suffer a continua-

The fuel crisis
Candle power and overcoats in the local during the winter of 1947.

tion and even an intensification of wartime restrictions (bread was rationed for the first time in 1946). At every level the government was intent upon reducing the import bill and directing all available resources into productive enterprises.

Yet all these efforts were not enough to prevent a new crisis in 1947. After the worst winter for generations, which disrupted industry and helped to cause a major fuel shortage, the economy was in no position to allow the free transfer of its currency. When it did, foreign investors, who had little faith in the £ sterling, sold off their reserves and there was a dangerous drain of gold from the country. Within weeks the restrictions had to be imposed once again and the Chancellor of the Exchequer, Sir Stafford Cripps, introduced more severe controls and taxes than ever before. Food imports were reduced, petrol strictly rationed and all foreign travel suspended. Although the country was producing more cars, more whisky, and more household appliances than ever before, these and other luxuries were reserved for the export markets. All these measures were meant to cut back personal spending and the next year the government's efforts were helped by the flow of Marshall Aid (see p. 177).

Yet two years later there was a new crisis brought on by Britain's inability to earn enough dollars to cover essential purchases from and payments to the United States. This time Cripps was forced to devalue the £ in relation to the dollar from 1:4·03 to 1:2·8. The effect of this was to make British goods cheaper on foreign markets, but it could only help the economy in the long run if the income from increased exports rose more quickly than the cost of imports which the devaluation made proportionately more expensive. To prevent inflation Cripps kept taxation at a high level and applied strict controls over prices and wages. Nevertheless there was a flourishing 'black market' in goods which were in short supply.

All these measures were necessary, but they were naturally very unpopular. There was very heavy emigration during these years. In 1950 55,000 people went to Australia and New Zealand alone and many people in Britain even looked back wistfully to the 'good old days' before the war.

The welfare state

Yet there were some compensations. In November 1942 Sir William Beveridge had produced his *Report on Social Insurance and Allied Services*. It was a plan for security from want from the cradle to the grave and the Labour party was committed to try and implement it and to maintain full employment even though such an ambitious programme increased the economic problems the government faced after 1945.

Austerity
Queuing for vegetables in 1946.

The heart of the plan was social insurance. Throughout a man's working life he and his employers were to pay weekly insurance

contributions and these would finance the grants to those in need and the maintenance of various social services. Although the Labour government was never able to fulfil the whole of Beveridge's plan, the series of acts they did pass between 1945 and 1949 constituted a major social revolution:

1945 The Family Allowances Act gave weekly grants for each child in a family after the first.

1946 The National Insurance Act provided a system of unemployment, old age, orphan's and widows' pensions.

1946 The National Insurance (Industrial Injuries) Act provided pensions for those wholly or partially incapacitated at work.

1946–8 The National Health Service Act provided free medical treatment of all sorts and state control over hospitals and other medical services.

1948 The National Assistance Act did away with the very last vestiges of the old Poor Relief and provided a special source of help for those not covered or inadequately covered by other schemes.

1948 The Children's Act made the counties and county boroughs responsible for all children without proper homes.

The Labour government was also largely responsible for the implementation of the 1944 Education Act which provided free secondary education for all and in 1947 they were able to raise the school leaving age to fifteen. They continued wartime food subsidies to help to keep the cost of living down and a series of housing acts provided the basis for a growing (though still inadequate) number of municipal housing schemes. The New Towns Act of 1946 and the National Parks Act of 1949 began to tackle the problem of providing a better environment for living and leisure.

This mass of social legislation was carried out in the face of considerable opposition and Churchill denounced the high level of government spending: 'In the last four lavish years the Socialist government have exacted upwards of £16,000 millions and spent them: over four times as much every year as was the cost of running the country in our richer days before the war.' Yet most people saw that this was not just extravagance, but a means of redistributing income and guaranteeing for all a better and more secure future.

The Cold War and the retreat from the empire

Britain's economic weakness was an important factor in determining her foreign policy. After 1945 it was more and more difficult for Britain to adopt an independent line and most of her initiatives had to be taken either as the junior partner in the alliance with the United States or as just one member of the European alliances. In the immediate post-war years the country had to hand over or share her responsibilities in Greece, Turkey and Germany with the United States. The government did manage to reduce defence expenditure every year until 1950, but the country still had to face a very heavy programme to garrison the empire and to pay for her troops in Germany. The Attlee government also supported the research project which was to lead to the explosion of the first British atomic bomb in 1952. Despite its difficulties the country was trying to keep pace with the super-powers.

By 1945 it was also clear that Britain would not be able to hold down the Indian subcontinent in the face of nationalist opposition. The main problem of the government was therefore to find some way of withdrawing with a minimum of bloodshed. In fact the partition settlement (see p. 252) pleased almost nobody and millions of Indians suffered and died in the terrible years 1946–8. Yet in many ways it was remarkable that the British had disengaged from its largest and most prized Imperial possession so swiftly and that India and Pakistan unlike Burma remained members of the Commonwealth.

The problem of communal violence and nationalism was repeated on a smaller scale in Palestine and here too Britain chose to withdraw as quickly as possible regardless of the fact that no satisfactory solution had been found for the future of the area (see p. 232). In general the British had neither the money nor the desire to fight to retain areas where the local population were united in arms against them.

The decline of the Labour government

In 1951 the government celebrated the centenary of the Great Exhibition, one of the high points of Victorian prosperity, by staging the Festival of Britain. The exhibition on the South Bank site and the many local efforts all over the country were supposed to be a demonstration to the British themselves and to the outside world that the country was on the road back to prosperity and greatness. But by 1951 the country was once more in difficulties.

In the late forties the reforming impetus had been lost and the nationalisation of iron and steel, which earned the government little popularity, was only carried after a long bitter battle at every stage. In the 1950 elections the discontent of the electorate with the speed of reconstruction was reflected in a swing away from Labour which left them with a majority of only half a dozen seats. In the middle of 1950 the Korean war broke out. The British despatched the second largest contingent in the UN army. This sent defence costs rocketing and it also upset international trade and finance. Sir Stafford Cripps, . one of the dominant figures in the Cabinet, retired, his health broken, and when his successor, Hugh Gaitskell, reimposed charges for the supply of spectacles and false teeth Aneurin Bevan, the fiery leader of the left wing of the party, and two other ministers resigned. The government was weakened still further by the death of Ernest Bevin in 1951.

In the autumn of 1951, faced with a mounting trade deficit, harried by an increasingly confident opposition, and worn out by the strain of governing with a tiny majority, Attlee called new elections. Once again the Labour party polled the largest share of the popular vote, but the Conservatives won an overall majority of seventeen in the Commons. The great reforming ministry had fizzled out in an atmosphere of frustration and disillusionment.

THE CONSERVATIVE DECADE

For the next decade British politics were dominated by the Conservatives, who increased their representation in the Commons at four successive elections until, in 1959, they had a majority of over a hundred. It was an unprecedented achievement and in many ways a surprising one. Churchill's peacetime ministry (1951–5) was undistinguished and under Eden (1955–7) Britain suffered a disastrous setback in world affairs with the failure of the Suez campaign (see p. 235). Under his successor, Harold Macmillan, there were many strains within the party on economic and colonial policy. And yet the Conservatives were uniquely successful at the polls.

One reason for this was the reorganisation of the party machinery carried out in the late forties by Lord Woolton and R. A. Butler. The party raised considerable funds from industry and was quicker than Labour to make use of the new techniques of advertising and television. Equally important, in Butler's Industrial Charter of 1947, and in their practical policies after 1951 they showed that they would not try to reverse Labour's social reforms. Only the nationalisation of steel and of road haulage were repealed and neither of these were issues on which the electorate were likely to be aroused.

During this same period the Labour party was passing through many difficulties. There was a fierce struggle between the moderates led by Herbert Morrison and later Hugh Gaitskell, who succeeded Attlee as leader in 1955, and the left wing led by Aneurin Bevan, Frank Cousins and Harold Wilson. The main points at issue were the extension of nationalisation, which Gaitskell believed would be both unnecessary and unpopular, and the maintenance of an independent British nuclear deterrent which the left bitterly denounced. It was only just before his death in 1963 that Gaitskell managed to recreate a united and confident party, and it was left to his successor and former rival Harold Wilson to reap the benefits.

Yet perhaps the most important single factor in these years was the growing prosperity of the British people for which the Conservatives claimed the credit.

The affluent society
Labour had governed through a period when Britain and the rest of the world were still recovering from the shocks of the war. It was not surprising that their administration seemed to be a grim and rather puritanical one. In contrast the fifties seemed much brighter. After the end of the Korean war there was a general upsurge in world trade and Britain benefited from the comparatively low cost of food and raw materials which formed the bulk of her imports.

The results showed in many ways. Rationing came to an end in 1954 and with freer hire purchase terms and fatter wage packets the British people were soon enjoying a higher standard of living than ever before. In 1950 average wages were £6 8s. od.; in 1959 they were £11 2s. 6d., while income tax had fallen from 9s. to 7s. 9d. in the £. Prices had also risen but people were still very much better off. The number of licensed vehicles rose in this decade from 4,500,000 to 8,600,000 and licensed televisions from 344,000 to 10,470,000. But if there was more spending there was also more saving. For instance by 1961 600,000 small investors had put £200,000,000 into unit trusts and there was a great increase in Post Office savings and the number of bank accounts. Prosperity even showed itself in death. The old killers of two generations before – bronchitis, tuberculosis and pneumonia – had been brought under control only to be replaced by cancer and heart diseases and there was a serious rise in deaths through motor accidents.

The Conservative government could hardly claim to be responsible for all these changes although they did cash in on the new wealth with their famous election slogan:

Life is better with the Conservatives – don't let Labour spoil it.

But in fact the Conservative governments were very unsuccessful in maintaining steady economic growth.

The economics of 'stop–go'

When R. A. Butler became Chancellor of the Exchequer in 1951, the country was beginning to feel the benefits of Labour's reconstruction work but there was an immediate problem of a heavy balance of payments deficit and a dangerous inflation. To check these developments income tax was raised, the defence budget spread over three years and the bank-rate, which controlled all other credit terms, and which had stood at 2 per cent since the war, was raised to 2½ per cent and then 4 per cent. These measures reduced spending power and checked the inflationary spiral and they also set the pattern for Conservative economic policy for the next decade. On the one hand Conservative Chancellors stimulated the economy by reducing taxes and restrictions, but when spending power was released faster than productivity increased, prices and wages chased each other up the familiar inflationary spiral and the country bought more than it could afford overseas. To check this the government had then to deflate, generally by increasing the bank-rate which reached 4½ per cent in 1955, 5½ per cent in 1956 and 7 per cent in both 1957 and 1958. This policy, which Labour critics called 'stop–go', was the most the Conservatives were prepared to do at this time in the way of economic planning and it certainly did not provide the conditions for steady economic expansion.

'The special relationship' and Suez

For almost the whole decade the cornerstone of British policy remained the 'special relationship' with the United States which was strengthened by close personal links between President Eisenhower and Churchill and Macmillan. It was during this period that Britain joined the United States in the construction of the world-wide western defence pacts – SEATO and the Baghdad Pact – and continued to play a role second only to that of the United States in NATO. In 1957 the first British hydrogen bomb was exploded and vast sums of money were put into the development of the Blue Streak missile. In theory at least Britain was still a great power and Macmillan, in particular, tried to take the lead in mediating between Russia and the West.

But in fact Britain took only one major initiative in defiance of the United States, with disastrous results. This was the Anglo-French expedition to Suez in 1956 and it demonstrated with brutal clarity that Britain had neither the economic strength nor the military power to play big power politics without American support (see p. 235 and p. 365). Immediately after the event there was considerable bitterness in Britain over the way in which the country had been 'let down' by her allies, but in time more and more people came to believe that Eden's action had been ill-judged and even highly dishonest. The experience of Suez hastened the necessary reappraisal of Britain's Imperial and world role.

Both before and after Suez Britain was involved in several clashes with armed resistance movements in the colonies – notably in Kenya and Cyprus. But generally after 1956 the process to independence was speeded up and violence avoided. The granting of freedom to Ghana and Malaya in 1957 had been planned for some time and the pace of change really quickened after Macmillan's tour of East and South Africa in 1959. Vast Imperial possessions were no longer seen as an asset but rather a costly liability.

But with Pakistan and India at loggerheads, South Africa increasingly uneasy in the company of the new African states, and Canada and Australia more and more under American economic influence, the new Commonwealth could not provide the context for a new world role for Britain politically, economically or psychologically. The alternative was Europe, but in the fifties the British were still half-hearted Europeans (see p. 180). Only in the less happy circumstances of the early sixties did the government decide that in this, as in so many other fields of policy, the time had come for more radical action.

THE PERIOD OF REAPPRAISAL

Europe and defence.
Macmillan's decision in 1961 to make a concerted effort to take Britain into Europe provoked a good deal of opposition. Some of his own party still clung to the idea that Britain's role was in the Commonwealth and that association with the EEC would destroy

national sovereignty, and there were many fears that membership would bring a dramatic rise in food prices and weaken still further the old depressed areas – in Scotland, Northern Ireland and the north-east – which would be farthest away from the focus of European affairs.

Against this the pro-marketeers claimed that Britain's trading future lay not with the Commonwealth but with Europe, which was the natural market for British industrial goods and a market which could afford to pay for them, unlike the emergent states in Africa and Asia. They also believed that membership of the group would give the country a new sense of purpose.

However during this same period the government was also facing a crisis in its defence programme. Despite a defence budget running at over £1,500,000,000 a year Britain was quite unable to keep pace with Russian and American war technology and its Blue Streak rocket programme proved to be a costly failure. The government then hoped to extend the life of its strike force by the purchase of the American Skybolt air-to-ground missile but in 1962 its plans were ruined when Kennedy announced that the Americans themselves were shelving the Skybolt programme. In a desperate effort to salvage his government's reputation Macmillan flew to Nassau and extracted from Kennedy a promise of a share in the Polaris nuclear submarine programme and a scheme for a NATO nuclear force backed by the United States.

But these manoeuvrings damaged Britain's prospects in Europe. They strengthened de Gaulle's conviction that Britain was too dependent on America to be a member of the EEC (see p. 185). In January 1963 in the face of a French veto, negotiations in Brussels were broken off. These events severely damaged Macmillan's reputation and Britain was left once more without a clear role in world affairs.

Economic planning and the decline of the Conservatives
During this time the Macmillan government was also seeking to develop a longer term economic programme to replace the discredited techniques of 'stop–go'.

Typical of the new mood was the appointment of Ernest Marples, a successful head of a civil engineering firm, as Minister of Transport and Marples's own appointment of Dr Beeching, an ICI director, to reorganise the railway system. Alfred Robens, a former Labour and

H

trade unionist leader, was brought in to rationalise the coal industry New long-term plans were drawn up to make good the omissions of the previous decade when no new hospitals had been built. In 1962 a plan was drawn up to spend £1,000,000,000 on the construction of much needed motorways and Professor Buchanan carried out a survey of the needs of the road system in the years to come. A whole series of Committees – Plowden, Newsom, Robbins, and Albemarle – were appointed to investigate the needs of all levels of education and the youth services.

Most pressing of all were the problems of economic development. Selwyn Lloyd, Chancellor of the Exchequer from 1960 to 1962, set up the National Economic Development Council to advise the government on economic expansion and representatives of both industry and the unions sat on it. Less successful was his National Incomes Commission which attempted to control inflation by checking wage increases. The unions refused to co-operate with the Commission and the Chancellor's 'wage freeze' was highly unpopular without being particularly effective. Conservative government no longer seemed to be a guarantee of prosperity and the shock by-election at Orpington in 1962 when the Conservatives lost a solid middle-class seat to the Liberals came as a dramatic demonstration of the decline in the government's fortunes. In 1962 Macmillan tried to revitalise his government by replacing a third of his cabinet and bringing in new young ministers, but the Conservatives continued to make a poor showing in the figures of the national opinion polls.

In 1963 unemployment rose to 800,000, the highest figure since the war. Even more spectacular was the revelation of a series of security failures, the most notorious of which was the Profumo affair, in which the Minister of War was shown to have misled both the Prime Minister and the Commons concerning a potential security risk involving himself. In the face of mounting unrest in his own party Macmillan resigned in the autumn but the subsequent struggle for power in the party did little to enhance its image. In the end the new leader was not Butler, the main architect of the post-war Conservative revival, but the Earl of Home who seemed, perhaps unfairly, to embody the old patrician Toryism. The new Prime Minister resigned his peerage and fought vigorously to revive his party's reputation, but in the 1964 elections Labour scraped in with a majority of four. Harold Wilson and his colleagues seemed to represent a radical reforming force better suited to the needs of the sixties and Sir Alec Douglas Home's successor, Edward Heath, was unable to prevent the Labour majority rising to a hundred in fresh

elections in 1966. It seemed enough, barring a major political
upheaval, to keep the Labour government in power into the 1970s.

Labour and the economic crisis

One of the reasons why the Labour party returned to power in 1964
was that the Conservatives had failed to find long-term solutions to
the nation's economic problems and almost immediately Harold
Wilson and his cabinet faced yet another major crisis. Once again the
problem was a huge trade deficit and a collapse of confidence in the £
which led to a flow of gold from the country. The government tried
to control the situation by imposing a 15 per cent surcharge on imports and fell back on the Conservative expedient of raising the bank-
rate but the crisis was only checked after a loan of $1,000,000,000
from the International Monetary Fund and $3,000,000,000 from the
European central banks. In 1966 there were signs of a recurrence of
the crisis but this time the central banks gave guarantees at an early
stage and in earnest of its intention to carry through a radical reform
of the economy the government imposed a rigid freeze on all increases
in prices, wages and dividends. The Prices and Incomes Board was
set up to control increases in the period after the freeze and the
government took upon itself greater powers of economic control and
coercion than ever before in peace-time.

Even so, in the autumn of 1967 the government was forced to make
a further devaluation to $2·40 to the £ and to make massive cuts in
expenditure on defence, education and the social services. Even this
was not enough to make the £ really secure and the world currency
crisis of 1968 was followed by still more restrictions on private
spending.

In 1969 and 1970 there was some improvement. The massive
international loans were paid off, there was a healthy credit balance
in international trade and a reduction in overseas military commitments. Without any great extension of state control there was an
attempt to manage the economy more effectively, to encourage
amalgamation and reorganisations in outdated industries and to
redeploy labour from depressed areas and dying trades. However
these reforms were bought at the cost of the highest level of unemployment since the war and a dizzy spiral of price inflation and wage
demands.

The government's attempts to control this situation were far from
successful and yet they managed to alienate many traditional Labour

supporters. At first they imposed a compulsory wage freeze and then attempted to negotiate voluntary wage control with the unions. But while the freeze was successful in the short term, it was followed by a deluge of wage claims when the controls were lifted. At the same time the government's efforts to reorganise and control the trade unions outlined in Barbara Castle's White Paper, *In Place of Strife*, ran into such stiff union opposition that they had to be abandoned.

On top of these difficulties the government's prestige suffered badly in foreign affairs. The renewed efforts to join the Common Market (see pp. 183) were wrecked by de Gaulle; the rebel regime in Rhodesia successfully declared independence and withstood all Wilson's attempts to resolve the situation by negotiations or by sanctions (see pp. 284); and finally the government was widely criticised by its own left-wing for its vacillating attitude towards United States policies, particularly in Vietnam.

In June 1970, however, Wilson was encouraged by the public opinion polls to hold a snap election. It was a disastrous mistake: many traditional labour voters stayed at home while others, won over either by Edward Heath's promises to cut prices at a stroke and control the militant unions, or by Enoch Powell's unofficial conservative line on immigration (see p. 225) turned again to the Tories who were able to form a new government with a comfortable majority of thirty.

The new Conservatives
Heath's new government was made up of men who contrasted sharply in style and policies not only with its Labour predecessors, but also with the middle-of-the-road, paternalistic Toryism of the Macmillan years. They were determined to carry through an extensive policy of denationalisation; to introduce powerful new controls over the trade unions; to withdraw from the close management of the economy and leave industrial development to free enterprise; and to modify the welfare state by cutting back generalised benefits such as council house subsidies and rely instead on benefits to be paid to individuals in great need, whose wants could be determined by a means test.

In the early months the new government acted vigourously to put these policies into effect, but very soon they found themselves baulked by a series of crises. First, the government's deflationary policies produced the most massive unemployment since the Depression, but did nothing to curb the rampant inflation. Several major industries such as Upper Clyde Shipbuilders and Rolls Royce were brought to a state of collapse and, against all their declared principles, the government found it expedient to come to their aid.

A new Industrial Relations Act was passed, setting up a register of trade unions, strict controls over their activities, and an Industrial Court to try breaches of the law. However the unions mostly refused to co-operate and, instead of imposing industrial peace, the law brought a series of crippling disputes between employers, unions, and the government. Indeed by 1974 the Act was being denounced and bypassed not only by the unions, but by many employers as well.

In 1972 the government suffered further setbacks in the face of miners' and dockers' strikes. The trade balance deteriorated sharply and the pound was allowed to float as an alternative to a further full devaluation. In yet another reversal of policy the government introduced first a complete wage freeze and then a phased wage control through 1973 and into 1974. At the time they launched a new policy of economic expansion which did reduce unemployment but did nothing to contain the ever-rising cost of living. Moreover Britain continued to show up very badly on all measures of economic activity—whether investment, productivity per head or growth rates. At the same time the government remained committed to prestigious but costly programmes such as the development of the Concorde airliner, the Channel Tunnel and the construction of a third London airport.

Only in one major policy area did the government wholly fulfill its programme—British entry to the EEC (see pp. 183), but the first year of membership did little to fulfill the hopes of those who had promoted it and the majority of the British people remained obdurately opposed to it.

Yet despite this the government seemed to be in a relatively strong position and the opposition weak and disorganised until Heath ran into a whole series of crises late in 1973. First, the country was desperately hard hit by the oil crisis which cut off supplies, and brought chaos to world trade and finance. Secondly, the govenment faced a series of major industrial disputes of which the most serious was a ban on overtime by the miners in the face of the government's wages policy. By Christmas the government had put the country onto a three-day working-week to conserve fuel, but the miners stood firm, apparently with a good deal of public sympathy. In the face of a full miners' strike in February 1974 the government called an election in the hope of winning on an emotive call to curb the unions. However, it appeared even from the government's own measurements that the miners did indeed deserve more money, and it was clear that the Conservative anti-inflation and industrial relations policies were in tatters. At the last moment Enoch Powell intervened with a plea to vote Labour in order to reverse the government policy on the EEC.

The result was that the Labour Party emerged as the largest party in Parliament by only a handful of seats and the balance was held by a motley collection of Liberals, independents, Scottish and Welsh Nationalists and Ulster Unionists. Harold Wilson improved his position marginally in a further election in October 1974, but the government's majority depended on the disunity of the minor parties and the Conservatives. In March 1976 Harold Wilson resigned and was replaced by Jim Callaghan as Prime Minister and leader of the Labour Party. Meanwhile the Conservatives had already replaced Heath with Margaret Thatcher, the first woman to lead a major British political party, and a spokeswoman for the right wing of the party.

These political shuffles seemed to do little to reinvigorate the political life of the country and they took place against the gloomy background of unresolved problems that had dogged post-war Britain and some of which were becoming increasingly acute.

The unresolved issues
Britain's international position was certainly ill-defined. The empire had gone, the Commonwealth was losing its purpose, but remaining colonial commitments, notably in Rhodesia, still bedevilled Britain's relationships with the third world. The old special relationship with America had vanished, but the initial experience within the EEC was an unhappy one and even after the referendum did not provide a clear new role. In 1974 Britain still had some of the pretensions and formal trappings of a great power but was lacking both the resources and the sense of purpose to sustain that role.

This was to a large degree a reflection of her internal problems. In the first place the integrity of the United Kingdom itself was increasingly open to discussion. In both Wales and Scotland there were small but vigorous separatist movements and these gathered popular support particularly at times of economic crisis when these relatively depressed areas suffered most. The discovery of oil in the North and Celtic seas strengthened the nationalists' position since they could argue that Wales and Scotland would suffer most from the environmental consequences without any assurance that they would reap the main benefits of the new resources. The 1974 general elections and subsequent local government elections revealed the increasing support for the nationalists and forced the major parties to produce their own alternative schemes for the devolution of power. However, the Labour government's devolution bill, with its proposal for elected assemblies in Scotland and Wales, did not go far enough for some nationalists while for its other opponents it heralded the break-up of the United Kingdom altogether. In any case the Labour government was unable to muster the votes to carry the bill through Parliament in 1977 — leaving the nationalists in a strong position to push for complete separation from England.

On a quite different scale were the problems of Northern Ireland. After the Treaty of 1921 (see p. 25) the southern part of the country had become increasingly estranged from Britain, finally leaving the Commonwealth in 1949. Almost all political groups were committed to the idea of a unified republic of Ireland and there remained a small but active minority in the paramilitary Irish Republican Army who maintained sporadic terrorist activities against Britain and Northern Ireland throughout the thirties and forties.

Meanwhile in the six northern counties political and economic life was controlled by the Protestant majority through their permanent grip on the provincial Parliament at Stormont. The large Catholic minority found themselves the victims of discrimination in many aspects of life and in particular housing, local government elections, and the search for work in an area suffering from endemic unemployment.

This situation remained frozen until the late 1960s when Catholic civil rights movements began to press their claims and were met to some extent by the liberal Unionist leader Terence O'Neill. But O'Neill was soon ousted by hardline Unionists. In the meantime Catholic civil rights demonstrations and Protestant counter-demonstrations escalated into intercommunal violence and the British army was called in to maintain law and order. But now the pace was set by extremists on both sides. The IRA was able to exploit Catholic fears and grievances and to launch armed attacks on the army. Meanwhile Protestant populist leaders such as the

Reverend Ian Paisley developed a mass following amongst the Protestant working class who were utterly opposed to concessions to the Catholics. In 1972 the Conservative government at Westminster took over direct responsibility for the government of the province while the Secretary of State for Northern Ireland William Whitelaw sought to reconcile the various groups in the North and work out a new constitution which would bring them together and lead to closer co-operation between the two parts of Ireland. But the new constitution collapsed almost as soon as it was established in 1974. Moderate Catholic and Protestant leaders, who had been prepared to try to share power, were denounced from the extremes and for a while a Protestant workers' strike brought the province to a standstill. The killings launched both by the IRA and Protestant paramilitary groups continued unabated and the indiscriminate bombing of civilians spread to the rest of Britain. In Britain itself all political groups seemed baffled by the irreconcilable hatreds of Northern Ireland and there were increasingly demands that the battered British troops should be withdrawn and the Irish should be left to resolve the problem on their own. Yet such a course seemed almost certain to plunge Ireland into a new civil war.

Another deeply divisive social and political issue for Britain was race relations. Britain had had a small black population for centuries, but the significant increase came in the late 1950s with some 40,000 black migrants arriving per year mainly from the West Indies but also from India and Pakistan. In 1958 there were brief but ugly anti-black demonstrations in Nottingham, Dudley and Notting Hill which led to a falling off in immigration. In 1961 the Conservative government introduced a law to restrict immigration and this produced a final large inflow of about 200,000 immigrants before the law came into action.

However it still remained possible for some immigrants to enter and for those who were already in Britain to bring in their dependants. As a result the actual flow remained at quite a high level and in 1965 the Labour government reversed all its previous pronouncements and introduced further restrictions. By this time most new immigrants were Indians and Pakistanis and in 1968 there were also a number of Kenyan Asians who held British passports dating back to the colonial period. The Heath administration introduced still further controls which also, incidentally, excluded a number of white Commonwealth citizens as well, but they too were forced to set aside their policies when President Amin ejected thousands of Ugandan Asians with British passports in 1972.

By 1977 the control had reduced the net inflow to a trickle, but of course there were by this time thousands of black Britons who had been born in the country, and the black population was probably growing faster in proportion than the white population. This situation brought to the surface deep fears and grievances amongst both blacks and whites. The blacks, with some justification, believed that they suffered from discrimination in many aspects of life despite the fact that the Labour government of 1964–70 had introduced two laws to make it an offence to utter racially inflammatory statements or to discriminate in public places, employment and housing. The whites, whose fears were articulated in particular by Enoch Powell, were suspicious of the strangers and seemed to dread in some ill-defined way that their presence was leading to unfair competition for jobs and housing, a rise in crime, and a breakdown of traditional British society. That these fears could not be substantiated in no way diminished their power and although Enoch Powell was expelled from the Conservative leadership for his racial views, he retained an enormous popular following. Heavy unemployment, especially amongst school leavers, exacerbated the situation. Clashes between West Indians and police in a riot in London in 1976; a noisy campaign of white racism by the National Front; demands from Enoch Powell for the repatriation of immigrants; and the deep division between the older and younger generations of black Britons were all symptoms of the continuing difficulty of creating a genuinely multiracial society.

If the black community was the outstanding example of a group suffering from the inequalities of modern society, the inequalities were by no means limited to them. Despite the welfare legislation and the high rates of taxation in post war Britain there remained enormous variations in wealth, in the quality of housing, education, and medical care available to different groups within society. There were also significant pockets of real poverty, particularly amongst pensioners and others living on fixed incomes during a period of massive inflation.

In education there were certainly attempts to broaden the range of opportunities open to all children. The 1960s had seen the great growth in universities and polytechnics; in the 1970s the process of changing from selective to comprehensive education was only temporarily delayed by the Conservative government. Much more serious for education and in turn for the future of the country was the fact that under all governments public services such as education bore the brunt of the cutbacks in the recurrent economic crises.

H*

This same period also saw a more general concern for the whole quality of life in a highly industrialised and densely populated state. More and more there was an awareness of the blight which could fall on people's lives through bad planning; by the indiscriminate destruction of houses to make way for motorways; by water and air pollution; and by the eating away of open spaces for development. This consciousness had brought in its turn increasing participation of people at the grass roots of political life. On the other hand most individuals remained personally wedded to the idea of an ever-increasing standard of personal wealth and consumption which would almost undoubtedly be incompatible with environmentalist controls and with Britain's increasingly shaky economic condition.

After 1974 the Labour government attempted to resolve the immediate problem of uncontrolled inflation and high unemployment by the establishment of a social contract with the employers and trade unions. This meant that the government passed a whole range of new legislation improving workers' terms of employment, protecting them against unfair dismissal and redundancy, and promising them an increasing participation in management. For their part the TUC bound their members to strictly controlled wage increases. The unions were in effect being given a substantial new part in national economic planning. This policy was in many ways a remarkable success. Inflation was checked and 1975–6 saw a dramatic drop in the number of strikes. But it was not enough. Unemployment remained high, national expenditure ran far ahead of income, productivity remained the lowest in the EEC, and a remorseless fall in the exchange value of the pound was an eloquent indication of the lack of faith the world money markets had in Britain's economic future.

The Conservatives demanded drastic cuts in public expenditure, including a ruthless reduction in welfare services. The left of the Labour Party called on the contrary for increased expenditure, more nationalization and the imposition of import duties. The Callaghan government sought a compromise with a massive loan from the International Monetary Fund, some cuts in government spending, a credit squeeze, and the promise of reduced standards of living for most Britons for several years to come. The hope was that the exploitation of North Sea oil would in a few years provide the basis for economic recovery – but oil alone was unlikely to be enough or to last long beyond the end of the century. Recovery depended much more on a popular will to succeed and the creation of the proper political and social conditions for recovery.

The Arabs and Israel   14

From the earliest days of civilisation the eastern Mediterranean has been a key area at the meeting point of three continents. Persians, Greeks, Romans, Arabs, Mongols, Turks and Europeans have fought for its control over the centuries. In the mid-nineteenth century it took on a new importance with the construction of the Suez Canal and today it lies across some of the world's busiest sea and air routes. It is a region of great poverty: only 5 per cent of the land area is cultivable, yet there are small areas of great fertility and it has one source of natural wealth most highly prized in industrial societies: oil. No less than 42 per cent of the world's known oil reserves are to be found in the Middle East. This alone is enough to make the Arab world a centre of international affairs.

It is a strangely hard area to define. The member states of the Arab League stretch from the Atlantic to the Persian Gulf and the region also encompasses non-Arab states such as Turkey, Persia, Cyprus and Israel. Within the Arab lands there is some unity: there is the religion of Islam which is common to most of the inhabitants of the Levant and North Africa; there is a common written language and culture; there is a common history of recent subjection to foreign rule. Finally almost all the states of this area share common economic problems. Although some are immensely wealthy like Kuwait and others pitifully poor like Jordan, all have gross inequalities of wealth, all lack industry and natural resources apart from oil, all have rapidly expanding populations which threaten to outrun the ability of their governments to provide even the miserable standard of education, nutrition and housing which they now receive.

In political terms it is much harder to find much in common be-

The Arab World

Arab League

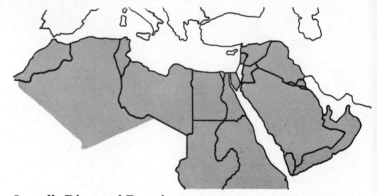

Israel's Disputed Frontiers

Palestine border

1947
awarded to Jews
by UN

1949
gained by Israel

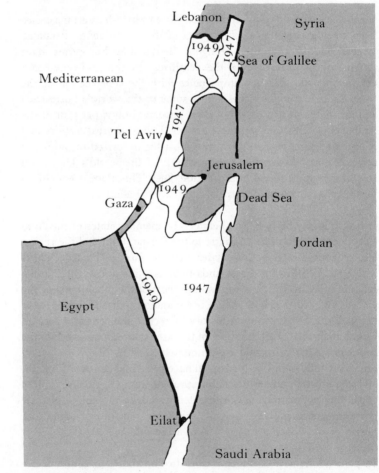

tween them. The states vary in size from Egypt which is bigger than France to Israel which is smaller than Yorkshire. Egypt is a one-party dictatorship, Israel a parliamentary democracy, Saudi Arabia a feudal kingdom. Mecca and Jerusalem are the religious centres, Beirut the financial capital and Cairo the political focus. The one common bond which does link most of the people of this area is Arab nationalism, yet it has also been a most disruptive force. To see why this has been so, it is necessary to trace the history of the region from the beginning of our period.

The Ottoman lands
Until the end of the First World War the states of Iraq, Syria, Yemen, Lebanon, Israel and Saudi Arabia were ruled by the brutal but inefficient despotism of the Turkish Empire. During the war the British and French encouraged the Arabs to revolt against their Turkish overlords and promised independence as their reward. Their offer was taken up by the Hashemite princes, Feisal and Abdullah, sons of the Sheriff of Mecca and with the help of Col. T. E. Lawrence they inflicted a number of damaging attacks on Turkish communications and succeeded in liberating Damascus ahead of the British. After the war the Hashemite princes expected their reward, but they were to be disappointed. During the war the British and French had already secretly earmarked most of the area for themselves by the Sykes-Picot agreement (see p. 10) and the British had chosen one part for a special project, the creation of a Jewish national home. On 2 November 1917 the British Foreign Secretary, Arthur Balfour, had announced that:

His Majesty's Government views with favour the establishment in Palestine of a National Home for the Jewish People and will use their best endeavours to facilitate the achievement of this object, it being clearly understood that nothing shall be done which may prejudice the civil and religious rights of the non-Jewish communities in Palestine or the rights and political status enjoyed by Jews in any other country.

This promise clearly contradicted earlier promises to the Arab leaders and it was hard to see how it could be fulfilled in an area which had a 90 per cent Arab population already. On the other hand it was the fulfilment of the aims of the Zionist movement to draw together the scattered Jewish peoples into their historical homeland where they would be free from their centuries' long persecution. It was also an astute move to please powerful Jewish interests in the United States, which had just joined the war.

Quite apart from the creation of the state of Palestine under British protection the Versailles settlement was a great blow to the Arab leaders. The French took over the protectorates of Lebanon and Syria and the British almost all the rest of the Turkish Empire. Only when Feisal and Abdullah threatened to attack Syria did the British buy them off by creating the kingdoms of Iraq and Transjordan for them to rule. Even these states remained under British protectorship until 1930 and 1946 respectively.

Egypt
In Egypt, too, relations between the British and the indigenous population were far from happy. The British became official protectors of the country in 1915 when the Turks declared war on the western allies, but this was no more than a recognition of the control which they had exercised since 1882. After the war the Egyptians demanded complete independence at Versailles but they soon found that Wilson's promises of national self-determination did not apply to them. There were a series of demonstrations and in 1922 Britain unilaterally declared that Egypt would become an independent monarchy, but that Britain would continue to control defence and the Suez Canal and maintain an army of occupation. Britain also remained in control of the Sudan which was technically part of the Egyptian monarchy. In 1936 the Egyptian nationalists and the King, fearful of Mussolini's ambitions in East Africa, came to an agreement with Britain. Egypt became completely independent, but Britain was to guard the Canal Zone for a further twenty years.

The Middle East and the Second World War
The Second World War had an extremely disruptive effect on the Arab world. The British had to face a pro-Axis revolt in Iraq in 1942. In the French mandates, the Vichy government had control initially but was defeated by the British and the old French system of government was destroyed in the process. Egypt was even more directly involved for the Axis armies actually penetrated the Western Desert and threatened to break through to Cairo and the canal. King Farouk and many other Egyptians favoured the Germans and at a critical point in Rommel's campaign the British surrounded the royal palace and forced the King to appoint a pro-ally Prime Minister. Although most Egyptian nationalists had no love for Farouk, this high-handed action only increased their fury with the way in which the British had involved them in the war without their consent.

At the end of the war Syria and Lebanon became independent states. Britain granted full independence to Transjordan although she kept a measure of control through the subsidies which she paid direct to the British commander of the Transjordanian army, Glubb Pasha. But despite the retreat of colonialism a number of old problems remained and there were several new ones, for Russia was anxious to extend her influence into the area and there was growing international rivalry for the control of the oil fields. There were two particularly pressing questions: the first was the future of Palestine and the second the relationship between Britain, which was still the main outside influence in the area, and the Arab nationalists, particularly in Egypt.

The Palestine crisis

In the years immediately after the Balfour declaration the creation of the Jewish national home did not pose an insuperable problem. Palestine was not an overcrowded land and the Jews came from Europe in small numbers. In 1917 Feisal himself said, 'We will wish the Jews a most hearty welcome. The Jewish movement is national and not imperialist. There is room . . . for both of us.' Between 1920 and 1930 about 100,000 Jews migrated to their new land which remained under British control and there was comparatively little inter-racial tension. However, once Hitler came to power the situation changed dramatically. His persecution drove Jews from Germany and the other countries which fell under Nazi control. In 1936 alone 60,000 newcomers arrived in Palestine and by 1939 there were some 600,000 Jews and 1,000,000 Arabs in the country. At this point, faced with mounting Arab protests and inter-racial violence the British decreed that a final quota of 75,000 Jews would be admitted and that all others would be refused entry. Those who were turned back were mostly condemned to die in Hitler's extermination camps.

The war ended the flow of migrants, and Jews both in and outside Palestine naturally felt very bitter against Britain. Those in Palestine determined that they would not be wiped out like their European co-religionists. They already had an armed force, the Haganah, which protected their kibbutzim (communal farms) from their hostile Arab neighbours. More extreme elements formed secret units such as the fanatical Stern Gang which waged open war against both the British and Arabs. As the war came to an end there was open conflict between the two communities in Palestine and the British troops and administrators were uncomfortably sandwiched between them.

The first Arab-Israeli war and the creation of Israel

Six million European Jews died at the hands of Hitler and all over the world there was sympathy with the desire of many of the survivors to migrate to Palestine. The British government, however, tried to reimpose restrictions and desperately sought to stem the flow of illegal entries. For two years the administration struggled to control Jewish and Arab terrorism and to end inter-racial violence. But their efforts were largely unsuccessful, and in 1947 all hopes of a compromise were lost when President Truman made an election speech obviously aimed at the American Jewish community in which he hinted that he would not support the British policy of controls. The British then decided to abdicate their responsibility for the country altogether. They referred the whole question to the United Nations and warned that they would leave the country by May 1948 whether or not a solution had been reached.

The United Nations sought to establish a partition of the country, but neither side would accept their division and when the British withdrew full-scale war broke out between the Jews and Palestinian Arabs, who were supported by other Arab states. When the UN finally arranged a truce in January 1949, the Jews had advanced far beyond the original partition lines although they were still left with a difficult frontier which split Jerusalem itself. Although the Arabs heavily outnumbered the Jews, they had fared very badly. The Syrians, Lebanese and Iraqis had played only a minor part and the Egyptians had been heavily defeated. Only the Transjordanians had been successful. They conquered a large part of eastern Palestine and Abdullah renamed his kingdom Jordan.

The state of Israel

The Jewish section of Palestine became the republic of Israel and the hastily-established government was immediately faced with enormous internal and external problems.

The tiny state was economically unpromising – it was a barren land with few natural resources and a desperate shortage of water. The Jews have done an enormous amount to build new industries, to create a merchant fleet and above all to irrigate and fertilise the desert. Yet the country would have had a permanently unfavourable trading balance but for the payments by the West German government to war victims and the gifts of Jews from all nations, especially the United States. By the mid-fifties the former source of income was drying up and the country's economy was more and more burdened with the heavy defence budget which the constant state of

hostilities with the Arab states made necessary.

David Ben Gurion
The dynamic leader of Israel in the early years.

There was also a cultural problem. The Jewish population grew from 700,000 in 1945 to 2,500,000 in 1967, but despite the common religion this population came from two very different sources. The first wave which almost died out by the mid-fifties was of literate urbanised Jews from Europe and America. The second wave which came mainly after 1945 was from North Africa, Yemen and Asia. These peoples were less well educated and less skilled and although they now form the majority they inevitably suffer from many social disadvantages.

Yet none of these difficulties are as dangerous as the external threats to the very existence of the state of Israel. The division of Palestine left both general bitterness and a series of specific grievances. There were problems over the exact demarcation of the borders; more serious there was the unresolved problem of the hundreds of thousands of Palestinian Arabs who fled from Israel and who mostly had to eke out a pitiful existence in refugee camps in Egypt, Syria and Jordan. There was another long standing dispute about the way in which the waters of the Jordan should be used for irrigation in the lands through which it flowed. In fact there is quite enough water

The new Israel
Israeli children on a
kibbutz, *or co-operative*
settlement, sweep their
own classroom.

for Syria, Jordan and Israel, but Israel and Syria in particular have clashed over their rival schemes for its diversion.

These are all specific problems capable of solution; much more dangerous was the fact that many Arab nationalists never accepted the right of the state of Israel to exist at all. It is this that has forced the Israelis to be in a state of constant readiness for a life and death war and has helped to make the Middle East one of the most explosive areas in international politics.

Britain and the Middle East 1948–56
After the débacle of 1948 Britain had to set about creating a new policy in the Middle East. It was traditionally a British sphere of interest and the British made many efforts to turn the Arab League (created in 1944) into an instrument of British policy against communist infiltration. However, this policy was doomed to failure as long as the British both occupied the Suez Canal Zone and controlled the Sudan, for her presence in these areas was an affront to the leading Arab nation, Egypt. Around the Canal Zone there was constant

skirmishing between the 80,000-man garrison and the nationalist guerillas and in 1951 Farouk unilaterally renounced the 1936 treaty and proclaimed himself King of the Sudan.

However, within a year a group of army officers led by Colonel Nasser, with the popular General Neguib as a figurehead, overthrew the corrupt and inefficient King and drove him into exile. At first the British found the new government much easier to deal with. In 1953 steps were taken to agree on the stages by which Sudan would achieve independence. In 1954 the British agreed to withdraw within twenty months from the Canal Zone subject to certain rights of re-occupation in time of war. This concession was made partly to improve Anglo-Arab relations and partly because Britain was finding it increasingly hard to defend and pay for the base in the face of a hostile native population.

The canal settlement opened the way for a constructive period of British diplomacy. In April 1954 Turkey and Pakistan on the fringes of the Middle East signed a mutual defence pact. In April 1955 Iraq under its young King, Feisal, and the powerful pro-western Prime Minister, Nuri es Said, joined the pact and a year later Great Britain and Persia became full members and the United States gave economic aid. It seemed that the western powers had succeeded in building a powerful bloc in the area with at least one Arab member. However, Egypt and the other Arab states remained suspicious of this British-dominated group known as the Baghdad Pact (after 1959 CENTO).

In fact Egypt took measures to counteract the influence of the pact in the Middle East. In 1955, she began to buy arms from Czecho-slovakia and signed an alliance with Syria. When the western powers tried to bring Jordan into the pact the young King, Hussein, found himself under Egyptian pressure through the Jordanian nationalist movements and had instead to dismiss Glubb Pasha. This was a serious set-back for the British and it seemed that by the beginning of 1956 their influence was declining, while that of Nasser, with eastern European support, was considerably enhanced.

The Suez crisis and the second Arab-Israeli war
Both America and Britain were disturbed by the growing influence of Russia and her satellites in the Middle East through Nasser and they determined to bring him to heel by economic blackmail. Nasser's plans for a new Egypt centred on the construction of the Aswan High Dam (see p. 241) which he hoped would be the core of a programme of irrigation, flood control and electrification. In 1955,

first Russia and then the western powers offered to help him finance this scheme. In July 1956, the western powers withdrew their offer, clearly because of Nasser's continued association with the communist powers. Nasser replied by nationalising the Suez Canal Company which actually ran the canal and was a private company owned partly by the British government and partly by private shareholders, most of whom were French. Nasser promised that he would compensate the company but insisted that the canal was properly Egyptian property and that the canal dues would be used to help finance the High Dam.

For several months the British made ineffectual attempts to unite world opinion against Nasser, but they were quite unable to bring pressure to bear on the Egyptians who held the trump card – the canal itself. During this same period there were a number of border clashes between Israel and her neighbours, but most people were taken utterly by surprise when the Israelis suddenly launched an all-out attack on the Egyptians late in October. In a lightning campaign the Israelis routed the Egyptian forces and sent them reeling back through the Sinai peninsula towards the canal. At this point Britain and France intervened and ordered both armies to withdraw ten miles either side of the canal. Ostensibly this was a police action,

Suez
British troops in action in Port Said, November 1956.

but it has since been shown that there was collusion between the Israelis and the two western powers who were seizing the opportunity to regain control of Suez. An Anglo-French force knocked out the Egyptian air force and landed at the north end of the canal, but within a couple of days their attack was halted. The Egyptians had blocked the canal with sunken ships and put up a solid resistance; the Russians had threatened to intervene; and the Americans had refused to support sterling in the currency crisis which the war brought upon Britain. Completely isolated, even within the Commonwealth, the British were forced to withdraw taking the reluctant French with them. A United Nations force moved in to clear the canal and to restore peace along the old Israel-Egypt border. Britain and France had lost all their prestige and goodwill in the Arab world. Israel had scored a considerable military success and had certain specific gains to show: in particular a United Nations force was posted at Sharm el Sheik at the entrance to the Gulf of Aqaba so that for the first time Israeli ships could sail through to the port of Eilat (see map). Yet ironically it was the Egyptians who emerged with the most prestige.

The Middle East 1956-67

The Suez fiasco emphasised a change that was already taking place in the Middle East before 1956. Egypt was becoming the dominant power there and Britain was unable to maintain her former commitments. The interests of the western alliance were increasingly taken over by the United States and under the policy of the Eisenhower Doctrine (see p. 292) the US 6th Fleet was used to support a pro-western régime in the Lebanon in 1957. But it was quite impossible for any outside power to control the kaleidoscopic politics of the Arab states. In 1958, a revolution in Iraq swept away the monarchy and Nuri es Said and in 1959 the left-wing military ruler General Kassem walked out of the Baghdad Pact. In the meantime Britain's new Middle Eastern base in Cyprus was virtually neutralised first by the long years of terrorism and violence between the Turkish and Greek communities on the island and then by the granting of independence in 1959. The British kept some bases there but it had never been a very suitable site for a strategic command. In fact by the mid-sixties, the British hold on the Middle East had been reduced to air bases in Libya, the protectorship of a few sheikdoms in the Persian Gulf and of Aden and the South Arabian Federation. In this last area their rule was increasingly resisted by local nationalists encouraged from Cairo and the British government evacuated their base in Aden in 1967.

During Britain's retreat from the area, no other outside power was able to establish a rival hegemony. Both Russia and America poured in a good deal of military and economic aid, but, although some Arab régimes were labelled pro-western and others pro-communist, in fact they mostly escaped any close alliance with either Moscow or Washington. Egypt remained the strongest local power but Nasser's leadership was challenged by Syria, Iraq and Saudi Arabia (see p. 243). This alone would have made the Middle East a potential flashpoint but the situation was made even more complex and unpredictable by the inflexible attitude of the Arabs to Israel after the 1956 war and by the fact that France, Britain, Russia and America all sold increasingly sophisticated weapons to both the Israelis and the rival Arab régimes.

Nasser and the new Egypt
If the situation in the Middle East had moved out of the control of any one power, it is still true that one man above all others was able to affect the course of events there: Gamal Abdel Nasser. Nasser was born in 1918. He came from a lower middle-class family and received a good education both at school and military academy during the thirties. As an eager student of history and politics he was keenly aware of the subordinate position of his country and the corruption of its government. From 1942 he was deeply involved with a revolutionary group of young officers. In the first Israeli war he was one of the few Egyptian officers to emerge with any glory and after the war he set about organising the overthrow of the monarchy which he regarded as responsible for his country's humiliation. In July 1952, he and his fellow-officers toppled the hated Farouk in an almost bloodless revolution and, under the nominal leadership of General Neguib, they set about reforming their land.

It was clear from the start that they could not rely on the old party political leaders to carry through the radical changes that Egypt needed and the officers, whose average age was only thirty-eight, retained absolute power for themselves. They soon found that Neguib was too conservative and insufficiently ruthless for their plans and he was pushed out of office. Until about 1960 Nasser and his colleagues were singularly successful. Their external enemies, Anthony Eden, Nuri es Said and General Kassem, were all in turn defeated. At home the only organised opposition came from the fanatical reactionaries of the Moslem Brotherhood and from the Egyptian Communist party, but both these groups were soon outlawed and driven underground. The military government was

unashamedly dictatorial, but for most Egyptians this was more than justified by its achievements.

The Voice of the Arabs
Gamal Abdel Nasser.

Nasser's reforms

When the officers staged their *coup* Egypt was in a deplorable state. The country was economically underdeveloped and disease-ridden; its people were mostly illiterate; there were fantastic inequalities of income. Many of the largest businesses were foreign-owned.

The government built rural clinics, hospitals and pure water supplies. School and university places doubled in ten years and the state provided free, and theoretically compulsory, primary education. With education came a considerable improvement in the position of women. For the first time, women were given opportunities in higher education and by the 1960s Egypt had women ministers and higher civil servants. Cairo soon became a cultural centre for both the Arab and African worlds and Egypt has its own radio service, 'The Voice of the Arabs', its own television service and many theatres and cinemas. All these are strictly under government control, but there is no doubt that intellectual life was revived by the revolution.

The effect of the revolution on the economy was even more dramatic.

For the first time in years Egypt was freed from direct foreign financial control. The state took over public utilities, heavy industry,
banking and foreign trade. Many foreign companies apart from the
Canal Company were nationalised and many of Egypt's native
capitalists (who were mainly Coptic Christians or Jews) have had
their wealth expropriated. Yet the results of these activities have not
been entirely satisfactory, despite the income from the canal and a
revived tourist industry. Although the number of industrial workers
has doubled, their productivity is pitifully low and the country's
balance of payments has depended on outside aid, in particular on
credits from east European states.

Seventy per cent of the population still work on the land and the
revolution certainly changed their lives. Before 1952, 6 per cent of
the landowners owned 65 per cent of the land. The others and the
landless labourers eked out a living at barely subsistence level.
Between 1952 and 1961 Nasser steadily expropriated the large estates
and distributed the land to the peasants or fellahin. The fellahin
were organised into rural co-operatives with government credits to
buy machinery and develop better methods. At the same time the
government sought to reclaim vast areas of the desert. In the west
there is a major plan to open up the New Valley by tapping great

underground water supplies which it is hoped will quite literally make the desert bloom.

At the heart of all Nasser's plans is the High Dam. When it is fully operational it will serve many purposes. It will be used for irrigation schemes; it will control floods and improve navigation on the Nile; it will supply abundant electricity. It will not be a magic answer to Egypt's economic problems, but it may give the country a chance to break away from the pattern of rural poverty and to exploit its industrial potential.

In achieving all this Nasser had to rely on communist aid, but he was always careful to stress the autonomy of Egypt and as a fervent nationalist he rejected the idea of an Arab communist: 'The Communists will find no-one in the whole Arab world who will listen to them except their agents, for the Communists themselves are agents who neither believe in the liberty of their land or their nation but only do the bidding of outsiders.' On the other hand his own methods had been dictatorial. There was a powerful bureaucracy, there was a watchful censorship, there was little political freedom, but then Egyptians have never been free from the control of either arbitrary administrators or foreign capitalists and Nasser realised that he had somehow to jerk Egypt out of its past and create a literate, responsible and self-reliant people:

We must always keep in mind that the most important, the most difficult, the most crucial of our problems is to create in this part of the world a dynamic and watchful nation and that human beings are the material from which a nation is made.
To build factories is easy, to build hospitals and schools is possible but to build a nation of men is a hard and difficult task.

Nasser and the Arab world

Nasser's work in Egypt could not be carried out in isolation. One of the ways in which the Egyptian people could be rallied behind their leader and one of the ways in which they could be diverted from their discontents with the inevitably slow progress he was making, was an appeal to Arab nationalism. Through his successes as the self-proclaimed leader of Pan-Arabism Nasser gained enormous prestige at home, but it also led him into many difficulties.

Nasser's influence among the Arabs as a whole was probably at its greatest in the late 1950s. Britain had been discredited; Iraq, always Egypt's main rival, was in political confusion; and Syria had united with Egypt to form the United Arab Republic. It appeared that the dream of a Pan-Arab state might really come true. Yet in the 1960s these hopes were dashed. In 1961 the Syrians broke off the relationship in which they were clearly junior partners. Relations with Iraq improved briefly after the overthrow of the pro-communist Kassem in 1963 but soon cooled again. In 1962 Egypt became involved in the civil war between republicans and royalists in the Yemen and this tied down 40,000 of Egypt's best troops and involved Nasser in a quarrel with the astute King of Saudi Arabia, Feisal, who supported the royalists. In the meantime Nasser's relations with his Arab neighbours in North Africa were also difficult. The Sudanese had established their independence in 1956 but showed no desire for a union with Egypt. Nasser quarrelled with both President Bourguiba of Tunisia and King Hassan of Morocco, who were less anti-western and less anti-Israeli than he was, and his closest ally in North Africa, the radical President Ben Bella of Algeria, was overthrown in 1965. During 1966 Nasser clearly felt that his position in the Arab world was weakening. The traditionalist King Feisal of Saudi Arabia was claiming the leadership of the less radical states while the Syrians were outbidding Nasser in their appeals for a united Arab front against Israel. It was this situation which forced Nasser to take the fatal steps which led to the third Israeli-Arab war.

The third Israeli-Arab war

For years the Egyptians and the Syrians had trained Arab Palestinian refugees to form a so-called 'liberation army' and they had always theoretically claimed that they were planning to drive the Israelis into the sea. Yet in fact this belligerent talk had led to no more than border skirmishes around the Sea of Galilee, while the Israel-Egyptian border was guarded by a small UN peacekeeping force on Egyptian soil. In the spring of 1967 tension mounted on the Syrian border and Nasser clearly felt the need to gain more attention for himself. Therefore in May he ordered the UN force to leave his territory and began to make belligerent gestures to Israel. No doubt to Nasser's surprise the UN Secretary-General, U Thant, immediately acceded to his order (see p. 366), and Egypt and Israel were once more face to face. Most dangerous of all, Nasser re-occupied Sharm el Sheik and announced that he would stop all ships going to the Israeli port of Eilat.

It was soon clear that war was imminent for the Israelis could not accept this situation. Once more the big powers took sides with Russia firmly behind the Arabs in speech if not in action; Britain demanding the opening of the Gulf of Aqaba; and America ambiguously asserting both her neutrality and her refusal to allow the destruction of Israel.

After some tense manoeuvring, Egypt and Jordan signed a military pact on 4 June. The next day the Israelis, once more heavily outnumbered, decided to take the initiative against large Egyptian formations along the Sinai frontier. In the lightning campaign that followed in the next five days the Israelis destroyed the Egyptian forces on land and in the air, reached the east bank of the Suez Canal, drove the Jordanian forces east of the Jordan and overran the Syrian defences which had dominated northern Israel. It was one of the most remarkable and complete military successes of recent times.

The political results of the Six Days' War

The war was certainly a blow to the status of the United Nations which seemed quite unable to control events before, during, or after the fighting. It was also a blow to the prestige of the big powers, none of whom wanted the war. For years they had been pouring arms into the area and apparently exercising economic control, but when the fighting broke out they were quite unable to restrain their allies or client states. For Nasser, who at one stage seemed on the brink of a major diplomatic victory only to suffer a disastrous military defeat, it was a terrible blow. He saved his position in Egypt by offering to resign, only to be swept back to power by popular acclaim, but his prestige suffered in the Arab world as a whole. At least for a while it was left to others less involved in the war, the leaders of Algeria and the Sudan, to convene an all-Arab meeting to solve inter-Arab problems and in particular to arrange for the withdrawal of both Egypt and Saudi Arabia from the Yemen civil war.

In 1970 Nasser died. He had been the outstanding leader of the Arab world and a leading spokesman of the non-aligned states. Yet so many of his plans for his country had been frustrated by war and the fear of war. He was suceeded by Anwar Sadat who soon emerged as a strong leader committed to reverse the effects of the 1967 war, though also determined to loosen the hold which the Russians had on the Egyptian economy and military policy.

Neither the breathtaking victory of June 1967 nor the removal of Nasser gave the Israelis any respite—in fact, on the contrary, they were increasingly embattled. New leaders in the Arab world, notably President Gaddafy of Libya, were determined to keep the struggle alive and although the military front was comparatively quiet the Arabs launched a diplomatic offensive to detach other developing countries, especially in Africa, from Israel's camp. Even in the West the Israelis very success and the tough line they took over the future of the occupied territories weakened the support Israel had previously won as the apparent underdog. In particular France swung away from her former policy of supplying the Israelis with arms and in consequence they became almost entirely dependent upon support from America.

During this same period Israel also had to face a mounting wave of Arab terrorism launched by various Palestinian guerilla groups. Suicide attacks on Israeli settlements and on Israeli diplomatic and commercial enterprises overseas, the hi-jacking of airplanes, and such headline-grabbing killings as the attack on Israeli athletes at the Munich Olympic games were all calculated to keep the fate of the Palestinian refugees before the world and to prevent the Arab governments from reaching a negotiated settlement with Israel. This was made all the more certain since each terrorist attack was followed by an Israeli counterblow against the refugee-camp headquarters of the terrorists or against the host countries, Syria and Lebanon.

The fourth Arab-Israeli War
It was always possible that the situation would explode once more as it had in 1967 and the moment finally came in October 1973. Egypt and Syria launched surprise attacks across the Canal in the south and onto the Golan heights in the north. Instead of the expected devastating Israeli counterblow there followed three weeks of hard fighting. In the end the Israelis did push the Syrians back towards Damascus but without achieving a decisive breakthrough. On the Canal front the Israelis carried out a characteristically daring counterthrust in the closing stages of the war that took them west of the Canal and cut off a major Egyptian army, but both sides were glad to settle for a ceasefire on October 24. It appeared that Russian training and arms had levelled the terms in the Middle East and indeed the Arabs might have been victorious if they had not, as always, suffered from their own disunity. But the Libyans had stood aloof and most other Arab states had only sent in token forces. So when the ceasefire was arranged, mainly through the activities of the American Secretary of State, Henry Kissinger, there was no clear-cut result.

Ironically this might well have been the best possible outcome. The

Arabs had for once emerged with some military honour and some bargaining power in the shape of a number of Israeli prisoners of war and could therefore afford to discuss terms. The Israelis, somewhat humbled and very much aware of their dependence on American support, were no longer in a position to be completely inflexible in negotiations. As a result in January 1974 Kissinger, with tacit Russian approval, was able to arrange for disengagement on the Suez front and the establishment on the east bank of a UN peace-keeping force. The canal was to be reopened and the way was open for permanent peace negotiations between the two states. With rather more difficulty the same sort of settlement was later achieved between Israel and Syria. In Israel the war was followed by a political crisis. Mrs Meir and other leading figures such as Moshe Dayan left the coalition government, but nevertheless the Kissinger ceasefire agreement was in many ways the most hopeful event in the area for many years. On the other hand there was no solution to the long festering problem of the refugees and the old pattern of terrorist attacks and Israeli reprisals. A most dramatic example of this pattern of events came in 1976 with the highjacking of a plane, carrying many Jews, to Entebbe in Uganda and their subsequent release by a long-distance Israeli commando raid.

Lebanon

A further act in the tragedy of the Middle East came with the outbreak of a vicious civil war in 1975 in the Lebanon, until then the relatively peaceful business centre of the region. On the one side was the right-wing Christian community who controlled most of the wealth of the country and on the other left-wing Moslem Lebanese and the Palestinian guerillas who controlled much of the south of the country from their refugee-camp bases. The Syrians intervened first on the side of the Moslems and then switched to the Christians. After appalling casualties to civilians and widespread economic disruption the Syrians were able to impose a rough and ready peace on the country with grudging Arab League approval.

Oil

For the outside world it was not the bloodshed on the sands of Sinai or the stones of Golan, but the queues at the local filling stations which brought home the seriousness of the crisis. In the years immediately before the war the oil-producing states had begun to take an increasingly militant attitude towards the western controlled oil companies. Gaddafy of Libya had set the pace in nationalising foreign oil concerns, but even more cautious Arab states were demanding higher prices for their oil and a larger stake in the oil companies' operations. The war gave all the oil-producing states the real opportunity to exploit their strength as possessors of the largest known oil reserves in the world on which a huge part of economic life in both the developed and developing countries was dependent.

Under the leadership of King Feisal of Saudi Arabia, the Arab oil producers made their contribution to the war not with men and arms but with a massive increase in the price of oil, a reduction in the quantity supplied to the Western world and a total embargo on exports to countries such as the United States and the Netherlands who were believed to be actively pro-Israeli. Even though supplies were resumed during 1974 the effects of these policies were dramatic. Major industrial states such as Britain faced a massive balance of payments crisis as a result of higher prices; some such as Japan were bullied into making pro-Arab policy statements in order to keep their industrial life on the move at all. Developing countries were even more hard hit by the price rise. Meanwhile the Arabs were able to negotiate favourable new trade and arms deals in return for guaranteed oil supplies and to strengthen their hold over the oil companies. Moreover the vast profits which they were making from the sale of oil became a major factor in the world currency markets and a major source of investment for industrial development and financial speculation all over the world. Sadly there was little hope that any significant amount would be made available for the re-settlement of the Palestinian refugees.

The crisis did of course also act as a spur to Britain and many other countries to speed up the exploitation of their own oil reserves and find alternative sources of power. But however fast this could be accomplished Middle East oil was bound to be one of the key economic and political factors for the coming decade—a powerful weapon in the hands of governments which, whether feudal monarchies, military dictatorships or one-party socialist republics, could none of them be regarded as very stable. Moreover it seemed virtually certain that by the late 1970s Israel, Egypt or the big non-Arab power in the area, Iran, would develop a nuclear capability with the help of western technological aid given in the wake of the war and the oil deals.

Empire to independence in South Asia   15

One-fifth of the people in the world live in the Indian subcontinent, an area which accounts for no more than 3 per cent of the world's land surface. They live in an area divided from the rest of Asia by almost impenetrable mountain ranges; an area which from the eighteenth century till 1947 was ruled by one Imperial power, Britain, and on which the British had imposed common systems of law, administration, army organisation and education. Even today these millions of people are divided into only three major states – India, Pakistan and Ceylon – and these states are separated by none of the ideological differences which have split Europe since 1945. Yet this area has suffered and continues to suffer from violent religious and racial conflict and its two largest member states have been on the brink of war for the whole of their independent history. Such a situation would be tragic anywhere. It is particularly terrible in South Asia, because here by far the greatest part of the community live at or below subsistence level and the population is increasing far faster than the means of supporting it.

The Imperial background
In 1917 Edwin Montagu, the Secretary of State for India, announced: 'The policy of H.M. Government . . . is that of increasing association of Indians in every branch of the administration, and the gradual development of self-governing institutions, with a view to the progressive realisation of responsible government in India as an integral part of the Empire.' It was 160 years since Clive had laid the basis of the British Raj in India at the battle of Plassey and the British government in India had come a long way since Clive had reported on the East India Company administration of Bengal, 'Such a scene of anarchy, confusion, bribery, corruption and

extortion was never seen or heard of in any country . . . nor such and so many fortunes acquired in so unjust and rapacious manner.' If the British had begun by plundering India, they were soon concerned to improve it, though still largely in their own interest. In those parts of the land they ruled directly they made roads, railways and hospitals. They developed coal mines and built steel mills. They encouraged the production of marketable crops like jute, tea and cotton, which did not compete with British industry. They administered their great possessions without corruption and generally with justice. However, their administration was always alien; no Indian could hope for any high official position in the life of his country. And the very success of British rule created an influential opposition. It led to the growth of a prosperous middle class who learned about the British parliamentary system and absorbed the democratic ideals behind it. Not surprisingly they came to resent their political exclusion and the social gulf which lay between them and their rulers.

From the late nineteenth century, various groups, of which the Indian National Congress was the most important, began to campaign for home rule. They were encouraged by changes elsewhere in Asia, by the Japanese victory over the Russians in 1905, and by the Chinese revolution of 1911–12. The 1914–18 war had an even more important effect, for the Indians gave generously both in manpower and money and they naturally aspired to the rights of national self-determination for which the victorious allies were supposed to be fighting.

For their part, the British were not blindly opposed to Indian political aspirations. Indeed, even in 1918 most British statesmen were agreed that sooner or later Indians should be given a measure of self-government. They disagreed, however, on how soon and how much. After the war, the Coalition government began to fulfil the Montagu declaration. A Council of State and a Legislative Assembly were set up with considerable powers based upon an electorate of 1,000,000 (in a population of 300,000,000). In the provinces local assemblies were also given wide powers including some financial control. However, both locally and at the centre the British administration retained the most important rights, in particular over the armed forces, external affairs and the maintenance of law and order. The new Constitution created two power systems, or a diarchy, in which the British were still really in control.

All the same, the new Constitution represented a concession which would have been gratefully accepted by Indians in 1914. By 1920, however, the Congress movement had come under new leadership.

Gandhi and the Indian National Congress

In 1918, Congress elected a new leader. He was a lawyer who had already made a name for himself as a defender of the Indian Community in South Africa. In the years to come he was to be revered almost as a deity for his simplicity, gentleness, humility and unquenchable nationalism. Though he died in 1948 his ideas continue to affect the course of Indian history. His name was Mohandas Gandhi.

Like many other leaders Gandhi regarded the 1919 Constitution as quite inadequate and determined to fight it. However, he fought with a new weapon – peaceful protest and civil disobedience. He sought to mobilise the people in great non-violent demonstrations in order to bring an overwhelming moral pressure to bear on the British as well as to disrupt their government. Support for Gandhi grew steadily especially after the 1919 'Amritsar Massacre', an incident in which British troops fired on an unarmed Indian demonstration. Congress boycotted the elections and in 1922, Gandhi was imprisoned along with his new and very able lieutenant, Jawaharlal Nehru.

Gandhi
The Indian leader at work with his spinning wheel after his release from prison in 1933.

Nehru was, like Gandhi, a lawyer, but they had few other similarities. Nehru came from a wealthy family and had been educated at Harrow and Cambridge. However, his father was a prominent nationalist and after the Amritsar affair, the younger Nehru joined the Congress movement. In a very short time his position in the party was second only to that of Gandhi himself.

Gandhi's policies were not very successful in the twenties. The new Constitution worked despite his boycott and for some time he abandoned political activity altogether to turn his attention to improving the lot of the 'untouchables', the lowest level in India's rigid social system. Meanwhile his fellow Congress leaders carried on the struggle and the British for their part soon felt that the Constitution needed review. In 1927, they sent the Simon Commission to investigate the situation. The Indians were furious when they found that only Englishmen were to be included on the Commission and this prompted Gandhi to take up politics again. In 1929, he led an effective demonstration against the unpopular salt tax but to his dismay, his followers were soon involved in violent clashes with the British. The British promised early dominion status with an executive responsible to an elected assembly, but by this time Congress was demanding full independence at once. Gandhi was reimprisoned though he was soon to be released and to reach a remarkable understanding with the liberal and humane viceroy, Lord Irwin.

In the meantime, the British turned their promises into the concrete form of the 1935 Constitution. This increased the authority of the provincial assemblies and promised much greater powers at the centre. But the diarchy remained, for the executive officers were still responsible to the viceroy who also reserved rights over defence and foreign affairs. In any case the central part of the Constitution never came into effect. It depended upon the princely states, which covered two-fifths of the country and which were largely self-governing, joining the other provinces in an Indian Federation. This the princes refused to do and the new Constitution was denounced both by the arch-imperialists in England like Churchill and by the Congress leaders. However, the latter decided to exploit and if possible, sabotage it from within. In the subsequent elections, they won control of a majority of the provincial assemblies.

The Muslim League
From about this time the struggle between the British and Congress was complicated by the emergence of a third force. Nearly three-quarters of India's people were Hindus, but most of the rest were

Muslims. They had a separate religion and culture and after the mid-thirties they were increasingly adopting a separate political role in their own organisation, the Muslim League. Congress was not a religious movement and had a number of prominent Muslim members, but Gandhi appeared to many Muslims to be the embodiment of the Hindu way of life and they were fearful that their own interests would be swamped by those of the Hindus. As the prospect of home rule grew nearer, so more and more Muslims were drawn into the League. During the late 1930s, the League, under the leadership of Ali Jinnah, began to campaign for separate Muslim states within the Indian federation and in 1940 they demanded that, if India was granted self-government, the large parts of the country in which Muslims predominated should form a completely separate state.

Congress and the war
Congress was completely opposed to any division of India and denied the necessity of religious separatism. However, at this stage they did not take the League's threat very seriously. They continued to campaign against the British until the whole situation was revolutionised by the war. Nehru summed up the new problem thus:

War and India. What were we to do? For years past we had thought about this and proclaimed our policy. Yet in spite of all this the British government declared India to be a belligerent without any reference to our people ... We had frequently condemned Fascism and Nazism but we were more intimately concerned with the imperialism that dominated us. Was this imperialism to go? ... The British Government's answer was clear. It left no doubt that they were not prepared ... to hand over control of the government to the representatives of the people.

Gandhi and the Congress preached pacifism while the League became increasingly militant for Muslim rights. When the Japanese entered the war India was brought into closer contact with the conflict, but some Indians argued that they would only be attacked because of the British presence in India. A few, like Subhas Chandra Bose, formerly a prominent Congress leader, believed that India would achieve independence as a result of a Japanese victory and fought alongside the Japanese.

In 1942, the British government sent Sir Stafford Cripps to India with an offer of dominion status with the right to secede from the

Commonwealth after the war. This offer was still hedged with conditions, however, and the Congress leaders would not accept it. Instead, Gandhi and Nehru launched the 'Quit India' campaign against the administration and were soon in prison yet again.

Independence

With the end of the war and the election of the Labour government in Britain, it was clear that some major concession would soon be made to India. But meanwhile, the situation had become much graver with the rapid growth of the Muslim League. In the 1945–6 provincial elections it became clear that Jinnah was now the acknowledged leader of most of the Muslim population and he would agree to nothing short of the partition of India. A cabinet mission sent out by Attlee advocated immediate dominion status without partition, but their opinion was soon overtaken by events. In Calcutta, Bihar, East Bengal and the United Provinces, Hindus were murdering Muslims and Muslims Hindus in a terrible wave of communal violence. The Muslim League took over several ministries in a coalition government at the centre, but then used their position to sabotage the efforts of their Congress colleagues. In vain Attlee called Nehru, Jinnah and the Sikh leader, Baldev Singh, to London.

Hindu v. Muslim
The aftermath of communal violence in Calcutta, 1946.

When they failed to agree, Attlee tried to force their hands by declaring that the British would leave India in a matter of months whatever happened and sent Lord Mountbatten as viceroy to India to organise the evacuation of British forces and officials. In this desperate situation the Congress leaders agreed to partition. Thus, amid scenes of mounting communal violence, on 15 August 1947 the independent states of Pakistan and India were created with Nehru as Prime Minister and Mountbatten as Governor-General of the latter and Liaqat Ali Khan and Jinnah holding these positions in the former.

The Indian Union
India had achieved independence and in a few years she was to become the first republic in the Commonwealth, but the nature of the victory was a bitter blow to Gandhi. First he loathed the idea of partition and secondly he was appalled by the merciless communal killings. In fact, a total of 400,000 people died during the partition and the number might have been very much greater if Gandhi had not used all his prestige to check the excesses. By a bitter stroke of irony, Gandhi himself was assassinated by a Hindu fanatic early in 1948.

The nation that Gandhi had done so much to create continued to face terrible difficulties. The 570 princely states became nominally independent in August 1947, when their treaties with Britain ended, but in fact by reason of their economic position and the nationalist aspirations of their peoples, they were forced to join either India or Pakistan. Most did this peacefully, but the Muslim Nizam of Hyderabad was made to bring his predominantly Hindu state into the Indian Union by force of arms, as were one or two other Indian rulers. More important for the future were the actions of the Hindu Maharaja of the predominantly Muslim state of Kashmir, which will be dealt with later.

Yet India was the largest parliamentary democracy in the world. With the enormous prestige of Nehru and Gandhi behind it, Congress easily won the elections against the communists, the Jan Sangh (Hindu traditionalists) and other small groups. Nehru remained Prime Minister until his death in 1964 and both his successors have headed Congress governments. However, this apparent stability has hidden considerable political difficulties. Congress has been subject to innumerable factional squabbles between pressure groups representing different regions, social castes and economic interests. In a primarily agricultural and largely illiterate community a great gulf has, not surprisingly, opened up between the ruling *élite* and the mass of the people. Politicians and administrators have all too often fallen into corrupt practices. Even while the respected Nehru was still alive, differences of language and religion led to a weakening of national unity and a consequent growth of local interests.

In 1967, the Congress government barely won control of the central parliament and lost its grip on many provinces to communists and Hindu traditionalists or a combination of smaller parties. While Nehru was alive, his personal popularity did a good deal to hold the country together, but under Lal Shastri and, still more, under Nehru's daughter, Mrs Indira Gandhi, the central government has been unable to check factionalism and separatism. In 1975 Mrs Gandhi suspended most democratic processes to keep herself in power.

The state of Pakistan

In 1947 the political problems of Pakistan were not the same as those of India, but they were no less pressing. The state which the Muslim League created was an unreal entity; it has no historical roots and its two parts are separated by 1,000 miles. The peoples of the two provinces were racially and linguistically different. Their economies had been badly disrupted by the partition, particularly in East Pakistan, where the jute-producing areas were cut off from their main outlet, Calcutta. Before 1947 the League's whole effort had been concentrated on the creation of Pakistan, and they had no concrete policy once this was done. Even more disastrous was the death of Jinnah and the assassination of Liaqat Ali Khan soon after independence. No other politicians had the stature to guide the country effectively and the League soon fell apart in a sordid competition for power. In 1956, Pakistan became a republic but the next year the army commander, Ayub Khan, seized absolute power. The army alone had the prestige and discipline to control the country, and Ayub Khan did a great deal to clean up the administration. For ten years his basically autocratic government remained apparently unshakeable and Ayub Khan successfully stood for re-election as President. Late in 1968 however he was faced with mounting opposition from radical students and the revived opposition parties. His promise not to stand again as President and to introduce more democratic elections did nothing to quieten his rivals or the separatists in East Pakistan. The latter province was swept by peasant uprisings in early 1969 which were only quelled by the resignation of Ayub Khan and the handing over of power to the army commander-in-chief, Yahya Khan. But the grievances of the East, long exploited by the Westerners, remained as did the claims of Socialists and separatists in the West.

The state of Ceylon
At this point it is worth looking very briefly at the third state of
South Asia, Ceylon. The island was always administered quite
separately by the British and moved through the various stages to
independence with much less trouble than India. In 1947, it became
a dominion ruled by a moderate pro-western party which remained
in power until 1956. Then a more radical and neutralist party was
elected until 1965, when the electorate returned the more conservative
party once more. From this outline it is clear that Ceylon has an
effective parliamentary system which has twice allowed the peaceful
transference of power from one party to another. On the other hand
the island does enjoy many advantages over its northern neighbours.
It is reasonably compact and prosperous, and most of its people are
Buddhists. And even here there has been a good deal of political
violence including the assassination of Prime Minister Bandaranaike
in 1959 and there have been many clashes between the Sinhalese and
Tamil sections of the population. However, such clashes are quite
insignificant when they are compared with the internal conflicts of
both India and Pakistan and the almost continual state of hostility
that has existed between the two countries.

India and Pakistan
Partition naturally led to a number of disagreements. There were
claims and counter-claims for refugee compensation. There were also
some relatively unimportant frontier squabbles which have since
been used as an excuse for conflict that was really concerned with
quite different issues – thus India and Pakistan fought for some weeks
in 1965 over the useless mud flats of the Rann of Kutch. More
important was the problem of the waters of the Indus. The head-
waters of many of the rivers which feed the Indus lie in Indian
territory and the Indians wanted to divert them for their own
irrigation schemes. The Indus was, however, vital for the irrigation
system of the western Punjab in Pakistan. Eventually the problem
was solved by a World Bank plan to build a new system of dams on
rivers which lay wholly within Pakistan, while the rivers within India
were used for the Indian system.

However, there was one problem which defied this sort of solution:
the status of Kashmir. In 1947, the rich north-western province of
Kashmir was one of the hundreds of princely states which had to
choose a new role. The Hindu Maharaja of this predominantly Muslim area at first seemed inclined to remain independent, but, after a
number of communal killings of Muslim refugees on his territory, he
found his state being invaded by the warlike Muslim tribesmen from

the North-west Frontier, who poured in from Pakistan both to avenge their co-religionists and to engage in plunder in the Vale of Kashmir. The Maharaja called in Indian troops and applied to join the Indian Union. In reply the Pakistanis sent their regular army units into Kashmir as well. After a complicated campaign, the United Nations arranged a truce which left the Pakistanis in control of the mountains and the Indians in the valley.

The UN ruled that a plebiscite should be held to determine the future of the province, but in the meantime both sides set about incorporating the areas they controlled into their home states. Nehru, whose family was Kashmiri, insisted that the state was an integral part of India, avoided the idea of plebiscite, and held elections instead, in which his friend Sheikh Abdullah was elected Prime Minister. However, once in power the Sheikh showed a preference for complete independence and was imprisoned in India.

The Kashmir problem has bedevilled Pakistani-Indian relations since 1947. In 1964, the Indians were persuaded to arrange a meeting with Ayub Khan, but Nehru died before it could take place. In 1965 a new war which neither side could afford, and which neither side seemed capable of winning, broke out in Kashmir and all along the Indian-Pakistan frontier. This time a dramatic bid to break the impasse was made by the Soviet premier, Kosygin, who arranged a meeting between Ayub Khan and the new Indian Prime Minister, Shastri, at Tashkent. A preliminary treaty was signed when the frail Shastri, worn out by the strain of his office, collapsed and died. Although the Tashkent agreement was not entirely lost, Shastri's successor, Mrs Indira Gandhi, was too concerned with India's terrible economic problems to be able to get any nearer a real solution in Kashmir.

Bangladesh

In 1971 the previous conflicts of the sub-continent were utterly overshadowed by a cataclysm in East Pakistan. Opposition movements in the East staged a general strike in an attempt to press their claim for self-government after a generation of domination and exploitation by the western Pakistanis. In the subsequent fighting the western-controlled army massacred tens of thousands of Bengalis and several million fled to India. There was mounting violence along the border as the Bengali guerillas counterattacked their oppressors and when India moved onto a full war footing the Pakistani effort in the East collapsed. In rapid succession in early 1972 the imprisoned Bengali leader Sheikh Mujibur Rahmann was freed and returned to the East to become leader of a new independent state of Bangladesh, while in the West Yahya Khan was overthrown and replaced by a more radical civilian leader Z. A. Bhutto. But these changes in themselves could not improve the terrible plight of the people of Bangladesh whose country had been smashed and ravaged. Pakistan itself had suffered a heavy military, psychological and economic blow and in 1977, after widespread accusations that he had rigged the general elections, Bhutto was overthrown by a new military Coup.

India, Pakistan and the outside world

Although India and Pakistan were so preoccupied with their local conflicts they have also, naturally enough, played an important role in Asian affairs as a whole. Initially Pakistan was neglected by the great powers. The Labour government had more sympathy with Nehru's moderate socialism than with the avowedly Islamic state of Pakistan. However, when the western powers came to build up their anti-communist alliances in Asia, this attitude changed. Pakistan became a founder member of both the Baghdad Pact and of SEATO and was apparently one of the pillars of western policies in Asia. However, the Pakistanis gradually became disillusioned about the value of western alliances for they felt that their American and British partners were failing to give them sufficient support in their disputes with India. They could not turn to Russia since the Soviet Union had always made a point of cultivating good relations with India. However, during the 1960s the Pakistanis found some interests in common with the Chinese, whose relationship with India has grown steadily worse.

Indian foreign policy has been quite different. Nehru refused to join any of the western military organisations and instead became a leading exponent of non-alignment. He sought to mobilise the new nations like Egypt and Indonesia into a third force in world affairs acting especially through the United Nations. From an Indian point of view it seemed more important to destroy the remnants of European colonialism and prevent the growth of American neocolonialism, than it did to join alliances against Russia who offered no immediate threat to India. In any case, neutralism proved to be fairly rewarding for India, unlike Pakistan, was able to get economic aid from both Russia and the western nations. After the 1962 war with China (see p. 258), India was forced to seek much more help from the West, but even then Nehru would not be stampeded into throwing over neutralism altogether. On the other hand the lack of western sym-

I*

pathy during the 1965 conflict with Pakistan and the cutting off of
military aid to both sides created a new wave of anti-western feeling.
Like Pakistan, India is in desperate need of outside help but, with
some reason, she is extremely suspicious of her benefactors' motives.

India and China

India and China are the two giants of Asia and indeed the most
populous nations in the world. They stand for two contrasting
political systems, and they share a long frontier which has always been
in dispute. For some years however the differences between them
were masked. Both seemed primarily concerned during the 1950s
in forwarding the independence of the Afro-Asian world. When
China invaded Tibet in 1951, India gave no support to Tibet's
traditional ruler, the Dalai Lama. However during the years 1954–9
there were a number of border clashes. In 1959 these suddenly
came into the open. First the Dalai Lama fled to India to seek refuge
from the Chinese communists and won considerable sympathy for
his cause. Secondly, the Indian government admitted that the Chinese
had built a military road through a section of Indian territory in the
remote province of Ladakh. India was swept by a wave of nationalist
fervour. Sino-Indian relations steadily deteriorated and after fruitless
negotiations, fighting broke out in 1962. Indian troops were not only
defeated at Ladakh, but a Chinese army penetrated many miles into
the north-eastern province of Assam. Although they later retired to

**The giants of
post-war Asia**
*Nehru with
Mao Tse-tung.*

their former line and a truce was patched up, the Chinese had clearly demonstrated their military superiority and consolidated their position in Ladakh. The Chinese threat has never been removed and India has remained open to pressure along her own frontier and through the Himalayan kingdoms she protects.

The social problems of the Indian subcontinent

The tragedy of South Asia has been that the governments have devoted so much of their time to international politics when the whole area lives permanently under the shadow of starvation and when so little impression has been made on mass illiteracy, gross economic inequality and social discrimination.

All agricultural societies face considerable difficulties in making the leap to a more industrialised economy, but in India the deeply entrenched social and religious traditions have made the change more difficult than usual. Hindu society is divided into a rigid hierarchy of castes and all social and religious influences have sought to persuade the individual that he should be content with the lot to which he has been born. Despite the efforts of both Gandhi and Nehru to break down the social barriers of the caste system it still operates powerfully in marriage, in appointment to jobs and even in political groupings. Hindu traditionalism has bred an attitude of fatalistic acceptance of the most appalling social and economic conditions and a lack of ambition for material progress which is almost incredible to western eyes. Despite the efforts of the educated *élite*, the great mass of the peasantry are unwilling either to aspire to, or strive for, a very much higher standard of living than that which they

Education in Bombay
An all-age class around a wireless bought with the help of UNESCO.

now enjoy. On the one hand, this makes them much less open to communist influence than their Buddhist neighbours in South-east Asia, but it also hampers the drastic economic plans which are necessary even to keep the present miserable levels of existence.

Traditionalism operates in other harmful ways. The Indians' veneration of the cow prevents scientific stock farming and any improvement in the protein level of the ordinary man's diet. Again, although India now has a woman Prime Minister and Pakistan has had a woman presidential candidate, most women still occupy a very lowly position in society. In practice, they do not have equal educational opportunities; they may still be married off as children, although this is illegal; and their lives are still dominated by their husbands and parents-in-law. Here again there is a great gulf between the practice of the educated *élite* in politics, business and the professions and of the overwhelming majority of the population. They exist almost in two different worlds.

The economic problem
India has a concentration of population second only to that of China amongst the large non-industrialised nations. It is increasing by over 2 per cent a year. That is to say that every year there are about 10,000,000 more mouths to feed, and because medical science now saves more babies and prolongs the life of the aged, an ever-larger proportion of the population is either too old or too young to work. Indian agriculture has some of the lowest yields in Asia. Both the organisation and methods of farming remain extremely primitive. The result is that the food situation is worse than it was fifty years ago and it is still deteriorating. Food production was the same in 1961 and 1964, but at the latter date the population was 28,000,000 larger. In 1966 the level of production was actually lower than in the previous two years.

The United Nations experts have agreed that the basic minimum diet for an adult should contain about 2,500 calories a day, but in India the average level is about 1,800. Moreover, the average Indian's diet is not only too small but it is made up of the wrong things. While the westerners get most of their calories from meat, dairy produce and fresh fruit and vegetables, the average Indian relies on cereals for 80 per cent of his food and this leads to widespread vitamin and protein deficiency diseases.

India is still dependent on imported foodstuffs to keep her people alive at all, and yet for an agricultural society to rely on imported

Famine
Bihar 1967.

foodstuffs is obviously economic madness. India is, in fact, an out-standing example of the problem facing all unindustrialised communities with expanding populations. In order to become more prosperous the country must be more self-sufficient both in food-stuffs and manufactured goods. However, to develop agriculture and industry the country needs vast amounts of capital which by definition it has not got. This necessary surplus capital can only come in two ways. Either the nation must save some surplus by actually reducing the present standard of living and completely controlling all economic resources, as China has sought to do, or it must rely on a good deal of outside help as India has done.

India's economic plans

India has made considerable efforts to stand on her own feet economically. Although the amount of aid the country has received from both East and West seems vast, per head of population India has had much less than most other countries. Since 1951, the government has launched three Five Year Plans. They have covered the whole range of industrial production with special emphasis on steel, cement and hydro-electricity. These are the basic materials for industrial expansion but they can of course have little effect in themselves. What affects the mass of the population immediately is agriculture and so far comparatively little has been achieved in the struggle to improve this vital sphere of the economy. Thus, despite the plans, India's balance of payments has got worse, and 1966–7, after widespread drought, was one of the worst years for a long time, with famine in many parts of the country. On the other hand 1968 was a record year and the Indians had high hopes that a new strain of wheat would make India a net exporter of food by the mid 1970s. Yet in 1973 and 1974 the country was hit yet again by food riots and famine.

India's future

In 1949, India either equalled China or led her in almost every sphere of economic activity, although China had well over 100,000,000 more people. Today, China's agricultural production is probably twice as high, her electricity production three times as high, her steel four times and her coal seven times. Such comparisons can be misleading. The problems of the two countries have not been identical and the statistics do not add up to a simple equation which proves that totalitarianism, not democracy, is the answer to Asia's economic problems – though Asians could not be blamed for reaching this conclusion. In any case it may be a piece of typical western arrogance to judge the progress of a country in such material terms.

Gandhi himself would certainly have applied more spiritual criteria. He once wrote: 'Industrialisation is, I am afraid, going to be the curse of mankind ... Industrialisation depends entirely on your capacity to exploit ... and why should I think of industrialising India to exploit other nations?' Gandhi judged nations by their probity, not their steel production, and he believed that India could only retain her spiritual well-being by rejecting industrialisation and relying on village society and village handicrafts. On the other hand Nehru placed great faith in industrialisation. No less than Gandhi, he wished to improve the quality of life in moral terms as well as in material benefits, but he believed that India could not have a just society without great material advance.

Birth control
The problem and one answer.

Despite continuing problems with food supply and the extra strains put on all developing economies by the inflation in oil costs, there was indeed economic advance, but it was very uneven. Hundreds of thousands of people in Indian cities have nowhere to sleep at night but the pavements; millions still live in a state of semi-starvation. One city such as Chicago has more privately-owned cars than the whole sub-continent and most westerners eat more meat in a week than the average Indian has in a year. Yet in 1974 India had the technological sophistication to explode her first nuclear bomb.

For all the difficulties the country faced, it did retain both in central and provincial government a lively parliamentary political life. At the centre, though not in the State Assemblies, the ruling Congress party remained completely dominant despite internal feuds and desertions. However, in 1975, faced with an attempt to topple her over alleged election malpractices, Mrs Gandhi declared a state of emergency, suspended the constitution and imposed a considerable degree of censorship. A number of her most outspoken critics were imprisoned.

Mrs Gandhi argued that the country could not afford the crisis that would have followed her overthrow and that the emergency was a temporary measure that could not be described as a dictatorship. However, many aspects of her rule – and especially those inspired by her son Sanjay – the head of the Young Congress movement did appear repressive. Particular hostility was created by the so-called voluntary sterilization campaign in which – no doubt through excessive efforts by local officials – many individuals were forced to participate. In 1976 Mrs Gandhi called elections and relaxed many of the earlier controls in an attempt to win back some popularity. However, when the elections finally came an alliance of the more conservative Janata Party and dissident Congress members defeated the mainstream Congress and Mrs Gandhi and the Congress movement lost power. The election left India with a totally inexperienced government dominated by Mrs Gandhi's elderly opponents and with none of the basic problems of the Indian economy resolved. On the other hand it did demonstrate that the democratic process could bring about peaceful change in the world's largest parliamentary system.

The making of modern Africa 16

The Negroes of Tropical Africa specialized in their isolation and stagnated in utter savagery. They may even have been drifting away from human standards back towards the brute when migratory impulses drew the Caucasian, the world's redeemer, to enter Tropical Africa ... and raise the mental status of these dark skinned, woolly haired, prognathous, retrograded men.
Sir H. H. Johnston, The Opening up of Africa, *1928*

They thought I didn't count
And pushed me round and round
From place to place;
They looked at my face,
And my kinky hair, and wouldn't share
Mankind's good fare
With me,
I'm African.

And yet I held my ground
Although in chains I was bound;
I strove against odds,
And prayed to my gods;
I rose above shame and grief;
Their scorn was brief:
I'm great,
I'm African.
From the poems of Michael Dei Anang,

Forty years separate these words of an English imperialist and a Ghanaian poet, and, though the contrast in tone is so striking, it is still not enough to express the enormous change that has come over the African continent during the last generation.

There are many signs that some form of human society developed very early in the Great Rift Valley of East Africa, long before it did in western Europe. Later there was contact between the African world and the Romano-Greek civilisation of the Mediterranean and Arab travellers of the Middle Ages brought back stories of large and well ordered African kingdoms in the 'Sudan'. But the European imperialists of the nineteenth century were quite unconscious of the African past. Until the 1880s they seldom penetrated beyond the coasts of West Africa where the slave trade, which they had exploited, had destroyed the old structure, and southern Africa where their first contacts were with the primitive Bushmen and Hottentots. When Leopold, King of the Belgians, began to open up the Congo basin and sparked off the 'scramble for Africa' in the last quarter of the nineteenth century Africa was still regarded as the 'dark continent', populated by savage tribes. The colonisers came in search of prestige, raw materials, or new markets for their manufactured goods. The more high minded came to bestow on the Africans the benefits of a supposedly higher civilisation and to preach Christianity to supposedly degraded pagans. Whatever their motives they were not concerned to see what the Africans had of their own that was worthwhile. Almost everywhere they broke down tribal resistance and soon African societies were being disrupted by the efforts of administrators, missionaries and engineers, and the relatively stable African economies were feeling both the benefits and strains of involvement with technically superior nations.

Africa after 1918

In 1919 the colonial partition of Africa was virtually complete and for the next thirty years the political map hardly changed. The great powers followed the period of conquest with the consolidation of their authority in the hinterland and the economic development of their territories. However even at this time there were signs that the old ideas of imperial control would have to change. The 1914–18 war had played an important part in this. African troops had fought for the allies both in Africa and Europe itself. Intelligent Africans could naturally see no reason why Wilson's ideal of national self-determination should not apply to them. Very few Africans were in a position to discuss such questions let alone bring any pressure to bear for their own rights, but some recognition of these rights was made in the disposal of Germany's African Empire. The former German colonies were shared between France, Britain, South Africa and Belgium not as outright possessions, but as mandates in trust for the League of Nations. In theory at least the mandatory power was supposed to develop the territory in the interests of the indigenous population and bring it to a state where it would be capable of self-government.

Thus although the European administrations affected more Africans than ever before and although the economic resources of the continent were more thoroughly exploited, the British and French at any rate were changing the theory of their empires from straight overlordship to paternal responsibility. At the same time, the economic development of the African territories produced a growing number of urbanised and educated Africans who questioned the position of the colonial rulers and who were likely to be influenced by news of resistance to colonial rule by other subjugated peoples – in Ireland, in Egypt and in India.

At this time there were considerable differences between the theory and practices of the various empires. The British tried to rule through the existing tribal structures wherever possible and, except through mission work, did comparatively little to export British culture to Africa. At least after 1918, the theory was that, ultimately, these territories would enjoy self-government within the empire. The 1924 and 1926 Ormsby Gore reports stressed the need to develop the economies of the African territories in the interests of the indigenous population and as early as 1923 the Devonshire report asserted that self-government in Kenya should not be granted to the white settler population if this would jeopardise the rights of Kenyans in the long term. However at this time no one supposed that the African territories would be enjoying self-government for many generations. The only colony which did advance towards this goal was Southern Rhodesia, where, in 1923, the white settlers were given control of most internal affairs.

The French theory was quite different. Their colonies were regarded as part of France and the whole population, black and white, were Frenchmen. The old tribal leaders were by-passed and the administration centralised and closely directed from Paris. Every attempt was made to spread the French language and a respect for French civilisation. The local population were offered, at some unspecified future date, complete equality with Frenchmen, but they would continue to be governed from France and might, in return, help to elect French governments. The Belgians and Portuguese also insisted on strict control from the metropolitan government, but they too paid lip-service to the idea that Africans would receive equal rights once they were educated. But in all the empires there was an almost unbridgeable distinction between black and white and discrimination was most obvious in the British colonies such as Kenya and Southern Rhodesia where there were large white settler populations.

During the interwar period there was some economic progress and the British and French were particularly active in building roads and railways, hospitals and primary schools, but far from the Africans advancing much towards self-government, the last African state with a centuries' long history as an independent country, Abyssinia, was overrun by Mussolini in 1935. However this conquest was soon overshadowed by the outbreak of the world war which was to have similar effects in Africa to that of 1914–18, but to a much greater degree. The colonial powers were weakened; the anti-colonial powers, Russia and the United States, were strengthened. Africans had learned more and expected more and soon after the war they had before them the example of free ex-colonial nations in Asia and the Middle East. Yet in 1945 it still seemed possible that the European empires would last in most areas for another half century.

Independence comes to Africa: the British Empire
In fact within little more than twenty years the British, French and Belgian empires had vanished. The British took the first steps. In theory they had always planned the devolution of power and by the late forties they had granted independence to most of their Asian dependencies. However the process of training Africans to take over the administration and giving them political experience in elected assemblies was speeded up considerably in the fifties. This was partly in recognition of the changed world atmosphere and the outside pressures for decolonisation, and partly as a result of the new attitude to overseas commitments which followed Britain's unhappy Suez expedition in 1956. The process became particularly marked after 1959 under the influence of Macmillan and his progressive Colonial Secretary, Iain Macleod. The result was that most territories were given their freedom with very little violence or bloodshed, but also without sufficient economic and political preparation.

The first steps were taken in West Africa. Here were relatively rich territories, without the complication of large white minorities and with a well developed urban life. There were well established trade unions and nationalist groups which dated back to before the war and were led by well-educated radicals such as Nkrumah in the Gold Coast and Azikiwe in Nigeria.

Independent Africa 1976

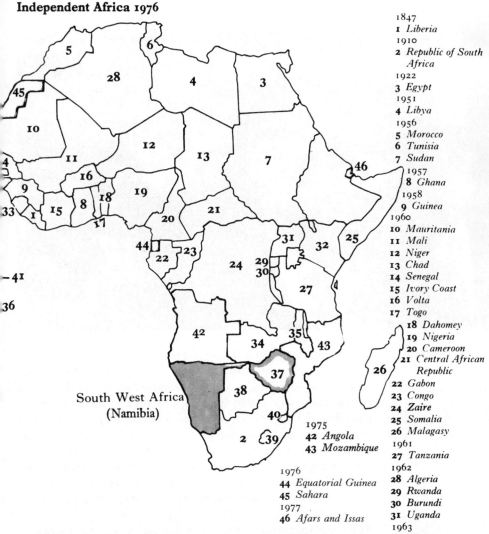

1847
1 *Liberia*
1910
2 *Republic of South Africa*
1922
3 *Egypt*
1951
4 *Libya*
1956
5 *Morocco*
6 *Tunisia*
7 *Sudan*
1957
8 *Ghana*
1958
9 *Guinea*
1960
10 *Mauritania*
11 *Mali*
12 *Niger*
13 *Chad*
14 *Senegal*
15 *Ivory Coast*
16 *Volta*
17 *Togo*
18 *Dahomey*
19 *Nigeria*
20 *Cameroon*
21 *Central African Republic*
22 *Gabon*
23 *Congo*
24 *Zaire*
25 *Somalia*
26 *Malagasy*
1961
27 *Tanzania*
1962
28 *Algeria*
29 *Rwanda*
30 *Burundi*
31 *Uganda*
1963
32 *Kenya*
1964
33 *Sierra Leone*
34 *Zambia*
35 *Malawi*
1965
36 *Gambia*
37 *Rhodesia (UDI)*
1966
38 *Botswana*
39 *Lesotho*
1968
40 *Swaziland*
1974
41 *Guinea Bissau*

1975
42 *Angola*
43 *Mozambique*

1976
44 *Equatorial Guinea*
45 *Sahara*
1977
46 *Afars and Issas*

Kwame Nkrumah was fortunate enough not only to receive a full secondary education in the Gold Coast, but to attend a Negro university in the United States and to study law in London. When he returned to Accra in 1947 at the age of thirty-eight it was therefore not surprising that he soon became a prominent figure in nationalist politics. However he found the nationalist United Gold Coast Convention much too moderate and soon founded his own Convention People's Party. He staged strikes, demonstrations and boycotts; and by 1950 it was clear that he was the dominant political figure in the towns and the southern part of the country. His activities landed him in gaol, but this did not prevent his party winning a majority in the

Kwame Nkrumah
*The Ghanaian
President on a visit to
London, 1961.*

first general elections for the representative assembly in 1951 and he was freed by the sympathetic governor of the Gold Coast to become the chief minister of the governor's executive council. In this position he was able to gain experience of government and build up his reputation in the country. In the mid-fifties the British decided that independence could be speeded up in West Africa and although Nkrumah was opposed by some conservatives and up-country chiefs, there was no one who could rival him as a national figure. It was therefore under his leadership that the Gold Coast, renamed Ghana, became the first new independent state in tropical Africa in 1957.

The pattern which Ghana had set was repeated with variations elsewhere. In Nigeria the country was too large and the regional and tribal variations were too great for one man to dominate the political scene. The Ibos in the east were led by Azikiwe, the Yorubas in the west by Chief Awolowo, while the northern tribes gave their allegiance to the Muslim emirs led by the Sardauna of Sokoto. When Nigeria did become independent in 1960 it was as a federation of the three regions. The northern conservatives allied with Azikiwe to control the central government with Awolowo in opposition and there were high hopes in Britain that the largest state in Africa would become a model of parliamentary democracy, but the deep tribal and regional differences were still unresolved.

The other, smaller West African colonies, Sierra Leone and Gambia, followed the same course to freedom a little more slowly. There too political alignments tended to follow tribal lines, but they were set up as independent parliamentary states with little or no violence.

In East and Central Africa, however, the process of decolonisation was much more troubled largely because of the existence of white settler communities. British Central Africa was made up of three territories: Southern Rhodesia, a comparatively prosperous country drawing its wealth from tobacco and sugar farms and from manufacturing industry in the towns, where there was a white population of about a quarter of a million outnumbered by 20:1 by the Africans; Northern Rhodesia, a mostly agricultural land but with very rich copper mining in the north and a small white community; and Nyasaland, a small and totally agricultural country with hardly any white settlers. In 1953 the British linked these three in the Central African Federation with the intention of granting the Federation dominion status in a matter of years. In the meantime they developed the Kariba Dam scheme on the Zambesi between the two Rhodesias and sought to show the economic advantages of co-operation between the parts of the Federation and between its people, black and white.

Kariba
The dam harnesses the Zambesi but cannot bridge the political gap between Zambia and Rhodesia on either bank.

However the Africans became convinced that the Federation was merely a way of perpetuating white settler government from Salisbury. They waged a concerted campaign against the Federation which was eventually broken up in 1963. The next year Northern Rhodesia and Nyasaland became independent as Zambia and Malawi. Southern Rhodesia remained a colony, for although the white settlers had enjoyed internal self-government for forty years, the British refused to grant complete independence until the African majority was given a larger share in the government. This the white settlers refused to do and the situation both within Southern Rhodesia and between Southern Rhodesia and her neighbours to the north became increasingly tense.

The problem of white settlement also created difficulties in the East African colony of Kenya. There a white population of 60,000 in a total of nearly 9,000,000 monopolised the best farming lands and occupied an exclusive and privileged social position. In 1952 the grievances of the Africans, and in particular the land hunger of the largest tribe, the Kikuyu, led to the eruption of the savage Mau Mau rebellion which was not brought under control until 1955 and in which some 10,000 lives were lost. However in 1957 the Africans were given their first chance to vote for the elective assembly and

Mau Mau
White policemen search Kikuyu suspects.

the nationalist leaders were able to press for freedom by more constitutional means. Finally in 1963 the country was granted full
independence with Jomo Kenyatta, who had been imprisoned by the
British in the Mau Mau crisis and emerged as the Kikuyu national
hero, as the first Prime Minister of a multiracial society with sizeable
European and Asian minorities.

The other British territories all over Africa achieved their independence by 1968. In some ways the British had done their work well.
In almost all territories there were African doctors, teachers, army
officers, administrators and judges who had gained considerable
experience before independence. On the other hand there were
seldom enough of these men and the new governments were faced
with enormous economic and social problems. Worse still there were
great political difficulties, at least some of which were the responsibility of the British.

The other empires

The experience of the French territories was quite different. During
the war French Equatorial Africa had been an important base for the
Free French forces and de Gaulle did what he could to reward the
African colonies. In the 1946 Constitution the colonies were given
fuller representation in the National Assembly and it was not long
before France was to have a Negro cabinet minister. On the other
hand the French policy of centralisation gave the French subjects in
Africa less experience of self-government at the lower levels. In the
mid-fifties, however, French policy began to change. Premier Mollet
passed the *Loi Cadre* in 1955 which broke up the West African and
Equatorial African regions into smaller units with a new emphasis on
local self-government. In 1958, with de Gaulle in power once more,
came an even more dramatic development. De Gaulle was determined to liquidate all France's colonial problems as quickly as
possible and therefore offered all the territories a choice between
immediate independence or self-government within a 'French
Community'. The Community offered considerable economic
advantages and all the territories except Guinea decided to join.
Guinea was immediately cut off from French aid and left to fend
for itself under the radical Sekou Touré, but within two years the
original idea of the Community broke down and all the former
French territories became completely independent – though many
remained closely aligned with France. The former French colonies
did not have the problem of large white settler groups or of powerful
traditional rulers, but they were generally smaller and economically
less viable than the ex-British states.

Of the other African empires the two most important were the Belgian and the Portuguese. The development of the Belgian Congo will be dealt with later, but it is worth noting here that the Portuguese territories formed the last significant European empire in Africa. They comprised the two large states of Angola and Mozambique, and a number of small but valuable enclaves and islands. The Portuguese showed a desperate determination to hold onto these underdeveloped but potentially quite wealthy colonies, despite the success of African nationalists movements in a series of exhausting wars. However the overthrow of the Caetano dictatorship in Portugal in 1974 spelled the end of Portuguese efforts to continue their debilitating struggle.

Politics and the problems of nation-building

Both the French and British left their African successors systems of legislation and administration modelled broadly on their own practices. However, not surprisingly, these European forms of government have not taken root or developed in the way the European powers had hoped.

None of the states of tropical Africa won their freedom by revolt as the nations of South America and some parts of Asia had done. Despite this several national leaders came to enjoy the prestige of a Bolivar or a Ho Chi Minh, and frequently they deliberately encouraged the cult of their own personalities both for private advantage and in an effort to build a sense of nationhood in territories which lacked other common bonds. On top of this parliamentary democracy lacked any deep roots in Africa and was, in some senses, a luxury which small and impoverished countries could hardly afford. Certainly opposition parties were weakened by the fact that the government was almost the only source of wealth and advancement in these countries. All these factors encouraged the emergence of charismatic national leaders ruling one-party states. This form of government was not necessarily a sort of African fascism. In Tanzania, for instance, the one-party government of President Nyerere was much more a national coalition of all available talent to cope with the enormous problems of a small impoverished state under a devoted and high-minded leader. On the other hand in some places, such as Ghana and Malawi, opposition was treated as disloyalty to the nation and opponents of the régime were gaoled or exiled. As a result opposition movements turned to conspiracy and violence, while genuine complaints against corruption and maladministration were silenced. The only effective check on the government in this situation was the army and in the mid-sixties a dozen African states witnessed

Biafra
*A young soldier beyond
the help of the Red
Cross and American
food parcels.*

army *coups*. An outstanding example was Ghana. Nkrumah had
become increasingly high-handed and silenced all open opposition,
but failed to check the corruption of his own supporters. He pursued
strongly anti-colonial foreign policies which lost him the co-operation
of western businessmen and governments, which in turn made the
state of the struggling economy more grave. The result in 1965 was
a military *coup*, strongly approved by western interests. The army
claimed that their intention was to purify the administration and
pursue more realistic economic and foreign policies.

Another difficulty, which has afflicted former British territories in
particular, has been the tension between the traditional rulers and
the party politicians. In most areas the new leaders have triumphed
without difficulty though sometimes the old chiefs have become
political leaders themselves. However in Uganda the rivalry between
the national leader, Milton Obote, and the Kabaka of Buganda,
strongly backed by his own people, led to a military showdown in 1966
and the exile of the Kabaka.

However the most common threat to nation-building in Africa has
been tribal separatism. The colonies which the European nations
created were not natural units and the imperial administrations often
found that it was in their own interests to play one tribal group off

against another. In the period after independence the aftermath of this situation has had terrible results. Political parties frequently coincided with tribal divisions, deepening bitterness between government and opposition, leading to unfair allocation of government funds and encouraging separatism. Nigeria has been a tragic example of the lengths to which this process can go. In 1966 there was a revolt against the northern-dominated federal government in which many prominent leaders were killed including the federal Prime Minister, Sir Abubakar Tafawa Balewa, and the Prime Minister of the Northern Region, the Sardauna of Sokoto. One group in the army seized power and tried to make the country a unitary state, only to be overthrown themselves by separatist interests. There followed terrible tribal killings directed particularly by the northerners against the Ibos. In 1967 the Ibos proclaimed their Eastern Region an independent republic, Biafra. This led to a civil war in which the Federal government, after some setbacks and with the political support of most of the major powers outside Africa destroyed the Ibo separatist movement. Happily the war was followed in 1970 by a rapid reconciliation of the peoples of Nigeria.

The economic problems
Africa is still a sparsely populated continent and vast areas support virtually no human life at all. Before the Europeans arrived there was almost no urban society and even now most Africans live as they always have done by some form of farming. But today there are growing numbers of towns especially in South and West Africa. Everywhere, but especially in the towns, the population is increasing by leaps and bounds. In a population of well over 200,000,000 two-fifths are under fifteen and at the present rate there will be 500,000,000 Africans by the year 2000.

Geography has not been kind to the continent. Most of southern Africa is a great plateau sloping sharply down to the sea. This has made access to the hinterland difficult even along great rivers such as the Zambesi and Congo. Great parts of the continent are either thick rain forest or waterless desert. In most of the tropical and equatorial belt soils are infertile and liable to erosion. Malaria, typhus, tuberculosis, bilharzia and many other killer diseases are endemic over a wide area, and there are still many places where the tsetse fly makes stock-farming impossible. In the south and east there are some highland areas which are free from these scourges and it was here that white settlers took up commercial farming. Almost everywhere else the majority of the people live as subsistence farmers or nomadic pastoralists, these peoples suffered appalling hardships in the extended droughts of the 1970s which hit a great belt through the heart of Africa.

In a few places there are highly valued natural resources: in South Africa gold and diamonds, in Zambia and Katanga copper, in Nigeria oil, in Rhodesia coal. Parts of West Africa as well as Kenya and Rhodesia produce cash crops for the world market such as cocoa, tobacco, coffee and fruit. These cash crops and the extractive industries are the only ones which have attracted large foreign investments, but cash crop farming employs a comparatively small number of workers and is dangerously vulnerable to variations in the world market demand. The products of mining are also mostly processed and consumed overseas. Almost all foreign investment is concentrated in Rhodesia, the Copperbelt, South Africa and the Nigerian oilfields. Only South Africa and Rhodesia have managed to develop healthy general industries apart from mining.

First steps in industrialisation
Skilled workmen in a mechanised Nigerian cement factory.

Neither cash crop farming nor mining can lead to a general improvement in living conditions or greater economic stability. Some African governments have built high hopes upon electrification schemes based on the continent's great hydro-electric potential, rather as the Egyptians hope that the Aswan High Dam holds the key to future prosperity. In 1959 the great Kariba Dam on the Zambesi came into action and Nkrumah developed the Volta Dam as part of a programme of electrification, irrigation, improved communications and new industry (in particular the production of aluminium). However it will be a long time before the ordinary Ghanaian peasant feels the benefit of the Volta scheme. What is needed above all is less prestigious, but more basic, investment in agricultural improvement and the development of simple diversified industries which can produce manufactured goods for the home market. At the moment 85 per cent of Africa's exports come from 5 per cent of her land mass and it is almost impossible to attract foreign commercial investment into the less profitable areas or activities. On the other hand it is extremely difficult for African governments to accumulate their own capital for development schemes. For this reason most African states are badly in need of planned economic aid from foreign governments and the international credit organisations.

However in Africa aid and overseas investment are deeply involved in political issues. Western investors have naturally been unwilling to put money into unstable countries or into those in which foreign-owned enterprises are likely to be nationalised. Western governments have, in the same way, been less than willing to grant aid to governments which have seemed too friendly with the communist states. On the other hand African leaders resent foreign-controlled firms making handsome profits out of African resources when the Africans themselves are still so poor, and they have reacted violently against attempts to exercise political control through the regulation of aid. It was Nkrumah himself who coined the word 'neocolonialism' to describe this sort of economic control and he and other African leaders have shown that they are willing, on occasions, to suffer financial loss rather than give in to such pressures. For instance, President Nyerere of Tanzania was prepared to forgo all West German trade and aid rather than suffer interference from Bonn in his right to recognise the East German government.

The Congo
The difficulties of nation building showed themselves in their most extreme form in the ex-Belgian Congo. Until the mid-fifties the

Belgians did a great deal to exploit the wealth of the Congo basin, and in particular of the copper-rich province of Katanga. They built railways, missions, hospitals and primary schools as well, but they did almost nothing to develop the higher educational level or political experience of the Congolese people. They were apparently planning to remain in the country for several generations to come and did all they could to shut out the influence of African nationalism. In the late fifties all this changed. A fall in world copper prices made the colony less valuable than before, and it was also clear that the colonial government could not prevent the development of African nationalism in the Congo. In these circumstances the Belgians decided to leave as soon as possible while safeguarding their remaining economic stake in the country as best they could. The Congolese had not even been allowed to vote in municipal elections until 1957, but at the beginning of 1960 the Belgians announced that they would be leaving in June. At this time the country had no African army officers, doctors or higher civil servants and only a handful of graduates in a population of 15,000,000 living in an area five times as large as France. The hurried elections in May 1960 gave a hint of what was to come. There were innumerable parties all based on tribal loyalties and in the end the Belgians had to hand over to an uneasy coalition headed by President Kasavubu, who had a following around the capital, Leopoldville, and Patrice Lumumba, the Prime Minister and the only party leader with anything like a national following. Meanwhile other regional leaders, notably Moise Tshombe in Katanga, were preparing to break away altogether.

Independence was followed almost immediately by an army mutiny and inter-tribal warfare. The outside world was shocked by the killing of white nuns and children, but the chief sufferers as the country disintegrated were the Congolese themselves. Belgian troops returned to evacuate white settlers and then a small United Nations force was sent in (see p. 365) to try to restore some sort of order and prevent the secession of rebel provinces. Their most formidable task was to control Katanga, where Tshombe's government maintained some sort of order with the support of powerful European business interests. In the meantime Kasavubu and Mobutu, the army leader, broke with Lumumba who commanded the support of most African leaders outside the Congo. Eventually he was captured by government forces and murdered while in prison in Katanga. However his influence grew with his death and he was soon to be regarded as a martyr in the cause of African freedom, struck down by the puppets of the neocolonialist powers. The government in Leopoldville still had to face a rebellion by his followers until they were brought more

Swedish troops in the U.N. army
On guard at a refugee camp in Katanga.

or less under control with the help of American aid and an army of white mercenaries. In Leopoldville there were a series of unstable governments and Tshombe himself became Prime Minister for a brief period, but in 1966 Mobutu staged a military *coup*. He in his turn came into conflict with rebellious mercenaries and an invading force of Katangese exiles from Angola in 1977. In the meantime hundreds of thousands of Congolese were killed in the fighting or died of starvation and disease as food supplies and medical services collapsed. Foreign technicians fled, the plantations returned to the jungle and the trade in minerals was badly disrupted.

The supporters of white supremacy in southern Africa have taken the Congo as the supreme example of the African's inability to rule themselves. But Africans have taken it rather as a demonstration of the way in which the colonial powers failed to exercise their responsibilities before independence and of the way in which African countries are manipulated by outside economic and political interests without any regard for the welfare of the African people themselves.

The problem of black and white

It is one of the tragedies of Africa that racial conflict has continued to be of such great importance in the post-colonial period. Southern and eastern Africa alone have 4,500,000 white men, nearly a million Asians and over a million half-castes living amongst the African majority. In Kenya, Zanzibar and South Africa there have been incidents between Africans and the Indians and Arabs who generally controlled retail trading and money-lending. In 1972 President Amin of Uganda launched a campaign of persecution against that country's Asian population ending with the ejection of the majority and the confiscation of their belongings. Yet in the long run the most explosive racial issue was relations between the black and white populations in Southern Africa.

Apartheid

The problem has reached its most acute form in the Republic of South Africa where the proportion of white men is very high – 3,500,000 whites live amongst 9,500,000 Africans, 1,000,000 coloured and 500,000 Indians. The white population has a history of three centuries or more in the country. In fact the first Boer settlers arrived in the Cape before the Bantus. They established permanent settlements after several bloody campaigns with the Zulu and other Africans moving in from the north-east and came to regard Africa as their home country. In the nineteenth century the main conflict was between the Boers, or Afrikaners, of Dutch stock, and the English government and settlers. In 1909 this seemed to be resolved by the establishment of the self-governing Union of South Africa, but the settlement showed no awareness of the problems of the African people. Both English and Afrikaners regarded the Bantu as their inferiors and allowed them few political rights. Between the wars the country was ruled by a coalition of moderate Afrikaners and English settlers led by Smuts and Hertzog, but even in this period the position of the Africans deteriorated politically – in the loss of limited voting rights – and economically – in the restriction of their rights to own land. In 1948 the Nationalist party, representing the extreme Afrikaners and led by Dr Malan, came to power and has remained in a majority in the all-white Parliament ever since. From then onwards racial discrimination became a rigidly applied political doctrine.

In theory the doctrine of apartheid, or separation of the races, was supposed to be in the interests of white and African. There were to be separate self-governing areas for the Africans to farm, separate schools and colleges, and a separate culture better suited to African

K

needs. But this 'separate' development meant in practice that the Africans always got inferior services, worked in lower paid and less skilled jobs, had to use different restaurants, buses and even churches, and were subject to a host of restrictions on movement and employment. Mixed marriages and even mixed social engagements became illegal.

The English and Afrikaner settlers either accepted or openly supported this system because they feared African control and because apartheid brought them prosperity. South Africa is by far the best developed country in Africa and the Africans themselves, though so much worse off than the whites, draw fatter wage packets than their fellows in other independent African states. South Africa exports gold and diamonds, wool and fruit and has well-developed local industry. Steel production alone increased nearly fourfold in the first ten years of Nationalist rule. However a small body of white liberals have joined the Africans themselves in bitter opposition to the theory and practice of apartheid. This in its turn has led the Nationalist governments to apply strict censorship and pass increasingly arbitrary and oppressive laws of arrest and detention for acts of opposition.

In the early years after the war the African leaders tried to pursue peaceful opposition through the African National Congress under the guidance of men such as Albert Luthuli, Nobel Peace Prize winner. But in Luthuli's own words:

Who will deny that thirty years of my life have been spent knocking in vain, patiently, moderately, and modestly at a closed and barred door. What have been the fruits of moderation? The past thirty years have seen the greatest number of laws restricting our rights and progress, until today we have reached the stage where we have no rights at all.

The younger generation of African leaders have turned to more violent methods, especially after the 1960 Sharpeville incident in which the police shot down unarmed African demonstrators. However the strong white police and security forces crushed all open opposition very effectively within the country, and for a long time South Africa seemed well placed both militarily and economically to ignore outside pressures.

Under Dr Verwoerd, Prime Minister from 1958 till 1966, the country became a republic (1960) and left the Commonwealth (1961). Verwoerd was a fanatical believer in apartheid in its fullest form and it was under his impetus that the first African area with local self-government was established in the Transkei. But paradoxically South Africa's prosperity is built not on the separation but the co-operation of the races. Her industry depends upon African labour and the Boer farmers and the white housewives in the cities have come to build their lives around African manpower. Moreover the government could never grant enough land for the Africans to exist completely separately unless it appropriated the farms of its own supporters. John Vorster, Verwoerd's successor, was an equally resolute defender of apartheid but he also recognised the economic facts and hoped that, without compromising the basic principles of white dominance, he could present a better image to the world for South Africa. In pursuit of this policy he allowed some minor relaxations in petty apartheid in public places, did not prevent the advancement of blacks and coloureds to skilled jobs in industry, and sought to create a hedge of allied and client states to the north. The Portuguese colonies and rebellious Rhodesia fulfilled this function in part and he also wooed Malawi and the former British High Commission territories, Botswana, Lesotho and Swaziland which were heavily dependent on South Africa economically.

However, by the mid-1970s this policy was crumbling in the face of both internal and external pressures. The collapse of the Portuguese empire was a major blow. Mozambique fell imme-

Apartheid
Bantu schoolchildren beside burning rubble after student riots in Soweto.

Apartheid
*One bench is marked
'Europeans Only'
and the other 'Nannies'
in this Johannesburg
park.*

diately under the control of the Marxist Frelimo movement and
this brought a hostile black government down to the borders of
the Republic and across the main supply line to Rhodesia. In
Angola, South African forces made a brief and unsuccessful intervention in the civil war from which the left-wing MPLA emerged
in a dominant position with the help of Russian aid and Cuban
armed units.

Whilst this pressure on South Africa and still more on Rhodesia
(see below) was becoming critical, Vorster had to face unprecedented problems at home. He had to find some solution to the
future of the trust territory of South West Africa or Namibia,
which could not be maintained under South African control
indefinitely, but in which the South Africans had a considerable
economic investment as well as a number of white settlers. In the
republic itself 1976 saw the creation of the first independent black
homeland, the Transkei, as a logical step in the process of separate
development, but the Transkei was denounced internationally as
a puppet state and received no diplomatic recognition.

Equally significant were the troubles within the great South
African cities. Here long-standing political and economic grievances combined in 1976 with the influence of changes elsewhere
in Southern Africa to produce a series of bloody and destructive
riots in the black townships around Johannesburg and amongst

the coloured population of the Cape. The government reacted with heavy-handed security measures, but also had to give way on some specific issues, such as the right of the Africans to be educated in English rather than in Afrikaans in the township schools.

By 1977 the position of South Africa had moved very considerably. The white government was still immeasurably more powerful militarily and economically than its neighbours. Its internal security control was still largely effective. America and the other western states still felt the need to trade with South Africa and reach some sort of political accommodation with the white regime despite its internal policies. On the other hand the government was having to reappraise its most fundamental policies and this was nowhere more evident than in relation to Rhodesia.

Rhodesia
A much less complete and less stable form of boss-ship has developed in Rhodesia. Between the wars the white settlers won control of all internal affairs and developed a social system which gave them exclusiveness and control of the best land without formally espousing the theory of apartheid. After the failure of the Central African Federation the white government fell into the hands of extremists who demanded complete independence from Britain while maintaining their loyalty to the crown. In 1965 the Prime Minister, Ian Smith, declared independence unilaterally after the British had demanded a new constitution which would give more rights to the African majority. This led to the application of economic sanctions approved by the United Nations and the position of the white Rhodesians seemed precarious since they were only a small proportion of the total population (220,000 in 4,400,000). However they have been helped by both South Africa and Portugal and individual businessmen from all over the world have broken the sanctions. Sanctions alone seem unlikely to bring down the Smith régime unless applied against South Africa as well. Few western states would be willing to take this course and the British government has rejected the use of force against Rhodesia. Into the early 1970s the Smith regime seemed to be quite capable of containing the spasmodic guerilla attacks from within and from over the border with Zambia. However, here too, the collapse of the Portuguese empire changed the situation dramatically. Rhodesia was now almost entirely surrounded by hostile states with only a slim life-line south into the Republic of South Africa. Guerilla activity increased sharply in 1976 and the success of Cuban intervention in

Angola caused deepening concern in Rhodesia. At this critical time the South African government seemed to have concluded that a defiant Rhodesia had become a liability and that the Smith regime must be pushed into a settlement. Vorster and the American Secretary of State, Dr Kissinger, held a series of meetings which finally forced Ian Smith to agree to go to the conference table in Geneva with the various black nationalist groups and under the chairmanship of the British.

However, the Geneva talks reached a stalemate early in 1977, partly because of Smith's delaying tactics and partly because of the deep divisions amongst the Rhodesian nationalist groups despite the attempts of the leaders of the neighbouring African states, Kaunda of Zambia, Nyerere of Tanzania, Seretse Khama of Botswana and Machel of Mozambique. Meanwhile however guerilla activity continued both internally and from Mozambique and it seemed clear that it could only be a matter of time before the white minority rule, which Smith had boasted would last a thousand years, gave way in the face either of diplomatic pressure or of force, leaving South Africa itself as the last area of white domination in the continent.

Africa and the world
In 1945 only three of the fifty-odd units in Africa were ruled by Africans. Today the whole continent except for the extreme south is made up of independent African states. The common emergence from colonial rule over the same period of years, the common economic and political difficulties and involvement in the racial issue in Africa and the world as a whole, has made Pan-Africanism – or continental unity – a popular slogan, especially for radical leaders such as Nkrumah. In practice the fruits of Pan-Africanism have been few. The projected union of Ghana, Guinea and Mali came to nothing and even attempts to set up an economic union in East Africa floundered. There have been a number of Pan-African conferences of heads of states and occasionally the African countries have voted as a solid bloc at the United Nations. On the other hand they have disagreed on many international issues – recognition of the state of Israel for instance, or the admission of communist China to the United Nations. Even more important they have divided on African affairs, such as the sides they supported in the Angolan civil war or their attitudes towards the brutal regime of President Amin in Uganda. There are unsettled territorial disputes between Ethiopia and Somalia and between Morocco and Algeria both of which have come to the edge of open warfare.

The creation of a new Africa

The concentration of Africans upon their continental problems and their suspicion of all outsiders is a product of Africa's colonial past and her present search for a new African culture. The European impact destroyed many links with the African past; Africans came to depend upon some form of European culture for advancement and the African countries were forced into European administrative, judicial and educational moulds. The influence of the colonial régime became a permanent part of the African scene, determining, for example, that some lands should speak French and others English, or that French Africa should have Roman Catholicism as its dominant form of Christianity while Presbyterianism flourishes in Malawi. Most of this is irreversible and in many ways Africa has gained by contact with societies which were able to speed the rate of technological development so much. On the other hand it has disturbed many African intellectuals that Africans should lose all contact with their own past and become, like many of the inhabitants of the South African shanty towns, divorced from their tribal society without finding any worthwhile new culture and society around which to build their lives.

The destructive impact of European culture has been a constant theme of African literature (see reading list). But African writers have moved on to modern African themes as well and have begun to develop for the first time a written African culture in French, English and African languages. African historians have been busy rediscovering their own past and there has been a conscious effort to revive folk culture. The very naming of countries such as Ghana shows an attempt to reach back to a national past, though possibly an historically inaccurate one. What the political and intellectual leaders are trying to do is to build up the dignity and self-respect of the African peoples in a post-colonial world so that they can echo the words of one nationalist, James Aggrey, written half a century ago:

If I went up to heaven and God said ' Aggrey, I am going to send you back, would you like to go as a white man?', I should reply, ' No, send me back as a black man . . . because I have work to do as a black man that no white man can do. Please send me back as black as you can make me' . . . I am proud of my colour; whoever is not proud of his colour is not fit to live.

Modern America 17

Today three powers dominate world affairs, the United States of America, Soviet Russia, and communist China. Of these three China has only recently become an open contender for world leadership and for most of the generation since the Second World War the rivalry was a simple one between Russia and America. The next three chapters are concerned with studies of these powers, one the most populous, another the largest, and the third the richest nation in the world.

The world war, which left the whole of Europe in a state of exhaustion, was a positive help to the United States in realising her enormous industrial and military powers. In 1945 America was by far the most powerful state in the world, the sole possessor of atomic weapons, and the only major combatant whose homeland was completely unscathed. Many American soldiers had died, but agricultural production was a third higher than in the depressed pre-war years and industrial output had risen threefold. There were American troops throughout Europe as far east as the Elbe and in all the key positions in the Far East. The United States was clearly in a position to establish her influence on a global scale in peace as in the war, but her future role was still uncertain in 1945.

The making of the Pax Americana: the Truman Doctrine
Between the wars America had refused to take up the responsibilities for which her material strength fitted her, and in 1945 Roosevelt gave no definite sign that he planned to make the American presence in Europe permanent. Complete isolation was, of course, out of the question. America had to establish strategic forward bases outside her own continent to protect her new economic interests, but there

was still a deep division between those who wished to limit American activities to areas of special interest, such as the Pacific, and those who already saw that the country might take up a general peace-keeping role throughout the non-communist world.

In this difficult period of re-adjustment America was led by a man who would never have become President in ordinary circumstances. Truman was a little-known party politician who had been chosen as Vice-President to win Mid-Western support; yet he soon showed a remarkable grasp of the broad issues which faced him. He kept on many of Roosevelt's key advisers, but modified his predecessor's policy, showing less faith in the Russians and more in his western European allies. His own position was weakened, as Woodrow Wilson's had been after 1918, by the Republicans' control of Congress, but he handled the situation with more tact than Wilson had shown. His delegate to the preliminary UN meeting in San Francisco (see p. 357) was a leading Republican senator and he was able to persuade Congress to vote 3 billion dollars to UNRRA and a further 5 billion for other loans and economic aid to devastated areas.*

Yet this could only be a beginning. It was not long before Truman and his advisers came to endorse Churchill's analysis of the world situation made in his 'iron curtain' speech at Fulton, Missouri: 'I do not believe that Soviet Russia desires war. What they desire is the fruits of war and the indefinite expansion of their power and doctrines.' When the British made it plain that they could no longer afford to support anti-communist régimes in Greece and Turkey, Truman persuaded Congress to accept an American commitment to 'free' Europe. In March 1947 he spelled out his vital policy decision:

I believe that it must be the policy of the United States to support free peoples who are resisting attempted subjugation by armed minorities or by outside pressures . . . The seeds of totalitarian régimes are nurtured in misery and want. They spread and grow in the evil soil of poverty and strife. They reach their full growth when the hope of the people for a better life has died. We must keep hope alive.

Congress voted a further 4 billion dollars and this was followed by an even wider scheme for European reconstruction – Marshall Aid (see p. 177). But even this massive economic effort was not sufficient; it

* Throughout this book, 'a billion dollars' means 'a thousand million dollars', not 'a million million dollars'.

Truman
Little known before 1945 but a key figure in the shaping of the post-war world.

had to be reinforced by an enormous military commitment with the creation of NATO (see p. 169).

Nor was Europe the only sphere of activity. Truman launched a great investment and loan programme in South America known as Point Four and the administration was heavily involved in Asia. The Pacific war had been dominated by the Americans and they were forced to take responsibility for the shattered state of Japan. In addition the government inherited the uneasy and expensive alliance with Chiang Kai-shek, although Truman resolutely refused to involve American troops in the Chinese civil war. Chiang was finally expelled from the mainland in 1949 and took refuge in Formosa (see p. 336), and this was followed by still more menacing developments. In September 1949 Russia exploded her first atomic device. In June 1950 came the outbreak of the Korean war in which America was the main western combatant and which threatened to escalate into an East Asian struggle when 250,000 Chinese 'volunteers' arrived to support the defeated communist North Koreans. At this point Truman had to face one of the stiffest tests of his career. The American commander in Korea, General MacArthur, stated publicly that he wished to use atomic weapons against China.

Truman was completely opposed to such a policy and he had no alternative but to sack MacArthur. However it was only with considerable difficulty that the President was able to discredit the views of the popular general.

The Eisenhower Doctrine: the extension of America's role

In 1952 Truman refused to stand again for the presidency and Adlai Stevenson, the Democrat candidate, was soundly defeated by General Eisenhower, the former world war hero and NATO Supreme Commander. Eisenhower was a man with a broad appeal and no strong party affiliations and was thus ideally suited as a candidate to regain the White House for the Republicans after twenty years in the political wilderness. He had little political experience and had to rely heavily on his party advisers, but he did not subscribe to the isolationism of a large section of the party. He made it clear that America would maintain her commitments in Europe and his appointment of the inflexible anti-communist John Foster Dulles as Secretary of State underlined his determination to continue America's new role.

Soon after his inauguration the world situation showed some signs of easing with the death of Stalin and the end of the Korean war, and Eisenhower himself showed a genuine desire to reach some sort of working *détente* with the Russians. However there were many reasons why this could not be achieved yet. There was a permanent threat to world peace in the existence of two Chinese régimes, separated only by the Formosan Straits and the presence of the United States Seventh Fleet. By 1954 the French colonial régime in Indo-China had collapsed and the American government felt impelled to extend her protection over non-communist régimes in Laos and South Vietnam. Then in the mid-fifties the United States became embroiled in yet another area, the Middle East. Faced with the extension of Soviet influence among the Arab nationalists and the complete discrediting of France and Britain after the Suez adventure (see p. 237), Eisenhower formally announced the extension of America's protective role over every part of the non-communist world, and particularly the Middle East. His words, spoken in January 1957, were strongly reminiscent of Truman's a decade before:

Building a peace with justice, in a world where moral law prevails . . . the United States has a deep involvement and responsibility in events that may lead to controversy in every part of the world, whether they touch the affairs of a vast region, the fate of an island in the Pacific, or the use of a canal in the Middle East.

The next year US Marines landed in the Lebanon to prevent a pro-Nasser *coup d'état.*

By 1959 America had alliances with forty-two nations either through the regional security pacts such as NATO and SEATO or in bilateral agreements. She was paying out 4 billion dollars a year to maintain them and Dulles had shown that America was prepared to take a tough line against the least sign of communist aggression. And yet the Pax Americana seemed to bring fewer and fewer rewards and costlier commitments. The new nations of Africa and Asia were wedded to the idea of neutralism which had no place in Dulles's clear-cut view of world politics. All too often Dulles's policy seemed to lead America into supporting unpopular right-wing strong men and left him open to charges of neocolonialism through economic control and the secret activities of the CIA. In the meantime Russia scored several propaganda victories, the most impressive of which was the orbiting of the first sputnik.

The American nightmare
Fidel Castro with Soviet leader Kruschev.

In 1959 it did appear as if there might be an improvement in Russo-American relations. Kruschev paid a visit to the United States which culminated in friendly discussions with Eisenhower at Camp David. But once again this proved to be a false start. A summit meeting in Paris the next spring broke down with the news that the Russians had shot down an American spy plane over their territory and the year became steadily more gloomy for the American government. In Cuba the radical revolutionary, Fidel Castro, seized American companies and when Eisenhower replied with an embargo on Cuban goods, Castro turned to Russia for help. In the Congo the new African government collapsed creating a dangerous political vacuum; in Laos there was a growing danger of a communist takeover. When Eisenhower handed over the presidency to John F. Kennedy in January 1961 he seemed to be leaving nothing but unresolved world problems and the task of refashioning American policy for the new decade.

Internal developments under Truman and Eisenhower

During the war the American economy enjoyed an enormous boom and there seemed to be a real danger that the post-war period would bring a recession. In fact, despite some difficulties in reconverting to peacetime conditions, the growth continued. In 1950 the country was producing no less than 45 per cent of the world's steel, 74 per cent of its cars and 86 per cent of its synthetic fibres and between 1946 and 1953 national income rose by 37 per cent. In these favourable circumstances Truman was anxious to continue the work of the New Deal but he was faced with a Republican majority in Congress. His own legislation was blocked while the Taft-Hartley Act which curbed the power of the trade unions was passed over his veto. In 1948 most people believed that Truman would not be re-elected; in fact the *Chicago Tribune* went so far as to print a front page headline 'Dewey Defeats Truman' before the results were announced. However Truman's energetic campaign against the 'do-nothing' Congress appealed to the underprivileged – the farmers, Negroes and less well paid urban workers and he secured his own re-election and a Democrat majority in the new Congress as well.

Even so he was not able to get far with his own 'Fair Deal' programme. Like his Democrat successors in the sixties, he found some of the most stubborn resistance to reform came from the conservative wing of his own party, especially from the representatives of the southern states. The congressional system which gave two seats in the Senate to every state regardless of population loaded the Senate with a disproportionate number of representatives from rural areas which were generally more conservative. In any case the deterioration of world affairs after 1948 meant that Truman was preoccupied with America's overseas commitments.

The most extraordinary development at home was closely connected with the 'cold war'. The collapse of Nationalist China, the explosion of the Russian atomic bomb and the unsatisfactory development of the Korean war created a feeling of frustration and suspicion which was ruthlessly exploited by a small group of political extremists and adventurers. Their opportunity came specifically with the revelation of a number of security leaks involving top atom scientists. But it was after the trial of a prominent diplomat, Algar Hiss, that Republican Senator McCarthy of Wisconsin began to use his position in the Senate Committees to launch a witch hunt against high ranking liberals and radicals within the administration and against anyone who had connections with the Communist party, as many young American intellectuals had done in the thirties. From the Un-American Activities Committee he harried officials throughout the administration. An unofficial censorship fell over literature and the film industry and for a while it seemed as though no one was safe as the McCarthy investigations turned on the army, the churches and the UN staff. But slowly sanity was restored and the end of the Korean war strengthened the few brave voices which had continued to speak out against him. In 1954 the Senate condemned his activities by 67 votes to 22 and his rule of fear was at an end.

By this time, of course, Eisenhower had moved into the White House and although the time was more auspicious for internal reforms the administration was no longer a reforming one. Eisenhower was inexperienced and frequently in ill health and the administration was once more dominated by big business interests. After the Korean war taxes were cut and the government fell under the control of a right-wing group which was opposed to any social reform and sought to keep government interference in the economy to a minimum. Until 1958 this did not matter so much for the economy was thriving, but thereafter the apparently invincible American economic structure showed signs of weakness. There was a trade recession and balance of payments difficulties.

The administration seemed to have no answer to the submerged problems of American society – rural poverty, bad housing, violent crime, and, most pressing of all, the position of the American Negroes. Altogether the country was in an unhappy state when Eisenhower's eight years at the White House came to an end. He had, himself, passed a bill which prevented a President standing for a third term of office and the Republican candidate was Vice-President Nixon.

The Democrats chose the young senator from Massachusetts, John F. Kennedy, with the experienced Senate leader from Texas, Lyndon Johnson, as the vice-presidential candidate. Nixon could claim superior political experience and Kennedy feared that he would suffer because of anti-Catholic prejudice, but in the end the handsome and charming Kennedy emerged with a narrow victory. He was the son of a millionaire and had not shown himself to be particularly liberal in the past, but there was something about him, a certain style and exuberance, which made it seem that his election was the beginning of a new era in American politics.

America in the sixties: the United States and Latin America
To the south of the United States lie twenty republics with a population of over 200,000,000 people. The largest of them, Brazil, is half as big again as the whole of Europe and the continent spans a great range of physical conditions. Most of this area has been independent for nearly 150 years, but it has remained outside the main stream of world politics. This is partly due to its physical isolation and partly to the fact that the people of Latin America have been absorbed in their own vast internal problems. It is an area of enormous untapped wealth, but the republics are mostly very poor and depend upon the export of raw materials such as oil, tin, copper, and foodstuffs, two-fifths of which go to the United States. The profits of this trade go to a small part of the population while the mass of the people live in great poverty. Except in some parts of the south, illiteracy, malnutrition and disease are the common conditions of life and do not supply a stable basis for democratic politics. For many years the republics were dominated by *caudillos*, or military dictators, who derived their power from their armies and a small ruling clique. By the 1960s few of the old-style dictators remained, but politics are still dominated by small oligarchies, are both corrupt and unstable, and are always open to interference by the armed forces.

Naturally this has been an area of particular interest for the United States for both strategic and economic reasons. She has resented any interference by outside powers, but has tended to adopt a paternalistic and protective role there herself. In the search for political stability, US administrations have supported unpopular and arbitrary strong men such as Batista in Cuba and Trujillo in the Dominican Republic. But they could not stem change indefinitely and they were naturally regarded with suspicion by the régimes which displaced the dictators. This mistrust of the United States was heightened by examples of direct interference. For example, in 1954 the CIA engineered a revolution against a left-wing régime in Guatemala. However the most serious disputes followed the overthrow of the corrupt Cuban régime of President Batista by the fiery revolutionary Fidel Castro in 1959. Cuba was on America's doorstep and there was a vast amount of American money invested there. By the time Kennedy came to power, trade relations had been broken off and Cuba had become a Soviet sphere of influence (see p. 294). In fact Kennedy inherited a CIA plan to send in a small army of anti-Castro refugees who had trained in Florida to overthrow the new régime. Kennedy did not stop their scheme, but he soon found that the CIA had grossly underestimated Castro and the tiny force was wiped out within a few days of landing at the Bay of Pigs. Kennedy would not allow direct American intervention and the island became even more firmly attached to Russia, while America was both humiliated and discredited.

Worse was to follow. On 14 October 1962 a US spy plane spotted Russian missile sites being constructed on the island. Kennedy once

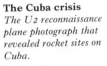

The Cuba crisis
The U2 reconnaissance plane photograph that revealed rocket sites on Cuba.

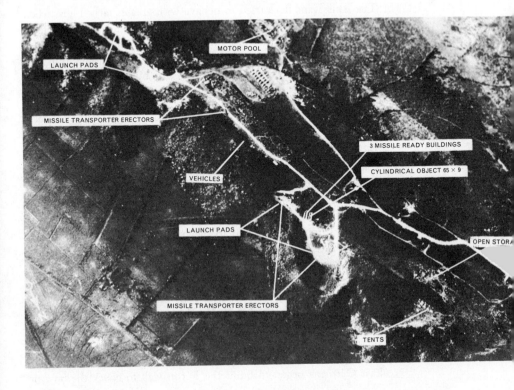

more acted forcefully but this time with more success. He placed a naval blockade around the island and warned the Russians that their ships would be stopped from reaching Havana. For a few tense hours it seemed that the final confrontation of the super-powers had come, but Kruschev was not prepared to fight on this issue. The missiles were removed though the Castro régime remained in power and more bitterly opposed than ever to American influence in Latin America.

Since that time the main concern of both Kennedy and later Johnson was to prevent the spread of Castroism to the rest of the continent but Kennedy did realise that Castroism was really just a symptom. In his own words: 'The big dangers in Latin America are ... unrelated to Cuba ... illiteracy, bad housing, maldistribution of wealth, balance of payments difficulties, the drop in the price of raw materials.' His administration poured aid into the Alliance for Progress which was founded in 1961 to help the Latin-American economies. The population of the region may well double by the end of the century and all the economic and social strains this is bringing cannot be solved without outside aid.

The Americans have tried to behave with greater tact. Thus, when Johnson was faced with a civil war in the Dominican Republic in 1965, he sought to associate other members of the Organisation of American States with his peace-keeping intervention. But the overthrow of the Marxist Allende in Chile by a right-wing military junta in 1973 seemed undoubtedly to have had the approval, and possibly help, of the Nixon regime.

The United States and Europe
In 1961 the general world situation was as bleak as that in the Caribbean, but the young and relatively inexperienced President threw himself into the problems of world peace with an energy that had been notably lacking in the last days of the Eisenhower administration. Soon after his inauguration he made an important trip to Europe. It took him first to Paris where he held talks with de Gaulle. But there was very little that Kennedy could do to change de Gaulle's dissatisfaction with the Atlantic alliance. In June he moved on to Vienna to confront Kruschev. The Soviet leader still had a low opinion of Kennedy and there was little progress on any of the grave problems they discussed – Berlin, Laos, nuclear disarmament. In fact things grew steadily blacker during subsequent months. Russia increased her defence spending and Kennedy demanded extra money for arms from Congress. On 13 August the Russians and East Germans began to build the Berlin wall to check the flow of

refugees which had reached 1,500 a day. The Soviet Union resumed nuclear testing and after a strong protest America followed suit. A three-year gap in nuclear explosions had been broken and Kruschev was threatening that Russia would soon have a monster 100 megaton bomb. In September the UN Secretary General, Dag Hammarskjöld was killed in a plane crash and Kruschev tried to paralyse the UN by blocking the election of his successor. On top of all this there were deepening crises in the Far East and Cuba (see p. 300 and p. 297).

Kennedy's reactions were not as clear-cut as those of his predecessors. He certainly emphasised over and over again that America would not be bluffed or bullied by Russia, but at the same time he showed that he saw the world situation in much more complex terms than Dulles. He saw that America could not dictate its will throughout the world and his more flexible attitude helped to win a new respect from the unaligned states:

We must face the fact that the United States is neither omnipotent nor omniscient – that we are only six per cent of the world's population – that we cannot impose our will upon the other ninety four per cent of mankind – that we cannot right every wrong or reverse each adversity – and that, therefore, there cannot be an American solution to every world problem.

During 1962 and 1963 the world situation remained tense. There was the second Cuban crisis and a deterioration in Laos and Vietnam. On top of this America was in difficulty with her allies. Kennedy shattered British defence plans by dropping the Skybolt missile programme (see p. 217); he offered Macmillan instead a share in the development of the Polaris nuclear submarines and he drew up a scheme for a co-operative multilateral nuclear force within the Atlantic Alliance. But within months de Gaulle had refused any part in the force, had vetoed Britain's entry to the Common Market, and France had exploded her own nuclear device.

However in 1963 there were some encouraging signs. On his trip to West Berlin Kennedy still stressed his complete opposition to communist ideology:

There are many people in the world who really don't understand . . . what is the issue between the free world and the Communist world. Let them come to Berlin. There are some who say that Communism is the wave of the future. Let them come to Berlin . . . And there are even a few who say that it is true that Communism is an evil system but it permits us to make economic progress. Lass sie nach Berlin kommen'.

But he and Kruschev did establish the 'hot line' on which they could contact each other rapidly to avert threats to world peace. Most hopeful of all, they negotiated the Partial Nuclear Test Ban Treaty – the first hesitant step back from the nuclear arms race.

This hopeful dialogue was broken by the assassination of Kennedy in 1963 and the fall of Kruschev in 1964. By the time the new leaders of both powers were ready to re-open communications the position had been complicated by the escalation of the war in Vietnam. As long as that struggle continued it seemed unlikely that the *détente* could make much progress (see p. 303).

Despite this there has been an overall change in the balance of US policy since the immediate post-war period. Kennedy in particular was anxious to turn back from military to economic aid and he saw that the despatch of young volunteer social workers of the Peace Corps was as important as the stationing of troops in developing lands. Aid of various sorts has reached neutralist and even communist states such as Yugoslavia. Both Kennedy and Johnson ran up against Congress attempts to control and reduce overseas spending; yet the change has continued and the United States continues to bear far and away the largest share of the costs of maintaining the United Nations and the Special Agencies.

The crisis in Asia

The long-standing American interest in Asia was strengthened in the post-war period by her occupation of Japan and her participation in the Korean war. Thereafter she found that her self-appointed task of containing communist China led to an expansion of her role. In 1954 the French abdicated their untenable position in Indo-China in the face of the brilliant guerilla victories of the communist leaders Ho Chi Minh and Giap and a fourteen-nation conference produced a new settlement for the area. Cambodia and Laos became independent and supposedly neutral kingdoms. Vietnam was divided in two. The northern part became a communist state under Ho Chi Minh. The south was established under President Ngo Dinh Diem as an American-protected republic. Yet the situation was most unstable. Laos was soon divided between rival factions and the north of the kingdom fell under the control of the communist Pathet Lao. Cambodia tried to remain neutral and non-aligned.

Kennedy
*The President with his
daughter Caroline
shortly before his
assassination.*

However the most dangerous situation developed in South Vietnam. After 1954 the Americans tried to fill the gap left by the French and gave considerable aid to Ngo Dinh Diem. But his régime was corrupt and arbitrary. He faced enormous economic problems and was soon under attack from a local communist guerilla movement succoured from the North. By 1958 the country was clearly in a state of civil war and by 1961 there were 20,000 Vietcong rebels in control of vast rural areas. Kennedy at once stepped up aid and in a few months of 1962 the force of American military 'advisers' swelled from 5,000 to 15,000. But in 1963 the Ngo Dinh Diem régime was overthrown and since that time the Americans have had to make greater and greater efforts to support a series of military régimes with doubtful local backing. Inevitably, after the death of Kennedy, the pressure to increase American activity to bring the civil war to an end led to a steady escalation. In 1965 the Americans became full scale combatants not just advisers. Later Australians, New Zealanders and South Koreans were sent in in token forces and a series of massive retaliatory raids were launched against North Vietnamese factories and military installations right up to the Chinese border. By 1967 there were over 500,000 Americans fighting in Vietnam and the cost of the war for the United States was running

Slaughter in Vietnam
Helicopters evacuate the wounded.

into millions of dollars a day. Yet there seemed to be no real hope of defeating the Vietcong who were able to penetrate into Saigon itself. American military leaders believed that they could win the war by sheer weight of arms, but the American government had to contend with world-wide criticism of their policy and widespread war-weariness at home. The war was jeopardising America's diplomatic relations both with the neutralist nations and with the Soviet Union, and it delayed the sweeping social reforms which both Kennedy and Johnson had promised.

Early in 1968 President Johnson made the surprising announcement that he would not contend the presidential elections that year but would concentrate instead upon finding a solution to the Vietnam situation. As a result preliminary negotiations between the United States and North Vietnam began in Paris and by the end of the year the South Vietnamese government and the Vietcong were drawn into the discussions.

However it was soon clear that the talks would not bring a swift settlement to the remorseless war. President Nixon's election seemed to open up new hopes for peace, for although he was a hardline anti-Communist on his past record, he was also determined to bring back the American troops if only for his own political gain. In June 1969 he began troop withdrawals and a policy of Vietnamisation—the process of training and arming Vietnamese to take over the role of the American ground forces. At the same time Nixon was engaged in an attempt to improve relations with China and the trade embargo was eased a little giving a hint of the diplomatic efforts which were soon to follow. On the other hand in April 1970 American and South Vietnamese troops made a thrust into Cambodia, hitherto little affected by the war although the Vietcong supply routes ran through its eastern border region. As a result Cambodia itself was soon being devastated by civil war. The next year the Americans gave massive air support to a South Vietnamese thrust into Laos again with the intention of cutting Vietcong supply routes. In 1972 the bombing of North Vietnam was resumed and reached a crescendo at the end of the year. Yet in fact America's overwhelming concern at this point was to get out of the war and to obtain the release of her prisoners of war. 1972 was the year of Nixon's major diplomatic visits to Russia and China and by January 1973 agreement had in fact been reached with the North Vietnamese and the Vietcong for the withdrawl of US forces, the repatriation of the American prisoners, and the stabilisation of the military position in the South with the help of various control commissions and observers.

In fact the settlement was merely a pause in the war. Fighting persisted until South Vietnam and Cambodia finally fell to the Communists in 1975. What was significant about it was that it marked the end of an era of American intervention in the area—a fact signalled by the American recognition of Communist China. Taiwan was not entirely abandoned, but otherwise the old American encirclement of China was more or less over. The military dictatorship in Thailand collapsed soon afterwards and the other major capitalist states in the Pacific such as Japan and Australia were also striving to improve their trade and diplomatic relations with Peking. The liquidation of America's disastrous military entanglement in South East Asia which seemed relatively successful at least from America's point of view had been largely the work of Nixon's Secretary of State Henry Kissinger. It was through Kissinger that Nixon also made a major effort to improve relations with the Soviet Union, though he visited the country himself in 1972 and 1974 and received Brezhnev in America in 1973. Both sides had much to gain from the improved relationship. Russia was anxious for trade and was obsessed by the threat of war with China. America saw a high level entente between the super powers as a means of replacing America's unmanageable and ineffective system of alliances and he hoped to be able to arrange for agreement on strategic arms limitation. Finally Nixon was hungry for successes in the field of foreign affairs to compensate for the disasters of the Watergate affair at home.

America in the sixties and seventies: problems of internal development

The United States enjoys material wealth quite out of proportion to the size of its population. Both absolutely and per head, the country leads the world in all the indices of economic development. She produces one-third of the world's oil, steel, energy supplies and manufactured goods. Agriculture is highly mechanised and its main problem is that it produces surpluses – which is a minor headache in a world where most people have to struggle to keep above the breadline. Although Russia has challenged America in certain technical and military fields there can be no comparison between their standards of living or general level of development. To take just one example, there is one car to every three people in the United States, one to every 300 in Russia.

Yet this great wealth is not evenly spread. Perhaps one-fifth of the population is poor by American standards (though of course most of these people are comfortably placed in Indian or African terms). Many of the elderly, large sections of the rural population, Negroes and Puerto Ricans are almost completely cut off from the 'affluent society'. Moreover, since the whole theory of American society is opposed to any form of socialism or the welfare state, there are few social services for the less well-off sections of the population to fall back on and the American economy operates with a level of unemployment.

The problems of the underprivileged include bad housing, inadequate schools and lack of medical facilities. There is a terrible crime rate, and the whole range of problems involved in the position of the Negroes (see p. 307). There were men in both the Kennedy and Johnson administrations who wished to tackle these problems, but they had to do so in a political system in which a large section of the majority party was opposed to reform and in which the federal government often had to seek devious ways to enforce its wishes on unwilling state administrations.

The New Frontier administration

Kennedy waded into the problems of American society with enormous vigour. In an attempt to distinguish his administration from its predecessors and to bring the best possible team together, he chose his ministers and advisers from far beyond the usual sources of party political leadership. The wealthy Republican businessman Mac-Namara became Secretary of Defence; Dean Rusk came into Foreign Affairs from the academic seclusion of the Rockefeller Foundation. Kennedy's own brother, Robert, became Attorney General. Historian Schlesinger, economist Galbraith and many other distinguished scholars and experts were prepared to serve under the dynamic new President and he soon won an extraordinary degree of loyalty from his talented team.

However those outside the administration did not always show him the same respect. Southern Democrats and Republicans did all they could to thwart his legislation and many powerful interests outside Congress were ready to defy him openly on occasions. The most remarkable instance of a clash with an entrenched vested interest came in the spring of 1962. This was a period of economic difficulty and the President had put forward a policy of pegging wages and prices in the national interest. However in April first United Steel and then a number of other large steel companies raised their prices. It appeared as though the small number of firms which controlled the industry was going to hold the country to ransom.

Kennedy reacted firmly. He directed a powerful publicity campaign against the steel bosses and began to place government orders with those firms which had not raised their prices. In the end he broke the steel men's resistance and prices were lowered again. It was a triumph for the administration and for the national interest but it was a dangerous one. Initially his actions had won widespread support, but later there was some backlash against such outright use of the presidential power and a heavy fall of prices on the stock market demonstrated the lack of confidence which the business community had in the President.

In fact Kennedy's so-called New Frontier schemes became little more than unfulfilled promises. He did win power to reduce tariffs, he did launch a bill which removed some of the disabilities of Negro voters in the south. He passed housing legislation and a minimum wage bill, but what got through was a shadow of what he planned. Throughout his brief administration he found his bills killed in the Senate Committees, especially after the mid-term 1962 elections brought new strength to the conservatives. In particular his plans for subsidised medical services for the elderly and his plans to extend New Deal welfare and labour legislation foundered. In fact the achievements of the Kennedy administration would have been even more flimsy had not the more subtle tactician Johnson steered parts of the programme through after Kennedy's death.

It is common to wonder at the premature death of a great man what he would have achieved had he lived longer. In Kennedy's case it seems quite possible that he might have been frustrated in most of his plans, even if he had not been killed in such strange circumstances in Dallas, Texas, in November 1963. Yet if he achieved little in legislative terms this alone was not the measure of his work. He set a new tone in American politics which inspired many young Americans who had little respect for the mainstream political leaders. His critics both to the left and right have frequently suggested that his greatest talent was as a self-publicist, and that his progressive attitudes were a sham. But he certainly did project an image of idealism and his death was mourned not just by Democrat supporters, but by ordinary people all over the world.

The Great Society administration
Kennedy's successor, Lyndon Johnson, was a man of a very different sort. Many years Kennedy's senior, he had enormous experience as majority leader in the Senate and was an outstanding political tactician without being a mere party hack. He had a long record of supporting progressive reforms, and in the remaining year of the

administration he did what he could to pass the remnants of the New Frontier programme.

In 1964 he scored a crushing victory in the presidential polls over the extreme conservative Republican, Senator Goldwater. But the very existence of Goldwater as a candidate shows how strong the reactionary groups – opposed to civil rights reform, social welfare and a *détente* with Russia – had become in the country as a whole. Johnson's own programme for the 'Great Society' was as wide-sweeping as Kennedy's and he had a much stronger position in Congress. It involved civil rights legislation, an attack on poverty, and major reforms in education and housing. Yet the plans for the Great Society made slow progress. The administration found itself more and more involved with the Vietnam war which led to vast overseas expenditure and a dangerous inflationary spiral at home. Moreover the war strengthened the conservatives and served as an excuse to let the programme slide into the background.

For the young to whom the Kennedy administration appealed so strongly these developments were very disillusioning, especially as more and more of them were conscripted to fight in Vietnam. This contributed to violent protest movements by student organisations on progressive university campuses such as Berkeley in California, or the retreat into pacifism and anarchism of the 'hippies' and 'beats' who opted out of established society altogether.

Civil rights
Of all the internal problems of American society none poses such a challenge to the American ideals of human rights and democracy as the position of the Negroes. For over a century there has been no slavery in the United States, but today the 18,000,000 American Negroes are still second-class citizens. In the southern states, where Negroes form a high proportion of the population, the white people have sought to erect legal barriers to prevent them enjoying equal social, educational and political rights and when these were broken down extreme groups tried to intimidate the Negroes with threats and violence. For years they have had to take the lowest jobs, live in the worst housing, and use separate public facilities, schools, hotels and transport. Side by side in Mississippi or Alabama would be public lavatories marked 'White Ladies' and 'Negro Women'. In the great northern cities the discrimination existed not by law but custom. The Negroes have had to live in slum ghettoes where they were cut off from the affluent society of the white man and where they suffered from inferior education and career opportunities. Despite

the efforts of a few prominent Negro leaders and white liberal sympathisers there was almost no concerted effort to improve their lot either between the wars or in the immediate post-war years – a period when Negroes in Africa and the West Indies were advancing towards self-government.

Gradually, in the early fifties, there was a change in the climate of opinion. In 1954 the Supreme Court ruled that it was illegal to impose segregation in state schools. Eisenhower backed this decision, but when nine little Negroes tried to enrol at an all-white school in Little Rock, Arkansas, in 1957, there was mob violence which the local authorities did nothing to check and federal troops had to be called in to restore order. Thereafter desegregation did make some progress in education but the pace was too slow for the younger generation of Negroes. The result was dissatisfaction with the moderate Negro leaders such as Martin Luther King. In 1960 the federal authorities sought to supervise elections and Johnson established a Civil Rights Commission while he was Senate Leader, but this was still only nibbling at the edges of the problem.

In 1961 Negro and white civil rights workers began a campaign to break segregation in public transport in the south and when they ran into trouble the sympathetic Kennedy administration did what it could to protect them against white extremists and hostile local authorities. The next year trouble centred on Oxford, Mississippi, in the heart of the racialist south, where a Negro student tried to enrol in an all-white college. There were riots in which several men died before federal marshals and troops restored order which the local governor had done nothing to protect. This pattern was repeated in Alabama where police used the most brutal measures against civil rights workers and Negro and white liberals went in danger of their lives while their murderers were sure of a sympathetic trial by local juries.

Kennedy faced a very difficult position. His civil rights legislation was sure to face a barrage of opposition in Congress but any attempt to modify it would only exasperate the Negro leaders. In the end it was left to Johnson to pass a bill which gave limited protection to the rights of Negroes in stores, theatres, cinemas and restaurants and Negroes who were brave enough to try to vote in elections in the south stood some chance of getting their names on the electoral roll. But the basic segregation in jobs and housing could not be changed so easily and demanded not just legislation but new attitudes.

Martin Luther King
*King leads a march
through the rain in
Montgomery
Alabama, 1965.*

Black Power
*Two Olympic medallists
at the 1968 games give
the Black Power salute
in silent protest.*

The moderation of the older generation of Negro leaders seemed to bring such poor results that the younger men turned to extremes. One example of this has been the Black Muslim movement founded by Elijah Mohammed. The Muslims reject the whole concept of integration and demand instead a separate Negro state in America. They are openly Negro supremacists and have been accused of stirring up race hatred.

In fact, the Muslims preached a strict moral code and a respect for women, hard work and education – which are normally hard to find in the Negro ghettoes. For those who do not have this code to confirm their self-respect, the only release is in outbreaks of violence and arson such as those which sent the Watts district of Los Angeles up in flames in 1965, shook Chicago and other northern towns in 1966 and turned Newark, New Jersey and Detroit into blazing battlefields with street fighting between armed Negroes and state troopers in 1967.   The final blow to moderation in the civil rights movements came in 1968 with the assassination of Martin Luther King by a white sniper in Memphis, Tennessee.

Yet the period of extreme racial violence which followed did moderate to some extent in the early 1970s. This was partly because of the brutal effectiveness with which the police and FBI pursued many of the leaders—many of the most prominent Black Panthers were killed and many more fled the country. But more significantly black Americans began to use their political power increasingly effectively to bring more and more black mayors and state and federal congressmen into power. But the gross inequalities did remain—full of potential for renewed racial violence.

Nixon and America

During the early years of Nixon's presidency the focus of government efforts was on foreign affairs. At home the President, whilst struggling as all other western leaders to contain the effects of inflation, pursued a fairly traditionalist Republican line—indeed there were growing suspicions that big business had an increasingly effective access to the favours of government.

The disillusion with established political life in America spread far beyond the alienated students and blacks during 1970s and reached its highpoint in the complex political scandals which surrounded the second Nixon administration and came to be known collectively as the Watergate affair.

Violence in the streets

Man on the moon

During the 1972 campaign a group of men apparently paid by Nixon supporters were found trying to install secret bugging devices in the Watergate Building headquarters of the Democratic National Committee. At the time this caused some stir but not enough to prevent Nixon winning a crushing victory over his democrat opponent the liberal MacGovern. Only afterwards as the affair came to be investigated by both Federal Grand Juries and the Congress itself, did it become clear that this was just one incident in a whole campaign of political espionage and bribery which had been used to discredit the President's enemies and to secure his re-election. Moreover following the discovery of the affair attempts had been made to interfere with the course of justice to protect those who had been initially involved in the break-in. Soon it was clear that men very high up in the government and perhaps even the President himself were involved in crimes and malpractices. The vice-president, Spiro Agnew, was forced to resign in a quite separate corruption case and there was a growing demand for the impeachment of the President himself. Finally it became clear that the President had lied to Congress and the people. In the face of pressure from all quarters including his own party, Nixon finally resigned in August 1974. In the remaining two years before the elections President Ford (who had succeeded Agnew as Vice-President and then Nixon as President) attempted to recapture some of the respect for the administration which Nixon had destroyed. In foreign affairs he retained Kissinger who continued to attempt a globe-trotting personal diplomacy, not only in the Middle East and South East Asia but in Africa as well. However, Ford lacked the personal appeal to overcome the enormous disadvantages which Nixon had left for the Republican administration and he was decisively defeated in 1976 by the Democrat Jimmy Carter of Georgia who promised honest government, liberal reforms, protection for minority groups, and open diplomacy in world affairs. Carter was viewed with some suspicion not only by the Republicans but also by many sophisticated radicals as something of a populist demagogue. Yet he certainly had a freshness of appeal and offered a promise of change after the tawdry image of Western democracy which the investigation of Nixon's America revealed in contrast to the aspirations of the American ideal which John Kennedy had expressed:

The unfulfilled task is to demonstrate to the entire world that man's unsatisfied aspiration for economic progress and social justice can be achieved by free men working within the framework of democratic institutions.

Russia and European communism

None of the allied powers suffered as badly as the Soviet Union in the Second World War. In 1939 the Soviet Union had a population of 170,000,000; within six years 8,000,000 soldiers and 11,000,000 civilians were dead and millions more disabled and homeless. The toll on the economy was just as heavy. A great part of the achievement of the Five Year Plans, for which the Russian people had sacrificed so much, was wiped out either by the ravages of the Germans or the Russians' own scorched-earth policy. The invasions swept across Russia's main industrial areas and richest agricultural land – at one time iron production fell by three-quarters, steel by one-half and railways were torn up, power supplies broken, millions of head of stock slaughtered. Over half the urban housing in Russia was left in ruins and the long-term effects on the standard of living were only just beginning to wear off in the sixties. It is not surprising that the sufferings of the war coloured Russia's home and foreign policy for so many years.

The last years of Stalin: foreign policy
At Stalingrad, Kursk and Kharkov the Russians destroyed Hitler's initiative in the East. By 1944 they were spilling into central Europe; in April 1945 they were in Prague, Vienna and Berlin and were free to dispose at will of the area east of the Elbe.

The policy which Stalin evolved for this vast new empire was determined by two considerations. The first was that Russia should extract whatever immediate compensation she could for the terrible losses she had suffered. The other was that she should build up a defensive system by transfer of territory and control of satellite governments to make sure that such an invasion could never be launched again,

L

either by the Germans or, as the Russians feared in 1945, by the western powers. Russia's policies in eastern Europe and the development of the cold war have already been dealt with in Chapter 11. But in this context it is worth noticing that the Russians were not engaged in an inexorable or completely successful expansion. Until 1947 they contented themselves with a consolidation of their power in the areas which the Red Armies had conquered and which had been recognised as Russian spheres of influence at Yalta. Though it did not seem so to westerners, Stalin's policies were still guided by defensive considerations and he was extremely cautious in the face of the American monopoly of atomic weapons.

The Russians did set up a communist régime in North Korea, but they adopted a very ambiguous attitude towards the struggle between the Chinese communists and nationalists (see p. 336) and soon withdrew from Manchuria, stripping the rich province of everything of value they could move. As in Europe, their attitude became more aggressive by 1947–8 and there was increasing local communist activity in Burma, Malaya and Indo-China with the approval of Moscow. This phase reached its climax in June 1950 when the North Koreans were encouraged to cross the 38th Parallel; but there, as elsewhere, the Russians avoided direct conflict with America.

In contrast to his successors, Stalin did little to establish good relations with the neutralist powers or to win world opinion – as the destructive policy of the Russians at the United Nations clearly showed (see p. 364). His goals were limited to the consolidation of the gains Russia had already made by the late forties. All the same there had been a revolution in Russia's world status. Before 1939 she had been an outcast and militarily underrated nation on the fringe of European and Asian politics. Within a few years she was one of the two super-powers and an arbiter of Europe's future, with a new and powerful ally in China.

The last years of Stalin: inside Russia

At home there were fewer policy changes after 1945. Stalin completely dominated the government and party, and was surrounded by those subservient lieutenants who had survived the purges. The two most influential were apparently Zhdanov and Malenkov, whom Stalin played off against each other. When Zhdanov died in 1948, Malenkov was able to oust many of his rival's followers, but he never achieved a really secure position as Stalin's heir-apparent. There were always others – Kaganovitch, Molotov, and the powerful Ukrainian party boss, Kruschev.

The most immediate task which Stalin and these men had to face was the reconstruction of the shattered economy. In 1946 a fifth Five Year Plan was launched which, yet again, gave priority to heavy industry. The government had tried to evacuate key industries east in front of the German invasion and they were now faced with the problem of redeveloping the shattered western regions. This concentration on heavy industry could only be achieved by neglecting both agriculture and consumer industries. By 1950 heavy industrial production was 40 per cent above the level of 1940, but thousands of people in cities such as Stalingrad were still living in the ruins of their old homes and there were fewer livestock than there had been in 1928, before the first Five Year Plan.

Inevitably the war was followed by an ideological purge for it had opened Russia to dangerous outside influences from a number of directions. Millions of Russians had lived for a while under German administration. There had been closer contact with the western powers and the Red Army had had a new world opened up for them as they moved into central Europe, where, despite the rigours of the war, the standard of living was still much higher than in Russia. Stalin's reaction was utterly ruthless. Beria's vast police organisation purged both the party and the people and racial groups which had shown signs of co-operating with the Germans, such as the Crimean Tartars and the Kalmuks, were deported wholesale to distant and inhospitable regions of Russia. During the Five Year Plans and still more during the war itself there had been a slight ideological thaw in order to strengthen national morale. This ended sharply with the peace. In every field of human activity a strict party line was laid down and Zhdanov and his henchmen were particularly active in crushing intellectual independence in literature and the arts.

By the early 1950s it was not just the intellectuals who were under pressure; even Stalin's closest subordinates were increasingly insecure as Stalin became more and more obsessed with the threat of treachery. In January 1953 nine doctors, seven of them Jewish, were accused of murdering Zhdanov, Malenkov's old enemy, and it seemed as though this might be the beginning of a new purge in which Malenkov himself was the ultimate victim. However, in March Stalin died. The iron hand which had ruled Russia for two decades was removed. He had been the author of millions of deaths, but he had also thrust his country through the first stages of industrial development and made Russia one of the dominant world powers. He was deeply feared and hated and yet, in the tradition of the Tsars, he had also been the 'little father' of the Russian people. The destruction of all the other great figures of the Bolshevik revolution meant that no one could possibly fill his role.

The interregnum

Initially all power passed to the collective leadership of the Praesidium (or Politburo). For a few days Malenkov held both the key posts of Prime Minister and party secretary, but his colleagues forced him to choose between them. He chose the premiership and Kruschev became first secretary of the party. Rivalling these two were Beria, the police chief, and Molotov, the foreign affairs expert, as well as Kaganovitch, Mikoyan and Marshals Bulganin and Voroshilov.

The struggle between these men was not long postponed and the first victim was the most hated and dangerous, Beria. He was declared responsible for the 1953 riots in East Germany and executed. It was the beginning of four years of manoeuvring which involved both a naked struggle for personal power and an ideological dispute about Russia's future development. The two leading figures were Malenkov and Kruschev. Both saw that the over-concentration on heavy industry had given the economy a dangerous imbalance and produced a desperate shortage of houses, consumer goods and even food. State planning was clumsy and over-centralised and agriculture had failed to keep pace with the needs of an advanced society. Productivity per head and the number of stock were no higher than before the First World War. Both men understood this, but for the sake of the power struggle they adopted different political attitudes.

Agriculture became the most important battlefield. Malenkov hoped to improve production by giving the peasants greater freedom and cash inducements. But Kruschev soon revealed to the Central Committee the failure to reach the planned levels and put forward his own plan which involved the replacement of the state planning authority, over which Malenkov had control, by local planning councils, in which party officials would have more influence. In 1954 Kruschev launched his own ambitious plan to develop the previously uncultivated 'virgin lands'. His radical agricultural schemes did not have the approval of the old Stalinists but he was able to strike up a working alliance with them on other key issues.

The far-sighted and able Malenkov had long-term plans to improve the standard of living in Russia and to remove some of the more objectionable features of Stalinist society. However he could only finance his reforms by reducing expenditure on defence and heavy industry. With the end of the Korean war and the explosion of the

Kruschev and Malenkov
Rivals for Stalin's throne.

first Russian hydrogen bomb in 1953, this did not seem an unreasonable policy but it provoked the bitter opposition of the traditionalists and the military interests with whom Kruschev was prepared to co-operate. Early in 1955 these men – Molotov, Kaganovitch and the marshals – were prepared to strike. In February they forced Malenkov to resign and made Bulganin Prime Minister in his place. Yet it was Kruschev who profited most from the reshuffle. From his key position as first secretary he was able to insinuate his supporters into key positions of power.

The evolution of a new foreign policy

With such an unstable situation at home the interregnum was not a period for decisive new initiatives abroad but there was a cautious change from Stalinist policies. For a while there was a slight thaw in East-West relations. The Korean war closed in an uneasy stalemate. The Russians withdrew from Austria and made tentative approaches towards the heretical Yugoslavs. In Europe they seemed to accept that a balance of power had been reached, but they were able to widen the possibilities for Soviet influence by adopting more friendly attitudes towards the neutralist states.

However the new line dictated from the Kremlin had disturbing effects in the satellite states. The local leaders who had been placed in power by Stalin found it hard to adjust to the new political climate and the notorious Stalinist boss of Hungary, Rakosi, had to step down in favour of the more liberal Nagy. Inevitably the Russian hold on the satellite states was weakened by their own internal party squabbles and there was also a gradual change in the relationship with China. Mao Tse-tung and his fellow veteran communist leaders could not be expected to treat the new Soviet leadership with the same respect that they had shown Stalin.

All these shifts were producing mounting pressure for a radical realignment of the leadership in Russia, of relationships in eastern Europe and of the Sino-Soviet alliance, but the full extent of the new situation was not apparent to the outside world until the dramatic year 1956.

The Twentieth Party Conference

The Twentieth Party Conference, held in 1956, was a landmark in Russian history. It was at this point that Kruschev felt powerful enough to break away from the cautious manoeuvrings of the interregnum. Before an astounded audience of Russian and foreign delegates he denounced Stalin, both for creating a cult around his own personality and exalting it above the party itself, and for instigating the atrocities of the Great Purges. This was remarkable enough, but what followed was even more revolutionary. Both at the Conference and during subsequent months he laid down a radical revision of Soviet policies both at home and abroad. He stated that communism and capitalism need not advance inevitably to open war. Communism would triumph in the end but it could do so by its innate superiority as a means of economic organisation. He also indicated that there might be several paths to the ultimate goal of communist society and that all countries need not slavishly follow the Russian model. This was clearly a concession to Tito and to more orthodox leaders such as Togliatti of Italy who was running a powerful communist party within the structure of parlimentary democracy.

Revolt in eastern Europe

The satellite states were already ripe for change and Kruschev's new line sparked off a chain reaction. The first sign of trouble came in Poland where rioting broke out in Poznan in June. The unrest soon grew into a national movement which swept back the popular, nationalistic Gomulka to the party secretaryship from which he had been dismissed by Stalin seven years before. At the same time the Russian general, Rokosovski, who had been installed by Stalin as Polish Defence Minister, was dismissed. At once the Russians closed ranks and Kruschev, Molotov and Kaganovitch flew to Warsaw to restore control. But the Polish communist leaders stood firm and the Russians had to accept a compromise which left Gomulka in power and allowed a general relaxation of social and intellectual controls in Poland. Things had gone further than Kruschev intended but he had to tolerate the new situation because of an even more serious challenge from Hungary.

In June 1956 the supposedly 'liberal' Prime Minister Gero had begun to carry through some cautious reforms. But the pace of change was too slow to prevent a full scale revolt in Budapest in October. The former Prime Minister Nagy was swept to power by an alliance of national communists, non-communists and army leaders. Within a day or two it became clear that the Hungarian revolt was not just an attempt to replace an unpopular leadership, but a full scale revolution which would reintroduce a multi-party system and take Hungary out of the Warsaw Pact. This the Russians could not afford to tolerate. Their troops swung into action and by 4 November the rebel government had been savagely crushed and a loyal communist régime under Kadar restored.

Budapest 1956

Kruschev versus 'the anti-party group'

The Twentieth Party Conference and the upheavals in eastern
Europe led to the final round in the power struggle in Russia.
Kruschev's rivals supported him in October and November but his
reputation had taken a heavy blow and by June 1957 Molotov,
Bulganin, Kaganovitch and Malenkov joined forces to out-vote him
in the Praesidium. However he had used his position as party boss
very carefully and had built up a formidable group of supporters
in the Central Committee. He therefore appealed from the Praesidium to the Committee and won a crushing victory over his enemies.
Malenkov, Molotov and Kaganovitch were immediately dismissed
from their posts in both the state and party structures and his other
enemies were all dropped within a year or so. In 1959 Kruschev's
absolute predominance was formally recognised by his assumption
of the premiership as well as the party secretaryship.

However he never became another Stalin. He had not been one of
the founding fathers of the revolution, nor did he have the personal
aura of the superhuman dictator. He was able to oust his enemies
from power, but he never liquidated them and some, especially
Molotov, remained unrepentantly critical. For his part, despite his
appalling record in the Stalinist years, he saw that purges and mass
killings no longer had a part in Russian society. Unlike Stalin he

tried to work through the proper channels of the party and government organisations and to this extent Russia had ceased to be a
totally arbitrary dictatorship.

Kruschev's Russia

Three years after the Twentieth Party Conference yet another meeting was called. This time the purpose was to give official recognition
to Kruschev's predominance and to announce his plans for the new
Russia. He was now optimistically announcing that Russia would
soon not only challenge the United States in heavy industry and
military potential, but that the Russian people could expect to enjoy
an unprecedented standard of living in a truly communist society.

It was a time of economic experiment. The old centralised state
planning authority, which had clogged rather than speeded economic
development, was replaced by 100 regional planning commissions.
There was a new drive to develop atomic energy and cultivate the
virgin lands. There was an attempt to reform the highly inefficient
heavy industries and in his efforts to rival the Americans Kruschev
was prepared to drop some of the constricting ideology of Soviet
economic theory. Hours were shortened and incentives increased,
while forced labour ceased to play any significant part in the economy.
Now that Malenkov was discredited Kruschev could afford – indeed
he was compelled – to adopt his old rival's policy of providing the
Russian people with a new range of consumer goods.

However the party leader's bubbling optimism could not disguise
important failures in the economy, of which the most dangerous was
in agriculture. At first his plans had done very well – between 1953
and 1958 there was a 50 per cent improvement in grain production
thanks to good weather and the first returns from the virgin lands.
However the country was still far behind America in productivity
and although the Russians' calorie intake was about as high as most
western Europeans', they had far less meat, fruit and dairy produce.
Paradoxically the greatest improvements came on the peasants'
private plots, not from the collectives or state farms. When Kruschev
tried to abolish these and force the peasants together into agricultural
towns from which they could work on huge state farms, he met with
the usual passive opposition. Production slumped in 1959 and the
new policy had to be almost totally abandoned. In 1954 Kruschev
had laid down that:

*We must produce more grain. The more grain there is, the more meat,
lard and fruit there will be. Our tables will be better covered. And*

L*

The new Russia
Morning exercises in a giant Russian watch factory.

if there is sausage and fruit, then people will say: give us grapes, and with grapes one must have wine and all sorts of other things. And all these are legitimate demands.

Certainly his years in power did witness an advance towards this goal of 'goulash communism', but he never succeeded in making Russia completely self-sufficient and in bad years the country was forced to import grain from Canada and other western sources.

Kruschev, the peasant's son, knew all about the grinding poverty of the old Russia and he realised that despite the industrial advances since the revolution, communism had still not given the people a sufficient improvement in their standard of living. As he shrewdly remarked in 1958:

Marxist theory helped us win power and consolidate it. Having done this we must help the people eat well, dress well and live well. You cannot put theory in your soup or Marxism in your clothes. If after forty years of Communism, a person cannot have a glass of milk or a pair of shoes, he will not believe Communism is a good thing, whatever you tell him.

Such a materialistic attitude was certainly in extreme contrast to the austere philosophy of Stalin and to the ideology of the Chinese communists. Yet it was a realistic recognition of the new mood of the Russian people and when Kruschev fell it was at least partly because he had failed to fulfill his own promises in agriculture and light industry.

The fruits of the revolution
A holiday by the Black Sea.

Some of the most objectionable features of Stalinism were also modified by Kruschev. The ordinary citizen was given a rather more secure position: the activities of the police were curbed and the law courts made less arbitrary. On the other hand persecution of the Church probably increased under his direction. and nothing was done to check sporadic attacks on the Jews. Students still had to spend 10–20 per cent of their time on political education. Kruschev himself was self-avowedly anti-intellectual and encouraged a concentration on practical subjects. Over 60 per cent of all students studied scientific and technical subjects – more than twice the percentage in the United States. The press, radio and television remained organs of propaganda and although a humorous magazine such as *Krokodil* was allowed to poke fun at bumbling officialdom, fundamental criticism of the régime could not be tolerated. Writers were freer but they were still open to pressure from the state. In 1958 Boris Pasternak, author of *Doctor Zhivago*, was forced to refuse his Nobel Prize and was thereafter hounded and humiliated as an 'enemy of the Soviet people'.

Yet, on balance, there was a considerable relaxation in Russian society. Even if he had wished it Kruschev could not have maintained the atmosphere of Stalin's day. Individual authors could be silenced but it was impossible to control the new social attitudes of the reasonably prosperous class of managers, technicians and party officials upon which the régime depended so heavily.

Kruschev and the outside world

Kruschev's Russia
The Soviet leader at the wedding of Valentina Tereshkova the first woman in space, and her astronaut husband.

In his foreign policy, Kruschev showed the same mixture of traditional attitudes and a new flexibility and freedom from ideology. He was very conscious of the great increase in Soviet power since the war. In some fields Russia led the Americans. They were the first nation to launch a space vehicle, the first to put a man in space, the first to send a rocket round the moon. They also controlled a vast

nuclear arsenal and Kruschev was still prepared to advance the Russian spheres of influence – in the Caribbean, for instance. On the other hand his actions showed a new sense of realism and even responsibility. He was aware that a rich and stable Russia did not have the same interest in the breakdown of the world order as Lenin and the early Bolsheviks; he was equally aware of the dangers of escalation into a nuclear war. Over and over again he stressed: 'one cannot propose to establish a communist revolution on the ruins of the centres of world civilisation'. It was this that led him to face American leaders at a series of summit meetings in America itself (1959), Paris (1960) and Vienna (1961) (see pp. 294–8). And it was this that led to the Partial Test Ban Treaty and to his retreat on the Cuban missile affair (see p. 298).

It did not mean that he pursued a 'soft line' even in Europe. He was particularly concerned to prevent West Germany controlling nuclear arms and to this end he sought to undermine the NATO alliance and to win recognition for the East German régime. Despite many attempts to settle its future, Berlin remained the most dangerous flashpoint in Europe. Outside Europe the Russians had more room for manoeuvre. This was especially true in the Middle East (see Chapter 14), but Kruschev soon found that Nasser was not prepared to play the part of a Russian stooge whilst pro-communist régimes in Iraq and Syria proved to be totally unstable. The most Kruschev could achieve was the disruption of the western alliances in the area and friendly though guarded relations with unaligned socialist régimes. And to win even this he had to tolerate the persecution of local communist parties.

In Asia he faced a similar problem. Certainly he established good relations with India, but India also accepted aid from the West and could not be wooed away from her neutralist position. Where communism did make rapid progress – for instance in Indonesia and Vietnam – the local parties had more in common with the Chinese than the Russians. In Asia and even more markedly in Africa, the Russians found it was no simple matter to win the friendship of ex-colonial peoples (see p. 286). Russia might be accepted as a source of aid but many leaders in emergent states echoed Nehru's words, spoken in 1962: 'They [the capitalist and European communist states] are changing, they are really approaching each other. The real difference today in the world is between the well-to-do countries and the underdeveloped countries. The other difference is a temporary one.'

The Sino-Soviet dispute

This distinction was an important factor in the most dramatic development of the Kruschev era – the rapid deterioration of relations between Russia and China.

The practical issues between China and Russia have a long history. They have disputed control over the Amur valley since the Russians first arrived in the Far East in the seventeenth century. There has been rivalry over Mongolia and the mineral-rich province of Sinkiang for several generations. More recently the Russians provoked ill-will by their depredations in Manchuria in 1945–6 and the Chinese communists were very keenly aware of the lack of support they received from Russia during the civil war (see p. 117). Even after 1949 they found that the Russians were extremely parsimonious with their aid and seemed more willing to help the neutralist Indians during the fifties. The Russian government was certainly not prepared to share its atom secrets with China and the Russians showed a contempt and fear of their Asian neighbours which was modified very little by their common ideology.

On top of this and closely connected with it were the ideological differences which developed in the mid-fifties. The world communist movement had always been dominated by the Russians for historical reasons, but once Stalin was dead Mao Tse-tung refused to accept that doctrine should be settled unilaterally by the Russian leadership, who lacked his own revolutionary experience. The suspicions of the Chinese were confirmed at the Twentieth Party Conference. They refused to accept that war with the capitalists was not inevitable or that atomic warfare would destroy socialism as well as capitalism, and they were dismayed by the lack of enthusiasm the Russians showed for promoting world-wide permanent revolution. Kruschev's retreat over Cuba and his backing for the Test Ban Treaty convinced them that he was a dangerous revisionist.

There was also disagreement on the nature of communist society. The Chinese saw across their borders an unhelpful neighbour which was beginning to enjoy the benefits of 'goulash communism' and was showing disturbing signs of succumbing to bourgeois social influences. The Chinese themselves were desperately poor by comparison, but they drew comfort from their ideological purity. Soon they not only denounced Kruschev's crude materialism but went so far as to claim that, with the introduction of the communes and the Great Leap Forward (see p. 345), China was actually nearer the achievement of true communism than Russia.

The tension between the two countries came into the open in the late fifties. After 1956 the Chinese turned to increasingly revolutionary internal and foreign policies just at the moment that the Russians were trying to re-assert their authority within the communist bloc. Inevitably there was friction and personal relations between the leaders and inter-party relations deteriorated steadily. The Chinese were particularly horrified by Kruschev's visit to America in 1959 and his apparently friendly contacts with Eisenhower. Their disapproval first took the form of attacks on Yugoslav 'revisionism', while the Russians replied by equally savage attacks on Albania, China's 'Stalinist' ally in Europe. By 1960, however, the fight was in the open. Russia withdrew her technicians from China, ruining a number of industrial projects, and Mao and Kruschev began to exchange public and personal abuse. Both sides sought to muster support for their line. The Russians appealed to the European communist parties against Chinese fanaticism, while the Chinese addressed themselves to Asian communists and to states such as Romania and Albania which were dissatisfied with Russian leadership for other reasons. They depicted Kruschev as a traitor to Marxism-Leninism and, in a variant of the Communist Manifesto of 1848, the Peking *Peoples' Daily* wrote: 'A spectre is haunting the world – the spectre of genuine Marxist Communism and it threatens you [Kruschev]. You have no faith in the people, and the people have no faith in you. You are divorced from the masses. That is why you fear the truth.' In the autumn of 1964 the quarrel seemed to be reaching its climax as Kruschev proposed, against the advice of many other party leaders, to call a meeting of all communist parties in Moscow in December in which he hoped the Chinese would be cast out of the communist bloc as heretics. But before the conference could meet there was a dramatic reversal of fortunes.

The fall of Kruschev
In the early sixties Kruschev faced mounting difficulties both at home and abroad. After 1959 agriculture failed to reach the planned levels and he never managed to provide the Russian people with the abundance of consumer goods he had promised. Yet his promises grew increasingly extravagant: Russia would beat America in all fields of production in a decade; there would be free public utilities; there would be more food, cars, televisions and refrigerators; there would be more houses; there would be tax reductions. But these things could not come fast enough and they could never come without cuts in defence expenditure which were bound to offend the powerful military interests. At the same time Kruschev was losing the confidence of his colleagues in other matters. They feared

the way in which he was becoming increasingly autocratic and his foreign policy was proving less and less successful. He had not solved the German problem and he had lost face over Cuba. Above all his fellow leaders believed that he was adopting an unnecessarily aggressive policy towards China. In October 1964, while Kruschev was out of the capital, the Praesidium decided that he must resign. He was summoned back and appealed to the Central Committee, but this time the vote went against him. The next day the astonished world heard that the man who had come to personify the new Russia had been replaced.

Russian policy after Kruschev

Once more Russia returned to 'collective leadership'. This time the most prominent men were Brezhnev (the new party chief), Kosygin (Prime Minister) and Podgorny (President). Kruschev went into peaceful and unrestricted retirement; it was the nearest thing to a constitutional change of government that Russia had ever enjoyed.

Despite the change of personalities there was little alteration in the country's overall policies. For a brief period it seemed that there might be a *rapprochement* with China, but the quarrel was not just a personal matter and the ideological battle was soon in full swing again. Early in 1969 Russian and Chinese frontier troops actually came to blows on the Manchurian border. Nor were the new leaders able to regain Russia's domination in eastern Europe. Romania, and to a lesser extent the other former satellites, showed increasing independence in their internal and foreign policies. (Romania disagreed with all her neighbours on the policy to be adopted in the 1967 Middle East crisis, for instance. For their part the new Russian leaders were more careful to consult their allies: in 1967 Brezhnev, Kosygin and Podgorny flew to Warsaw to co-ordinate attitudes towards the upheavals in China.)

Inevitably the dialogue with America, which Kruschev had begun to conduct, was interrupted and American commitments in Vietnam made it very hard to reopen. In fact it was not until the Middle East crisis in 1967 that the leaders of the two super-powers, Johnson and Kosygin, met face to face. Their meeting in America in July did not produce any dramatic changes, but there were signs that the Russians were anxious to reduce their conflicts with the West to a minimum, if they could do so without loss of world prestige. It appeared, in fact, as though the Russians were beginning to play a much more constructive role in world affairs. An outstanding example of this was the Russian mediation in the Indo-Pakistan dispute of 1965 which brought Shastri and Ayub Khan together at Tashkent in January 1966 (see p. 257).

This apparent shift in Russian policies left many people in the West quite unprepared for the Russian reaction to the Czechoslovak liberalisation in 1968. President Novotny of Czechoslovakia was the last of the old Stalinist leaders to retain a rigid hold on his party and his country, but in 1967 opposition to him within the Czechoslovak Communist party developed and more and more positions of power were filled by moderate socialists of quite a different mould. In the early part of 1968 these men led by party secretary Dubcek and Premier Cernik launched a programme of political liberalisation which won immediate support from the Czech people. Although the Czech leaders granted much greater freedom to the press and even promised to allow the emergence of some form of opposition to the government they continually re-emphasised their desire to remain within the eastern bloc and the Warsaw Pact.

However the Russians and their allies in the bloc were deeply disturbed by these developments. They believed that the Czechs were in danger of being swept along the path of the Hungarians in 1956 to a complete rejection of the Russian alliance; that the intellectual ferment in Czechoslovakia would spill over the frontiers and threaten the communist establishment in East Germany, Poland and even the Soviet Union itself; that the Czechs' desire to develop economic links with the West would split eastern Europe open and ruin their own plans for the Comecon area. Finally they probably totally underrated the unity of the Czech people behind this new style of communist leadership.

For some months they were content with threats and diplomatic pressure, but quite suddenly in August Russian troops supported by Poles and East Germans invaded the country and took over the government. The world outcry did not deflect the Russians from their course, but they found to their embarrassment that such was the support for Dubcek that it was quite impossible to form a credible alternative government loyal to Moscow. In the end Dubcek and his fellows were left in power, but forced to accept some pro-Moscow colleagues in positions of power (though not the fallen Novotny); to suffer the continued occupation of the country by Warsaw Pact forces; and to withdraw the great bulk of their liberal reforms. Yet such a solution could at best be a temporary situation. When the Russians finally achieved the dismissal of Dubcek as party chief in April 1969 there was another wave of student unrest.

Prague 1968
A young Czech waves a bloodstained flag in front of impassive Russian soldiers.

The Czechoslovak crisis did much to revive the old fears of Russian aggression amongst the western European states and provoked criticism from some western European Communist parties. On the other hand the Russians undoubtedly felt they were behaving defensively to protect their own sphere of interest much as the Americans might against a Communist regime in Latin America.

At all events the affair did not prevent Nixon and Brezhnev carrying on a series of talks to improve trade relations between the two countries and to agree on the limitation of arms. There also appears to have been a good deal of tacit agreement between the super powers in the face of the Middle East crisis in 1973, when once again neither of them had effectively controlled their allies.

Russian society

One of the factors which did make closer accord between the western states and Russia more difficult was the line which the Russian government continued to take against its critics and others whom it regards as a menace to the Soviet Union. After the fall of Kruschev the recurrent bouts of official anti-semitism and the persecution of intellectuals who criticised the regime grew steadily worse. The Russians claimed that western societies had their own rather different ways of silencing unacceptable views but such incidents as the exiling in 1974 of the world famous novelist Alexander Solzhenitsyn, produced a hostile reaction in the west.

Westerners would find conditions, even in Moscow and the big cities, rather austere. There is still a lack of new housing, especially for young married couples, and private cars, refrigerators and television sets are still luxuries rather than the possessions of every reasonably prosperous family as they are in America and much of western Europe. On the other hand young Russians have an excellent chance of further education especially if they live in a town. They will find full provision for all sorts of training beyond school, especially in science and technology and there is no real problem of unemployment. Russia certainly offers women greater equality of opportunity in both education and careers than western societies. Housing may be poor, but there are good public services and excellent medical care, at least in the towns.

Nor are the pressures to conform as oppressive or all-pervasive as they were under Stalin. In Russia as elsewhere the younger generations constantly adopt new standards even against the disapproval of their elders. Despite official criticisms, western influences such as pop music and Beatle haircuts have been eagerly accepted by Russian teenagers. Russian women have become highly fashion conscious and Russia and Britain have exchanged fashion displays, which provoked the following comment from the Chinese News Agency:

The swimming costumes, mini-skirts, evening gowns etc., all had the foul smell of the decadent bourgeoisie . . . The blatant peddling of these filthy things was described by the Soviet revisionist group as 'developing economical, technical and cultural ties' and promoting 'progress' and 'world peace'. These undignified performances held in the Sports Palace named after the great Lenin clearly show how far Brezhnev, Kosygin and the other renegades and scabs have gone in their degradation as revisionists. They show they are sliding further down the road of restoration of capitalism.

On a much more serious level the party itself has made important modifications in its social and economic thinking. In particular, under the influence of the economist Professor Liberman, they have cautiously re-introduced elements of competition and the profit motive into the economy.

The improvement in standards for some sections of society has emphasised the sad state of rural society. Fifty years ago five-sixths

The new Russia
*Western mini-skirts and
Asiatic designs in a
fashion show in Alma
Ata, capital of
Khazakstan.*

of the Russian people lived in the country; now the proportion is down to a half and the drift to the towns continues. However those that remain form the most depressed class in Russia. Many of them still live in conditions of extreme poverty. Their housing is often primitive by European standards and they do not have access to such good medical or educational facilities as the townspeople. Certainly they are the last section of society to feel the increase in consumer goods. The poor peasant has been a permanent feature of Russian society and the new leaders have still not been able to eliminate his disabilities.

The economy
Russia is the largest country in the world by size and the third largest by population. It stretches more than 5,500 miles across, a ten-day train journey. Most of the population lives in the western third of the country, but its sheer size still poses enormous problems. It has vast variations in climate and physical geography from tundra and forest to desert and mountain or the Riviera climate of the Black Sea coast. For all its size it is not a very favourable land for agri-

culture. Less than 30 per cent of the land is suitable for farming and only 11½ per cent for arable cultivation.

In other senses however it is well endowed. There are almost limitless supplies of timber and vast resources of coal, iron, gold, oil and other minerals. Great rivers have enormous potential for the generation of electricity. But Russian planners still face great difficulties. The full development of agriculture has been particularly pressing and rapid industrial growth has revealed inadequacies in both the road and rail systems. The failure of Soviet agriculture is the greatest problem of all since it both presents practical difficulties and brings the whole theory of collectivisation into question. Kruschev tried to solve it by opening up the uncultivated 'Virgin Lands' of Central Asia but the benefits were short-lived. The agricultural failure contributed to his downfall but his successors did no better. Grain had to be purchased from the West in the 1960s and again after the disastrous harvests of 1972 and 1975.

As long ago as 1932, the Russian author Lunacharsky wrote:

When we build the biggest blast furnace in Europe, when we complete the largest dam in the world, when we set up the biggest ball-bearing factory in Europe, each occasion is a great struggle won, a bloodless struggle. We are giving concrete proof that a planned socialist economy, even in a technically backward country with a low level of culture that has been enslaved for centuries by one of the most barbarian governments the world has known, can produce brilliant results in a short time . . .

For us war is an encumbrance. We have no need of it.

These words, which are worth comparing with those of John Kennedy at the end of the previous chapter, represent Russian attitudes at their most idealistic. There are of course those, in both the European communist and the western capitalist societies, who still believe that competition will inevitably take a more violent form, but the hopes and ambitions of most ordinary Russians probably differ very little from those of millions of other people all over Europe and North America.

An aggressive giant?
Massed Chinese militiamen on the march.

A Chinese family at the seaside.

The new China 19

In pre-revolutionary days the Chinese called their land the Middle Kingdom and regarded all other countries as mere tributary states. For over a hundred years this was the flimsiest fiction which could not conceal the fact that China was a helpless giant at the mercy of the industrialised nations. Today all that has changed. Despite enormous natural difficulties and the hostility or indifference of all the great powers, China once more occupies a central position in world affairs; has developed her own nuclear weapons; and is carrying out a great social and political revolution which may well rank, in the long view of history, as of greater significance and even more far-reaching in its human consequences than the revolutions in France and Russia which have hitherto stood as the great turning points in the history of the modern world. Certainly the transformation of modern China from its miserable state in the thirties is an outstandingly dramatic story even in the centuries' long history of that country.

China and the end of the war

By 1942, after the first desperate efforts and the headlong retreat into the hinterland, the war in China had settled down to a fairly static pattern. Both the nationalists based in Chungking and the communists at Yenan believed that the defeat of the Japanese could only be accomplished by outside intervention and they concentrated upon improving their own power prospects in the long term. For Chiang this meant stockpiling American military aid and preserving his troops from major combats. The communists received very little aid from outside and devoted their efforts to building up a network of guerilla bases and to propaganda work. They carried out considerable social and agrarian reforms in their base areas while in

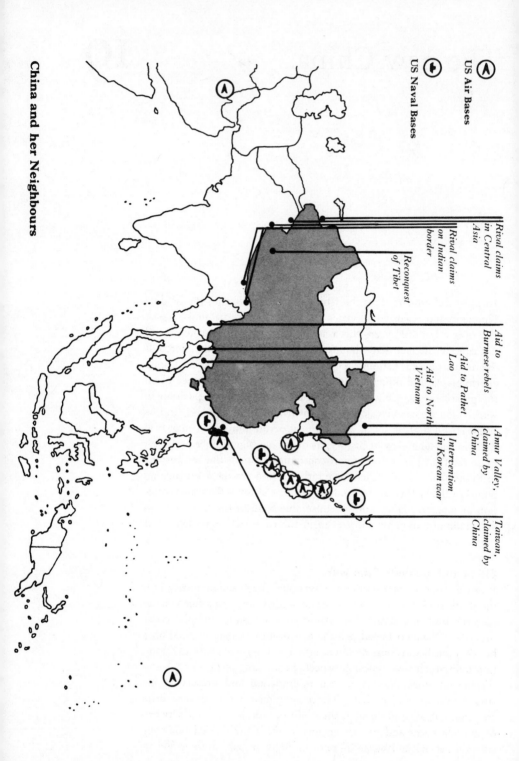

China and her Neighbours

US Air Bases

US Naval Bases

Rival claims in Central Asia

Rival claims on Indian border

Reconquest of Tibet

Aid to Burmese rebels

Aid to Pathet Lao

Aid to North Vietnam

Amur Valley, claimed by China

Intervention in Korean war

Taiwan, claimed by China

nationalist-held lands there was raging inflation and obvious government corruption. The communists made a good impression on American emissaries and the Americans continually tried to improve relations between Chungking and Yenan. This became even more urgent with the sudden collapse of the Japanese in September 1945, which was followed by a race between the two Chinese governments for control of key areas, especially in Manchuria. The Americans did manage to bring about the first face-to-face meeting between Mao and Chiang since 1926, but Chiang was quite unwilling to compromise and the Americans were left with the delicate problem of deciding upon their role in the civil war which was bound to follow. The same difficulty faced the Russians for Stalin was still far from sure that it would serve Russia's interests to side openly with the Chinese communists in a civil war which they seemed unlikely to win.

The civil war

The first round went to the nationalists. The Americans airlifted thousands of their troops to Manchuria and the Russians handed over the main towns to them after plundering all movable wealth. The communists, who had to move on foot, established a few bases in the countryside though the Russians, hedging their position, did pass on to them quantities of Japanese arms. Both the big powers were still interested in an *entente* between the communists and nationalists and in January 1946 General Marshall managed to arrange a temporary truce. The communists were prepared to accept this as a breathing space in which to strengthen their position and even to join a coalition government, but Chiang was sure that the whole weight of American arms would eventually be thrown in on his side and this led him to adopt a highhanded and provocative attitude. By the summer of 1946 open fighting had broken out again and the Americans were drawn into giving the nationalists more aid.

Despite this and despite the 5 : 1 numerical advantage with which they had started, Chiang's forces suffered a series of defeats. Corruption, mismanagement and treachery paralysed the nationalist leadership and demoralised the troops. In 1947 they suffered major setbacks in Manchuria and the next year the whole province was lost in a campaign in which a million men changed sides in four months taking with them quantities of American arms. During 1948 the communists began to win positional battles as well as the guerilla combats in which they had always been superior. In January 1949 the communists took Peking and in April they crossed the Yangtse and took Nanking. Though some people, including Stalin, believed that the communists could not win a complete victory and would have to be content with control of the north, the war was as good as over. By the end of the year all but a few pockets of nationalist resistance had been wiped out and the nationalist administration had evacuated with the remnants of its forces to the island of Formosa.

The communist success

Chiang's defeat had been rapid and spectacular. He had been one of the Big Five, enjoying the backing of the Americans and the recognition of the Russians. Numerically and technically his armies had begun with enormous advantages and yet he had lost almost everything in a few years. In retrospect it is easy to see that his whole structure was rotten. He relied for his power upon an alliance of warlords, landlords and financiers and this alliance killed any plans he had once had to check the inflation, put down corruption or carry out land reform. In the words of Mao Tse-tung's American confidant, Edgar Snow, Chiang

was no great tyrant, only a petty one; he failed not because he was Caesar or killed too many people, but because he killed too few of the right people; he never understood that his worst enemies were inside his own camp. Chiang was not resolute, only obstinate; not wise, only obsolete; not disciplined, only repressed; not original, only a scavenger among the relics of the past; not ruthless, merely vain – as none knew better than the greedy parasites who surrounded and finally consumed him.

The qualities which Chiang and his entourage lacked were just those which Mao and his colleagues appeared to have in full measure. The party contained a core of utterly dedicated and incorruptible leaders of the greatest ability; it possessed a reasonable record of resistance to the Japanese which was carefully inflated by an excellent propaganda machine. It supported a programme of social reform with great appeal to the peasants. It was in a position to appeal to sections of the middle class and the intelligentsia, who were opposed to Chiang's oppressive measures and resented outside interference in China's affairs. In personal terms their leadership was outstanding, with theorists and administrators such as Liu Shao-chi and Chou En-lai and outstanding guerilla generals such as Chu Teh, Peng Teh-huai and Lin Piao, all of whom had more than two decades of gruelling military and political experience. In fact the communists won not because of their narrow Marxist ideology, which had a limited appeal, but because they appeared to be the patriotic party – the only force which offered a genuine national renaissance.

There was one other factor of the greatest importance in the final decision. In the past China's political fate had often been decided by outside intervention and there is no doubt that Chiang Kai-shek believed that the intervention of the United States would save him. In this he was fatally mistaken for Truman and his advisers had a growing contempt for the administration of the Generalissimo, and although they continued to supply him arms and credits almost till the end, they absolutely refused to shed American blood in Chiang's cause, let alone employ atomic weapons as the nationalist leader hoped.

China and the communists in 1949

On 1 October 1949, thirty-two years after the Bolshevik revolution in Russia, Mao and the other communist leaders in Peking formally inaugurated the Chinese People's Republic. It is natural to draw comparisons between the two events, but in fact it is the differences between them which are most significant.

In November 1917 Lenin and his supporters seized power in a dramatic *coup d'état*. Their success transformed them from a small group of theorists and conspirators into the rulers of a great state. They lacked experience and commanded little support outside a few big cities. They only gained political and military experience and established their reputations in the country after a bitter civil war.

In contrast the communist leaders in China were men of enormous experience who had been national figures for years and commanded support all over the country. Even amongst those who did not support them there was initially general acceptance of their régime except from the numerically unimportant upper classes. They defeated their main enemies before coming to power and could begin their programme with far less internal opposition than the Bolsheviks had faced. They did have to face external threats, but unlike the Bolsheviks they were not completely isolated in a totally hostile world. The first steps in the revolution could be taken with the friendship and advice of Russia and her satellite states.

All these factors help to explain why the new government in Peking was so unlike that of the Bolsheviks. It could afford to tolerate a certain amount of diversity and could adopt a broad national policy rather than a narrow class or party one, at least at first. In all, fourteen political parties attended the preparatory constitutional congress and, although the communists dominated the meeting, two groups – the Left Kuomintang which had broken with Chiang and the Democatic

League which represented the middle-class intellectuals – did have some influence and even places in the government. Mao was at pains to show that his government represented the great majority of the people:

Who are the people? At the present stage in China they are the working class, the peasantry, the petty bourgeoisie and the national bourgeoisie; under the leadership of the working class and the Communist party, all these classes unite to build up their own state and they elect their own government to enforce their dictatorship over the jackals of imperialism, the landlord class and the bureaucratic bourgeoisie.

In contrast to the period of War Communism in Russia there was not an immediate attack on the middle class as a whole because, in Mao's words:

It will take many years for China to attain economic independence . . . To meet imperialist pressures and raise China from her low economic position, China must utilise all elements of urban and rural capitalism that are beneficial to the national economy . . . Our present policy is to control not to eliminate capitalism.

In fact from the very first there were two driving forces behind Mao's work. On the one hand he was a nationalist leader determined to give the country true political independence and economic development. For this task he needed a broad support beyond the confines of those ideologically committed to the Communist party. On the other hand he was a passionate and dogmatic revolutionary whose background had convinced him that ideology could overcome any technical difficulties and that any material gains China might make would only be worthwhile if it maintained the purity of its revolutionary Marxist creed. Sometimes these two forces have worked in harmony but at other times they have been plainly contradictory and this helps to explain the erratic course of Chinese policies at home and abroad since 1949.

The early years: foreign policy
After the brief period of intervention, post-revolutionary Russia was able to work out her internal problems in comparative isolation. In contrast China's internal transformation was carried out simultaneously with the development of a major role in world affairs.

In December 1949 Mao flew to Moscow and won from Stalin a military security pact and some economic and technical aid. The result was, of course, an even more serious rift with the United States which was exacerbated by the American refusal to acknowledge the communist government and their decision to re-equip Chiang's army and support his retention of the Chinese seat in the United Nations. Yet relations might not have been so bad had Mao been free to direct foreign policy as he wished. In the immediate future he was concerned with China's internal problems and the assertion of Chinese control over the 'lost provinces' of the old empire such as Tibet (completed in 1951). His hand was forced, however, by the defeat of the North Koreans by the United Nations forces (see p. 364). China had suddenly to pour in hundreds of thousands of men to support her routed neighbours and although China was doing Stalin's work for him she received very little in return – a fact that was not easily forgotten. All the same they did manage to establish a deadlock in Korea which convinced them more than ever that American technical superiority could be defeated by Marxism and mass armies and that the nuclear deterrent was all bluff. It was a theory that Mao had enunciated as long ago as 1945 and which he has held fast to ever since: 'The atom bomb is a paper tiger used by the US reactionaries to scare people. It looks terrible, but in fact it isn't. Of course, the atom bomb is a weapon of mass slaughter, but the outcome of a war is decided by the people, not by one or two new types of weapons.'

But it was a limited and costly success and provoked a series of American counter-measures. By 1954 the Americans had constructed a cordon around China from Japan, through Taiwan with whom Eisenhower signed a new security pact, to the SEATO group and the ANZUS pact in the south. The Americans were also preparing to step into the political vacuum left by the French in Indo-China.

In 1955 it seemed as though there might be open fighting in the Formosa Straits but in general the Chinese followed a softer line in the years after the Korean war. Certainly they did nothing to improve relations with the West, but in concert with the Russians they made a serious effort to woo the uncommitted nations in Africa and Asia. This effort reached its climax in 1956 at the Bandung Conference of Afro-Asian states when the shrewd and cosmopolitan Chou En-lai established good relations with neutralist leaders such as Nasser, Nehru and Sukarno, and seemed to endorse their desire to stand aside from European power struggles.

In fact this was not so. At this very time the Chinese were beginning to play a major role in the direction of the communist world strategy. In the great crisis of European communism in the autumn of 1956 Mao flew once more to Moscow to support and advise the Russian leaders. It was a critical moment in post-war history, for despite the united front the Chinese and Russians presented to the outside world, the two leaderships drew a quite different moral from the uprisings and by mid-1957 the great schism in the communist world had opened up.

The early years: internal policy
The communists were determined to carry out a drastic reshaping of Chinese society, but in the early years they were restrained from the excesses of the Bolsheviks by a realistic appraisal of their problems. The property of the leading nationalists who had fled with Chiang was seized and the state took control of major banking, public service and heavy industrial enterprises, but this was done slowly and with some compensation for the owners. The government wanted both the capital and the expertise of the middle class. However the middle classes could only be allies in the revolution if they behaved loyally. The government launched the Three Anti-Movement (to purge corruption, waste, and government inefficiency) and then the Five Anti-Movement (against tax evasion, bribery, theft of government property, theft of industrial secrets and fraud) in a conscious effort to wipe out traditional bad practices in government and business. And one way and another these policies began to take effect. In 1949 production was 30 per cent below the level of 1935; by 1952 it had crept to 15 per cent above and the really dramatic efforts were still to come.

Initially agriculture changed much more than industry and commerce. The Land Reform of June 1950 took over most of the property of the landowners, including the monasteries and shrines, and distributed it to the peasants. Unlike the urban middle class, the landlords as a whole were regarded as enemies of the people, but even they were left with some property unless they had been particularly repressive in the past. In the meantime the peasants themselves were encouraged to form marketing and producing co-operatives for greater efficiency.

There were also many other changes in society. The emancipation of women, who had occupied a lowly position in Chinese society, and the extension of education ranked particularly high in communist priorities. The last remnants of European privileges in China were abolished and all foreign investments were seized. The only exception to this was made in the case of Russia which continued to hold two treaty ports for some years and ran a number of joint-stock companies with the Chinese.

There was of course ideological reform. Many time-servers, who had joined the winning side in the last stages of the civil war, were ousted from the party and the ideological purge became particularly harsh during the Korean war (an interesting parallel with McCarthyism). There were constant propaganda campaigns, anti-religious demonstrations and a communist take-over of youth movements and unions. However there was comparatively little bloodshed. The Chinese – in contrast with Stalin's cruder methods – were concerned not only with coercion but conversion. To take an extreme case, they were determined that Pu Yi, the last of the Manchu Emperors and the Japanese puppet ruler in Manchukuo, should not only become a Peking municipal gardener but that he should be a *happy communist gardener*. The whole justification for the great powers of the state and party was the creation of conditions in which people could be reformed and

shake off the influence of domestic and foreign reactionaries, rid themselves of the bad habits and ideas acquired in the old society, not allow themselves to be led astray by reactionaries and continue to advance . . . toward a socialist and communist society . . . As for the reactionary class . . . so long as they do not rebel, sabotage or cause trouble . . . land and work will be given to them as well to allow them to live and remould themselves through work.
Mao Tse-tung

Mao's communism had become a form of secular evangelicalism, with Marxism-Leninism as a doctrine through which the human will can achieve anything: 'Of all things in the world people are the most precious. As long as there are people, every kind of miracle can be performed under the leadership of the Communist party.'

It was in this spirit that the first Five Year Plan was launched in 1953. Anything could be achieved if the people followed the right path, and the path chosen for them was a crash programme of heavy industry and collectivisation. The country was to follow the same pattern as Russia in the thirties, but it was starting from a lower level and it was planning to move faster, with even less attention to the

Backyard steelmaking
A small commune's works.

standard of living or individual interests of the people.

The difficulties were enormous and there was little outside help. People and equipment were driven ruthlessly in the battle for steel, cement and chemicals. It was, in Mao's words, 'the progressive exaltation of the human will over the rational analysis of the facts'. Inevitably it was accompanied by the extinction of most private enterprise in industry and further ideological attacks on those who were not willing to throw themselves, body and soul, behind the revolution.

Alongside the drive for heavy industry came collectivisation. Some agricultural reform was desperately needed. China was primarily an agricultural country but it was a net importer of food – caught in the vicious economic spiral which prevented the accumulation of capital to invest in modernisation and industrialisation. Once more the Chinese leaders chose to follow the Russian pattern and to push the peasants from individual farming, or at best small co-operatives, into full-scale collective farms. Moreover they achieved this with much less difficulty than Stalin had met in Russia.

The result of the first Plan was impressive. Between 1953 and 1957 there was an annual increase in industrial production of 14 per cent. Steel production alone went up by 300 per cent and coal by 200 per cent. Agriculture did not do so well – indeed it was hard pressed to keep pace with the annual increase of over 2 per cent in the population. All the same the leadership had grounds for satisfaction. It may well have been this that led them to ease ideological restrictions and allow freer discussion of China's problems. 'Let a Hundred Flowers bloom and a Thousand Schools contend' said Mao, but the intellectuals and the middle class took him too literally and within a few months the leadership quickly suppressed the tide of criticism which they had released. At the same time the crisis of European communism convinced them of the danger of allowing any further freedom to opponents of the party line. Instead they decided to launch a yet bolder and more rapid campaign to transform society – the Great Leap Forward.

The Great Leap Forward
The Great Leap Forward was a plan to telescope the whole process of social and economic revolution into a few years. The country was to be transformed:

Why can't 600,000,000 paupers by their own efforts create a socialist country rich and strong? The wealth of society is created by the workers, the peasants, the working intellectuals. If they take their destiny in their own hands, use Marxism-Leninism as their guide, and energetically tackle their problems instead of evading them, there is no difficulty in the world that they cannot overcome.
Mao Tse-tung

And this economic growth was to be accompanied by a social and political one in which, at one bound, China would overtake Russia and achieve a truly communist society.

The two sides of the revolution were to complement each other. Industrial production was to increase by 30 per cent in a year and steel production was to increase by 100 per cent, but this was not to be achieved only through the construction of new steel mills. The people were to establish backyard furnaces in the country and the suburbs and every man become a part-time steel maker. A mass movement of the people was to do what the experts and managers could never hope for by traditional methods.

M

It was to be the same in agriculture. China had to have more food both to feed the people and to earn foreign currency. This could only be achieved by new methods and new social organisation. Three-quarters of a million collective farms were to be changed into 24,000 enormous communes covering, perhaps, 10,000 acres and providing work for thousands of people. The land was no longer the property of the peasant or the collective, but of the whole people. To work more efficiently the peasants gave up their private plots and even their tools. Often they moved from their houses to communal dormitories and refectories and men and women, young and old, worked in the fields and workshops while the little children were cared for in collective nurseries. The family, like the other relics of the old order, was to be undermined and swept away. White collar workers and officials were made to work in the fields in their spare time so that they did not lose touch with the masses, and students and teachers joined together in self-criticism to maintain their ideological purity.

Improving agriculture
Experts instruct youths on a communal farm.

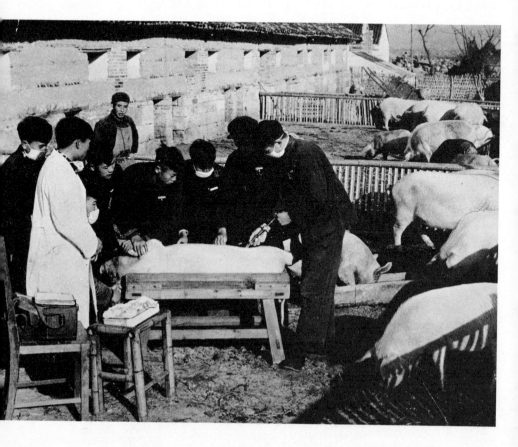

It was a dramatic social experiment, but it soon ran into trouble. The peasants resented the loss of their personal property and the crude attacks on their way of life. They treated communal property with little care and in many areas the amount of land actually under cultivation decreased. At this particularly inopportune moment China suffered from a series of natural disasters which ruined an already inadequate crop. By 1960 food production was down to the level of 1952 and millions of tons of grain had to be imported from Canada and Australia. Much of the energy devoted to industrial production was also wasted – steel output was boosted by the frenzied efforts of the workers, but enormous quantities produced in the backyard steelworks were useless.

The party leaders were forced to step back. In the first year of the Great Leap Forward Mao himself concentrated on the formulation of ideology from his position as Chairman of the party and passed the position of head of state to Liu Shao-chi. Liu and Chou En-lai, the Prime Minister, were also devoted veteran communists, but they realised that ideology had to be sacrificed to save the economy. The peasants were given back their gardens and houses and backyard steelworks were quietly abandoned. The commune structure was broken down so that the communes controlled only major pieces of capital equipment and overall planning, while day to day running of the farms and factories devolved upon the brigades, made up of groups of villages, or on the teams (individual villages).

The scheme had failed because of the passive resistance of the people. The revolution was going too far too fast and 'thought reform' had been unable to prepare the masses for the upheaval. Moreover, in practice the new mass methods were chaotic and wasteful. On top of this Mao and his fellow leaders had been unable to solve the problem of the experts and bureaucrats. Inevitably the managerial class were either drawn from old middle-class elements or began to take on new social attitudes as they were promoted. They became concerned with problems of efficiency rather than ideological purity. A major purpose of the Great Leap Forward had been to combat such attitudes and to keep alive in the hearts of the people and the party the revolutionary guerilla spirit of the thirties. Yet in the end the leadership had to admit that it needed the experts in the steel mills and chemical plants whether they were ideologically reliable or not.

Yet the Great Leap Forward was not a total loss. After 1962 production began to climb again and many features of the experiment were retained in a modified form. Certainly Mao and the other leaders did not renounce their plan to lead China into their version of the communist Utopia.

The Sino-Soviet dispute and permanent revolution

The main issues of the Sino-Soviet dispute have already been described in Chapter 18. However in the context of this chapter it is worth stressing once more the importance of genuine ideological differences. The personal rivalry between Mao and Kruschev was bitter but it was not decisive, as subsequent events have shown. The territorial disputes were of great significance, but they do not explain why the dispute broke out as and when it did. For this it is necessary to turn to the fundamental differences which had developed between the world views of the two leaderships. In the late fifties the Chinese were fighting their desperate battle against centuries of backwardness and the natural elements in the Great Leap Forward, while the Russians were enjoying the first fruits of technological development. The Chinese were seeking to create a new communist man – the product of relentless thought reform and social reorganisation – while Russia seemed to be slipping back to a new version of western bourgeois society.

In foreign affairs the Chinese saw the same contrast. In 1957 the Russians had launched their sputnik and developed effective inter-continental ballistic missiles. To the Chinese it appeared that the communist bloc at last had both technical and ideological superiority on their side and the time had come to launch the world revolution. But they found that the Russians refused to share their knowledge and reacted with horror to Mao's arguments that, ' If the worst came to the worst and half mankind died, the other half would remain while imperialism would be razed to the ground and the whole world would become socialist; in a number of years there would be 2,700,000,000 people again.'

In 1958 and 1959 China moved towards a new crisis in the Formosan Straits, crushed a rebellion in Tibet driving the Dalai Lama into flight to India, and began an open quarrel with India herself. During the same period, despite some setbacks, Kruschev was taking the first steps to lower tension between Russia and the western powers.

In 1960 the quarrel moved into the open at the 22nd Conference of the Russian Communist party and the Russians withdrew their much needed technical aid from China. In the Ladakh crisis (see p. 258) and the Cuban missile crisis of 1962 the rift between the two states was even more obvious and the two sides were soon openly denouncing each other. One advantage of the open breach for the Chinese was that they could bid freely for the leadership of the poor non-white nations of the world. China could hardly hope to over-throw her enemies in America or Russia yet, but she could try to spread permanent revolution through the Third World.

China and the Third World

China's bid for supremacy amongst the 'have-not' nations began well but soon suffered severe setbacks. There were many reasons why this should be. In South America the Chinese had very little to offer except their austere political philosophy. The area bred its own form of revolution and even Castro did not take long to decide that his best interests lay with the Russians however cautious they might be in their attitude to the United States. In the Middle East, too, the Chinese slogans could not compete with the solid economic and military aid of the two super-powers, even when, as in the 1967 crisis, the Russians seemed to have failed their Arab allies. Africa was basically more promising for the Russians had been singularly unsuccessful there and many African leaders could be expected to echo Peking's violently anti-imperialist line. Chou En-lai made two well-publicised tours and several countries – notably Mali and Tanzania – accepted small amounts of Chinese aid and some military instructors. But the emergent African states did not wish to be tied to China's world plan and found little relevance in Chinese experi-ences. It was a blow to Chinese prestige when Nkrumah's government was overthrown while he was in Peking and several Chinese missions have been expelled from African states for interfering in internal politics.

The most suitable area for Chinese revolutionary activity was obviously Asia itself. In their own continent the Chinese leaders employed a variety of tactics – with India open conflict, with Pakistan a temporary alliance of convenience, with Japan some tentative economic links. In all these Chinese behaviour seems to have been guided more by national power interests than international revolu-tionary planning. In Indonesia the Chinese-supported Communist party seemed to be on the point of seizing power in 1966 when a sudden reversal of fortunes led to the most disastrous defeat of a communist movement since 1945. Nor was this the only setback. By 1967 both the North Koreans and the North Vietnamese showed signs of moving out of the Chinese orbit in the dispute with the Soviet Union.

The most desperate challenge of all to the Chinese position in Asia was in Vietnam, traditionally part of the greater Chinese empire. The American presence in the southern part of the country and their bombing raids right up to the Chinese border provoked violent denunciations from Peking, but the Chinese were not able to give much aid to Ho Chi Minh and after the war a united Vietnam challenged rather than supported Chinese influence in South East Asia.

In fact from early 1971 onwards there were signs of steadily improving relations with America. In October of that year China at last was given her seat at the United Nations and on the Security Council and in February 1972 President Nixon visited China and the process of developing full trade and diplomatic relations began. Through enormous efforts the country had developed as a nuclear power on her own, but China's leaders were still very well aware that they needed trade and technical exchanges with the West and above all support in the face of the ever present Russian threat.

The great Cultural Revolution

The disasters of 1959 and 1960 led to a pause in the radical policies of Mao Tse-tung and probably a setback for Mao within the party itself. Unlike Stalin he had not wiped out the men who had made the revolution with him, and some of his closest collaborators were in favour of more realistic reforms. During the early sixties there was probably a good deal of tension within the leadership. Liu and Chou were dealing with the immediate economic problems while Mao was still exercised by the difficulties of reaching the ultimate goal of communist society. No doubt he was urged on by the problem of the succession to the leadership. Mao and his fellow leaders were ageing veterans and he was concerned that the next generation of leadership should not lack the guerilla spirit of the thirties and the purity of their ideology. He had before him the example of Russia, where, in his view, the revolutionary faith had been allowed to die out. He feared that the creation of a new class of functionaries and experts in China might have just the same effect. There was also the problem of China's position in the world, especially in the face of the American presence in Vietnam. The Chinese had come to fear that they might well be attacked by America, or even Russia and America, and that that attack might involve the use of nuclear arms. If this happened, Mao believed that China's only defence could be the hold of communism on the hearts of the people. Central government might collapse and a vast new guerilla war might have to be fought. At any rate the people had to be kept in a state of

The old leadership of China

Mao Tse-tung (centre), and Chou En-lai (left) with Lin Piao

ideological preparedness and all unreliable elements purged from positions of power. These problems appear to have brought to the surface many disagreements, both personal and ideological, within the top leadership and these in turn released the extraordinary forces of the 'Cultural Revolution'.

In 1966, the army press controlled by Defence Minister Lin Piao, launched the first attacks against those who disagreed with Mao's line. The first victims were members of the academic staff at the University of Peking who were denounced by their own students, but gradually more and more prominent men in the party and army were also identified as enemies of the revolution. Peng Chen, the Mayor of Peking, who had formerly been regarded as a loyal Maoist, was publicly disgraced and then the attacks in the papers and the wall posters in the streets of Peking turned upon Liu Shao-chi, the head of state and Teng Tsia-peng, the Communist party secretary. The vanguard of the Maoist attacks were the students and school-children of the Red Guard movement who marched, demonstrated and wrote the wall posters. Established figures such as Liu and Teng

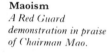

Maoism
*A Red Guard
demonstration in praise
of Chairman Mao.*

commanded support within the state and party structures, but the Guards denounced and intimidated local party officials and municipal officers. Managers, teachers and professors were overthrown by their subordinates and pupils and any individual who showed signs of succumbing to western influences, by wearing lipstick or expensive clothes or possessing small luxuries, was liable to be attacked. This was the answer of Mao and his group to the threat of those in the leadership at all levels who placed efficiency and expertise above ideology or who showed hankerings after goulash communism – building China's economy on false incentives of wage differentials and the promise of consumer goods. Mao was appealing back to the masses and seeking to break down the structure of the party and government and to rule through permanent revolution.

The result was mounting chaos in which it became increasingly unclear who, if anyone, was in control. Work stopped in schools, universities and many factories and the structure of government was undermined in the centre and the provinces. The young Red Guards exalted Mao in the most idolatrous way:

Every character in Chairman Mao's works is gold and every sentence is truth. Mao Tse-tung's thought is the red sun in the hearts of the entire Chinese people and of the revolutionary people the world over; it is their life line and their treasure. Fish cannot live without water and without Mao Tse-tung's thought how can people make revolutions.

The study of his thought became the only worthwhile knowledge and it was supposed to be equally effective in boosting production or improving efficiency in table tennis. But this was no way to run a country of 700,000,000 people. In Shanghai and Wuhan party officials and workers fought back and there was bloodshed in battles with Red Guards. In distant provinces in the south and west local governors refused to allow the Red Guards to operate, in defiance of Peking. During 1967 and 1968 the nature of the power struggle became even more obscure but there were some attempts, especially by Chou En-lai, to bring the Guards under control and turn the attention of the state and party to the desperate economic problem of supporting a population of 700,000,000.

In the end the extreme excesses of the Revolution were brought under control by the army and Lin Piao who emerged as Mao's successor. For a while the army came to play the dominant role in Chinese internal affairs, but there appears to have been a further

M*

split in the leadership. Perhaps Mao and Lin disagreed over the new policy towards America, perhaps Lin Piao was intending to stage a coup. At all events the official version claimed that he was killed in a plane crash in Mongolia in 1971 while fleeing from China after an abortive coup. The government remained apparently in the hands of Chou En-lai and his aides while Mao occupied an increasingly remote role as the fountainhead of ideological othordoxy conveyed to the people through his wife and her radical young allies. In 1976, however, the leadership was transformed first by the death of Chou and then of Mao himself. After a struggle for power which could only be remotely monitored from the West, Mao's wife and her supporters were disgraced and driven from power by an alliance of government officials and generals who appeared to be following the general policy lines laid down by Chou En-lai and Teng Hsia-ping, who regained major influence in the government of the new Chairman Hua Kuofeng and the generals and party members who supported him.

The economy and the future
The population of China has long been a favourite subject for statisticians. Its growth may be expressed as 15–20,000,000 a year or a net increase of 1,700 an hour, night and day.

The attitude of the Communist party has generally been that the population presents no problem. However in the mid-fifties even Mao went so far as to back a birth control programme and he admitted that: 'the population growth must be of great concern to us all . . . The increase in the grain harvest for the last two years has been . . . barely sufficient to cover the needs of our growing population . . . Steps must be taken to keep our population for a long time at a stable level of, say, 600,000,000.' But the campaign was badly received by the peasants, who placed great value on large families and regarded it as a sign that the government would be unable to feed them. The programme was soon dropped and then quietly resurrected, this time not as a way of controlling population, but of protecting the health of women. By 1974, with an admitted population of 800,000,000 the party switched to an open programme to control population growth.

Certainly the cause for concern remained. At present little more than one-ninth of the land is cultivated and although party experts have claimed that this could be doubled, the new lands would necessarily be less productive. The steady growth in grain production up to 1959 has apparently not been maintained consistently while the population has continued to grow. There is still a grave lack of machinery and chemical fertilisers and these are essential for improved yields. Yet this is not to deny what has been achieved. Conditions such as those suffered in 1959-60 would no doubt have led to widespread famine in the old days and China, unlike India, has had to struggle with her enormous problem without outside aid.

The country has reasonable supplies of coal and iron and of a number of special minerals including uranium in the distant province of Sinkiang. She lacks timber, oil and most tropical goods. For such a vast country the internal transport system is still underdeveloped and normal industrial progress has been held up because such enormous quantities of power, technical expertise and industrial materials have been devoted to military development and especially the construction of nuclear weapons. Yet in industry too it is important to recognise how much has been achieved especially considering the desperate state of the country when the communists took over in 1949. The communists have acted with a mixture of brute force and revolutionary conviction, but one way and another there seems no doubt that the lot of the ordinary people has been improved in material terms and that Chinese society had been purged of many evil features. With the tentative opening up of the country to foreign visitors over recent years a clearer picture of the sort of new society which the Chinese are trying to create has emerged. Some western commentators see it as regimented and utterly conformist. Certainly the Chinese have had no experience of the sort of freedom and parliamentary democracy which are so highly prized in some western societies. On the other hand they would claim to enjoy another sort of freedom and democracy where grassroots organisations, such as street committees, are responsible for social control and law and order and where political discussion and idealism permeate every aspect of human endeavour.

At all events the great part which the Chinese people must play in the future of the world is undeniable. In the nineteenth century the Europeans and Americans broke into the old Middle Kingdom and destroyed her political and economic structure. For more than half a century the country was a prostrate hulk. The regime of Mao Tse tung was the first this century to unite the country, to rescue it from exploitation by the foreigners, and to give its people material welfare and a faith in their own future. In Mao's own words the Communists have taught China to 'walk on two legs' again.

UN Membership

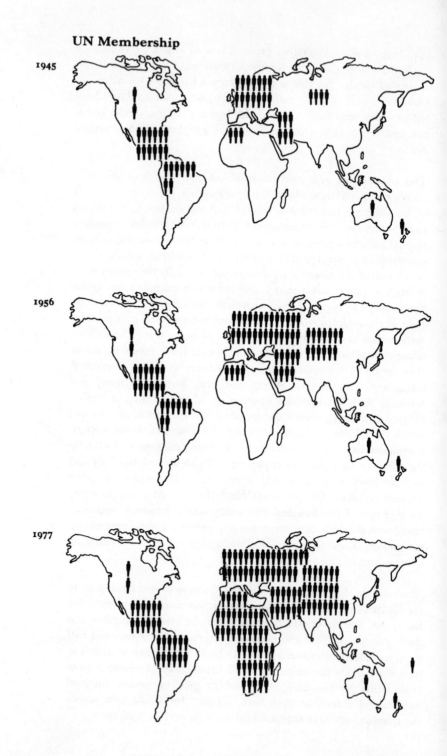

The United Nations and the post-war crises 20

When the delegates at the preliminary conference of the United Nations met in San Francisco it was the second time in little more than a generation that the leading nations of the world gathered together to create a body which aimed not only to keep the peace, but to improve the whole quality of human life. Like its predecessor, the League of Nations, the United Nations was born of a terrible war; like the League it incorporated the highest aspirations of men throughout the world; like the League it found all too soon that unanimity in principle was no guarantee of practical success. In some ways, the conditions under which it has had to operate have been even more difficult than those in the 1920s and 1930s.

The new body came into being at a time when the great split between communist and anti-communist powers was already threatening the world with yet another war and throughout its existence the United Nations has functioned in a world under the menace of nuclear destruction.

The creation of the United Nations
One advantage which the UN did enjoy was that it was not created as part of the peace treaties; indeed the first steps were taken to bring it into being long before the war was won. When Roosevelt and Churchill met in a warship off the coast of Newfoundland in August 1941 to sign the Atlantic Charter, they pledged their two nations to provide the world with peace, national self-determination, freedom of trade and the assurance 'that all men in all lands may live out their lives in freedom from fear and want'. In January 1942 twenty-six nations endorsed the Charter which became the Declaration of the United Nations. From this point onwards the allied

powers began to plan a new international organisation to replace the League of Nations.

The first detailed scheme was drawn up at the Dumbarton Oaks Conference which met in August 1944, under the joint sponsorship of the United States, the Soviet Union and Great Britain. Yet already there were important points on which the Big Three disagreed and these had to be thrashed out at the Yalta Conference in February 1945. At Yalta they decided that they, together with China and France, should be permanent members of the Security Council (see p. 163) and that they should each have the power to veto any decision even if it was approved by all the other members of the council. They also agreed that the constituent republics of the Soviet Union should have only three seats (RSFSR, Ukraine and Byelorussia), rather than the sixteen they claimed. In the spring and early summer a preparatory meeting of delegates was held in San Francisco, but it had none of the atmosphere of a great occasion which had accompanied the birth of the League. Roosevelt had just died; the war was still being fought and none of the big-power leaders attended. There was tension between the Russians and the other big powers and the smaller nations were angry about the veto decision. However, a general agreement was reached and in January 1946, the first full meeting was staged in London.

In the meantime much better progress had been made in the creation of various subsidiary agencies. The International Labour Office had continued to function throughout the war from Geneva and it was absorbed into the new structure. From 1943, the United Nations Relief and Rehabilitation Administration (UNRRA) was coping with the problems of refugees and emergency relief in the wake of the victorious allied armies. In the same year the Food and Agricultural Organisation (FAO) was set up and in 1944 the International Monetary Fund and the International Bank for Reconstruction (the World Bank) were established. So by the end of the war the basic structure of the peacekeeping body with associated functional agencies had already been created.

The structure of the United Nations
Despite the wishes of its founders, the basic structure of the United Nations turned out to be very like that of the League. There was a forum for the representatives of all member nations – the General Assembly; there was an executive committee with wide powers to take action on behalf of the other members – the Security Council; there was an international court, a series of special agencies and a

The United Nations

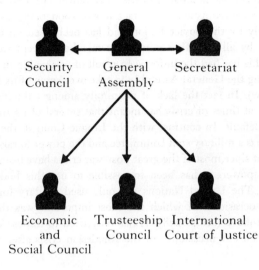

Security   General   Secretariat
Council   Assembly

Economic   Trusteeship International
and   Council   Court of Justice
Social Council

ILO FAO EEC WHO IMF IBRD UNESCO

permanent international civil service. Yet despite this formal similarity, there were important differences from the pattern of the League.

The Security Council
In an attempt to remedy the weaknesses of the League Council, the Security Council was given very wide powers. From the first it included the five greatest powers: the United States, Russia, Britain, China and France. In addition, there are a number of temporary members (their number has increased from six to eleven over the years) who sit for two-yearly terms, and, by convention, these include at least one representative from each of the world's major regions and blocs.

A most important feature of the Council has been the veto power of each of the permanent members. Originally this was meant as a protection against an alliance of the small powers, only to be used in very special circumstances. In fact it was soon being used indiscriminately by the Soviet Union and has been used on important occasions by all the other permanent members except the United States. This has had the unforeseen result of weakening the Council and forcing the General Assembly to take over some of its functions (see below). In fact the lack of unanimity amongst the big powers especially at times of crisis has meant that several of its rights have gone by default. In contrast with the League Council, the Security Council has a military staff committee and the power to raise its own forces, but since most of the great post-war crises have been between the great powers it has been impossible to use this body as was intended. The United Nations has only used military forces on a very few occasions, of which the most important was the Congo crisis of 1960–1 (see p. 278). It has only tried to impose economic sanctions on one occasion – in the Rhodesian crisis after 1966 (see p. 284).

Of course, the Council does have a number of other important activities apart from the ultimate powers of sanction and military action. Within the organisation it controls the election of the Secretary-General and the admission of new members. It has the duty to investigate disputes and to attempt to conciliate – as it has sought to do between India and Pakistan in 1947 and between the Netherlands and Indonesia in 1961, for instance. It has a responsibility for world disarmament and it acts as a world tribunal to which appeals can be made at very short notice. In all these functions it has had both its successes and failures. Yet it is probably true to say that it has played a smaller part in the maintenance of world peace than was expected whilst the General Assembly has been considerably more active than most people would have foretold in 1945.

The General Assembly

Unlike the Council, the Assembly is not in permanent session. It normally meets in September every year and its sittings last altogether no more than a few weeks. Every nation has one vote in the Assembly and may send up to five delegates to sit in it. Each year they choose a President who, with a powerful vice-presidential committee, controls the agenda. The delegates also elect members to the Security Council and to the other councils and committees where a good deal of the real work is done. The most important subsidiary bodies apart from the Security Council are the Economic and Social Council, which co-ordinates the work done by the agencies, and the Trusteeship Council, which is responsible for overseeing the proper government of the old League mandates. Most of the territories directly under its supervision achieved their independence by the mid-sixties, but the Council has also assumed a general responsibility for all colonial peoples and has consequently occupied an important but controversial role during the period of the break-up of the European empires.

In 1945, it was assumed that the Assembly would act as a general forum for international debate and as the ultimate authority to which both the Security Council and the Secretariat would have to answer. It was also given a vague power to recommend the form of settlement in international disputes. However this relatively limited role in the handling of international crises has been considerably extended by a practice known as Uniting for Peace, which was adopted by the Assembly at the beginning of the Korean crisis in 1950. The Uniting for Peace resolution stated that:

If the Security Council, because of lack of unanimity amongst its permanent members, fails to exercise its primary responsibility for the maintenance of peace and security . . . the General Assembly shall consider the matter immediately with a view to making appropriate recommendations to members including, in the case of a breach of the peace or an act of aggression, the use of force.

This method of getting round a big power veto combined with the change in the composition of the organisation has meant that it differs in many important ways from the intentions of the powers who founded it in 1945.

Membership
The break-up of the old colonial empires and the emergence of a host of new states in Africa and Asia has brought about a considerable shift in the balance of the organisation, (see p. 356). On issues where they can maintain their own bloc discipline the uncommitted nations of the world can prevent either the American or Russian power blocs pushing any motion through the Assembly. In this way the organisation which was meant to perpetuate big power control of world affairs, has become rather more like a genuine protective organisation for smaller nations.

The greatest anomaly in the UN membership was the fact that the

Chinese seat, including the permanent place on the Security Council, was controlled by the nationalist government in Taiwan from 1949–1971, when at last it was transferred to the Peking government. Another anomaly was removed in 1973 when both East and West Germany were given seats. Both of these moves were signs that the old hard lines were breaking down in the organisation, which could now claim to be a truly world-wide assembly representing almost the whole of humanity.

The Secretariat

The United Nations has about 4,000 permanent officials drawn from many nations, but, unlike the national delegates they are supposed to give their first loyalty to the organisation as a whole, not to a particular country. Most of them are involved in purely administrative duties running the vast UN Headquarters in New York, or applying various technical aid schemes and special funds throughout the world. However, the Secretary-General and his top aides have come to exercise a much more important role in world affairs. Far from being merely the top international civil servants, the Secretaries-General have all played the part of international statesmen and have taken the initiative in settling world crises. They have had no force at their command worth speaking of, and have always stood in danger of being disowned by their own organisation, but they have been able to wield considerable moral authority.

The first Secretary-General was Trygve Lie of Norway. In the difficult post-war situation he frequently sought to take the initiative, but his outspoken and generally pro-Western attitudes earned him the enmity of the communist bloc, especially after the part he played in the early stages of the Korean war (see p. 364). In the face of implacable Russian hostility he resigned in 1952.

His successor, Dag Hammarskjöld of Sweden, was an experienced civil servant, not a politician, and acted at first with much more caution. He won praise from all quarters for his organisation of the United Nations emergency force which cleared the Suez Canal after the 1956 war and patrolled the border between Israel and Egypt (see p. 237). As a result he was re-elected in 1959 and soon began to take a more and more active role in world affairs.

Hammarskjöld's most important initiative came in 1960. When the newly independent state of the Congo collapsed in anarchy and civil war, it was Hammarskjöld who brought the crisis before the Security Council and created an international army of 20,000 men to help restore order in a country more than four times the size of France. It was Hammarskjöld too, who called up the resources of the World Health Organisation and the FAO to try to prevent famine and epidemics. His activities brought criticisms from all sides and the Russians tried to have him replaced by a triumvirate of officials, but Hammarskjöld certainly commanded the loyalty of the majority of UN members. In the end he died in a mysterious air crash while still struggling to prevent the break-up of the Congo, but by that time he had established two vital principles. The first concerned the nature of the organisation:

It is not the Soviet Union or indeed any other big power who needs the United Nations for their protection; it is the others . . . I shall remain at my post in the interest of all those other nations, as long as they wish me to do so.
Dag Hammarskjöld refusing Kruschev's demand that he should resign in 1962

The second concerned the right of the Secretary-General to act on his own initiative:

The Secretary-General should be expected to act . . . without guidance in order to help in filling any vacuum that may occur in the systems which the Charter and traditional diplomacy provide for the safeguarding of peace and security.

After his death the Russians revived their idea of a triumvirate or troika, but the uncommitted states whom Hammarskjöld had defended joined with the western powers in insisting that Hammarskjöld's deputy, U Thant of Burma, should succeed him with full powers. He in his turn has built up the authority of his office, and when he threatened to refuse re-election in 1966, all powers, large and small, communist and anti-communist, persuaded him to stay on. In 1971 Kurt Waldheim of Austria succeeded him.

The agencies and the Court
A most important part of the United Nations has been the system of functional agencies (see p. 359). Most of the agencies are simpler and specialised versions of the central body with assemblies, councils and secretaries or directors-general. Like the central body they also depend upon co-operation from their member states for their success. They can gather together all the necessary information and resources and have plans drawn up by the world's foremost experts, but a project, for instance the control of locusts, may founder on the

obstructionist and short-sighted attitude of one small member state. All the same, the achievements of the agencies in non-political fields have been one of the brightest spots in the history of international affairs in the past generation.

The International Court of Justice which succeeded the League's Permanent Court of Justice at the Hague has not had such a happy history and has been noticeably less successful than its predecessor. The difficulty has been that few of the major post-war problems could be solved by a judicial decision and even where they could, few states have been prepared to accept the ruling of the Court unconditionally. Its most important decision was to reaffirm South Africa's jurisdiction over the mandate territory of South-west Africa in 1965. This controversial judgement, made on the narrowest of majorities, largely discredited the Court in the eyes of the African and Asian states.

The United Nations and the post-war crises
The United Nations was the product of a terrible war and even before its headquarters had been established in New York its future was being jeopardised by the split between Russia and the western powers. As early as January 1946, there was a dispute between Russia and the other powers over the presence of Russian troops in northern Iran and from then onwards the Russian representatives blocked motion after motion in the Security Council by the indiscriminate use of their veto. Partly as a result of this the United Nations was either not consulted on or failed to provide a solution to such post-war trouble spots as Kashmir, Trieste and Palestine. As the cold war become more and more open both the Security Council and the Disarmament Commission were almost immobilised.

This unhappy development reached a climax in 1950. At the beginning of the year the Soviet Union began to boycott the Council because they had failed to have the Chinese seat transferred to the communist government in Peking. They were still maintaining this boycott when the North Koreans began their invasion across the 39th Parallel. The Council at once declared that this was an act of aggression and approved the dispatch of a predominantly American army to South Korea. Eventually sixteen nations sent forces to fight in the United Nations force and forty-five gave some sort of aid. As a result the independence and territorial integrity of South Korea were preserved. However, delegates were well aware that this had only happened because of Russia's absence. In August 1950, Russia returned to the Council and their representative used his position as chairman of the Council for the month of August to paralyse it once more. The result was the Uniting for Peace motion (see p. 361) which passed the Assembly by 50 votes to 2 with 2 abstentions. This was a qualified success for the United Nations but it was followed by a period in which Russia harassed Trygve Lie into resignation and denounced the Uniting for Peace motion, while the McCarthyites in America were attacking the organisation as a hotbed of communism.

The next great tests for the organisation arose almost simultaneously in the autumn of 1956. First in late October came the Anglo-French landing at the Suez Canal. This time it was the two western powers who tried to paralyse the UN by the use of their veto powers and the Uniting for Peace machinery had to be turned against them. By a majority of 64 votes to 5 with 15 abstentions the Assembly demanded a cease-fire. On 3 November the invaders, under diplomatic pressure from all directions but especially from the United States and the Soviet Union, agreed to withdraw. By the 15th, a hastily assembled UN force moved in to clear the canal and separate the Israelis and the Egyptians. The whole operation was extremely efficient and effective, and a token UN force was left to patrol the Egyptian side of the border with Israel. It might well have been regarded as a major success for the UN had it not coincided with a crisis of a very different nature.

On 2 November the Hungarian rebels appealed for help against the Russians (see p. 319). Yet again Uniting for Peace was used but the Assembly could do no more than appeal for a cease-fire. A few months later an investigating committee of the Assembly condemned the Russians for open aggression in Hungary. But these motions could not disguise the fact that the United Nations had been totally ineffectual in the Hungarian crisis. Britain and France had been checked because both super-powers opposed their action but when the super-powers were divided there was almost nothing that the UN could do.

Four years later the operation in the Congo seemed to suggest that in some areas at least the UN could play a really vital role. Under the initiative of the Secretary-General a large force was raised and though the Congo operation came under criticism from many directions there can be very little doubt that the people of the Congo would have suffered even more if the polyglot army of Indians, Ghanaians, Nigerians, Irish and many others had not been there.

Yet during the 1960s this promise of a really strong world organisation has not been fulfilled. The organisation has failed to bring about any reduction in world armaments. It played a negligible part in the Cuban crisis and despite the efforts of U Thant it has not been able to prevent the escalation of war in Vietnam. In 1966 for the first time it imposed economic sanctions against the rebel government in Rhodesia. All members were supposed to apply them, but one, South Africa, openly stated that it would not co-operate and the sanctions failed to produce the immediate collapse of the rebel government.

Perhaps the most serious setback of all came in June 1967. Relations between Israel and her Arab neighbours were worse than at any time since 1956 (see p. 243) and Nasser ordered the UN emergency force which patrolled the border with Israel to withdraw from Egyptian territory. To the amazement of many outsiders, U Thant almost immediately complied and within a few days a full-scale war swept across the border they had been guarding. The United Nations was unable to prevent the war, to stop it until the Israelis had reached all their main objectives, or to draw up a satisfactory new settlement

The UN in action
A Greek doctor working for WHO instructs young Congolese.

for the area. U Thant's withdrawal seems to have been brought about not only by his uncertainty about the legal position of his force, but because the states which had provided the soldiers were threatening to withdraw them unilaterally; whatever the reason it has undoubtedly done a good deal to discredit the UN as an effective peacekeeper. Once the war broke out the organisation was hampered by the fact that the communist bloc gave their full support to the Arabs whilst the western powers were committed to preventing the destruction of Israel. Yet again this fatal division left the organisation impotent. On the other hand the organisation was given an important new role in peace-keeping in the area after the 1973 war (see pp. 244-5).

The United Nations and the world
At Yalta, Roosevelt claimed that with the creation of the United Nations there would 'no longer be any need for spheres of influence, for allies, for balance of power, or any other of the special arrangements through which in the unhappy past, nations strove to safeguard their security or promote their interest'. In fact, the post-war world has witnessed the creation of huge global security pacts such as the Warsaw Pact and NATO; there have been wars or threats of wars in almost every quarter of the globe; and looming over all humanity the possibility of an ultimate nuclear cataclysm.

The United Nations has been able to do comparatively little about these tragic developments, but this is not to say that it has been a complete failure. Certainly by comparison with the League it has achieved some qualified success. It has seldom been completely ignored and by-passed as the League so often was, and it has retained the membership of almost all the great powers. Despite setbacks its functions have been evolving and growing rather than stagnating or retreating as the League's did. Above all it still exists twenty-odd years after its creation and is still a vital centre of world affairs. Twenty years after the creation of the League, that body was falling apart and the whole of Europe was plunging into war.

Its real weakness remains, as Harold Macmillan pointed out in 1962, that: 'The United Nations can never be made to work unless political conditions can be created in the world which allow the Security Council to operate not as a body permanently divided, but gradually as a team'. Under these conditions it might perhaps be able to fulfil the high aspirations of its charter.

Children of two worlds

The Indian child is the older of the two.

Postscript: what sort of world?

A great deal of this book has been concerned with political rivalries and military alliances which have split the world in the last fifty years, but the deepest divide in the world today is not ideological, or racial, or religious, or military. It is simply the gulf between wealth and poverty. It is reflected in every aspect of human life:

	USA	India
Calories per head per day	3,200	1,800
Doctors per 10,000 people	12	2
Literacy rate (per cent)	99	19
Cars per 1,000 people	390	1
Population in agriculture (per cent)	12	70
Population in towns (per cent)	70	20

What is even more disturbing is the fact that the differences between the rich and poor are growing greater. The FAO planners reckon that the annual average income in the underdeveloped lands is about $133 per head while in the industrial states it is $1,500. But in 1985 the Indian level will probably still only be a miserable $160 while the Americans could be enjoying $5,000 a head. Most people in the developed lands are scarcely aware of the pockets of deprivation in their own societies; the poverty of the other world must therefore be almost beyond comprehension.

The problem of population and food
The greatest single problem of the poor nations is the most basic: food. In October 1966 Dr Sen, the Director-General of FAO, introduced the Indicative World Plan for Agricultural Development with these words: 'The next twenty-four to twenty-eight years are going

to be crucial . . . if the rate of food production cannot be significantly increased, we must prepare for the Four Horsemen of the Apocalypse.' He was not overdramatising the situation, for during the next twenty years the population of the world will probably increase from 4,000,000,000 to 6,000,000,000 and by far the largest part of that increase will be in those countries which are already suffering from food shortage and overpopulation. The sheer size of the population is hard to grasp: today there are more people alive than existed in the whole of man's history up to this century and the net increase is 5,000 an hour and accelerating.

The first problem is to feed these new mouths. In the autumn of 1966 the Prime Minister of India had to appeal to all her people to eat a little less so that *fewer* of their compatriots would starve to death in the coming months. At the same time it was costing the United States something like $1,000,000 a year to destroy food surpluses. Yet even if the surpluses of the rich could be given to the poor the problem would not have been solved. In the words of the 1966 FAO report: 'Sending your rice pudding to the starving millions and large scale efforts to harness charity to meet the world's food needs can make a valuable contribution, but a final solution cannot be found through a piecemeal approach.' In fact the only solution is to create a situation in which the poorer nations can feed themselves or can earn enough money to pay for their imports. At present they can do neither: India has over 70 per cent of her population engaged in agriculture, but all their efforts cannot produce enough food. And in the meantime the raw materials she exports are not increasing in value as quickly as the imports she needs to survive. Cotton and jute are being challenged by synthetic materials and tea and tropical luxury foods are sold overseas to the people of the rich nations whose populations are only growing slowly.

Eighteenth-century Britain fed her growing population by improving irrigation and drainage, by experimenting with new crops, by selective stock breeding and by the use of new fertilisers and machinery. These things could all be of immense value to the developing lands today but they all require capital and technical knowledge which are both in desperately short supply. Moreover the problem grows remorselessly every year. In 1950 there were probably no more than 3,000 tractors in the Middle East. Today there are perhaps 90,000 but if FAO's plans are to succeed there will have to be at least 300,000 more within the next two decades.

In 1977 it was clear once more that food supplies were falling

behind population growth. There was more than ever a consciousness of the imminent shortage of all commodities including food
and of the tremendous wastage for which the industrialised states
are largely responsible.

Industrial development

When the British population was surging upwards in the eighteenth
and early nineteenth centuries the process was accompanied by the
growth of the towns and a rapid development of trade and industry.
In these circumstances the new population was actually an advantage,
providing as it did both a labour force and an expanding home
market. Britain and the countries which followed her in industrial
expansion now dominate world commerce and manufacture. By far
the greatest part of the world's industrial strength can be found in
about half a dozen areas – California and north-east America, north-
west Europe and central Europe, Japan, west-central Russia and
north-east China. North America, western Europe and the Comecon
produce 85 per cent of the world's steel, North America and western
Europe alone produce 85 per cent of the world's cars, and North
America, western Europe and the Comecon produce well over two-
thirds of the world's energy supplies.

The developing countries are therefore not at all in the position of
Britain 200 years ago. Their infant industries lack capital, but, even
when they do develop, they are faced with competition from the
giant corporations of the technically developed countries. On the
other hand when the developing country has some natural wealth it
is developed by foreign companies and a good deal of the profit
syphoned off.

Yet the way forward for the less industrialised states must be through
co-operation with the rich countries. What is needed is aid without
strings and massive investment not only in mining or commercial
plantation farming, which bring quick returns, but in basic industries,
especially those which can be integrated with the agricultural pattern
of the country.

Education and society

A third problem of development is cultural. The transition of Britain
from an agricultural to an industrial state took place over more than
a century under relatively favourable conditions. The increase in
population, due largely to a decrease in the death rate though with
some increase in births, took place within a context of economic and
social evolution. As a result the increase slowly levelled out as the

The Growth of World Population

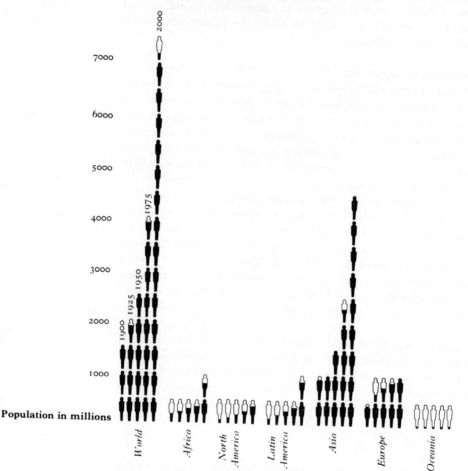

birth rate fell to match the death rate.

In the less developed countries this has not happened because population changes have been revolutionary. For instance in some places the population pattern has been disturbed by the introduction of some Western medical discovery. In Ceylon the death rate per thousand fell from twenty-two to twelve in the course of seven years thanks to DDT spraying which wiped out the malarial mosquito. But this was much too short a time for a cultural readjustment and the birth rate remained at about forty per thousand. The only difference was that many more children lived to adulthood. In the same way an increase in food supplies or the development of industry and urban life may merely lead to a proportionate increase in the popula-

tion. In many of these societies large families are still regarded as
socially desirable, in many more there are religious objections to
birth control. Above all it is very difficult to educate people in
methods of family planning where most adults are illiterate and there
is a chronic shortage of clinics and doctors. Under these circumstances
it is hardly surprising that some governments have been tempted
as the Indians have by the drastic idea of compulsory sterilisation.

In fact all the problems of developing poor societies make democratic
and evolutionary methods seem a luxury. To overcome traditionalism
and ignorance the methods of Stalin or Ataturk may sometimes seem
to be the only answer. The temptation, too, is to divert a deprived
and discontented people with an aggressive nationalist foreign
policy as Sukarno did in Indonesia. Poverty and political extremism
all too often go hand in hand.

The problems of development
Not surprisingly, in a world so full of poverty, planners have concentrated on the problem of development towards industrialised
society and to a better balanced food-population ratio. But many
people have now come to see that the conquest of the subsistence
problem is not in itself enough. The rich western societies have their
own problems and the developing countries are running into them
as they advance to a materially superior level.

The first problem is that poverty, unlike starvation, is a comparative
environmental matter. Most of the poor in Britain or the United
States are not poor in the Indian sense, but they still suffer from a
sense of deprivation because they live in a rich society. Their suffering is made worse when they also suffer racial discrimination as the
Negroes do in the United States. In some senses poverty is more
bearable where the whole society is poor.

A second problem is the loss of values, of individuality and of social
stability which often comes with industrialisation and urbanisation.
This is true even in a country like Britain where cities have developed
fairly slowly; it is more noticeable in the United States which had
eleven cities of over a million people in 1900 and forty-nine in 1950;
it is most true in Africa and Asia where many individuals are drawn
straight from a stable tribal society into the life of huge new cities
like Johannesburg. The historian Arnold Toynbee has painted a
vivid picture of this process:

People herded together in mammoth cities without social cohesion . . .

having their individuality ironed out of them by the demand for
docile employees to serve mammoth organisations private and public
... The country people crowding into the cities of the United States,
Australia, Indonesia, Pakistan, Peru, Mexico, and Saudi Arabia
alike ... the children of peasants and shepherds living in shanty
towns.

This is not just a problem of shanty town poverty. Many American sociological studies have pointed out the pressure to conform in wealthy middle-class society. Others have traced the increase of both crime and neurotic illness in the big cities. The naturalist Konrad Lorenz has shown that when rats and other animals are crowded together their behaviour patterns change and they become more aggressive even though they are well fed. There are good reasons to believe that men are likely to react in the same way.

In the wealthy societies, too, there are many pressures against the proper functioning of democracy. The sheer complexity of administration produces powerful bureaucracies and more and more state direction in even the details of human life. The need to conform, to co-ordinate, to organise on a grand scale leave less and less room for individuality. Indeed an answer to all these social problems may be in a scientifically controlled, test-tube society such as that prophetically described by Aldous Huxley in *Brave New World* but to many people this would seem to be a negation of humanity itself.

The problem of destruction

Twentieth-century man appears to be the highest living form at the end of millenia of evolution and there is at least a hope that scientists and doctors, economic planners and psychologists will be able to overcome the problems of both poverty and wealth – even though this may mean accepting quite new concepts of human existence. But in the meantime man has also to live with the constant threat of destruction by his own sophisticated war technology. Even before Hiroshima eminent scientists, such as the seven signatories of the Franck Report and the great nuclear physicist Niels Bohr, warned the American government that the use of the bomb would start a terrible arms race with unforeseeable results. In fact within a dozen years the even more destructive hydrogen bomb had been discovered, world range had been achieved with the inter-continental ballistic missile, and there were three atomic powers. Even at this stage while the race was only between Russia and America and the danger of war by mistake was relatively controlled, the mere testing of bombs was a danger to humanity. Radioactive fall-out can cause bone cancer and leukaemia and it can also cause genetic changes. Already many children have been born defective because of fall-out and as early as 1958 the zoologist Curt Stern wrote, 'By now everyone in the world harbours in his body small amounts of radioactivity from past H. bomb tests: "hot" strontium in bones and teeth, "hot" iodine in thyroid glands . . .'

It was in recognition of this awful danger that Russia, America and Britain promoted the Partial Test Ban Treaty in 1963, but their tests did not halt completely and, what was worse, proliferation continued. France became a nuclear power in 1961 and China in 1964. In 1974 India exploded an atomic bomb and many other countries from Sweden and Switzerland to Japan and Israel could soon achieve nuclear capacity. So the problem becomes more dangerous and more complicated. Russia and America have now such complex and massive armouries that neither could escape the other's attack, but the aggressor would in his turn be unable to prevent the counter-blow. Both are now concerned with defence systems to deal with China and there is always the danger that some form of nuclear weapons might be introduced into the Middle East arms race.

The postscript of a book on the development of the world since 1918 could hardly be optimistic without wilfully ignoring the awful challenges which face mankind. In the face of these we cannot say there is nothing mankind can do; but we must recognise that Dr Sen's words (p. 369) apply to a wider context: the next generation will be decisive. Either we resolve these problems or face the Four Horsemen of the Apocalypse.

Books for further reading

This list is not intended to be all-inclusive. I have not mentioned standard textbooks but most of my suggestions are readily available, often in paperback.

General
The following are primary works of reference for a study of modern world history: *Whitaker's Almanack*, *The Statesman's Yearbook* and *Keesing's Contemporary Archives*. Other useful general books include: D. W. Crowley, *The Background to Current Affairs*; A. Boyd, *Atlas of World Affairs*; J. P. Cole, *Geography of World Affairs*; M. Gilbert, *Recent History Atlas*; and B. Catchpole, *A Map History of the Modern World*.

Introduction
D. Thomson, *Europe since Napoleon* provides a good introduction and an excellent source of reference for most of the period on European affairs. A. J. P. Taylor, *The First World War* is probably the best short introduction to the war. The First World War produced a good deal of first class literature: *Goodbye to All That* by Robert Graves and *All Quiet on the Western Front* by E. M. Remarque are 'anti-war' novels written respectively from a British and a German viewpoint; *The Men Who March Away*, ed. Ian Parsons, is a collection of some of the best First World War poetry.

Chapter 1
D. Thomson, *Europe since Napoleon*; E. J. Passant, *A Short History of Germany*; B. Catchpole, *Twentieth Century Germany*; and *Portraits of Power* (on Kemal) by G. Ayling.

Chapter 2

On America, Hugh Jones, *Woodrow Wilson and American Liberalism*. On Britain there are two large books which can be used for reference: C. L. Mowat, *Britain between the Wars* and A. J. P. Taylor, *Britain 1914–45*. C. L. Mowat also provides an excellent short biography of the outstanding British politician of the period in *Lloyd George*. The social effects of the war on Britain are covered in A. Marwick, *The Deluge* and the Irish troubles in E. Holt, *Protest in Arms*. France is dealt with very adequately by P. Holland, *Twentieth Century France* and more fully by A. Cobban, *History of France Vol. III*.

Chapter 3

The best short introduction is probably S. Pickering, *Twentieth Century Russia*. The revolutionary period is also covered very well in C. Hill, *Lenin and the Russian Revolution*. I. Deutscher, *Stalin* is long but well worth referring to. The novels and stories of G. Sholokhov give some excellent background on the revolutionary period, as does B. Pasternak, *Dr. Zhivago*. A vivid picture of the great purge trials is conveyed by A. Koestler, *Darkness at Noon* of the labour camps in the novels of Alexander Solzhenitzyn and G. Orwell, *Animal Farm*, is an outstanding parable of the revolution and its aftermath. See also B. Catchpole, *A Map History of Russia* for maps of the whole period.

Chapter 4

For a very brief outline R. Nye and J. Morpurgo, *A History of the United States*, Vol. II. The outstanding work on Roosevelt is A. Schlesinger, *The Age of Roosevelt* but there is a short introduction in J. A. Woods, *Roosevelt and Modern America* and C. P. Hill, *Franklin Roosevelt*. The novels of Scott Fitzgerald and the *Grapes of Wrath* by J. Steinbeck help to fill in the social background as does *The Aspirin Age*, ed. Isabel Leighton.

Chapter 5

See Chapter 2 above. There are introductory accounts in D. Thomson, *The Twentieth Century* and E. Reynolds and N. Brookes, *Britain in the Twentieth Century*. Ronald Blythe, *The Age of Illusion* and R. Graves and A. Hodge, *The Long Weekend* give an account of social developments. G. Orwell, *The Road to Wigan Pier* and *Coming up for Air* and J. B. Priestley, *English Journey* convey something of the atmosphere of the thirties.

Chapter 6

On Italy, C. J. Sprigge, *The Development of Modern Italy*; C. Hibbert,

Mussolini; C. Bayne Jordan, *Mussolini and Italy*. On Germany see above, Chapter 1, and in addition B. Elliot, *Hitler and Germany*; H. Mau and H. Krausnick, *German History 1933–45*. Two longer but very valuable accounts of Nazi Germany are A. Bullock, *Hitler: a Study in Tyranny* and W. Shirer, *The Rise and Fall of the Third Reich*.

Chapter 7
R. Storry, *A History of Modern Japan* is a first rate introduction. The best short book on China at this time is R. North, *Chinese Communism*. Rather longer but also very useful are C. P. Fitzgerald, *The Birth of Communist China*; O. Clubb, *Twentieth Century China*; and H. Macaleavy, *The Modern History of China*.

Chapter 8
National histories mentioned above mostly contain sections on foreign policy. D. Thomson, *Europe since Napoleon* and E. H. Carr, *International Relations between the Two World Wars* give straightforward accounts of the period. M. Gilbert, *Britain and Germany between the Wars* is an excellent short account. L. Snellgrove, *Franco and the Spanish Civil War* is a good introduction; H. Thomas, *The Spanish Civil War* is a very full analysis. E. Hemingway, *For Whom the Bell Tolls* is the outstanding novel of the war and G. Orwell, *Homage to Catalonia* a fine personal view.

Chapter 9
Details of the campaigns can be followed in the Purnell *History of the Second World War* or more concisely in C. Falls, *The Second World War*. J. Reeves and P. Flower, *The Second World War* provide a complete history through first hand accounts, some of which are quoted in this chapter. A. Werth, *Russia at War* focuses attention on the enormous part played by the Russians. B. Collier, *The War in the Far East, 1941–1945* is a very good detailed account and J. Hersey, *Hiroshima* is an important book on the atomic holocaust.

Chapter 10
Apart from the national histories mentioned below it is worth looking at H. Higgins, *The Cold War* and G. Connell Smith, *The Pattern of the Post-War World*.

Chapter 11
There are many books on the debate on the European movement and the Common Market but perhaps it is best to look at N. Pounds and R. Kingsbury, *An Atlas of European Affairs* to follow their development in outline.

Chapter 12
Apart from the books already mentioned in chapters 1 and 2, A. Werth, *de Gaulle* and Dorothy Pickles, *France*.

Chapter 13
See general histories in chapter 5. Also R. J. Cootes, *The Making of the Welfare State* and M. Sissons and P. French, *The Age of Austerity*. Detailed economic information is to be found in J. Livingstone. *Britain and the World Economy* and P. Donaldson, *A Guide to the British Economy*.

Chapter 14
J. Parkes, *A History of the Jewish People* puts the emergence of Israel in its historical perspective. E. Hodgkin, *The Arabs* is a short general account. P. Mansfield, *Nasser's Egypt* looks at the work of the most important single figure in modern Arab history.

Chapter 15
Taya Zinkin, *India* is a brief introduction. R. Segal, *The Crisis of India* analyses the post independence problems. F. Watson, *Gandhi* is a good short biography. I. Stephens, *Pakistan* traces the emergence and problems of the new state.

Chapter 16
The Penguin African Histories provide a steady flow of new material on Africa. Note in particular R. Segal, *African Profiles*; J. Fage and R. Oliver, *A Short History of Africa*. Also very useful are A. Boyd and P. van Rensburg, *Atlas of African Affairs* and P. Fordham, *Geography of African Affairs*. For a better understanding of Africa it is important to read some African creative writing such as that to be found in *African Writing Today*, ed. E. Mahahlehe and the Heinemann African Writers Series (note especially the novels of Chinua Achebe and James Ngagi).

Chapter 17
A brief introduction can be found in A. Buchan, *The U.S.A.* Of the many books on President Kennedy, R. Schlesinger, *The Thousand Days* is long but particularly good. M. Harrington, *The Other America* gives a picture of the darker side of American society and James Baldwin states the Negro case brilliantly in *The Fire Next Time* and in his novels such as *Go Tell It On the Mountain*. See also B. Catchpole, *A Map History of the United States*.

G. Pendle, *A History of Latin America* and H. Blakemore, *Latin America* introduce the history of the neglected continent.

Chapter 18

Good accounts are to be found in R. Pethybridge, *A History of Post-War Russia* and M. Frankland, *Kruschev*. It is also worth looking at A. Palmer, *Yugoslavia* and G. Ionescu, *Break up of the Soviet Empire in Europe*. See also B. Catchpole, *A Map History of Russia*.

Chapter 19

S. Schram, *Mao Tse-tung* and Jerome Ch'en, *Mao and the Chinese Revolution* are both quite advanced books but most readable. The most up-to-date recent accounts are C. Bown, *China 1949–1977* and B. Catchpole, *A Map History of Modern China*. Ping Chia kuo, *China* gives a very brief introduction. See also North, Macaleavy, Clubb, etc. under chapter 7.

Chapter 20

C. Connell Smith, *The Pattern of Post War Affairs*; J. Hornby, *The United Nations*; A. Boyd, *United Nations: Piety, Myth and Truth*; H. Nicholas, *The United Nations*; G. Evans (ed.), *Human Rights*; C. Bown and P. Mooney, *Cold War to Détente*.

Postscript

On Population, C. Park, *The Population Explosion* and C. Cipolla, *The Economic History of World Population*. On nuclear weapons, B. Russell, *Has Man a Future?* and R. Jungk, *Brighter than a Thousand Suns*. On some problems of advanced society, W. White, *The Organisation Man* and V. Packard, *The Hidden Persuaders*. Three prophetic novels worth considering in this context are Aldous Huxley, *Brave New World* (and *Brave New World Revisited*), George Orwell, *1984* and Mordecai Richler, *Level 7*.

Index

ACKNOWLEDGEMENTS

Thanks are due to the following for permission to reproduce photographs:

Radio Times Hulton Picture Library   frontispiece, pp. 6, 12, 16, 27, 36, 38, 41, 53, 57, 73, 76, 78, 84, 86, 91, 101, 117, 118, 138, 142, 209, 210, 233, 239, 240, 317, 320

The Mansell Collection   pp. 25, 136

Keystone Press Agency   pp. 33, 105, 121, 133, 145, 198, 199, 201, 204, 234, 245, 252, 270, 277, 291, 293, 351

Miss Mary Pickford   p. 50

United Press International   pp. 53, 104, 192, 205, 271, 275, 297, 301, 309, 330, 334

Associated Press   pp. 61, 92, 195, 236, 284, 304, 309, 322

Camera Press   pp. 98, 221, 258, 261, 263, 280, 283, 288, 311, 332, 334, 344, 346, 352, 366 (United Nations Picture)

Museum of Modern Art, New York   p. 132

Imperial War Museum   pp. 151, 152, 154, 160, 165, 190

Press Association   p. 156

UNESCO   p. 259

Novosti   pp. 323, 324

Trustees of the British Museum   p. 55

OXFAM   p. 368

The New York Times   p. 55

Thanks are due to the following for permission to quote at length from their works:
Michael Dei Anang for his poem *The African.*
M. Junod and Messrs Jonathan Cape for the extract from *Warrior without Arms.*
R. W. Pethybridge and Messrs Allen and Unwin for the translation from the works of A. Lunacharsky.
J. K. Galbraith and Messrs Hamish Hamilton for the passage from *The Great Crash.*
The author also wishes to express his debt to the authors of all those books mentioned in the suggestions for further reading on which he has drawn in the preparation of this book.

ACKNOWLEDGMENTS